THE
NEOCLASSICAL THEORY
OF PRODUCTION AND
DISTRIBUTION

C. E. FERGUSON

Professor of Economics
Texas A & M University

CAMBRIDGE UNIVERSITY PRESS

CAMBRIDGE

LONDON · NEW YORK · MELBOURNE

CAMBRIDGE UNIVERSITY PRESS
Cambridge, New York, Melbourne, Madrid, Cape Town, Singapore, São Paulo

Cambridge University Press
The Edinburgh Building, Cambridge CB2 8RU, UK

Published in the United States of America by Cambridge University Press, New York

www.cambridge.org
Information on this title: www.cambridge.org/9780521074537

First published 1969
Reprinted with corrections 1971, 1975
Reprinted 1979
This digitally printed version 2008

A catalogue record for this publication is available from the British Library

Library of Congress Catalogue Card Number: 75–92248

ISBN 978-0-521-07453-7 hardback
ISBN 978-0-521-07629-6 paperback

FOR MICKEY AND THOSE WHO LOVED HIM

Until the laws of thermodynamics are repealed, I shall continue to relate outputs to inputs—i.e. to believe in production functions. Until factors cease to have their rewards determined by bidding in quasi-competitive markets, I shall adhere to (generalized) neoclassical approximations in which relative factor supplies are important in explaining their market remunerations ...a many-sectored neoclassical model with heterogeneous capital goods and somewhat limited factor substitutions can fail to have some of the simple properties of the idealized J. B. Clark neoclassical models. Recognizing these complications does not justify nihilism or refuge in theories that neglect short-term microeconomic pricing.

PAUL A. SAMUELSON

CONTENTS

PREFACE   *page* XV

1 INTRODUCTION   1
   1.1 Scope   1
        1.1.1 *Neoclassical theory*   2
        1.1.2 *Macroeconomic theory*   3
   1.2 Method and level of presentation   5
   1.3 Definitions   5
        1.3.1 *Inputs and outputs*   6
        1.3.2 *The short run and the long*   6
   1.4 Assumptions   7
        1.4.1 *The production function*   7
        1.4.2 *Fixed and variable proportions, limitational and
               limitative inputs*   8
        1.4.3 *Full employment*   11
   1.5 A caveat   11

PART I: THE MICROECONOMIC THEORY
OF PRODUCTION

2 THE TECHNICAL THEORY OF PRODUCTION UNDER
   CONDITIONS OF FIXED PROPORTIONS   15
   2.1 Introduction   15
        2.1.1 *Elementary inputs*   15
        2.1.2 *Complex inputs*   17
        2.1.3 *A caveat*   18
   2.2 Technical production with elementary inputs   19
        2.2.1 *Production with fixed coefficients*   19
        2.2.2 *Production with fixed proportions*   25

v

CONTENTS

2.3 Technical production with complex inputs   *page* 29

2.3.1 *An example of production with complex inputs*   29

2.3.2 *Marginal products, single limitational inputs*   31

2.3.3 *Marginal products, mutual limitationality*   32

2.3.4 *The Pareto region*   34

2.3.5 *The economic region of production with complex inputs*   39

2.3.6 *The elasticity of substitution*   41

2.4 The theory of production with elementary inputs and multiple production processes   43

2.4.1 *Marginal products*   44

2.4.2 *The elasticity of substitution*   45

3 THE ECONOMIC THEORY OF PRODUCTION UNDER CONDITIONS OF FIXED PROPORTIONS   47

3.1 Introduction   47

3.2 The expansion path   47

3.3 Graphical determination of the expansion path   48

3.4 Restrictions imposed upon the interpretation of the expansion path   50

3.4.1 *The Pareto ray as an isocline*   50

3.4.2 *The Pareto ray as the expansion path*   52

3.4.3 *The inapplicability of certain marginal equalities*   53

3.5 The technical and economic theory of production with discontinuous production functions   55

3.5.1 *Concavity of the production isoquants*   55

3.5.2 *Economic efficiency*   57

3.5.3 *Efficiency and input demand*   58

3.5.4 *Profit maximization and input demand*   58

3.5.5 *Conclusion*   59

4 TECHNICAL ASPECTS OF CONTINUOUS PRODUCTION FUNCTIONS: GENERAL THEORY   60

4.1 Introduction   60

4.2 The production function   61

4.2.1 *Algebraic and tabular representations*   *page* 61

4.2.2 *Graphical representation*   63

4.2.3 *Isoquants*   63

4.3 Single input variations   66

    4.3.1 *Marginal product*   67

    4.3.2 *Marginal returns and input relations*   69

    4.3.3 *Average product*   71

    4.3.4 *Average returns*   71

    4.3.5 *Relations among the product curves*   72

    4.3.6 *Output elasticity and the elasticity of average
         product*   76

    4.3.7 *The stages of production*   77

4.4 The function coefficient   79

    4.4.1 *Proportional input variations and the function
         coefficient*   79

    4.4.2 *Derivation of the function coefficient*   81

    4.4.3 *Relation of the function coefficient to output
         elasticities and the elasticity of average product*   83

4.5 Simultaneous input variations   84

    4.5.1 *The marginal rate of technical substitution*   84

    4.5.2 *Production isoclines*   86

    4.5.3 *The substitution region*   86

    4.5.4 *The diminishing marginal rate of technical
         substitution*   88

    4.5.5 *The elasticity of substitution*   90

5 TECHNICAL ASPECTS OF CONTINUOUS PRODUCTION
   FUNCTIONS HOMOGENEOUS OF DEGREE ONE   93

5.1 Introduction   93

5.2 Homogeneous functions   94

    5.2.1 *Mathematical properties of functions homogeneous
         of degree one*   94

    5.2.2 *The elasticity of substitution*   95

    5.2.3 *Classes of linearly homogeneous production
         functions*   97

CONTENTS

5.3   Production functions and the isoquant map: the general case   *page* 111

 5.3.1   *Marginal and average products*   112

 5.3.2   *Isoclines*   113

 5.3.3   *Output elasticities and the economic region of production*   114

 5.3.4   *Cross-section product curves*   116

 5.3.5   *The isoquant map*   120

5.4   Numerical example   122

5.5   Homothetic production functions   124

Appendix: A note on Professor Knight's production function   125

6   ECONOMIC THEORY OF PRODUCTION WITH FIXED INPUT PRICES   127

6.1   Introduction   127

 6.1.1   *Isocost curves*   127

 6.1.2   *Shifting the isocost curve*   129

6.2   Optimal input combinations: cost minimization approach   130

 6.2.1   *Special case, two variable inputs*   130

 6.2.2   *General case, multiple inputs*   131

 6.2.3   *Interpretation of the first-order conditions*   132

6.3   Optimal input combinations: output maximization approach   133

 6.3.1   *Special case, two variable inputs*   133

 6.3.2   *General case, multiple inputs*   134

6.4   Isoquants and comparative statics   136

 6.4.1   *The second-order conditions*   136

 6.4.2   *Comparative static changes: constant-output demand curves*   138

 6.4.3   *Comparative statics: changes in output*   141

6.5   The expansion path   142

6.6   Input demand functions   144

 6.6.1   *A two-factor model of input demand*   145

 6.6.2   *A multi-factor model of input demand*   149

 6.6.3   *Conclusion*   153

CONTENTS

7   THE THEORY OF COST WITH FIXED INPUT PRICES   *page* 154

   7.1   Introduction   154

     7.1.1   *The expansion path and long-run cost*   154

     7.1.2   *Viner revisited*   155

   7.2   Analysis of long-run cost   157

     7.2.1   *Cost functions*   157

     7.2.2   *Elasticities of the cost functions*   158

     7.2.3   *Cost elasticities and the function coefficient*   159

   7.3   Two examples of cost functions   163

     7.3.1   *The Cobb–Douglas function*   163

     7.3.2   *The CES function*   166

8   THE ECONOMIC THEORY OF COST AND PRODUCTION WITH VARIABLE INPUT PRICES   169

   8.1   Introduction   169

     8.1.1   *Demand and supply functions*   169

     8.1.2   *Cost and the marginal expense of input*   170

     8.1.3   *Isocost curves*   171

   8.2   Economic theory of production   172

     8.2.1   *Minimizing the cost of producing a given output*   172

     8.2.2   *Maximizing output for a given level of cost*   173

     8.2.3   *The expansion path*   174

     8.2.4   *The second-order conditions*   174

   8.3   The theory of cost   176

     8.3.1   *Cost functions and their elasticities*   177

     8.3.2   *Cost and the function coefficient*   178

   8.4   Profit maximization and the derived input demand functions   179

     8.4.1   *Profit maximization*   180

     8.4.2   *Input demand functions*   181

     8.4.3   *Summary*   185

   8.5   Conclusion   186

CONTENTS

9 'INFERIOR FACTORS' AND THE THEORIES OF
PRODUCTION AND INPUT DEMAND   *page* 187

   9.1 Introduction   187

   9.2 The model   187

   9.3 'Inferior factors' of production   189

   9.4 Inferior inputs and commodity price   191

   9.5 Inferior inputs and the cross-elasticity of derived input
demand functions   192

   9.6 Inferior inputs and the output effect of an input price
change   193

   9.7 Numerical example   199

   9.8 Conclusion   200

10 THEORY OF THE MULTI-PRODUCT FIRM   201

   10.1 Introduction   201

   10.2 The Kuhn–Tucker theorems   202

      10.1.1 *Constrained maximization*   202

      10.2.2 *Constrained minimization*   203

   10.3 Economic efficiency: constrained cost minimization 204

      10.3.1 *The Kuhn–Tucker conditions*   205

      10.3.2 *Economic interpretation*   206

      10.3.3 *Conclusion*   209

   10.4 Profit maximization in a multi-product firm   209

      10.4.1 *The Kuhn–Tucker conditions*   210

      10.4.2 *Economic interpretation*   210

      10.4.3 *Conclusion*   211

PART II: MACROECONOMIC THEORIES OF
DISTRIBUTION AND TECHNOLOGICAL PROGRESS

11 TECHNOLOGICAL PROGRESS AND THE NEOCLASSICAL
THEORY OF PRODUCTION   215

   11.1 Introduction   215

11.2   The classification of technological progress   *page* 216

    11.2.1   *Short-run effects of technological progress:*
            the Hicks approach   217

    11.2.2   *Long-run effects of technological progress:*
            the Harrod approach   219

    11.2.3   *Relation between Hicks- and Harrod-*
            neutrality   222

    11.2.4   *Two special cases*   222

11.3   A general neoclassical model of technological progress   224

    11.3.1   *The model*   224

    11.3.2   *Hicks- and Harrod-neutrality in a one-sector*
            model   228

    11.3.3   *The model again: two sectors*   229

    11.3.4   *Hicks-neutrality in a two-sector model*   231

    11.3.5   *Harrod-neutrality in a two-sector model*   232

    11.3.6   *Comparison of Hicks- and Harrod-*
            neutrality

11.4   Conclusion   234

12   TECHNOLOGICAL PROGRESS AND THE NEOCLASSICAL
    THEORY OF DISTRIBUTION   235

12.1   Introduction   235

12.2   Derived demand and the Marshall–Hicks rules   235

12.3   Technological progress and relative factor shares   239

    12.3.1   *Neutral technological progress and relative*
            factor shares in a one-sector model   240

    12.3.2   *Biased technological progress and relative*
            factor shares in a one-sector model   241

    12.3.3   *Biased progress in a purely factor-augmenting*
            model   243

    12.3.4   *Relative shares in a multi-sector model*   245

    12.3.5   *Relative shares in a two-sector model*   246

    12.3.6   *Conclusion*   250

12.4   Simple neoclassical theory   251

    12.4.1   *Neoclassical views of capital*   251

    12.4.2   *Real capital and neoclassical theory*   253

CONTENTS

12.5 The Cambridge Criticism: a first view   page 254

12.6 Professor Samuelson's parable   255

12.7 The Cambridge Criticism: second view   257

     12.7.1 *A small deviation from Samuelson's model*   259

     12.7.2 *Parametric representation of the factor-price frontier*   261

     12.7.3 *A graphical view of reswitching*   262

     12.7.4 *Conclusion*   265

12.8 Technical considerations   266

     12.8.1 *Elasticity of a nonlinear frontier*   266

     12.8.2 *Conditions for reswitching*   268

12.9 Conclusion   269

13 VINTAGE MODELS AND FIXED PROPORTIONS IN NEOCLASSICAL THEORY   271

13.1 Introduction   271

13.2 Vintage models, or the 'new view' of investment   272

     13.2.1 *The Cobb–Douglas vintage model*   272

     13.2.2 *A factor-augmenting vintage model*   275

     13.2.3 *The new view and the old*   278

13.3 Vintage models with fixed proportions   280

     13.3.1 *Structure of the model*   280

     13.3.2 *Wage determination*   281

     13.3.3 *Determining the type of machines built*   282

     13.3.4 *Marginal product of labor*   283

     13.3.5 *Marginal product of 'capital'*   284

     13.3.6 *The interest rate*   285

     13.3.7 *The factor-price frontier*   285

13.4 An extension of Solow's model   287

     13.4.1 *Notation*   287

     13.4.2 *Equations of the model*   288

     13.4.3 *Operation of the model*   290

14 LEARNING BY DOING   293

14.1 Introduction   293

14.2 Arrow's model   293

CONTENTS

14.2.1 *Notation*   page 294

14.2.2 *Output and the wage rate*   295

14.2.3 *Social and private returns*   296

14.2.4 *Marginal products and relative shares*   298

14.3 The growth path   300

14.3.1 *Stability of the growth path*   300

14.3.2 *Properties of the growth path*   302

14.4 Conclusion   305

Appendix: Professor Frankel's variant   305

15 MONOPOLY AND AGGREGATE DEMAND AS DETER-
MINANTS OF RELATIVE FACTOR SHARES   308

15.1 Introduction   308

15.2 The degree of monopoly and labor's relative share   309

15.2.1 *Kalecki*   310

15.2.2 *Mitra*   311

15.3 Theories based upon aggregate demand   314

15.3.1 *Kaldor's model*   314

15.3.2 *A two-sector variant of Kaldor's model*   317

15.3.3 *Mrs Robinson's model*   323

Appendix: Capital valuation in Mrs Robinson's model   333

16 INDUCED BIAS OF INVENTION AND THE THEORY OF
DISTRIBUTIVE SHARES   336

16.1 Introduction   336

16.1.1 *Hicks on induced bias*   337

16.1.2 *Fellner's rehabilitation*   338

16.1.3 *Ahmad's rehabilitation*   341

16.2 Induced bias and the theory of distribution   343

16.2.1 *Kennedy's basic model*   343

16.2.2 *Interpretation*   345

16.2.3 *The theory of distribution*   346

16.2.4 *Technical progress in the capital sector*   348

16.2.5 *Ahmad's criticism*   349

xiii

CONTENTS

16.3 Induced innovations and production functions: the Samuelson model   *page* 351

   16.3.1 *Basic model*   351

   16.3.2 *Stability with Hicks-neutral progress*   353

   16.3.3 *Dynamic properties of the Hicks-neutral model; the Cobb–Douglas case*   354

   16.3.4 *Dynamic properties; general case*   356

   16.3.5 *The model with changing factor prices*   356

   16.3.6 *Variable factor supplies*   358

   16.3.7 *Summary*   360

16.4 Generalization of Samuelson's model   361

16.5 Conclusion   364

REFERENCES   365

AUTHOR INDEX   379

SUBJECT INDEX   382

PREFACE

The first half of this book deals with *the* microeconomic theory of production, cost, and derived input demand. *The* is italicized because there is no truly alternative theory to explain the phenomena and behavior in question. This body of theory may validly be called neoclassical theory, but one should emphasize that it is neoclassical microeconomic theory dealing chiefly with microeconomic pricing. I doubt that there are many who would reject this approach to microeconomic behavior, especially that portion of the theory which does not involve the assumption of profit maximization.

The second half of the book is another matter because there I turn to the neoclassical theory of aggregates, especially technological progress and relative factor shares. In this part, the book is *discursive* in that neoclassical theory is presented in its most favorable light, though its limitations are noted and appraised in chapter 12. Correspondingly, those aggregate theories that purportedly 'compete' with neoclassical theory are criticized without constructive suggestions. In short, my point of view is uncompromisingly neoclassical. While I personally think the resulting work constitutes a fair appraisal of modern aggregative theory, there are some who would disagree.

Something more should be said about chapter 12. In the initial draft this chapter formally ended with the multi-sector model of technological progress and relative factor shares. Since the exposition of neoclassical aggregate theory in chapters 11 and 12 depended entirely upon the assumption of J. B. Clark real homogeneous capital, I added an appendix on Samuelson's 'Parable and Realism in Capital Theory' in order to show that the results of neoclassical analysis could be obtained from fixed-proportions, heterogeneous capital models. Shortly after this was completed, the 'Symposium on Capital Theory' appeared in the *Quarterly Journal of Economics*; and it then became quite apparent that the Cambridge Criticism, as I call it, must be accorded more careful consideration. As it now stands, the last half of chapter 12 is given over to an exposition of the Cambridge Criticism of neoclassical theory. Its validity is unquestionable, but its importance is an empirical or an econometric matter that depends upon the amount of substitutability there is in the system. Until the econometricians have the answer for us, placing reliance upon neoclassical economic theory is a matter of faith. I personally have the faith; but at present the best I can do to convince others is to invoke the weight of Samuelson's authority as represented, for example, by the flyleaf quotation.

This manuscript was begun while I was at Duke University. The initial work was greatly facilitated by a grant from the Duke University Council on Research and by a fellowship and an Auxiliary Research Award, both granted by the Social Science Research Council. The manuscript was completed while I was at Michigan State University. It was expertly typed by Miss Sue Slover, whose work for me was supported by an All-University Research Award granted by Michigan State University.

At various stages, different parts of the manuscript were read by quite a number of people. In draft or lecture form, most of the contents of this book were inflicted upon the Duke graduate students who attended my seminar in advanced theory in the academic years 1965–6 and 1966–7. All of the participants contributed helpful suggestions. The same statements apply to the Michigan State graduate students in the academic year 1967–8. One of these especially, Roger Blair, made very useful suggestions concerning chapters 6 and 9.

The first half of the book was given a very careful treatment by my colleague John R. Moroney. There is scarcely a page in this section that has not been improved by his thoughtful suggestions. Murray Brown read the entire manuscript; and I have benefitted greatly from his detailed critique. In particular, the last half of chapter 12 would have been hopeless without his help. I wish to express my deep appreciation to all of these people and, of course, absolve them of responsibility for the finished product. Finally, acknowledgement is made to the editors of *Economica* and *The Southern Economic Journal* for permission to publish, with some changes, portions of articles that previously appeared in these journals.

C.E.F.

College Station, Texas

1

INTRODUCTION

1.1 Scope

The object of this book is to present a systematic and thorough statement of the neoclassical theory of production and distribution. A decade or so ago this would not have required much space; and whatever the final product, it could only have been an embellishment of Carlson and Shephard, or of Samuelson's beautifully concise 'Comprehensive Restatement of the Theory of Cost and Production.'[1] To be sure, one would have had to add something on the microeconomic theory of distribution; but this could have been easily done by relying upon the works of Hicks, Stigler, Chamberlin, and others.[2]

But matters have changed dramatically within the past few years. Emphasis and professional interest have shifted significantly. Now most research centers on macroeconomic theory, on *aggregate* production functions and their implications for aggregate input substitution, distribution and technological progress (even though there now seems to be a trend toward microeconomics again). Since the behavior of these aggregates has a material effect upon the national economy, there has been a concomitant rise in the interest attached to econometric studies of production, distribution, and technological progress.

In a sense the chronical above is parochial because it concentrates upon developments whose origins are found predominantly on this side of the Atlantic.[3] A group of English economists, centered around Cambridge, has taken an altogether different view of the macroeconomic aspects of distribution and technological progress. While there are certain differences within the group, the tenor of thought is reflected in the works of Kaldor.[4] He argues that it is impossible, or at least meaningless, to distinguish

---

[1] Carlson [1939], Shephard [1953], and Samuelson [1947, pp. 57–89].
[2] Hicks [1932], Stigler [1939], Stigler [1946], and Chamberlin [1936].
[3] Without serious overstatement, I think one can say that the *origins* are to be found largely in the works of Samuelson and Solow.
[4] Kaldor [1955], [1957], [1959], [1961], and Kaldor and Mirrlees [1962]. See especially Kaldor [1959, pp. 220–4]. I have quoted Kaldor because he is somewhat more out-spoken than the rest. Mrs Robinson has doubtless done the most significant work in this vein of theory.

1

between shifts of a production function and movements along it (i.e. the substitution of capital for labor). In his words, '...just as technical progress causes accumulation, the process of accumulation stimulates the growth of knowledge and know-how. Hence it is useless to analyze the effects of capital accumulation in terms of a production function which assumes a given state of knowledge.' [1959, p. 221.] Instead, Kaldor thinks it more sensible to take as given, not the relation between capital stock[1] and output that underlies the production function, but the relation between the rate of accumulation and the rate of change of output.

Upon this foundation several Cambridge economists have built macroeconomic theories purporting to explain capital accumulation, technical progress, and distribution.[2] These theories occupy an important place in the literature and have given rise to no small amount of debate. Hence a coverage of these developments is also necessary if the claim of thoroughness is to be made. But the line is drawn at this point. Other macroeconomic theories of distribution are ignored, and the reader is referred to Davidson's excellent account of them.[3]

Throughout the study primary emphasis is attached to neoclassical theory and, within this framework, to microeconomic theory. Thus Part I is devoted to the microeconomic theories of production and distribution. The (neoclassical) macroeconomic theory of production and distribution is the subject of Part II. The concluding chapters, 15 and 16, are devoted to an exposition and critique of some 'alternative' theories of aggregate distribution and technical change.

1.1.1 Neoclassical theory[4]

The terms 'neoclassical theory' and 'macroeconomic theory' have so far been used without regard to precise definition. In a way this does no great damage because they are well established in our jargon. Yet these terms enter significantly throughout the book; so we must pause for exact description.

'Neoclassical theory' has different implications to different people; but on two counts there would seem to be a uniformity of opinion. These concern the ways in which 'neoclassical theory' differs from 'classical

---

[1] Kaldor's terminology is used here. As we shall presently see, concentrating upon the flow of capital services, the relevant variable for the production function, allows one to incorporate changes in the state of knowledge and know-how in the production function.

[2] The reader may think that *Cambridge* has been overemphasized. However, on this score see the explicit statement of a leading member of the group, Pasinetti [1962, p. 267]. [3] Davidson [1960].

[4] For a similar treatment, see Ferguson [1965c]. In writing this section I have had the advantage of comments by Professor J. J. Spengler.

theory', a term I shall conveniently leave undefined except to say it refers to the world of Malthus and Ricardo. First, neoclassical theory is based upon the assumption that there are no fixed, nonaugmentable factors of production. This contrasts sharply with the classical assumption of a fixed supply of land. Second, in neoclassical theory the rate of growth of population or of the labor force is assumed to be determined exogenously.[1] This too contrasts sharply with classical theory, in which population is very much an economic variable.

Beyond these points there is less accord. To some, neoclassical theory implies that the production function is smoothly continuous and at least twice differentiable. Others add the stipulation that marginal products are positive and continuously diminishing. Neither of these requirements is imposed in Part I. Indeed the subject matter of chapters 2 and 3 is production with fixed technological coefficients; and in chapters 4 and 5 the 'uneconomic regions' of production are discussed. However, when we come to macroeconomics in Part II, the aggregate production function is usually assumed to be smoothly continuous and twice differentiable, with first partial derivatives always positive and second partial derivatives always negative.

1.1.2 Macroeconomic theory[2]

The type of macroeconomic theory discussed here needs two comments, the first of which may be disposed of quickly. So far as this book is concerned, macroeconomic theory deals with *real* aggregate magnitudes; the nominal price level is neither a variable nor a parameter in any model presented. It might seem more appropriate to label this type of analysis 'general equilibrium theory'; and I would raise no objections because the macroeconomic theory of this book is squarely, if somewhat tenuously, based upon general equilibrium theory.

The last statement leads to the second point. General equilibrium theory is essentially microeconomic in character, dealing with the price-output decisions of individual businessmen and the price-purchase decisions of households. Aggregates appear only when they are well defined and when the process of aggregation does not impose restrictive conditions. Indeed, aggregates usually appear only as market balance equations or industry equilibrium conditions. The logical unity of general equilibrium theory is

---

[1] This statement does not imply that the rate of participation of the labor force is exogenously determined. However (see 1.4.3 below), we are concerned only with full employment situations; the cyclical behavior of output and employment is not under consideration.

[2] A discussion along these lines may be found in Ferguson [1964b]. Also see Kuenne [1963, pp. 22–39] and Solow [1959].

beautiful; and once one has worked his way through the complete model, he may stand back and admire its beauty. But that is about all he can do. Some simplifying assumptions are necessary if the theory is to be rendered usable.

There are at least three avenues of approach. First, one may choose to adopt Marshall's approach: to ignore the general interdependence of the economic system, to impound most variables in a *ceteris paribus* assumption, and to analyze the behavior of individual economic units in this carefully circumscribed environment. This is, in fact, the approach adopted in Part I of this book.

Second, one may reduce the general equilibrium system to manageable proportions by making some drastically simplifying (linearizing) assumpions concerning behavioral or technological relations that appear in the model. This is the method of Leontief; and it seems to be powerful indeed for a certain set of problems, mainly of a short-run nature. It is not, however, the set of problems upon which our attention is focused.

Finally, one may aggregate. One way is to define special aggregates and special techniques of aggregation, so that the underlying microeconomic relations entail the existence of corresponding macroeconomic relations. The rigor of general equilibrium theory is thus preserved; but two objections may be raised. First, this method, even if practicable, is not practical.[1] The second objection has been demonstrated forcefully by Grunfeld and Griliches [1960]. Their principal argument is that *in practice* we do not know enough about the underlying microeconomic relations to specify them perfectly. Thus each micro-equation will contain specification errors, and these errors tend to be magnified when aggregated. Consequently, they conclude that a direct aggregate '...equation may explain the aggregate data better than all micro-equations combined if our micro-equations are not "perfect". Since perfection is unlikely,... aggregation is not necessarily bad if one is interested in the aggregates.'[2]

Alternatively, the macroeconomic system may be constructed *by analogy* with the corresponding microeconomic system. Thus one may assume, for example, that the aggregate economic system possesses an aggregate production function, that the system behaves as though it minimizes the cost of producing a stipulated output, and that the system rewards each input according to competitive imputation. In constructing macroeconomic systems by analogy one sacrifices the rigor of general equilibrium theory in favor of empirical feasibility. Index numbers and conventionally defined aggregates are used in lieu of the specially defined aggregates required for precise aggregation. Whether this method is successful or not is itself an

---

[1] For abundant evidence on this score, see Theil [1954].
[2] Grunfeld and Griliches [1960, p. 10].

empirical question whose answer is treated very lightly in this book. But the macroeconomic theory discussed is the macroeconomic theory constructed by analogy with the corresponding microeconomic theory.

1.2 Method and level of presentation

The pure theory of production and distribution is our exclusive concern; and little or no effort is made to show the relevance of the analysis to issues of current economic policy. Theory is the concern of the theoretician, and to him the book is directed. In no way is this a practical man's guide to production; the method is strictly that of model analysis of model situations. What Dewey has said of his own book applies to this as well: '...this book employs the method of austere, sustained, and, I regret, largely humorless abstraction that has served economics so well in the past. Given the excruciating complexity of so many of the problems encountered..., I cannot see that any other method will allow us to cut through to first principles and deal with these problems according to their importance.'[1]

The level of presentation varies quite widely. Some chapters or parts of chapters are elementary indeed; other passages are relatively advanced. The differences in level stem from my desire to present a thorough and comprehensive statement of the theory under consideration. The method of presentation varies as well. For the most part, mathematical models of production and distribution are discussed; and except for Part II, no effort is usually made to reduce the number of variables under consideration. Yet whenever it seemed helpful, I have not eschewed graphical analysis, numerical examples, or drastic simplification by reduction in the number of variables.

The subject matter of this book is taken from the public domain of economic literature, hopefully with citation. The published works of many economists comprise the sources from which the material was developed. The intended merit of the book lies in the systematic exposition and analysis of the theory and in the explanation and interpretation of some of its more difficult aspects. Nonetheless, portions of chapters 2, 3, 6, 9, and 11–14 are believed to contain original material.

1.3 Definitions

The jargon of production theory is well established and broadly understood. Nonetheless, some possible ambiguity might be removed if careful definitions are given to a few terms.

[1] Dewey [1965, p. vii].

1.3.1 Inputs and outputs

For our purposes an *output* or *product* is any good or service whose fabrication or creation requires one or more scarce resources. When concrete examples are cited, they refer exclusively to goods output simply because it is easier to conceive of the precise set of resources used. Furthermore, one important dimension of products is ignored throughout the book; in particular, our discussion is generally applicable only to that set of outputs whose production does not involve 'time' or 'storage' in an essential way. Thus, for example, the production processes that convert new wine into vintage wine and May wheat into January-consumable wheat are not included. To do so would take us rather far afield into the dynamics of speculation. Still worse, it would make our dangerous skirting of the theory of capital and growth even more perilous.

Next, a *factor of production* or an *input* is defined as any scarce resource[1] used in the production of a good or service. According to the paragraph above, one class of inputs is excluded, namely 'time' or 'storage'. The remainder may conveniently be divided into two broad groups. First, there is a set of inputs, called *ingredient inputs*, that are used up or consumed in the process of production. At times, especially in Part II, we assume that ingredient inputs must enter the production process in fixed proportions one to the other. The recipe, or 'blueprint' in modern terminology, is given and cannot be changed without altering the nature of the product. Since this class of inputs is assumed to enter in fixed proportions, one is able to subtract its cost from the market value of the commodity and thereby determine the 'value added' by those inputs whose proportions are not fixed.

The second class is composed of those inputs that render a flow of services, which are 'consumed' in the production process; but the inputs themselves are not consumed. Capital and labor are the principal, and certainly the most interesting, inputs belonging to this set. In Part II our attention is focused upon these two inputs, which are usually assumed to be homogeneous aggregates.

1.3.2 The short run and the long

For many years economists have indulged in a bit of circularity that has been rewarding. More specifically, it has become customary to define the *short run* as that period of time during which the quantity of one or more inputs cannot be changed. The quantity of input or of its maximum

---

[1] Using the term 'scarce resource' in these two paragraphs is, in a sense, begging an important economic question. However, it is a question whose answer demands a full model of general equilibrium, rather than a model of the output side alone.

flow of services is fixed and can be neither augmented nor diminished. Such an input is called a *fixed input* in the short run. The *long run* is then defined as that period of time (or planning horizon) in which all inputs are variable, none fixed. The circularity enters because a fixed input is defined as one whose quantity or flow of services cannot be changed in the short run.

It is sometimes argued that no inputs are ever fixed and, consequently, that one cannot distinguish between short and long runs. Whether or not certain inputs are instantaneously augmentable or not seems to be a moot question, which fortunately does not require an answer. No input must, of necessity, be fixed to permit one to take a partial derivative or a cross-section of a production surface. The cross-section may be analyzed for one or more values of the variables conceptually held constant. In what follows the study of these cross-sections is referred to as short-run analysis. It is recognized that a 'short run' might not exist; yet to act as though it exists creates a convenient analytical fiction that is fully justified by the mathematical processes used to define it.

1.4 Assumptions

A large number of assumptions are employed throughout the book. Most of these are specific to the topic immediately under consideration; others apply uniformly throughout (with the exception of Part II, chs. 15, 16). Whenever particular assumptions arise, e.g. the assumption of either perfect or imperfect competition in the input or output markets, they are explicitly noted. However, there are two pervasive assumptions of such importance as to merit discussion at the outset.

1.4.1 The production function

A production function, which may be specified in a mathematical or tabular form, is assumed to exist for each good or service. According to conventional definition,[1] a production function shows the *maximum* output attainable from any specified set of inputs, i.e. any set of quantities of ingredient inputs and flows of services of other inputs. In general, no further limitations are imposed except that the set of outputs and inputs must be nonnegative. Finally, the production function is a single-valued mapping from input space into output space inasmuch as the maximum attainable output for any stipulated set of inputs is unique.

Two broad classes of production functions are discussed in Part I, *fixed-* and *variable-proportions production functions*. A production process is

---

[1] See, for example, Samuelson [1947, p. 57]. For a somewhat different view, see Smithies [1935, pp. 122–9].

characterized by fixed proportions if, and only if, each level of output technologically requires a unique combination of inputs. If the technologically determined input–output ratio is independent of the scale of production for each input, the production process is characterized by *fixed input coefficients*. In this case, the fixed-proportions production function is homogeneous of degree one. If the input–output ratios are not independent of scale, but if all pairs of input ratios are constant, the fixed proportions production function is homogeneous. However, it is not homogeneous of degree one throughout; in this case, the degree of homogeneity may be constant or it may change with the scale of operation.

One more variant of the fixed-proportions production function is conceivable: the pairs of input ratios are technologically fixed for each level of output, but they change as output changes. This specification is, of course, inconsistent with homogeneity of degree one. It is not discussed in what follows because it would seem to imply that some of the inputs change qualitatively when the scale of production changes. If such cases must be discussed, it would seem more reasonable to suppose that there are several different production functions, each of which is relevant within a certain range of output.

A variable-proportions production function is one in which the same level of output may be produced by two or more combinations of inputs. For convenience, we always assume that variable-proportions functions are smoothly continuous. This assumption restricts us to a subset of the full class of variable-proportion functions, and it rules out boundary solutions.[1] However, the essential *technological* feature of variable proportions is preserved: one input may be substituted for another while maintaining a constant level of output. Of course, as we shall see, the production coefficients are in fact 'fixed' by economic considerations, given the set of ratios of input prices. At efficiency points, observable economic behavior is much the same regardless of the class of functions. Yet there is an important technological difference, and it is important to preserve it.

1.4.2 Fixed and variable proportions, limitational and limitative inputs

At this point it is convenient to pause for an additional definition or classification of inputs. The origin of this classification is presumably Frisch [1931]; but it has been refined and elaborated by Georgescu-Roegen.[2] His formulation is adopted here, especially as presented in

---

[1] Any member of the excluded group, in which there is only a finite number of input combinations that will yield the same level of output, may be viewed as a set of fixed-proportion production functions. This approach is briefly treated in Part I, chs. 2–3.

[2] Georgescu-Roegen [1935], [1951], [1955], and [1960]. On this point, also see Schneider [1934] and Zassenhaus [1935].

[1955, pp. 299–302]. The definitions are illustrated graphically by figures 1 and 2 under the assumption that there are only two inputs. These figures show two isoquants, labeled Q_0 and Q_1, derived from the following production functions:

$$Q = \min\left(\frac{x_1}{\alpha}, \frac{x_2}{\beta}\right), \tag{1.4.1}$$

and

$$Q = f(x_1, x_2), \tag{1.4.2}$$

where x_1 and x_2 are the amounts of inputs X_1 and X_2, α and β are constants, and f is continuous and everywhere differentiable.

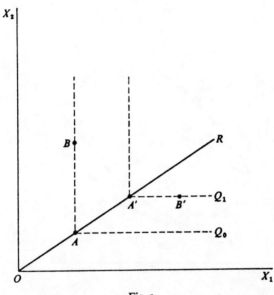

Fig. 1

Now for the definitions. An input is said to be *limitational* if an increase in its usage is a necessary, but not sufficient, condition for an increase in output. According to this definition, both X_1 and X_2 are limitational at points A and A' in figure 1. An increase in either input, the usage of the other remaining constant, would not expand output. Thus increased usage of either input alone is only a necessary condition. It should be noted that no points such as A or A' appear in figure 2. In other words there are no limitational inputs if the production function is characterized by variable proportions.[1] Limitationality imposes a special structure upon the pro-

---

[1] When ingredient inputs enter the production function as fixed coefficients, while other inputs have technologically variable coefficients, the production function is a mixture of fixed and variable proportions. In this case, the ingredient inputs may become limitational at certain points. This situation, which is treated briefly in Part I, chs. 4 and 5, has been analyzed by Smithies [1936].

duction function, namely, for every level of output, there is a factor combination such that all inputs are limitational. If the limitational production function is also homogeneous, as assumed above, it is completely defined by a single process. This single process is represented by the ray OR in figure 1.

Limitativeness, on the other hand, is a characteristic of every production function. An input is said to be *limitative* if an increase in its usage is both a necessary and a sufficient condition for an increase in output. Every pro-

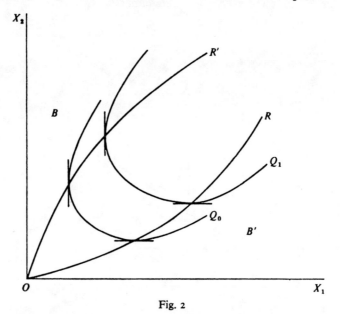

Fig. 2

duction function has a domain of limitativeness for each input. In figure 1, factor X_1 is limitative at point B and at every point on the vertical portions of the isoquants. Similarly, X_2 is limitative at point B' and at every other point on the horizontal segments of the isoquants.

In figure 2 the domains or regions of limitativeness are more pronounced. In the open region B (the open curvilinear cone $X_2 OR'$), X_1 is limitative. In the region B' (the open curvilinear cone $X_1 OR$), X_2 is limitative. On the other hand, X_2 is superfluous in region B and X_1 is in region B'. Similarly, X_2 is superfluous at B in figure 1 and X_1 is at B'. More generally, in figure 1, X_2 is superfluous within the open linear cone $X_2 OR$ and X_1 is superfluous within the open linear cone $X_1 OR$. Along the common boundary OR, both inputs are limitational rather than limitative. This points to another technological characteristic that distinguishes fixed-from variable-proportions production functions.

The open curvilinear cones of input limitativeness in figure 2 do not have a common boundary. The curvilinear cone $R'OR$ separates the regions of single-factor limitativeness; and within this cone and on its boundary lines, both inputs are limitative.[1] Thus the so-called 'economic region of production' is that region within which all inputs are simultaneously limitative. An economic *region* can generally be defined only for the variable-proportions case; the region degenerates into what might be called an *economic ray* when the inputs obey a limitational law.[2] This merely reflects the absolute impossibility of input substitution when inputs are limitational.

1.4.3 Full employment

In Part I emphasis is placed strictly upon an individual entrepreneur; hence an assumption concerning the aggregate level of employment is not required. However, it is assumed that no relevant input has an absolutely inelastic input supply curve. Part II, on the other hand, is based upon the assumption of continuous full employment of all (both) inputs. Thus the type of macroeconomic theory discussed here may not be applicable to economies in which there is a substantial volume of secular unemployment.

1.5 A caveat

Before embarking upon the body of this work, a caveat is in order. There is basically *one* neoclassical theory embracing production, distribution, capital, and growth. In this work production and distribution are the center of attention, capital and growth are more or less arbitrarily ignored. This is justifiable in Part I, which is devoted to static microeconomic theory. The omission is much more serious in Part II, where issues concerning capital and growth come to the surface.

On the aggregate level the theory of production must allow for technological progress. At this stage one must ask, for example, whether technological progress occurs simply because capital and labor become better and better day by day, or whether technological advances must be embodied in new capital that replaces old capital. Similarly, the aggregate

---

[1] In case the production function possesses an absolute maximum for variations in all directions, the cone of mutual limitativeness is closed. Otherwise it is an open cone. If the production function is homogeneous of degree one, the cone of mutual limitativeness is an open linear cone.

[2] The 'economic region of production' is the subject of further discussion in chs 4 and 5 below. Among other things, we will note that the 'economic region' has been defined as the region between: (a) the points at which the marginal products are zero, and (b) the points at which average products are a maximum. If the production function is homogeneous of degree one, the two definitions are identical. Otherwise, they are not. The argument in this section will be repeated when we subsequently select definition (a).

theory of distribution is set in the context of equilibrium growth. Thus the segment of neoclassical theory treated in Part II fundamentally relies upon the segment of neoclassical theory that is (almost) not discussed.

Omitting one segment of the theory would not be particularly serious if the capital-growth half upon which production–distribution is based were above reproach. But it is not; and this is a fact that has only recently come to light (even though the crucial difficulty is certainly implicit in Wicksell's *Lectures*).

Let us get at this somewhat differently. Neoclassical theory is a beautiful edifice erected upon the foundations of microeconomic production functions (and input-output pricing processes). If these production functions, and the aggregate production function derived from them, possess certain characteristics, the central results of neoclassical theory are obtained and the theory of production and distribution is validated.[1] That is, if certain production relations hold, one may prove that the permanently sustainable consumption stream varies inversely with the rate of interest and that the maximum sustainable consumption per capita is attained when the rate of growth equals the rate of interest (or capital rent).

In proving these theorems, one also proves that the capital–labor ratio varies inversely with the wage–rent ratio; and the *elasticity* of this functional relation is the ratio of aggregate relative factor shares. Thus neoclassical distribution theory is obtained, as it were, in the process of deriving the central propositions of neoclassical capital and growth theory.

The analysis leading to the results described above may be based either upon a real-capital model or a period-of-production model *providing* heterogeneous capital goods may be reduced to a homogeneous capital aggregate. This is necessary in order to obtain a unique relation between the aggregate capital–labor ratio and the wage–rent ratio. Otherwise, the relation is between the wage–rent ratio and what Hicks calls the 'capital-capital' coefficient and the 'labor-consumption' coefficient.[2] In this case, the elasticity of the factor-price frontier does not give the ratio of aggregate relative shares.

Thus the J. B. Clark homogeneous capital model, which is chiefly discussed in this book, depends crucially upon the structure of production processes. In particular, there may exist production relations that jeopardize not only the simple neoclassical theory of capital and growth but the simple neoclassical theory of production and distribution as well. This issue has been the subject of much recent research and debate, and it is by no means settled. The caveat stated here is that the issue exists and that it is relegated to discussion in chapter 12.

---

[1] As Samuelson would probably say, the J. B. Clark homogeneous capital 'fairy tale is a useful approximation of a full-blown M.I.T. model involving heterogeneous capital goods.   [2] Hicks [1965, pp. 139–40].

PART I

THE MICROECONOMIC THEORY
OF PRODUCTION

2

THE TECHNICAL THEORY OF
PRODUCTION UNDER CONDITIONS
OF FIXED PROPORTIONS

2.1 Introduction

In chapter 1 various characteristics of fixed-proportions production functions were discussed and defined. There is one additional feature that must be noted before proceeding to the technical theory of production under conditions of fixed proportions. More specifically, it is necessary to distinguish between fixed-proportions production functions in which the inputs are not technically related and those in which they are. As we shall see, this is tantamount to distinguishing between simple fixed-proportion production functions and those requiring linear programming techniques for a solution.

2.1.1 Elementary inputs

First, let us define a *fixed-proportions production function with elementary inputs* as one in which all pairs of input ratios are constant at all efficiency points, but in which there is no other technical relation among the inputs. A production function of this type may be written as

$$q = \min \left(\frac{x_1}{\alpha_1}, \frac{x_2}{\alpha_2}, \dots, \frac{x_n}{\alpha_n} \right), \qquad (2.1.1)$$

where q is physical output, the α_i's are constants or variables that are functions of q and always change proportionately, and the x_i's are the physical quantities of inputs X_i. At any observable production point (or efficiency point),[1] the following relation must hold:

$$\frac{x_1}{\alpha_1} = \frac{x_2}{\alpha_2} = \dots = \frac{x_n}{\alpha_n}. \qquad (2.1.2)$$

---

[1] A 'production point' or an 'efficiency point' is a point at which no input is redundant. Any such point, of course, lies on the production ray determined by the technical relations given by equations (2.1.3).

Thus in any efficiency point, the constant input ratios are

$$\frac{x_i}{x_j} = \frac{\alpha_i}{\alpha_j} \quad (i, j = 1, 2, ..., n). \tag{2.1.3}$$

Equations (2.1.3) are the only technical conditions governing input relations.

If one assumes that the maximum available quantity of each input is fixed, a geometrical interpretation may be given. Consider the n-dimensional input space, or the two-dimensional space shown in figure 3. Each

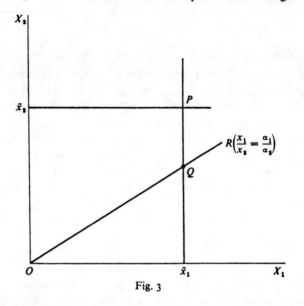

Fig. 3

input availability determines a one-dimensional hyperplane; and the hyperplanes taken together form an input-availability 'hyperbox' that imposes precisely n potential constraints upon output (one constraint for each elementary input). In figure 3, $O\bar{x}_1$ units of X_1 and $O\bar{x}_2$ units of X_2 are available; the input-availability box is thus $O\bar{x}_2P\bar{x}_1$. The production function (2.1.1) or the technical input relation (2.1.3) determines an $(n-1)$ dimensional hyperplane that intersects the hyperbox on one of its facets or at the junction of two or more facets. In figure 3 the technical relation determines the ray OR, which intersects the facet $\bar{x}_1P$ at Q.

Rephrasing the discussion in terms of linear programming shows there is no 'linear programming problem' at all:

$$\left.\begin{aligned} \text{maximize} \quad & q = \min\left(\frac{x_1}{\alpha_1}, \frac{x_2}{\alpha_2}, ..., \frac{x_n}{\alpha_n}\right), \\ \text{subject to} \quad & x_i \leqslant \bar{x}_i \quad (i = 1, 2, ..., n), \end{aligned}\right\} \tag{2.1.4}$$

16

where $\bar{x}_i$ is the maximum available amount of X_i. Nothing but simple arithmetic is needed to solve the 'problem' in equations (2.1.4): divide $\bar{x}_i$ by α_i for all i and determine the minimum ratio.

2.1.2 Complex inputs

The other situation, which is called a *fixed-proportions production function with complex inputs*,[1] is more difficult both to describe and to analyze. Basically the case arises when the maximization problem involves more restraints than imposed by the input-availability limitations. Suppose the technical conditions of production impose the following requirements: $g_j(x_1, x_2, ..., x_n) \leqslant 0$ for $j = 1, 2, ..., m$. The linear programming problem then becomes:

$$\left. \begin{aligned} \text{maximize} \quad & q = \min\left(\frac{x_1}{\alpha_1}, \frac{x_2}{\alpha_2}, ..., \frac{x_n}{\alpha_n}\right), \\ \text{subject to} \quad & x_i \leqslant \bar{x}_i \quad (i = 1, 2, ..., n), \\ & g_j(x_1, ..., x_n) \leqslant 0 \quad (j = 1, 2, ..., m). \end{aligned} \right\} \quad (2.1.5)$$

There are now $n+m$ upper bounds on the problem; but from the theory of linear programming, we know that at most n of these will be least upper bounds.

Graphically, the case of complex inputs is illustrated by figure 4, in which it is assumed that only one additional constraint exists. The input-availability box is $O\bar{x}_2 P\bar{x}_1$, and the extra constraint is represented by the line CF. When this constraint is imposed, the input-availability box is transformed into an *input-possibility* polyhedron, shown as $O\bar{x}_2 Q'Q\bar{x}_1$.[2] The production process ray may intersect the polyhedron along any facet or at one of the junctions. If the production ray lies beneath OR or above OR', one of the input availabilities is the only effective constraint. On the other hand, the production ray may intersect the facet corresponding to the additional constraint CF, as shown by OS in figure 4. In that case, neither input is used to the full extent of its availability, i.e., $x_1^* < \bar{x}_1$ and $x_2^* < \bar{x}_2$.

Production with complex inputs presents somewhat different possibilities of limitativeness and limitationality.[3] We consider the possibilities that are

---

[1] The terms 'elementary inputs' and 'complex inputs' have not, to my knowledge, appeared in the literature. The former, of course, refers to the class of fixed-proportions production functions conventionally discussed. The latter case has received little or no attention. The only discussion I know of appears in Frisch [1965, pp. 232–5]. Frisch uses the terms 'independent limitation factor' and 'mixed factor ring' to describe the cases.

[2] In n-dimensional input space, the input-availability hyperbox is transformed into an input-possibility polyhedron, the 'convex polyhedral cone' that is familiar from linear programming.

[3] In discussions involving limitativeness and limitationality the absolute input availabilities are usually ignored.

17

apparent from figure 4, although the multidimensional interpretation is analogous. First, suppose the production ray is given by OR' or any other ray showing a higher $X_2 - X_1$ input ratio. X_1 is limitative in the *closed* cone OCQ', as compared with an open cone of limitativeness when inputs are elementary. Similarly, if the production ray is OR or any other ray showing a lower $X_2 - X_1$ input ratio, X_2 is limitative in the *closed* cone OFQ.

The second difference lies in the fact that complex inputs lead to regions of limitationality. Thus X_1 is limitational in the open polyhedron $X_2CQ'R'$ and X_2 in the open polyhedron X_1FQR. Furthermore, the inputs are

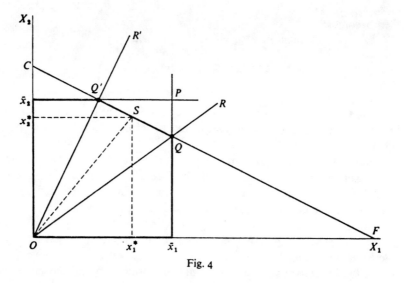

Fig. 4

mutually limitational along any production ray lying between OR' and OR. Thus, as we shall later see, there may exist a region, rather than a ray, of mutual limitationality when production is subject to complex inputs. Finally, one might note that production with complex inputs may give rise to a region of mutual limitativeness; hence an economic region of production may exist.

2.1.3 A caveat

Throughout this chapter the discussion concerns *technologically* feasible situations without regard to their *economic* feasibility (i.e. efficiency). As shall become apparent in chapter 3, the set of economically feasible situations is a very small subset of the set of technologically feasible events.

2.2 Technical production with elementary inputs

In this section our concern is the theory of production when the production function is characterized by fixed proportions and elementary inputs. The case of fixed coefficients, or homogeneity of degree one, is analyzed first, followed by a discussion of production with proportionately variable coefficients (i.e. the input ratios remain constant but the input–output ratios vary).

2.2.1 Production with fixed coefficients

As the reader will recall, when the production function is characterized by fixed proportions and fixed input–output ratios, output is said to be produced according to fixed coefficients. In this situation the production function may be written as

$$q = \min \left(\frac{x_1}{\alpha_1}, \frac{x_2}{\alpha_2}, ..., \frac{x_n}{\alpha_n} \right), \qquad (2.2.1)$$

where q represents the physical output of a single good, the x_i's are the physical quantities of inputs X_i, and the α_i's are fixed coefficients.

Equation (2.2.1) gives rise to two basic situations. The first, and less interesting, of these occurs when a proper subset of the inputs satisfies the minimal relation. Without loss of generality we may assume that inputs $X_1, ..., X_i$ comprise the *minimum subset*. Thus

$$\frac{x_1}{\alpha_1} = \frac{x_2}{\alpha_2} = ... = \frac{x_i}{\alpha_i} < \frac{x_j}{\alpha_j} \quad (j = i+1, ..., n). \qquad (2.2.2)$$

The inputs in the minimum subset are mutually limitational; the others are redundant. Furthermore, if all inputs in the minimum subset are expanded or contracted so as to preserve the input ratios, the minimum subset may be regarded as a single limitative input. As discussed in chapter 1, in the two-input case the ray of mutual limitationality is OR. Inputs X_1 and X_2 are limitative in the cones X_2OR and X_1OR respectively. These two open cones are the graphical counterpart of the minimum subset concept. That is, by assumption all inputs are not mutually limitational; hence the position under consideration cannot lie on the ray OR.

Average and marginal products, limitational and limitative inputs. Let us turn now to average and marginal products, first considering the inputs in the minimum subset. From equations (2.2.1) and (2.2.2), we obtain

$$q = \frac{x_1}{\alpha_1} = \frac{x_2}{\alpha_2} = ... = \frac{x_i}{\alpha_i}. \qquad (2.2.3)$$

19

The average product of any input is, by definition, the corresponding output–input ratio. Denoting the average product of the hth input by AP_h,

$$AP_h = \frac{1}{\alpha_h} \quad (h = 1, 2, \ldots, i). \tag{2.2.4}$$

If we consider the two-input case, or more generally the case in which the minimum subset contains only one element, the average product of the input in question is a constant. This is illustrated by the horizontal line labeled AP in figure 5. In the situation under consideration, the *single* minimum input is a limitative factor; over the range of its limitativeness, the average product function is constant and smoothly continuous.

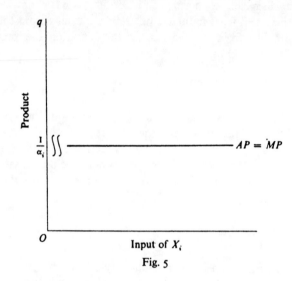

Fig. 5

When the minimum subset contains two or more inputs, the average product function is generally not continuous. If all the inputs in the minimum subset are expanded or contracted in the proper proportions, the average product functions are constant and smoothly continuous, i.e. the subset may be treated as a single limitative input. Otherwise, average product behaves differently according to the direction of input change.

As previously defined, an input is limitational if an increase in its usage is a necessary, but not sufficient, condition for an expansion of output. But so long as an input is not redundant, i.e. when it is either limitational or limitative, a *contraction* in its usage is both a necessary and a sufficient condition for a decrease in output. Now consider a change in the quantity of one, and only one, input in the minimum subset. From an initial limitational point, any decrease in the usage of the input under consideration causes a proportional decrease in output. Hence the average product is constant and smoothly continuous for reductions in the quantity of input.

An expansion of input usage, on the other hand, would cause no change in output. As a consequence, the average product of the input would decline. At the point where the input becomes limitational (and ceases to be limitative), there is a kink in the average product curve. The curve is continuous; but the average product function itself is neither smoothly continuous nor constant over the whole range. Its behavior is shown graphically in figure 6.

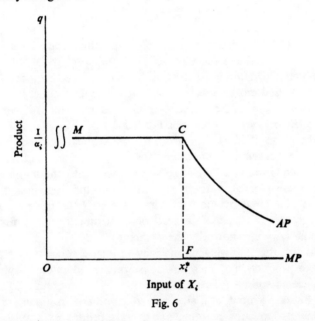

Fig. 6

Very similar considerations apply to the marginal product functions, which are denoted MP_h for the hth input. From equation (2.2.3), one obtains

$$MP_h = \frac{\partial q}{\partial x_h} = \frac{1}{\alpha_h} \quad (h = 1, 2, ..., i). \tag{2.2.5}$$

However, one must exercise caution because equation (2.2.5) is true if, and only if, input h is limitative at the point under consideration.

First, as we have seen, if all the inputs in the minimum subset are either increased or decreased in the proper proportion, the minimum subset may be treated as a single limitative input. In this case, equation (2.2.5) holds for all inputs in the minimum subset. Average and marginal products are equal, constant, and smoothly continuous, as illustrated in figure 5. One

21

might also note that the same reasoning applies exactly when there are only two inputs or when there is only one input in the minimum subset.[1]

Next, suppose there are two or more inputs in the minimum subset and, further, consider the variation of only one input at a time. In particular, let X_i be one of the minimum inputs and let its quantity be x_i^* at the point of mutual limitationality. We then have

$$(MP_i)^- = \left(\frac{\partial q}{\partial x_i}\right)^-_{x_i^*} = \frac{1}{\alpha_i} \qquad (2.2.6)$$

and

$$(MP_i)^+ = \left(\frac{\partial q}{\partial x_i}\right)^+_{x_i^*} = 0, \qquad (2.2.7)$$

where ' $-$ ' and ' $+$ ' indicate, respectively, reductions and increases from the value $x_i = x_i^*$. When the input of X_i is reduced, while $x_j = x_j^*$ for $j \neq i$ and j in the minimum subset, output is reduced proportionately. Thus for backward movements from x_i^*, the marginal product is constant, smoothly continuous, and equal to average product.[2] This is illustrated in figure 6 by the heavy horizontal line labeled MC.

When the usage of X_i expands from the limitational point x_i^*, all other limitational inputs remaining constant, the marginal product of X_i is zero, as shown in equation (2.2.7). For forward movements, the marginal product is constant (zero), smoothly continuous, and less than average product, as illustrated by the heavy line labeled FMP in figure 6. The significant feature is that the marginal product function has a finite discontinuity at $x_i = x_i^*$, shown by the dashed segment CF.

In summary, the following points may be made concerning marginal and average products and their relations when production is subject to fixed coefficients and all inputs are not mutually limitational: (a) if there is a single limitative input, or if all inputs in the minimum subset are varied in the proper proportions, marginal and average products are constant and positive, smoothly continuous, and equal for input changes in either direction, so long as the variation is restricted to the region of input limitativeness (see figure 5). (b) If two or more inputs are mutually limitational,[3] marginal and average products behave differently according as the input of one factor is augmented or diminished from the point of *group* limitativeness. For input reductions marginal and average products are

---

[1] It might be well to recall that we are now dealing with the situation in which all inputs are not mutually limitational. Thus in the two-input model, one input must be redundant and the other limitative.

[2] Needless to say, MP and AP are constant, continuous, and equal for positive changes in X_i when $x_i < x_i^*$. In this use, however, X_i would be a *single* limitative input.

[3] Notice that under conditions of fixed proportions with elementary inputs, a combination of inputs cannot be mutually limitative. They are limitative as a *group*.

constant and positive, smoothly continuous, and equal. At the point of group limitativeness, there is a kink in the average product curve and a finite discontinuity in the marginal product curve. Beyond this point, the average product curve is smoothly continuous and monotonically decreasing, and it approaches the horizontal axis asymptotically. Over this range, the marginal product curve is constant at zero and (presumably) smoothly continuous (see figure 6).

Marginal and average products; redundant inputs. Let us now retain the assumption that all inputs are not mutually limitational. Equation (2.2.2) is valid:

$$\frac{x_1}{\alpha_1} = \frac{x_2}{\alpha_2} = \ldots = \frac{x_i}{\alpha_i} < \frac{x_j}{\alpha_j} \quad (j=i+1, \ldots, n). \tag{2.2.2}$$

Our attention is focused upon X_k in the redundant subset and, when necessary for comparison, upon X_h in the minimum subset.

Suppose X_k is present in the amount $x_k > x_k^*$, where x_k^* is the amount that would cause X_k to be in the minimum subset. In this case the output–input ratio, which is the average product of the input, is not equal to the fixed input coefficient:

$$\frac{q}{x_k} < \frac{q}{x_k^*} = \frac{1}{\alpha_k}. \tag{2.2.8}$$

Equation (2.2.8) shows very little about the average product of a redundant input; however, a good bit of information can be gained by introducing an input from the minimum subset. Using equations (2.2.3) and (2.2.4) in equation (2.2.8), one may write:

$$AP_k = \frac{q}{x_k} = \frac{1}{\alpha_h} \frac{x_h^*}{x_k} = AP_h \left(\frac{x_h^*}{x_k}\right) > 0. \tag{2.2.9}$$

Thus the average product of the redundant input at any redundancy value equals the average product of any minimum input multiplied by the actual input ratio.

Holding the minimum input fixed, the slope of the average product curve over the region of redundancy may be determined from equation (2.2.9):

$$\frac{\partial(AP_k)}{\partial x_k} = -\frac{x_h^* AP_h}{x_k^2} < 0. \tag{2.2.10}$$

Thus the average product function is positive, negatively sloped, and smoothly continuous over the region of redundancy. Furthermore, it should be perfectly obvious that

$$MP_k = \left(\frac{\partial q}{\partial x_k}\right)^- = \left(\frac{\partial q}{\partial x_k}\right)^+ = 0 \tag{2.2.11}$$

for all $x_k > x_k^*$. Thus the marginal product of a redundant input does not depend upon the direction of variation; it is constant at zero and (presumably) smoothly continuous. The marginal and average product curves for a redundant input are shown in figure 7.

Marginal and average products; all inputs mutually limitational. Mutual limitationality of all inputs is the economically relevant case, at least at the microeconomic level. An entrepreneur who must pay a positive price for an input will not employ it in superfluous quantity.[1] Hence all observed situations will lie upon the production ray OR (figure 1), which may be called the *Pareto ray* inasmuch as its properties are much the same as Pareto optimality conditions.

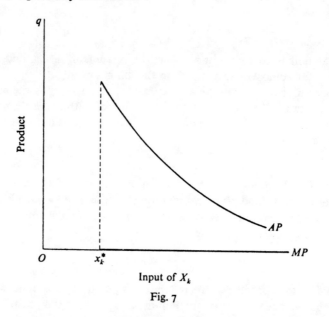

Fig. 7

Along the Pareto ray, all inputs are mutually limitational; the minimum subset is the entire set of inputs. When all inputs are simultaneously varied in the correct proportions, the whole set behaves as a single limitative input. The marginal and average products of the whole set are equal, constant and positive, and smoothly continuous for variations in either direction. The situation is precisely the one shown in figure 5. Similarly, when one input is varied, all others held constant, the situation is exactly the same as the one shown in figure 6; marginal and average products are equal for backward movements and diverge for forward displacements from the point of limitationality.

---

[1] This statement, of course, presupposes perfect divisibility of inputs. In any production situation, indivisibilities in the acquisition of inputs may cause 'excess capacity' in the stock of the inputs concerned.

2.2.2 Production with fixed proportions

When production is subject to fixed coefficients, the production function is homogeneous of degree one. This is the 'fixed proportions' case most frequently treated in the literature. Yet there may be increasing or decreasing returns to scale even though the production function is of the fixed-proportions variety. There are several ways in which non-constant returns may be introduced; in this section a simple method is analyzed.

We have so far assumed that the production coefficients α_i are constants. Let us now modify that assumption so as to make the coefficients functions of the level of output, i.e. $\alpha_i = \alpha_i(q)$. We shall further impose the condition that the input ratios remain constant irrespective of the level of output. Thus if q_0 and q_1 represent different levels of output, the condition may be stated as

$$\frac{\alpha_i(q_0)}{\alpha_n(q_0)} = \frac{\alpha_i(q_1)}{\alpha_n(q_1)} \quad (i=1, 2, ..., n-1). \tag{2.2.12}$$

The production function, in this case, becomes

$$q = \min\left(\frac{x_1}{\alpha_1(q)}, \frac{x_2}{\alpha_2(q)}, ..., \frac{x_n}{\alpha_n(q)}\right), \tag{2.2.13}$$

where equations (2.2.12) comprise a set of auxiliary relations that must be satisfied.

Equation (2.2.13) is characterized by increasing, constant, or decreasing returns to scale according as

$$\frac{\partial \alpha_i(q)}{\partial q} \lessgtr 0 \quad (i=1, 2, ..., n). \tag{2.2.14}$$

Conditions (2.2.12) require the signs of the partial derivatives in equations (2.2.14) to be the same. Thus there are increasing or decreasing returns to scale according as the input coefficients diminish or increase as output increases.

A further requirement must now be imposed. In particular, two economically meaningless possibilities must be precluded: 'something for nothing' and 'nothing for something'. In terms of inequalities (2.2.14), increasing returns to scale must not be so strong as to permit a greater output to be produced by a smaller set of inputs, and decreasing returns to scale must not be so great as to require a larger volume of inputs to produce a smaller level of output. Consequently, along the Pareto ray, we must require that

$$\frac{\partial x_i}{\partial q} > 0 \quad (i=1, 2, ..., n). \tag{2.2.15}$$

Inequalities (2.2.15) must obviously be required; but they are not them-

25

selves very meaningful. To obtain a rationale, note from equation (2.2.13) that along the Pareto ray, the following relation must hold:

$$x_i = \alpha_i q \quad (i = 1, 2, ..., n).$$ (2.2.16)

Next, take the elasticity of input with respect to output along the Pareto ray (θ):

$$\theta_i = \frac{\partial x_i}{\partial q} \frac{q}{x_i} = \alpha_i \frac{q}{x_i} + q \frac{\partial \alpha_i}{\partial q} \frac{q}{x_i}.$$ (2.2.17)

From equation (2.2.16), the first term on the right-hand side of equation (2.2.17) is unity. Further, $q/x_i = 1/\alpha_i$, so the second term may be written

$$\theta_i = \frac{\partial \alpha_i}{\partial q} \frac{q}{\alpha_i} = \frac{\text{the elasticity of the input}}{\text{coefficient with respect to output.}}$$

Using these results and the sign conditions imposed by inequalities (2.2.15), one obtains

$$\theta_i = 1 + \theta_i > 0 \quad (i = 1, 2, ..., n).$$ (2.2.18)

Thus to eliminate the economically meaningless situations, the elasticity of the input coefficients, when negative, must be less than unity in absolute value.

Inequalities (2.2.15) may be given a different interpretation, which will be of use in the following subsection. Denote $\partial \alpha_i / \partial q$ by α_i'. From equations (2.2.16),

$$\frac{\partial x_i}{\partial q} = \alpha_i + q \alpha_i' > 0 \quad (i = 1, 2, ..., n).$$ (2.2.19)

Consider the right-hand inequality and divide by $q > 0$, preserving the inequality:

$$\frac{\alpha_i}{q} + \alpha_i' > 0 \quad (i = 1, 2, ..., n).$$ (2.2.20)

Consequently, the average value of the input coefficient must exceed the absolute value of the marginal input coefficient when the latter is negative.

It is now convenient to introduce an alternative definition of increasing and decreasing returns to scale. Specifically, increasing or decreasing returns to scale exist according as $\partial^2 x_i / \partial q^2 \lessgtr 0$. Consequently, using inequality (2.2.19), increasing or decreasing returns exist according as

$$\frac{2\alpha_i'}{q} + \alpha_i'' \lessgtr 0 \quad (i = 1, 2, ..., n).$$ (2.2.21)

Because of the prior conditions on the sign of α_i', inequalities (2.2.21) do not permit an inference concerning the sign of α_i''. However, in case increasing or diminishing returns occur at a constant rate, $\alpha'' = 0$, and inequalities (2.2.21) are clearly satisfied.

Marginal and average products for variations along the Pareto ray. It is apparent from subsection 2.2.1 that marginal and average products behave exactly the same whether the minimum subset is a proper subset or the entire set. Hence we shall only discuss the situation in which all inputs are mutually limitational at the initial production point, i.e. the initial point is on the Pareto ray. In this subsection our attention is further restricted to proportional variations of all inputs. Thus all variations are along the Pareto ray, and the entire set of inputs behaves as a single limitative input.

For movements along the Pareto ray, average and marginal products are given by

$$\frac{q}{x_i} = \frac{\partial q}{\partial x_i} = \frac{1}{\alpha_i} \quad (i = 1, 2, ..., n). \tag{2.2.22}$$

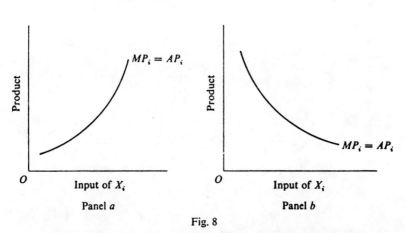

Fig. 8

Hence marginal and average products are positive and equal for variations in either direction. Furthermore, both functions are continuous if $\alpha_i = \alpha_i(q)$ are themselves continuous. Assuming they are, the slope of both curves is given by

$$\frac{\partial(q/x_i)}{\partial x_i} = \frac{\partial(\partial q/\partial x_i)}{\partial x_i} = \frac{\partial(1/\alpha_i)}{\partial q} \frac{\partial q}{\partial x_i} = -\frac{\alpha_i'}{\alpha_i^3} \quad (i = 1, 2, ..., n). \tag{2.2.23}$$

Thus the average and marginal product curves are positively or negatively sloped according as $\alpha_i' \lessgtr 0$, i.e. according as increasing or decreasing returns to scale exist. Panel a, figure 8, illustrates the case for increasing returns; panel b is relevant when decreasing returns prevail.[1]

---

[1] When the production function is characterized by variable proportions, one must carefully distinguish among average returns, marginal returns, and returns to scale. It is interesting to note that for variations along the Pareto ray of a fixed-proportions production function, the distinction is not so material. In this situation average returns, marginal returns, and returns to scale are all decreasing, constant, or increasing according as the degree of homogeneity of the production function is less than, equal to, or greater than unity.

The curvature of the average and marginal product curves is determined by taking the partial derivatives of equations (2.2.23):

$$\frac{\partial^2(q/x_i)}{\partial x_i^2} = \frac{\partial^2(\partial q/\partial x_i)}{\partial x_i^2} = \frac{3\alpha_i'^2 - \alpha_i\alpha_i''}{\alpha_i^5} \quad (i=1, 2, ..., n). \quad (2.2.24)$$

Since $\alpha_i > 0$, the sign of equations (2.2.24) depends entirely upon the numerator. In general the sign is not determinable since the sign of α_i'' is not known. As a pivotal case, suppose returns to scale increase or decrease at a constant rate. Then $\alpha_i'' = 0$, and equations (2.2.24) are always positive,

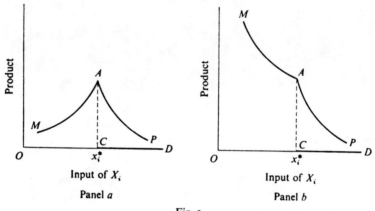

Input of X_i

Panel a Input of X_i

Panel b

Fig. 9

i.e. the average and marginal product curves are everywhere concave from above, as illustrated by both panels in figure 8. If returns to scale increase at an increasing rate or decrease at a decreasing rate, the curves are *a fortiori* concave from above. The curves can be concave from below only if returns increase at a strongly decreasing rate or decrease at a strongly increasing rate.

In summary: for variations along the Pareto ray, average and marginal products are positive and equal, smoothly continuous if $\alpha_i(q)$ is continuous, and usually concave from above. The curves are positively or negatively sloped according as returns to scale are increasing or decreasing.

Marginal and average products for single-input variations. When only one input is varied from a point of mutual limitationality, due heed must be paid to the direction of variation. Since a decrease in the usage of an input from a limitational point is both a necessary and a sufficient condition for a decrease in output, marginal and average products on decrease are given by

$$\left(\frac{q}{x_i}\right)^- = \left(\frac{\partial q}{\partial x_i}\right)^- = \frac{1}{\alpha_i} \quad (i=1, 2, ..., n). \quad (2.2.25)$$

The slope and curvature properties are identically the same as in figure 8 for reductions from the point $x_i = x_i^*$, as shown in panels a and b, figure 9, where MA represents both marginal and average products over the range $0 < x_i \leqslant x_i^*$.

For an increase beyond the input level $x_i = x_i^*$, average product is

$$\frac{q}{x_i} < \frac{q}{x_i^*} = \frac{1}{\alpha_i} \quad (i = 1, 2, ..., n). \tag{2.2.26}$$

Beyond the point of mutual limitationality, the average product curve declines as input increases because output is fixed. This portion of the average product curve is shown by the segment AP in figure 9. Consequently, the average product curve MAP has a cusp at the initial point of mutual limitationality.

Finally, in both the increasing (panel a) and decreasing (panel b) returns cases, the marginal product for increases from $x_i = x_i^*$ is

$$\left(\frac{\partial q}{\partial x_i}\right)^+ = 0 \quad (i = 1, 2, ..., n). \tag{2.2.27}$$

This portion of the marginal product curve is shown by the segment CD in figure 9, and the whole curve is given by $MACD$. The marginal product curves have a finite discontinuity at the limitational point, and marginal and average products diverge for increased input usage beyond the initial point of mutual limitationality.

2.3 Technical production with complex inputs

Production with complex inputs, which was described in subsection 2.1.2, has been largely ignored in the literature. To my knowledge, Frisch is the only author who has dealt with the case at all.[1] However, it is potentially important and differs from the theory of production with elementary inputs in several significant respects. The object of this section is to analyze the theory of production with complex inputs; however, this is accomplished largely by relying upon a specific example.

2.3.1 An example of production with complex inputs

Consider a producer of pipe tobacco who packages two blends, burley and bright (whose quantity is denoted x_1) and straight burley (whose quantity is denoted x_2). Our focus is upon the total production of pipe tobacco; in order to eliminate all but the technical aspects of production, it is assumed that the market price of the two blends is identical. Finally, the burley and bright blend contains the basic tobaccos in equal proportion.

---

[1] Frisch [1965, pp. 232–51]. He uses the term 'mixed factor rings' to denote what is here meant by complex inputs. Parts of this section follow Frisch's development.

29

Denote the total output of pipe tobacco in pounds by q. Thus necessarily

$$q \leqq x_1 + x_2. \tag{2.3.1}$$

Expression (2.3.1), however, specifies only one aspect of production. Due heed must be paid to the auxiliary processes of stemming and drying, cutting, and packaging. The cutting operation is denoted by x_3, and it is assumed that a constant amount α_3 of cutting-machine time is required per pound of tobacco, irrespective of blend. Similarly, packaging is denoted by x_4, and α_4 represents the constant amount of packaging-machine time per pound of tobacco. Thus the output of pipe tobacco is further subject to the following upper bounds:

$$q \leqq \frac{x_3}{\alpha_3}, \tag{2.3.2}$$

and

$$q \leqq \frac{x_4}{\alpha_4}. \tag{2.3.3}$$

Finally, x_5 denotes the stemming and drying process. It is assumed that bright tobacco requires a constant amount α_1 of stemming and drying time per pound, while burley requires the constant amount α_2. Since bright tobacco is more highly processed by the grower, it requires less stemming and drying time than burley; hence $\alpha_2 > \alpha_1$. The burley and bright blend is half-and-half; hence the drying and stemming time per pound of this blend is $\frac{1}{2}(\alpha_1 + \alpha_2) < \alpha_2$. Since the blends sell for the same price, the stemming and drying facilities are first devoted to the burley and bright blend. If the available quantity of bright tobacco is sufficiently great, the burley and bright blend might exhaust the stemming and drying facilities. In that case, production would be subject to the following upper bound:

$$q \leqq \frac{2x_5}{\alpha_1 + \alpha_2}. \tag{2.3.4}$$

If the stemming and drying facilities are not exhausted by the burley and bright blend, the following amount of straight burley can be stemmed and dried:

$$x_2 = \frac{x_5 - \left(\frac{\alpha_1 + \alpha_2}{2}\right) x_1}{\alpha_2}.$$

Thus the final upper bound for the problem is

$$q \leqq \frac{2x_5 + (\alpha_2 - \alpha_1) x_1}{2\alpha_2}. \tag{2.3.5}$$

The production process contains five elementary inputs; but there are restrictions that convert elementary inputs into complex inputs and accordingly impose five upper bounds [expressions (2.3.1)–(2.3.5)]. Hence the production function for total pipe tobacco output may be written

$$q = \min\left[x_1 + x_2, \frac{x_3}{\alpha_3}, \frac{x_4}{\alpha_4}, \frac{2x_5}{\alpha_1 + \alpha_2}, \frac{2x_5 + (\alpha_2 - \alpha_1) x_1}{2\alpha_2} \right]. \tag{2.3.6}$$

For notational convenience, the production function may be written schematically as

$$q = \min [f_1(x), ..., f_5(x)], \qquad (2.3.7)$$

where $f_i(x)$ represents the ith complex input, and x without subscript simply indicates the particular set of elementary inputs contained in the complex input. In this particular example, x_3 and x_4 are actually elementary inputs in every sense; x_1, x_2, and x_5 enter the problem as complex inputs.

2.3.2 Marginal products, single limitational input

In certain respects marginal products are much the same in the elementary and complex input cases. From a point of mutual limitationality, marginal products are always positive on decrease but are only positive on increase when all inputs in the minimum subset are expanded proportionately. Yet there are differences as well; in particular, the marginal product of an elementary input depends upon the complex inputs contained in the minimum subset. For example, if f_1-f_4 comprise the minimum subset, the marginal product of x_1 is precisely unity. On the other hand, if f_2-f_5 is the minimum subset, the marginal product of x_1 is $(\alpha_2-\alpha_1)/2\alpha_2$. The situation in which both f_1 and f_5 are in the minimum subset is dealt with in subsection 2.3.3 below.

From the production function in equation (2.3.6) it is clear that if the ith complex input is the only limitational input, the marginal product of the jth elementary input on decrease is

$$\left(\frac{\partial q}{\partial x_j}\right)^- = \frac{\partial q}{\partial f_i}\frac{\partial f_i}{\partial x_j} \quad (i,j=1, ..., 5). \qquad (2.3.8)$$

In all cases, however, $\partial q/\partial f_i \equiv 1$; thus the marginal products are actually determined exclusively by $\partial f_i/\partial x_j$ (when the ith complex input is the only limitational input). The calculations for equation (2.3.6) are shown below:

$$\left.\begin{aligned}
&\frac{\partial f_1}{\partial x_1} = 1, \quad \frac{\partial f_1}{\partial x_2} = 1, \quad \frac{\partial f_1}{\partial x_3} = 0, \quad \frac{\partial f_1}{\partial x_4} = 0, \quad \frac{\partial f_1}{\partial x_5} = 0; \\[2mm]
&\frac{\partial f_2}{\partial x_1} = 0, \quad \frac{\partial f_2}{\partial x_2} = 0, \quad \frac{\partial f_2}{\partial x_3} = \frac{1}{\alpha_3}, \quad \frac{\partial f_2}{\partial x_4} = 0, \quad \frac{\partial f_2}{\partial x_5} = 0; \\[2mm]
&\frac{\partial f_3}{\partial x_1} = 0, \quad \frac{\partial f_3}{\partial x_2} = 0, \quad \frac{\partial f_3}{\partial x_3} = 0, \quad \frac{\partial f_3}{\partial x_4} = \frac{1}{\alpha_4}, \quad \frac{\partial f_3}{\partial x_5} = 0; \\[2mm]
&\frac{\partial f_4}{\partial x_1} = 0, \quad \frac{\partial f_4}{\partial x_2} = 0, \quad \frac{\partial f_4}{\partial x_3} = 0, \quad \frac{\partial f_4}{\partial x_4} = 0, \quad \frac{\partial f_4}{\partial x_5} = \frac{2}{\alpha_1+\alpha_2}; \\[2mm]
&\frac{\partial f_5}{\partial x_1} = \frac{\alpha_2-\alpha_1}{2\alpha_2}, \quad \frac{\partial f_5}{\partial x_2} = 0, \quad \frac{\partial f_5}{\partial x_3} = 0, \quad \frac{\partial f_5}{\partial x_4} = 0, \quad \frac{\partial f_5}{\partial x_5} = \frac{1}{\alpha_2}.
\end{aligned}\right\} \quad (2.3.9)$$

2.3.3   Marginal products, mutual limitationality

In the example above, suppose f_1 and f_5 are mutually limitational at an initial point. Furthermore, suppose the elementary input x_1 is varied. Finally, as illustrated in figure 10, suppose $(\alpha_2 - \alpha_1/2\alpha_2) < 1$. Our concern is the marginal product of x_1.

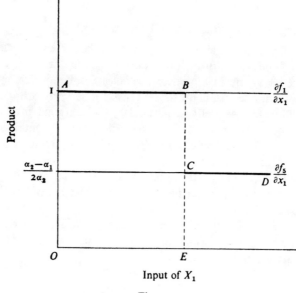

Fig. 10

For an increase in x_1 from the initial point E, total output is augmented by the lesser of the marginal products. Hence on increase,

$$\left(\frac{\partial q}{\partial x_1}\right)^+ = \left(\frac{\partial f_5}{\partial x_1}\right)^+ = \frac{\alpha_2 - \alpha_1}{2\alpha_2}. \qquad (2.3.10)$$

On the other hand, if the input of x_1 is reduced, total output is reduced by the greater of the marginal products. Hence on decrease,

$$\left(\frac{\partial q}{\partial x_1}\right)^- = \left(\frac{\partial f_1}{\partial x_1}\right)^- = 1. \qquad (2.3.11)$$

Thus in effect, when x_1 alone is increased, f_5 becomes the single limitative complex input. Similarly, when x_1 alone is decreased, f_1 becomes the single limitative input. Consequently, the marginal product curve is $ABCD$ in figure 10, having a finite discontinuity BC at the initial point E.

More generally, the marginal product curve for each elementary input will contain a finite discontinuity when production is subject to complex inputs. Let the production function take the form

$$q = \min(f_1, f_2, ..., f_m), \tag{2.3.12}$$

where $f_i = f_i(x_1, x_2, ..., x_n)$ or some subset of the n elementary inputs. Further, suppose all complex inputs are mutually limitational at some initial point E (see panel b, figure 11).[1] Finally, we consider a more general situation in which some or all elementary marginal product functions are negatively sloped and linear within a small neighborhood of the initial point.[2] Two graphical views of the situation are shown in panels a and b,

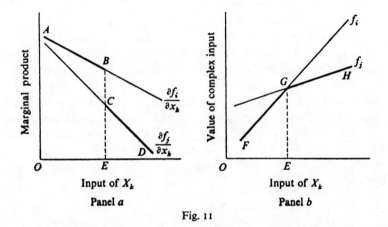

Panel *a*

Panel *b*

Fig. 11

figure 11, where it is assumed that f_i and f_j are the most limiting complex inputs on decrease and on increase respectively.[3]

Suppose the organization of production establishes the initial point E. We are concerned with the change in total output resulting from the variation in usage of the elementary input X_k. Suppose the input of X_k is increased. Total output will expand; but it can only expand by an amount equal to the *least* increment in the set of complex inputs. At the initial point, $f_1 = f_2 = ... = f_m$. When the usage of X_k expands, the value of each

[1] The assumption of mutual limitationality of the entire set is not in the least restrictive. As we have previously seen, the results are the same irrespective of the dimensions of the minimum subset.

[2] The reader may easily prove for himself that if *one* elementary marginal product function is negatively sloped, it will dominate all the rest. If there are two or more negatively sloped functions, figure 11 represents the most general situation.

[3] While not specially constructed for this algebraic form, the complex inputs might be represented as:
$$f_i = ax_h^\alpha x_k^\beta \quad (0 \leqq \alpha, \beta < 1)$$
and
$$f_j = ax_h^\alpha x_k^{1-\alpha}.$$

33

complex input utilizing X_k also expands. But in general, they do not expand proportionately; and the expansion in output cannot exceed the least expansion in the complex inputs. Furthermore, the marginal product of X_k on increase equals the increase in the least expansive complex input. Thus

$$\left(\frac{\partial q}{\partial x_k}\right)^+ = \min\left(\frac{\partial f_1}{\partial x_k}, \frac{\partial f_2}{\partial x_k}, \ldots, \frac{\partial f_m}{\partial x_k}\right). \qquad (2.3.13)$$

In figure 11 it is assumed that f_j is the least expansive complex input. Thus on increase from point E,

$$\left(\frac{\partial q}{\partial x_k}\right)^+ = \left(\frac{\partial f_j}{\partial x_k}\right)^+, \qquad (2.3.14)$$

and the relevant section of the marginal product curve is shown by the segment CD in Panel a. The *value* or magnitude of the complex input is shown in panel b. At point E, all complex inputs are mutually limitational and hence are equal. The fact that f_j is the least expansive input is illustrated by the segment GH in panel b.

Next, consider the marginal product of X_k on decrease. When X_k is decreased from the initial point, each complex input utilizing X_k decreases as well. Output diminishes and, by equation (2.3.12), it must diminish by an amount equal to the greatest diminution in the complex inputs. Since the marginal product of X_k on decrease equals the greatest of the decreases in the complex inputs,

$$\left(\frac{\partial q}{\partial x_k}\right)^- = \max\left(\frac{\partial f_1}{\partial x_k}, \frac{\partial f_2}{\partial x_k}, \ldots, \frac{\partial f_m}{\partial x_k}\right). \qquad (2.3.15)$$

In figure 11 it is assumed that f_i has the greatest decrease. Hence on decrease

$$\left(\frac{\partial q}{\partial x_k}\right)^- = \left(\frac{\partial f_i}{\partial x_k}\right)^-, \qquad (2.3.16)$$

and the relevant section of the marginal product curve is shown by the segment AB in panel a. Similarly, in panel b, FG illustrates that f_i diminishes most rapidly when the input of X_k is reduced.

Generally, the marginal product curve for an elementary input will always look like the curve $ABCD$ in panel a. There will always be one finite discontinuity, which occurs at the initial point. Naturally, the complex inputs involved and the marginal product curve itself depend upon the initial point.

2.3.4 The Pareto region

The Pareto ray has previously been defined as the *ray* along which all elementary inputs are mutually limitational. When the production function contains only elementary inputs, the points of mutual limitationality lie on *the* ray whose slope is determined by the $(n-1)$ pairs of input ratios. At any point not on the ray, one or more inputs are redundant and one or more are limitative.

In a Pareto point, all elementary inputs have positive marginal products on decrease.[1] This brings to light another way in which production with complex inputs differs from production with elementary inputs: in the former situation, the set of Pareto points may comprise a *region* instead of a ray.

To see this, let us compare an example of production with elementary inputs with the example of complex inputs used throughout this section. Let the elementary production function be

$$q = \min\left(\frac{x_1}{\alpha_1}, \frac{x_2}{\alpha_2}, \frac{x_3}{\alpha_3}, \frac{x_4}{\alpha_4}, \frac{x_5}{\alpha_5}\right). \tag{2.3.17}$$

Thus at any limitational or limitative point, the marginal product of the ith elementary input on decrease is

$$\left(\frac{\partial q}{\partial x_i}\right)^- = \frac{1}{\alpha_i} \quad (i=1, ..., 5). \tag{2.3.18}$$

Now consider table 1. The elementary inputs contained in the minimum subset are specified in the left-hand stub, while the body of the table shows the sign of each marginal product on decrease. In the first block, there is only one input in the minimum subset. The sign matrix is a diagonal matrix with 'plus' along the principal diagonal and 'zero' elsewhere. The entries continue in the same way for all possible combinations of two, three, four, and five inputs in the minimum subset. It is especially important to notice: (a) in the fourth block, the sign matrix is a 'reverse' diagonal matrix, with a diagonal of zeros; and (b) only in the last block, the unique case in which all inputs are in the minimum subset, are all marginal products positive on decrease. This is another way of viewing the fact that the set of Pareto points lies on a one-dimensional ray.

The corresponding situation for complex inputs is portrayed in table 2. The complex inputs in the minimum subset are specified in the left-hand stub; and the signs of the marginal products of the *elementary* inputs, obtained from equations (2.3.9), are shown in the body of the table. There are, to be sure, differences in the first three blocks in the two tables; however, these differences are not particularly significant. Furthermore, the final blocks are identical: when all inputs are in the minimum subset, all elementary marginal products are positive on decrease. The crucial difference lies in the fourth block. In two of the five combinations, all

---

[1] Notice that at any point not on the Pareto ray, redundant inputs have zero marginal products on increase and decrease.

TABLE I *Minimum subsets and marginal products, Elementary inputs*

Elementary inputs in the minimum subset	Marginal product of elementary input				
	X_1	X_2	X_3	X_4	X_5
X_1	+	o	o	o	o
X_2	o	+	o	o	o
X_3	o	o	+	o	o
X_4	o	o	o	+	o
X_5	o	o	o	o	+
$X_1 X_2$	+	+	o	o	o
$X_1 X_3$	+	o	+	o	o .
$X_1 X_4$	+	o	o	+	o
$X_1 X_5$	+	o	o	o	+
$X_2 X_3$	o	+	+	o	o
$X_2 X_4$	o	+	o	+	o
$X_2 X_5$	o	+	o	o	+
$X_3 X_4$	o	o	+	+	o
$X_3 X_5$	o	o	+	o	+
$X_4 X_5$	o	o	o	+	+
$X_1 X_2 X_3$	+	+	+	o	o
$X_1 X_2 X_4$	+	+	o	+	o
$X_1 X_2 X_5$	+	+	o	o	+
$X_1 X_3 X_4$	+	o	+	+	o
$X_1 X_3 X_5$	+	o	+	o	+
$X_1 X_4 X_5$	+	o	o	+	+
$X_2 X_3 X_4$	o	+	+	+	o
$X_2 X_3 X_5$	o	+	+	o	+
$X_2 X_4 X_5$	o	+	o	+	+
$X_3 X_4 X_5$	o	o	+	+	+
$X_1 X_2 X_3 X_4$	+	+	+	+	o
$X_1 X_2 X_3 X_5$	+	+	+	o	+
$X_1 X_2 X_4 X_5$	+	+	o	+	+
$X_1 X_3 X_4 X_5$	+	o	+	+	+
$X_2 X_3 X_4 X_5$	o	+	+	+	+
** $X_1 X_2 X_3 X_4 X_5$	+	+	+	+	+

marginal products are positive even though only four complex inputs are in the minimum subset.[1]

In this example, a Pareto point is attained where

$$q = f_1 = f_2 = f_3 = f_4, \qquad (2.3.19)$$

or where
$$q = f_1 = f_2 = f_3 = f_5. \qquad (2.3.20)$$

[1] It might be well to reemphasize that this is based upon the example introduced at the beginning of the section. In general, if $f_i = f_i(x_1, x_2, ..., x_n)$ contains all of the elementary inputs, all marginal products will be positive on decrease when f_i alone constitutes the minimum subset.

TABLE 2 *Minimum subsets and marginal products, Complex inputs*

Complex inputs in the minimum subset	Marginal product of elementary input				
	X_1	X_2	X_3	X_4	X_5
f_1	+	+	o	o	o
f_2	o	o	+	o	o
f_3	o	o	o	+	o
f_4	o	o	o	o	+
f_5	+	o	o	o	+
f_1f_2	+	+	+	o	o
f_1f_3	+	+	o	+	o
f_1f_4	+	+	o	o	+
f_1f_5	+	+	o	o	+
f_2f_3	o	o	+	+	o
f_2f_4	o	o	+	o	+
f_2f_5	+	o	+	o	+
f_3f_4	o	o	o	+	+
f_3f_5	+	o	o	+	+
f_4f_5	+	o	o	o	+
$f_1f_2f_3$	+	+	+	+	o
$f_1f_2f_4$	+	+	o	o	+
$f_1f_2f_5$	+	+	o	o	+
$f_1f_3f_4$	+	+	o	o	+
$f_1f_3f_5$	+	+	o	+	+
$f_1f_4f_5$	+	+	o	o	+
$f_2f_3f_4$	o	o	+	+	+
$f_2f_3f_5$	+	o	+	+	+
$f_2f_4f_5$	+	o	+	o	+
$f_3f_4f_5$	+	o	o	+	+
** $f_1f_2f_3f_4$	+	+	+	+	+
** $f_1f_2f_3f_5$	+	+	+	+	+
$f_1f_2f_4f_5$	+	+	+	o	+
$f_1f_3f_4f_5$	+	+	o	+	+
$f_2f_3f_4f_5$	+	o	+	+	+
** $f_1f_2f_3f_4f_5$	+	+	+	+	+

In the first case, f_5 is redundant; and f_4 is redundant in the latter. Thus a Pareto point can exist when some input(s) are redundant, as well as when all inputs are mutually limitational, i.e. when

$$q = f_1 = f_2 = f_3 = f_4 = j_5. \qquad (2.3.21)$$

Using the production function in equation (2.3.6), equations (2.3.19)–(2.3.21) may be written as follows:

$$(a) \quad x_1 + x_2 = \frac{x_3}{\alpha_3} = \frac{x_4}{\alpha_4} = \frac{2x_5}{\alpha_1 + \alpha_2};$$

$$(b) \quad x_1 + x_2 = \frac{x_3}{\alpha_3} = \frac{x_4}{\alpha_4} = \frac{2x_5 + (\alpha_2 - \alpha_1)\, x_1}{2\alpha_2};$$

$$(c) \quad x_1 + x_2 = \frac{x_3}{\alpha_3} = \frac{x_4}{\alpha_4} = \frac{2x_5}{\alpha_1 + \alpha_2} = \frac{2x_5 + (\alpha_2 - \alpha_1)\, x_1}{2\alpha_2}.$$

(2.3.22)

These three alternatives all represent Pareto points, and they exhaust all possibilities for Pareto points. However, these alternatives can be reduced somewhat. First, equations (2.3.22 a) are irrelevant because they can only hold if $x_2 < 0$. If equations (2.3.22 a) hold, the fifth complex input is redundant, implying

$$2x_5 + (\alpha_2 - \alpha_1)\, x_1 > 2\alpha_2(x_1 + x_2). \tag{2.3.23}$$

Substitute the value of x_5 obtained from (2.3.22 a) into (2.3.23), obtaining

$$\frac{(\alpha_1 + \alpha_2)\, (x_1 + x_2) + (\alpha_2 - \alpha_1)\, x_1}{2\alpha_2} > x_1 + x_2. \tag{2.3.24}$$

Upon reduction, inequality (2.3.24) becomes

$$0 > (\alpha_2 - \alpha_1)\, x_2. \tag{2.3.25}$$

But since $\alpha_2 > \alpha_1$, $(\alpha_2 - \alpha_1) > 0$; consequently, inequality (2.3.25) can only be satisfied if $x_2 < 0$. Therefore, equations (2.3.22 a) may be discarded as economically irrelevant.

Equations (2.3.22 c) can also be eliminated inasmuch as they are a special case of equations (2.3.22 b) when $x_2 = 0$. To see this, first solve equations (2.3.22 b) so as to express x_3, x_4, and x_5 as functions of x_1 and x_2:

$$(a) \quad x_3 = \alpha_3(x_1 + x_2);$$

$$(b) \quad x_4 = \alpha_4(x_1 + x_2);$$

$$(c) \quad x_5 = \frac{2\alpha_2 x_2 + (\alpha_1 + \alpha_2)\, x_1}{2}.$$

(2.3.26)

If equations (2.3.22 c) are solved in the same way, one obtains equations (2.3.26) and one additional equation:

$$x_5 = \frac{(\alpha_1 + \alpha_2)\, (x_1 + x_2)}{2}. \tag{2.3.27}$$

For consistency, equations (2.3.26 c) and (2.3.27) must be equal, implying

$$2\alpha_2 x_2 = (\alpha_1 + \alpha_2)\, x_2. \tag{2.3.28}$$

But since $\alpha_2 > \alpha_1$, $2\alpha_2 > (\alpha_1 + \alpha_2)$; consequently, equation (2.3.28) can be satisfied if, and only if, $x_2 = 0$. Hence the set (2.3.22 c) may be eliminated as a special case of the set (2.3.22 b).

The relevant set of Pareto points is fully characterized by equations
(2.3.22b), or their equivalent form contained in equations (2.3.26). From
equations (2.3.26) it is clear that the set of Pareto points does not lie upon
a one-dimensional ray. Indeed, the Pareto set constitutes a three-dimen-
sional *region* embedded in a five-dimensional space. When production is
governed by complex inputs, there is a region rather than a ray of mutual
limitationality. However, there is neither a point nor a region of mutual
complex-input limitativeness.

2.3.5 The economic region of production with complex inputs

The economic region of production was mentioned in chapter 1; and it
has been emphasized that when production is subject to fixed proportions,
there is only an economic *ray* if all inputs are elementary.[1] But just as there
is a Pareto region, rather than a Pareto ray, when inputs are complex, so
also is there an economic region of production rather than an economic
ray. The object of this subsection is to demonstrate the existence of the
economic region by means of a very simple example.

The economic region of production is examined in considerable detail in
Chapters 4 and 5; let it suffice at present to give the following definition: the
economic region of production is that portion of the isoquant map over
which all marginal products are positive on increase and on decrease. Thus
for an economic region to exist, there must exist a region in which all
elementary inputs are mutually limitative.

Before introducing the example, it might serve well to emphasize that
the 'Pareto region' and the 'economic region' are not the same when
production is subject to fixed proportions and complex inputs. The Pareto
region is the region in which all elementary inputs are mutually limitational,
i.e. all marginal products are positive on decrease. To qualify as an
economic region, all inputs must be mutually limitative, i.e. all marginal
products must be positive on increase and on decrease. Thus an economic
region exists if, and only if, *one* complex input is limitative and all others
redundant. The economic region and the Pareto region are the same only
when both degenerate into a ray; and then they are the same only for
proportional variation of all the inputs, i.e. the entire set of inputs behaves
as a single limitative input.

The discussion can be made more concrete by turning to an example,
which is illustrated by figure 12. Let the complex-input, fixed-proportions
production function be given by

$$q = \min\left(\frac{x_1 + x_2}{\alpha_1}, \frac{x_2}{\alpha_2}\right), \tag{2.3.29}$$

[1] In this case the 'economic ray' has a limited meaning in that marginal products are all
positive if, and only if, all inputs are varied in the proper proportions.

where, as shown below, $\alpha_1 > \alpha_2$ of necessity. First, the two complex inputs are mutually limitational when

$$\frac{x_1 + x_2}{\alpha_1} = \frac{x_2}{\alpha_2}, \qquad (2.3.30)$$

or

$$\frac{dx_2}{dx_1} = \frac{\alpha_2}{\alpha_1 - \alpha_2}. \qquad (2.3.31)$$

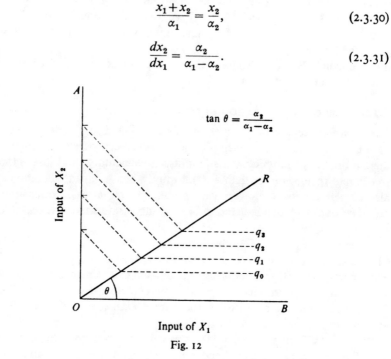

Fig. 12

Equation (2.3.30) determines the production ray OR in figure 12; equation (2.3.31) shows its slope and also shows that $\alpha_1 > \alpha_2$ is required for an economically meaningful situation.

Next, suppose the first complex input is the single limitative input. Thus in some region the marginal products are

$$\left(\frac{\partial q}{\partial x_1}\right)^+ = \left(\frac{\partial q}{\partial x_1}\right)^- = \left(\frac{\partial q}{\partial x_2}\right)^+ = \left(\frac{\partial q}{\partial x_2}\right)^- = \frac{1}{\alpha_1}. \qquad (2.3.32)$$

The region in which equations (2.3.32) are valid is easily determined by considering the condition that must hold if the first complex input is to be limitative:

$$\frac{x_2}{\alpha_2} > \frac{x_1 + x_2}{\alpha_1}. \qquad (2.3.33)$$

Rearranging inequality (2.3.33), one obtains

$$\frac{x_2}{x_1} = \frac{dx_2}{dx_1} > \frac{\alpha_2}{\alpha_1 - \alpha_2}. \qquad (2.3.34)$$

40

Therefore, the economic region of production comprises the semi-interior of the open linear cone AOR in figure 12. That is, the economic region is the set of points within the cone AOR plus the points on the boundary OA. The points on the boundary OR are excluded from the economic region because all marginal products are positive only on decrease.

Within the linear cone ROB and along the boundary OB, X_1 is redundant. Therefore, the isoquants in this region are horizontal lines parallel to the abscissa, i.e. the marginal product of X_1 is zero on increase and on decrease, so the marginal rate of technical substitution is zero. In the economic region, the isoquants are not vertical lines. Indeed, since both inputs are mutually limitative, the marginal rate of technical substitution is positive and, indeed, it is precisely unity throughout the entire economic region. This may also be seen from the equation of the isoquant within the economic region:

$$x_1 + x_2 = \alpha_1 \bar{q}, \tag{2.3.35}$$

where $\bar{q}$ represents any constant level of output. From equation (2.3.35) it is apparent that along the isoquant

$$\frac{dx_2}{dx_1} = -1. \tag{2.3.36}$$

Hence the isoquant is negatively sloped throughout the economic region; and the entire isoquant map is typified by the isoquants labelled $q_0, \ldots, q_3$ in figure 12.[1]

2.3.6 The elasticity of substitution

The elasticity of substitution, just as the economic region of production, is the subject of intense analysis in Chapters 4 and 5. However, the concept must be introduced briefly at this time because the existence of an economic region of production implies the possibility of a non-zero elasticity of substitution.

At this stage let the following statements suffice to describe the elasticity of substitution: (a) the elasticity of substitution is the proportional change in the input ratio attributable to a proportional change in the marginal rate of technical substitution (MRTS), or

$$\sigma = \frac{\Delta(x_2/x_1)}{x_2/x_1} \div \frac{\Delta(MRTS)}{MRTS} = \frac{\Delta \ln (x_2/x_1)}{\Delta \ln (MRTS)}; \tag{2.3.37}$$

and (b) the elasticity of substitution is defined only for movements along an isoquant.

A simple case is illustrated in figure 13, where q_0 is an isoquant and

[1] Throughout this section on complex inputs, complex inputs of the kind shown in footnote 3, p. 33, are excluded from this analysis. While applicable to all of section 2.3, it is especially relevant to note this caveat when reading subsections 2.3.5 and 2.3.6.

X_2OR is the economic region of production. So long as each complex input contains the elementary inputs in linear combinations, the marginal rate of technical substitution is a positive constant throughout the economic region of production, e.g. the segment AB. Similarly, in the uneconomic region the marginal rate of technical substitution is a constant whose value is zero, e.g. the segment BC.

For movements along AB within the economic region, the inputs are perfect substitutes, i.e. $\sigma \to \infty$. This may readily be seen from equation

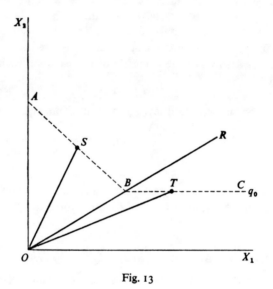

Fig. 13

(2.3.37) since $\Delta(MRTS) = 0$ and $MRTS > 0$ [see equation (2.4.3) or (3.4.5)]. The opposite situation prevails along BC within the uneconomic region. The inputs cannot be substituted one for the other, i.e. $\sigma = 0$, the usual case with fixed-proportions production functions. This cannot be derived directly from equation (2.3.37) since both $\Delta(MRTS)$ and $MRTS$ are zero. The denominator is an indeterminate form; by convention the elasticity is set equal to zero.

Finally, for movements from one region to the other, the elasticity of substitution takes on some finite, positive value. Consider the movement from S to T in figure 13. The input ratio declines by the difference between the slopes of OS and OT. Thus $\Delta(x_2/x_1) < 0$. Similarly, the marginal rate of technical substitution declines from some positive magnitude to zero. Hence $\Delta(MRTS) < 0$. Measuring the input ratio and the marginal rate of technical substitution from the initial point S, both are positive quantities.

The two negative signs cancel, leaving equation (2.3.37) positive; since each term is also finite, the elasticity of substitution is positive and finite as well.

2.4   The theory of production with elementary inputs and multiple production processes

It is quite conceivable that at a certain moment in time a particular commodity may be produced by a variety of production processes. That is to say, there may exist two or more alternative fixed-proportions production

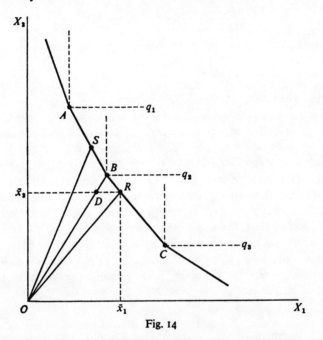

Fig. 14

processes capable of producing an identical output. In point of fact one might never observe more than one process in use; however, it is technologically possible for two processes to be used concurrently.

The object of this section is to discuss multiple-process production when all processes use elementary inputs. Without loss of generality, our attention may be restricted to a situation in which two inputs may be used in three different fixed-proportions processes to produce a single homogeneous output. The production function may be written

$$q = \min\left(\frac{x_{1i}}{\alpha_{1i}}, \frac{x_{2i}}{\alpha_{2i}}\right) \quad (i = 1, 2, 3). \tag{2.4.1}$$

Unit isoquants for the three processes are represented in figure 14 by q_1, q_2, and q_3; and the points of mutual limitationality for the individual processes are indicated by A, B, and C. Throughout the discussion our attention is restricted exclusively to points of mutual limitationality because, whatever the input endowment ratio, two processes may be combined so as to obtain a production point in which all inputs are mutually limitational.

2.4.1 Marginal products

For expansion or contraction of both inputs in the proper proportions, the marginal products in the points of single-process limitationality are

$$\frac{\partial q}{\partial x_j} = \frac{1}{\alpha_{ji}} \quad (i=1, 2, 3; j = 1, 2). \tag{2.4.2}$$

Hence in any limitational point, the marginal rate of technical substitution on decrease is

$$MRTS_{21, i} = \frac{\alpha_{2i}}{\alpha_{1i}} \quad (i=1, 2, 3), \tag{2.4.3}$$

as explained in chapter 3, subsection 4.1.

Equations (2.4.2) and (2.4.3) are simple extensions of the theory of production developed in section 2.2 above. However, this does not exhaust the technical possibilities when more than one production process is available. More specifically, in the present situation two production processes may be combined so as to obtain *any* desired input ratio.

To explain this point, let us assume that there are fixed endowments of the two inputs: $\bar{x}_1$ units of X_1 and $\bar{x}_2$ units of X_2. If only a single production process were used, the maximum output would be attained by using process 2 at the level indicated by OD. Since each of the isoquants represents unit output, it is clear that output would be less than one if a single process were used. However, if it is possible to produce at point R, one unit of output can be obtained. As a matter of fact this can easily be accomplished.

Suppose the point R lies $100p_2\%$ of the distance between B and C $(0 < p_2 < 1)$. Then the unit output corresponding to point R may be obtained by producing $100(1-p_2)\%$ of a unit by process 2 and $100p_2\%$ of a unit by process 3. The total input of X_1 is $(1-p_2) x_{12}+p_2 x_{13} = \bar{x}_1$, and an analogous expression holds for X_2. The inputs are fully utilized and output maximized by using a linear combination of processes 2 and 3.

When a linear combination of processes is used, it is reasonable to assign marginal products to each input by means of the same linear combination. Thus at point R, the marginal products are

$$\frac{\partial q}{\partial x_j} = (1-p_2)\frac{1}{\alpha_{j2}}+p_2\frac{1}{\alpha_{j3}} \quad (j=1, 2), \tag{2.4.4}$$

or

$$\frac{\partial q}{\partial x_j} = \frac{\alpha_{j3}+p_2(\alpha_{j2}-\alpha_{j3})}{\alpha_{j2}\alpha_{j3}} \quad (j=1, 2). \tag{2.4.5}$$

Since at B and C processes 2 and 3 are in points of mutual limitationality, point R is a point of mutual limitationality. Thus equations (2.4.4) or (2.4.5) hold on decrease and on increase when the inputs are expanded or contracted in the ratio given by the slope of OR. Furthermore, since any point on the locus ABC may be obtained by the proper linear combination of processes, every point on ABC is a point of mutual limitationality. At any such point, both marginal products are positive on decrease; hence the locus ABC, together with its radial projections, comprises the Pareto region.

In this case, however, there is not an economic region of production.[1] There are many economic rays of production in the circumscribed sense in which that term is used. Nonetheless, there is no point in the whole space in which both marginal products are positive on increase and decrease when the marginal products are taken individually.[2]

2.4.2 The elasticity of substitution

While there is not an economic region of production, there are an infinite numbers of economic rays; and this alone permits one to define the elasticity of substitution between points of mutual limitationality. From figure 14 it is obviously possible to shift from point A, through points such as S, B, and R, to point C. In the process, X_1 is substituted for X_2 in producing a constant level of output. Hence substitution is technologically possible; and the elasticity of substitution is positive and finite over the Pareto region. This statement is true whether one moves from one single-process point to another (from A to B, or B to C) or from one linear-combination point either to a single-process point (S to B) or to another linear-combination point (S to R).

From equations (2.4.3) and (2.4.5) it is clear that the marginal rate of technical substitution is a positive quantity at all points on ABC. Furthermore, it is easy to show that the marginal rate of technical substitution diminishes as the production point moves downward along ABC (i.e. from

---

[1] Despite this, there are positive elasticities of substitution.

[2] It should be emphasized that sections 2.3 and 2.4 are largely descriptive rather than analytical because these cases had to be developed by examples. Indeed, a general analysis is not possible because an infinite number of complex relations may exist. The reason for including these two sections is, in my opinion, an important one: to demonstrate that input substitution is possible in many different kinds of fixed-proportions technologies. All readers of the manuscript did not share my opinion. One wrote: 'You have forced fixed proportions production theory into a neoclassical mold in order to be able to define marginal products, elasticities of substitution, etc. But these are all emasculated versions of their variable proportions counterparts. It comes down to this: if you take care about directions, or if you know all inputs change proportionately, or if inputs have a neoclassical property (like your complex inputs), then you can use neoclassical analysis.' Quite true; the object of these two sections is to demonstrate this important fact.

point A in the direction of B (cf. chapter 3, subsection 4.1)). The proof is given for a movement from A to B, but by analogous reasoning, the statement holds for any movement.

Since A and B are points of mutual limitationality, at each point

$$\frac{x_{2i}}{x_{1i}} = \frac{\alpha_{2i}}{\alpha_{1i}} \quad (i = 1, 2). \tag{2.4.6}$$

Thus the input ratio equals the marginal rate of technical substitution. It is obvious that

$$\frac{x_{21}}{x_{11}} > \frac{x_{22}}{x_{12}}, \tag{2.4.7}$$

so equations (2.4.6) imply that

$$\frac{\alpha_{21}}{\alpha_{11}} > \frac{\alpha_{22}}{\alpha_{12}}. \tag{2.4.8}$$

Thus
$$\Delta(MRTS) = \frac{\alpha_{22}}{\alpha_{12}} - \frac{\alpha_{21}}{\alpha_{11}} < 0 \tag{2.4.9}$$

by inequalities (2.4.8).

The changes in the input ratio and in the marginal rate of technical substitution are both negative; the elasticity of substitution is accordingly positive. Furthermore, since all terms entering into its calculation are finite, one may conclude that the elasticity of substitution is positive and finite for movements along the unit-output locus ABC.

3

THE ECONOMIC THEORY OF
PRODUCTION UNDER CONDITIONS
OF FIXED PROPORTIONS

3.1 Introduction

The presence of fixed input proportions establishes a *technological* production ray. Economic considerations do not play so crucial a role as they do when production is subject to variable proportions. Indeed, the only two economic questions posed are: (*a*) should the product under consideration be produced; and (*b*) if so, in what quantity. All questions pertaining to the organization of production are settled on strictly technological grounds.[1] Thus the exposition in this chapter is considerably more limited than in chapters 4 and 5 below.

Throughout the discussion several familiar terms are used. All of these are defined in detail in chapters 4 and 5; except for noting the particular circumstances of their use, we rely upon the reader's prior knowledge of their meaning.

3.2 The expansion path

When treating variable-proportions production functions, it is convenient to define and distinguish between an *isocline* and an *expansion path*. The former refers to a path along which the marginal rate of technical substitution is constant, the latter to the path along which the marginal rate of technical substitution equals the corresponding input-price ratio. The expansion path is a special isocline, of course, if all input prices are independent of the quantities of inputs used.

An isocline is strictly determined by technological conditions, while economic considerations determine the expansion path. Indeed, the latter is a path of economic efficiency in the sense that either cost is minimized for each level of output or output is maximized for each level of cost. When

---

[1] The object of this book is not to provide either a criticism or a critique of other works. However, at this point I should like to note my exception to the way in which the economic theory of production under fixed proportions is developed in Frisch [1965, pp. 252–6], especially equation (13.b.1).

the production function is smoothly continuous, the expansion path is easily determined by means of the Lagrange technique for constrained extrema. When the production function is characterized by fixed proportions, however, the constrained maximum or minimum does not occur at an interior point. The extremum occurs at a boundary or corner, so the differential calculus is not a particularly useful tool for determining the expansion path.

In what follows we first determine the expansion path graphically. Next, some limitations upon the interpretation of the expansion path are discussed. Finally, the technical and economic theory of production is analyzed for the general case in which production functions are not continuously differentiable. This, of course, includes 'fixed proportions' as a special case.

3.3 Graphical determination of the expansion path

It is assumed throughout that the economic objective of the entrepreneur is to maximize profit. For the most part, however, it is possible to work with a weaker assumption, namely the entrepreneur strives to attain economic efficiency in the sense that a given level of output is produced at minimum cost or that output is maximized for a given level of cost. As a consequence, when the weaker condition is used, as it is here, the basic assumption is not incompatible with a variety of postulates concerning entrepreneurial behavior. For example, attaining a point of economic efficiency is consistent with minimax behavior, with Baumol's sales-maximization hypothesis, and with even broader classes of 'satisficing' behavior.

As in most of chapter 2, it is assumed that the production function is given by

$$q = \min\left(\frac{x_1}{\alpha_1}, \frac{x_2}{\alpha_2}, ..., \frac{x_n}{\alpha_n}\right), \qquad (3.3.1)$$

where the x_i's are all elementary inputs. The price of the ith input is denoted p_i; and it is generally assumed that

$$p_i = p_i(x_i), \quad p_i' \geqq 0 \quad (i = 1, 2, ..., n). \qquad (3.3.2)$$

The cost of production (c) is accordingly given by

$$c = \sum_{i=1}^{n} p_i x_i. \qquad (3.3.3)$$

Attaining a point of economic efficiency requires either (a) minimizing cost (3.3.3) subject to producing a given level of output, or (b) maximizing output (3.3.1) subject to a given level of cost. The locus of all efficiency points is the *expansion path* although, as shown in section 3.4, this path must be interpreted in a circumscribed way.

The general conditions for establishing the expansion path are discussed in section 3.5. At present the constrained extremum problem is treated graphically under the assumption that there are only two inputs. In figure 15, q_0 and q_1 are two isoquants representing contours of the production function, and CF and $C'F'$ are two constant-input-price isocost curves obtained by setting $c = \bar{c}$, a constant, in the cost function (3.3.3). Our object is to prove that the Pareto ray OR is the expansion path.

Suppose the organization of production is initially represented by a point not on OR, say point A (or A') in figure 15. At point $A(A')$ input

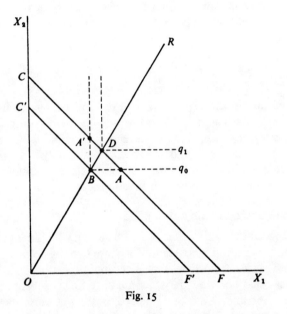

Fig. 15

$X_1(X_2)$ is redundant and input $X_2(X_1)$ is limitative. If the object is to maximize output for the level of cost represented by CF, it is quite apparent that output may be expanded from the q_0-level to the q_1-level by reducing the employment of the redundant input and expanding the usage of the limitative input. This process must continue until point D is reached, at which the inputs are mutually limitational. It is not possible to attain a higher isoquant without increasing the level of total expenditure on inputs. Hence point D is an efficiency point.

The analysis is exactly the same if the object is to minimize cost subject to producing a stipulated level of output, say q_0. Again suppose that the q_0-level is produced by the input combination represented by point $A(A')$. It is again apparent that $X_1(X_2)$ is redundant at $A(A')$; thus its usage may be diminished without reducing the volume of output. By disposing of the redundant input, cost may be reduced from the CF-level to the $C'F'$-level at point B. No further reduction is possible, however, so long as q_0 units of output are to be produced. Hence point B is a point on the expansion path.

Generalizing, the expansion path associated with equations (3.3.1) and (3.3.3) is given by the equations

$$\frac{x_i}{\alpha_i} = \frac{x_n}{\alpha_n} \quad (i = 1, 2, \dots, n-1).$$ \hfill (3.3.4)

There are $n-1$ equations in (3.3.4); this set of equations therefore determines a one-dimensional ray in the n-dimensional input space. This ray is the expansion path.

3.4 Restrictions imposed upon the interpretation of the expansion path

As indicated above, the expansion path determined by equations (3.3.4) cannot be interpreted in quite the same way as the expansion path associated with a variable-proportions production function. We now show that the Pareto ray is an isocline and an expansion path only in a circumscribed sense and that it is not determined by the marginal conditions applicable to variable-proportions production functions.

3.4.1 The Pareto ray as an isocline

Let us first recall that an isocline is a locus along which the marginal rate of technical substitution is constant. There are two possible interpretations of the Pareto ray as an isocline. First, since input substitution is impossible, one might say that both the marginal rate of technical substitution and the elasticity of substitution are zero. Indeed, in a strict sense they are.[1] The marginal rate of technical substitution is defined for movements along an isoquant; and the simple fact is that inputs cannot be substituted for one another while maintaining a constant level of output. Thus the Pareto ray is an isocline because the marginal rate of technical substitution is exactly zero at every point on the ray.

The interpretation just given is the logically correct one; however, a somewhat less precise interpretation may be given. The exact definition of the marginal rate of technical substitution ($MRTS$) between two inputs is

$$MRTS_{ji} = -\frac{dx_j}{dx_i}\bigg]_{dq=0}.$$ \hfill (3.4.1)

---

[1] In an even stricter sense, the marginal rate of technical substitution is not defined *at any point* on the Pareto ray, even though it may be defined as '∞' above the ray (where X_2 is redundant) and as zero below the ray (where X_1 is redundant).

As in the paragraph above, $MRTS_{ji} = 0$. However, if the production function is continuous, the definition in equation (3.4.1) may be expressed in an alternative form. Suppose the production function is given by

$$q = f(x_1, x_2, ..., x_n), \tag{3.4.2}$$

where f is continuous and f_i denotes the first partial derivative with respect to x_i. Along an isoquant

$$dq = \sum_{i=1}^{n} f_i dx_i = 0. \tag{3.4.3}$$

One may thus solve for (say) $-\dfrac{dx_j}{dx_i}\bigg]_{dq=0}$, obtaining

$$-\frac{dx_j}{dx_i}\bigg]_{dq=0} = \frac{f_i}{f_j} + \sum_{k \neq i,j}^{n} \frac{f_k}{f_j}\frac{dx_k}{dx_i} \quad (i,j=1, 2, ..., n). \tag{3.4.4}$$

When there are only two inputs, or when variation is strictly limited to two inputs, $dx_k = 0$ for $k \neq i,j$. Thus the conventional definition of the marginal rate of technical substitution is obtained:

$$MRTS_{ji} = -\frac{dx_j}{dx_i}\bigg]_{dq=0} = \frac{f_i}{f_j} \quad (i,j=1, 2, ..., n). \tag{3.4.5}$$

Verbally, the marginal rate of technical substitution is equal to the ratio of the marginal products when only two inputs are varied and the production function is continuously differentiable. However, the differentiability provision is sometimes ignored; the marginal rate of technical substitution is simply defined as the ratio of the marginal products. Under this definition, another interpretation of the Pareto ray as an isocline may be given.

From the discontinuous production function in equation (3.3.1), we obtain the following marginal products on decrease:

$$\left(\frac{\partial q}{\partial x_i}\right)^{-} = \frac{1}{\alpha_i} \quad (i=1, 2, ..., n). \tag{3.4.6}$$

Thus using the restricted definition, along the Pareto ray the marginal rate of technical substitution on decrease is

$$MRTS_{ji} = \frac{(\partial q/\partial x_i)}{(\partial q/\partial x_j)} = \frac{\alpha_j}{\alpha_i} \quad (i,j=1, 2, ..., n). \tag{3.4.7}$$

Since the ratio of the fixed coefficients is itself fixed, the Pareto ray is characterized by a constant marginal rate of technical substitution on decrease. It should be reemphasized, however, that this interpretation depends upon the questionable definition of the marginal rate of technical substitution.[1] That is, the continuity requirement must be ignored in case the production function is discontinuous.

[1] See footnote 1, p. 50 above.

3.4.2 The Pareto ray as the expansion path

In section 3.3 it was shown that the Pareto ray is an expansion path in the sense that economic efficiency is attained only by input combinations represented by points on the ray. That is to say, these input combinations are the only ones that minimize the cost of producing a stipulated output or maximize output for a given cost. Thus any change in output may be represented by a movement from one point on the Pareto ray to another point also on the ray.

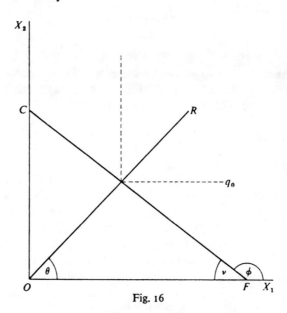

Fig. 16

When the production function is continuously differentiable the expansion path has a unique property; namely, at every point on the path, the marginal rate of technical substitution is equal to the corresponding input-price ratio. It should be quite clear that the expansion path associated with a discontinuous production function does not possess this characteristic. If the marginal rate of technical substitution is zero, the condition is obviously not satisfied given any 'economic' definition of inputs.[1] Yet even if the more restricted definition of the marginal rate of technical substitution is used, the expansion path does not (generally) have this characteristic, as illustrated in figure 16.

In the figure, OR is the Pareto ray, q_0 is a representative isoquant, and CF is the isocost line determined from equation (3.3.3). The marginal rate

---

[1] That is, $p_i > 0$ for $i = 1, 2, ..., n$.

of technical substitution, using the restricted definition is

$$\frac{(\partial q/\partial x_1)}{(\partial q/\partial x_2)} = \frac{\alpha_2}{\alpha_1}. \tag{3.4.8}$$

Next, observe that along the Pareto ray, $x_2/x_1 = \alpha_2/\alpha_1$. Finally,

$$\tan\theta = \frac{x_2}{x_1} = \frac{\alpha_2}{\alpha_1}. \tag{3.4.9}$$

Thus the marginal rate of technical substitution (restricted definition) is the tangent of the angle θ.

The input-price ratio is the negative of the slope of the line CF, i.e. for $c = p_1 x_1 + p_2 x_2$,

$$\frac{p_1}{p_2} = -\frac{dx_2}{dx_1} = -\tan\Phi = \tan(180 - \Phi) = \tan\nu. \tag{3.4.10}$$

Equality between the marginal rate of technical substitution and the input-price ratio would occur if, and only if, $\tan\theta = \tan\nu$. This could, of course, happen; but it would be entirely fortuitous. Production will occur at a point on the Pareto ray, if it occurs at all, irrespective of the input-price ratio.

3.4.3   The inapplicability of certain marginal equalities

In general, the economic task confronting an entrepreneur is to determine the profit-maximizing level of output. Considerations of economic efficiency then determine the quantity of each input employed and the composition of inputs, i.e. the various input ratios. In the case of fixed proportions, the input composition is determined by the technologically given coefficients; nonetheless, the entrepreneur must determine the volume of output and of input usage.

If the production function is continuous, the output-input decision may be based upon either of two different calculations: (a) equating marginal revenue and marginal cost, or (b) for each input, equating marginal revenue product with the marginal expense of input. To illustrate this, let the production function be given by equation (3.4.2) and the input cost function by equation (3.3.3). Further, let the commodity price be denoted by p, where

$$p = p(q), \quad p' < 0. \tag{3.4.11}$$

Thus profit (π) is the difference between revenue (r) and cost (c), or

$$\pi = r - c = pq - \sum_{i=1}^{n} p_i x_i. \tag{3.4.12}$$

The maximization of equation (3.4.12) may be performed with respect

FIXED PROPORTIONS: ECONOMIC THEORY

to output or with respect to the inputs. The former approach leads to the marginal revenue-marginal cost criterion:

$$\frac{d\pi}{dq} = \frac{dr}{dq} - \frac{dc}{dq} = p\left(1+\frac{1}{\eta}\right) - \sum_{i=1}^{n} p_i\left(1+\frac{1}{\theta_i}\right)\frac{dx_i}{dq} = 0, \qquad (3.4.13)$$

where η is the elasticity of commodity demand and θ_i is the elasticity of supply of the ith input. If the production function is of the fixed proportions variety, and if the analysis is restricted to movements along the Pareto ray, $(dx_i/dq) = \alpha_i$. Thus the entrepreneur has the following criterion: expand output so long as

$$p\left(1+\frac{1}{\eta}\right) \geq \sum_{i=1}^{n} \alpha_i p_i\left(1+\frac{1}{\theta_i}\right). \qquad (3.4.14)$$

Alternatively, equation (3.4.12) may be maximized with respect to the inputs. In this case the criterion is

$$\frac{\partial\pi}{\partial x_i} = \frac{\partial r}{\partial x_i} - \frac{\partial c}{\partial x_i} = 0 \quad (i = 1, 2, ..., n). \qquad (3.4.15)$$

There are n equations in expressions (3.4.15) to solve for the n quantities of inputs; knowing the quantities of inputs, equation (3.4.2) may be used to determine the profit-maximizing level of output.

Let us now consider equations (3.4.15) more carefully. First, note that

$$\frac{\partial r}{\partial x_i} = \frac{dr}{dq}\frac{\partial q}{\partial x_i} = p\left(1+\frac{1}{\eta}\right)\frac{\partial q}{\partial x_i} \quad (i=1, 2, ..., n) \qquad (3.4.16)$$

is the marginal revenue product (MRP_i) of the ith input. In case the production function is given by equation (3.3.1), the expression is

$$MRP_i = \frac{p\left(1+\frac{1}{\eta}\right)}{\alpha_i} \quad (i=1, 2, ..., n). \qquad (3.4.17)$$

Next, $$\frac{\partial c}{\partial x_i} = p_i\left(1+\frac{1}{\theta_i}\right) \quad (i=1, 2, ..., n) \qquad (3.4.18)$$

is the marginal expense of the ith input (MEI_i). Thus the criterion states that the marginal revenue product must equal the marginal expense of input for each input entering the production process:

$$MRP_i = MEI_i \quad \text{or} \quad p\left(1+\frac{1}{\eta}\right)\frac{\partial q}{\partial x_i} = p_i\left(1+\frac{1}{\theta_i}\right) \quad (i=1, 2, ..., n). \qquad (3.4.19)$$

The criterion expressed in equations (3.4.13) and (3.4.14) is applicable to all production situations; however, the criterion expressed in equations

(3.4.19) is applicable only if the production function is continuous. To be sure the criterion might hold, but it would be a fortuitous circumstance; more precisely, it would be the same fortuitous circumstance that brought about equality between the marginal rate of technical substitution and the input-price ratio. In general, only an aggregate criterion is applicable: output should be expanded if, and only if, marginal revenue exceeds marginal cost or, what is the same, the aggregate of the marginal revenue products exceeds the aggregate of the marginal expenses of input. There is no way by which a relation may be imposed upon the individual marginal revenue products and marginal expenses of input.

3.5 The technical and economic theory of production with discontinuous production functions[1]

In this concluding section the analysis of chapters 2 and 3 is broadened so as to include not only the fixed-proportions type of production function but all discontinuous production functions. In passing, some general properties of derived input demand are determined.

3.5.1 Concavity of the production isoquants

In chapters 6 and 7, it is shown quite rigorously that the constrained extremum problem associated with economic efficiency dictates that production isoquants be concave from above over the relevant (economic) range of production. A similar property can be shown to hold for production isoquants derived from discontinuous production functions.

Let the production function be

$$q = f(x_1, x_2, \ldots, x_n), \tag{3.5.1}$$

where f is single-valued but need not be continuous or have continuous partial derivatives. For consistency, f must further be such that

$$\Delta q \geqq 0 \quad \text{for} \quad \Delta x_i \geqq 0 \quad (i = 1, 2, \ldots, n). \tag{3.5.2}$$

Finally, while unique partial derivatives need not exist at all points, it is assumed that left-hand and right-hand partial derivatives do exist, i.e. one may calculate

$$\left(\frac{\partial q}{\partial x_i}\right)^- = f_i^- \quad \text{and} \quad \left(\frac{\partial q}{\partial x_i}\right)^+ = f_i^+ \quad (i = 1, 2, \ldots, n). \tag{3.5.3}$$

As before, all inputs are independent variables. In the spirit of chapter 2, it is never true that the inputs *must* be used in fixed proportions; it is merely unprofitable not to do so. Given fixed input prices, the same state-

---

[1] The development in this section follows Samuelson [1947, pp. 70–81].

ment holds for continuous production functions. Thus, to quote Samuelson, 'The only difference between these cases is that in the discontinuous case the required optimum point may be more obvious and less sensitive to changes in the prices of all factors of production.'[1]

It is assumed that all isoquants are concave from above in the following sense. Let an arbitrary point on an isoquant be represented by the column vector $x^0 = \text{col}\,(x_1^0, x_2^0, ..., x_n^0)$. There must exist a column vector of constants $\beta^0 = \text{col}\,(\beta_1^0, \beta_2^0, ..., \beta_n^0)$, which is generally not unique, such that[2]

$$\beta^{0\prime}(x^1 - x^0) \geqq 0, \qquad (3.5.4)$$

where $x^1 = \text{col}\,(x_1^1, x_2^1, ..., x_n^1)$ is any other point on the isoquant and 'prime' denotes the transpose of the column vector. Inequalities (3.5.4) simply imply that, at each point, there exists one or more tangent planes that touch but do not cross the isoquant.

Correspondingly, at the point x^1 there must exist one or more column vectors of constants $\beta^1 = \text{col}\,(\beta_1^1, \beta_2^1, ..., \beta_n^1)$ such that

$$-\beta^{1\prime}(x^1 - x^0) \geqq 0. \qquad (3.5.5)$$

As above, inequalities (3.5.5) imply the existence of tangent planes at the point x^1.

For convenience, let $\Delta x = x^1 - x^0$ and $\Delta\beta = \beta^1 - \beta^0$. Since the points chosen are purely arbitrary, attention may be concentrated upon x^0. For movements along an isoquant, i.e. $f(x^0) = f(x^0 + \Delta x)$, inequalities (3.5.4) imply that

$$\beta^{0\prime}\Delta x \geqq 0; \qquad (3.5.6)$$

and inequalities (3.5.4) and (3.5.5) together imply that

$$\Delta\beta^{\prime}\Delta x \leqq 0. \qquad (3.5.7)$$

Indeed, it can be shown that for inequalities (3.5.6) to hold, it is necessary and sufficient for the vector of constants to satisfy the following inequalities:

$$\frac{f_i^+}{f_n^-} \leqq \frac{\beta_i^0}{\beta_n^0} \leqq \frac{f_i^-}{f_n^+} \quad (i = 1, 2, ..., n-1). \qquad (3.5.8)$$

At a continuity point, the marginal products are the same on increase and decrease, and inequalities (3.5.8) reduce to

$$\frac{\beta_i^0}{\beta_0^n} = \frac{f_i}{f_n} \quad (i = 1, 2, ..., n-1). \qquad (3.5.9)$$

[1] *Ibid.* p. 72.
[2] For the production function in equation (3.3.1), *one* possible vector of constants is

$$\beta_i = \frac{1}{\alpha_i} \quad (i = 1, 2, ..., n).$$

Similarly, for the production function in equation (3.3.1) it is true that

$$\frac{f_i^-}{f_n^-} = \frac{\beta_i^0}{\beta_n^0} = \frac{\alpha_n}{\alpha_i} \quad (i=1, 2, ..., n-1). \tag{3.5.10}$$

3.5.2 Economic efficiency

Continuing the notation of section 3.3, let p_i represent the price of the ith input, where the set of input prices is taken to be the column vector $p = \mathrm{col}\,(p_1, p_2, ..., p_n)$. The cost function from equation (3.3.3) thus becomes

$$c = p'x. \tag{3.5.11}$$

Suppose we are given a set of prices p^0 for which there is a unique point x^0 at which cost is minimized for the given output q^0. Thus at the point x^0,

$$\Delta c \gtreqless 0 \quad \text{for} \quad \Delta q = 0 \quad \text{and} \quad \Delta x_i^0 \gtreqless 0. \tag{3.5.12}$$

For any other point x^1 on the isoquant q^0, i.e. $f(x^0) = f(x^1)$, it must be true that

$$p^{0\prime}x^1 \geqq p^{0\prime}x^0, \tag{3.5.13}$$

or

$$p^{0\prime}\Delta x \geqq 0. \tag{3.5.14}$$

Comparing inequalities (3.5.6) and (3.5.14), it is clear from inequalities (3.5.8) that inequalities (3.5.14) imply

$$\frac{f_i^+}{f_n^-} \leqq \frac{p_i^0}{p_n^0} \leqq \frac{f_i^-}{f_n^+} \quad (i=1, 2, ..., n-1). \tag{3.5.15}$$

It is instructive to compare inequalities (3.5.8) and (3.5.15). In a continuity point, inequalities (3.5.15) become

$$\frac{f_i}{f_n} = \frac{p_i^0}{p_n^0} \quad (i=1, 2, ..., n-1). \tag{3.5.16}$$

Thus in light of equation (3.5.9), we have

$$\frac{\beta_i^0}{\beta_n^0} = \frac{p_i^0}{p_n^0} \quad (i=1, 2, ..., n-1). \tag{3.5.17}$$

The full import of equations (3.5.17) will be discussed in chapters 6 and 7. At this time it is only necessary to note that, in a continuity point, there is a *unique* tangent plane whose slope equals both the input-price ratio and the marginal rate of technical substitution. The same does not apply to the discontinuous case. In this situation there are limiting tangent planes; but the input-price ratio and the marginal rate of technical substitution must only lie within the limits. As stated above, their equality would be a purely fortuitous circumstance.

3.5.3 Efficiency and input demand

Let us now suppose that the given set of input prices is p^1, for which there is a point x^1 at which the cost of producing the output q^0 is a minimum. That is, for any point x^0 on the isoquant q^0

$$p^{1\prime}x^0 \geqq p^{1\prime}x^1, \tag{3.5.18}$$

or
$$-p^{1\prime}\Delta x \geqq 0. \tag{3.5.19}$$

Adding inequalities (3.5.14) and (3.5.19) yields

$$\Delta p'\Delta x \leqq 0 \quad \text{for} \quad \Delta q = 0. \tag{3.5.20}$$

If only the price of the ith input varies, inequalities (3.5.20) reduce to

$$\Delta p_i \Delta x_i \leqq 0 \quad (i = 1, 2, ..., n). \tag{3.5.21}$$

Inequality (3.5.20) states that an increase (decrease) in all input prices cannot result in an increase (decrease) is all input usages. Inequalities (3.5.21) refer, in turn, to specific input demands. In particular, for a given level of output, an increase (decrease) in the price of an input cannot result in an increase (decrease) in the usage of the input. Thus for each input, the constant-output demand curve is negatively sloped. If the equality sign holds in (3.5.21), the demand curve is perfectly inelastic (and is no longer single-valued).

3.5.4 Profit maximization and input demand

Whatever the discontinuities present, a point of profit maximization can be represented by the following inequalities:

$$\Delta \pi = \Delta r - \Delta c \leqq 0 \quad \text{for} \quad \Delta x_i \gtreqless 0 \quad (i = 1, 2, ..., n). \tag{3.5.22}$$

In the special situation in which only one input changes, inequalities (3.5.22) reduce to[1]

$$\left.\begin{aligned}\frac{\Delta r}{\Delta q}\frac{\Delta q}{\Delta x_i} < p_i + x_i \Delta p_i \quad \text{for} \quad \Delta x_i > 0, \quad \Delta x_j = 0, \\ \frac{\Delta r}{\Delta q}\frac{\Delta q}{\Delta x_i} > p_i + x_i \Delta p_i \quad \text{for} \quad \Delta x_i < 0, \quad \Delta x_j = 0.\end{aligned}\right\} \tag{3.5.23}$$

Inequalities (3.5.23) simply state that it must not pay to vary one input in either direction.

In the very special case of fixed coefficients, inequalities (3.5.23) obviously hold at a profit-maximizing point on the Pareto ray. In that situation the left-hand side of the inequalities, which represents marginal revenue

---

[1] These inequalities essentially appear in equations (100) and (101) in Samuelson [1947, p. 80]. Samuelson's equations, however, are somewhat different inasmuch as he implicitly assumes that input prices are fixed.

product, always has a magnitude that satisfies the inequalities. If the input of x_i is expanded, all other inputs remaining unchanged, marginal revenue product is zero. The right-hand side, which represents the marginal expense of input, is always positive. Hence the inequality is satisfied for an increase. If the production point under consideration is truly a maximum, the inequality must hold on decrease as well, for otherwise the point would not be a maximum.

The conditions placed upon constant-output demand curves by inequalities (3.5.21) may also be deduced from profit maximization. Suppose a given vector of input prices p^0 implies a corresponding vector of inputs x^0 at the point of profit maximization. Then

$$r[f(x^1)] - p^{0\prime}x^1 \leqq r[f(x^0)] - p^{0\prime}x^0, \qquad (3.5.24)$$

where x^1 is any other vector of inputs. Similarly, let p^1 be the vector of input prices that would establish x^1 as the profit-maximizing vector of inputs. Then $\quad r[f(x^0)] - p^{1\prime}x^0 \leqq r[f(x^1)] - p^{1\prime}x^1. \qquad (3.5.25)$

Adding inequalities (3.5.24) and (3.5.25), one obtains

$$\Delta p' \Delta x \leqq 0, \qquad (3.5.26)$$

which is precisely the same as inequality (3.5.20). For a variation in the price of the ith input only, inequality (3.5.26) reduces to

$$\Delta p_i \Delta x_i \leqq 0. \qquad (3.5.27)$$

Inequality (3.5.27) is exactly the same as inequality (3.5.21), and it is subject to the interpretation given in the paragraph following that inequality.

3.5.5 Conclusion

In concluding the exposition of chapters 2 and 3 it seems appropriate to quote Samuelson at some length because he has given a succinct statement concerning the effect of discontinuities:

> ... the general case is simpler than that of the special continuous case. Moreover, the method of finite increments appears to be mathematically simpler in the sense that it is possible to state the qualitative direction of changes without solving inversely for the actual demand functions. The method employed here is that which underlies Le Chatelier's principle in physics. By making use of Professor E. B. Wilson's suggestion that this is essentially a mathematical theorem applicable to economics, it has been possible to gain increased generality without increased complexity and emptiness. It is important to realize just how much content there is to a particular economic theory. As far as the single firm is concerned, everything fundamental which can be said is implied in the statement that in equilibrium there must exist no movement by which the firm can improve its profits, i.e. $\Delta \pi \leqq 0$ for all movements of variables possible to the firm.[1]

[1] Samuelson [1947, p. 81].

4

TECHNICAL ASPECTS OF
CONTINUOUS PRODUCTION FUNCTIONS:
GENERAL THEORY

4.1 Introduction

Throughout this chapter and the next the production function is assumed to be single valued, everywhere continuous, and well defined over the range of inputs yielding nonnegative outputs.[1] A second assumption, which increases generality without sacrificing content, is that the production function belongs to a class of functions with continuous first and second partial derivations. Third, it is assumed that the inputs are continuously variable, i.e. the inputs are real variables defined over the nonnegative domain of real numbers.

A fourth assumption, which is sometimes not invoked, concerns the unchanging character of the production function and of the inputs. Specifically, unless otherwise stated, the production function is given and fixed; there is neither technological progress nor retrogression. Similarly, the inputs remain unchanged in character and are assumed to be homogeneous within themselves. Finally, our attention is chiefly focused upon the production of a single commodity and the behavior of a single-product firm.

As mentioned in chapter 1, it is both convenient and instructive to examine the behavior of output when only one input is varied, all other inputs being held constant. In the conventional terminology of economics such investigations are called short-run analyses; the inputs held constant are called 'fixed inputs', the one allowed to vary is called a 'variable input'. Otherwise, one may simply regard such investigations as the study of cross-sections of the production surface or of the behavior of a single partial derivative.

Finally, it might be well to note that inputs are sometimes classified as 'general' and 'specific'. General inputs are those used in producing a variety of different outputs; specific inputs are those used to produce the

[1] For a more thorough discussion of the concept of a production function, see Smithies [1935], Smithies [1936], and Carlson [1939, pp. 14-16].

commodity under consideration but not used in the production of any other good. For example, 'unskilled labor' is a general input used in some phase of production of most goods, while 'neurosurgeon' is a specific input efficiently utilized only in cerebral operations. Often the category in which an input is placed depends upon the stage of processing it has reached. Thus the input 'cotton' is widely utilized, whereas 'percale' is virtually specific to the fabrication of bed linens.

This dichotomy of inputs is not important so far as the technical theory of production is concerned. It is relevant only when economic considerations are introduced, especially in determining input demand functions. For the most part it is assumed that all inputs are 'general'. Thus their prices may be regarded as parametric data to the firm. In chapter 8, however, the economic theory of production with variable input prices is discussed.

4.2 The production function

Production functions must generally be given an algebraic representation; however, if the number of inputs is sufficiently small, graphical and tabular representations are possible. In this section primary emphasis is placed upon algebraic formulations; graphical and tabular forms are sometimes shown for purposes of illustration.

4.2.1 Algebraic and tabular representations

In principle the variety of equations that may validly represent a production function is virtually limitless. Three special features, however, deserve notice. First, the production function might have an additive constant term; however, this would imply that a positive level of output could be obtained without the use of inputs. This is a 'something for nothing' condition that violates one's established notions of the real world, not to mention the real economic world. Hence we assume that the production function does not contain an additive constant.

Second, the variables could enter singly, in pairs, etc., or they may enter only in universally multiplicative groups. The more reasonable assumption seems to be that a positive usage of all inputs simultaneously is required to produce a positive output. Let the production function be written

$$q = f(x_1, x_2, ..., x_n), \qquad (4.2.1)$$

where q is output and x_i is the usage of input X_i. Thus, we assume that

$$f(0, 0, ..., 0) = f(0, x_2, ..., x_n) = f(x_1, 0, x_3, ..., x_n) = ...$$
$$= f(x_1, x_2, ..., x_{n-1}, 0) = 0. \qquad (4.2.2)$$

Third, the production function may be homogeneous or inhomogeneous. Chapter 5 is devoted to a special analysis of homogeneous functions. In this chapter our attention is directed chiefly to the more general class of inhomogeneous functions.

Specific examples of production functions are easy to come by. Perhaps the simplest form is

$$q = \sum_{i=1}^{n} a_i x_i \quad (0 < a_i). \tag{4.2.3}$$

However, this function does not satisfy our general requirement concerning second partial derivatives. Perhaps the two best known production functions are the Cobb–Douglas function and the Arrow–Chenery–Minhas–Solow function shown, respectively, by[1]

$$q = A x^\alpha y^\beta \quad (0 < \alpha, \beta < 1), \tag{4.2.4}$$

and

$$q = \gamma[\delta x^{-\rho} + (1 - \delta) y^{-\rho}]^{-1/\rho} \quad (0 < \gamma, \delta). \tag{4.2.5}$$

Other examples of homogeneous functions are listed below:

$$q = 2axy - bx^2 - cy^2 \quad (0 < a, b, c \text{ and } a^2 > bc), \tag{4.2.6}$$

$$q = \frac{2axy - bx^2 - cy^2}{dx + cy} \quad (0 < a, b, c, d, e \text{ and } a^2 > bc), \tag{4.2.7}$$

$$q = a_1 x^{\alpha_1} y^{\beta_1} + a_2 x^{\alpha_2} y^{\beta_2} \quad (0 < \alpha_1, \alpha_2, \beta_1, \beta_2, a_1, a_2), \tag{4.2.8}$$

$$(\alpha_1 + \beta_1 = \alpha_2 + \beta_2)$$

$$q = a \left[\frac{bx^3 y^2 + x^2 y^3}{x^4 + y^4} \right] \quad (0 < a, b). \tag{4.2.9}$$

An example of an inhomogeneous function, which is used illustratively in this chapter, is:
$$q = a[x^2 y + xy^2 - \tfrac{2}{3} x^4 - \tfrac{2}{3} y^4] \quad (0 < a). \tag{4.2.10}$$

The function above satisfies all the criteria introduced above, and it is uniquely defined over the range from (0, 0) to (1·5, 1·5). A tabular representation of this production function (for $a = 10,000$) is presented in table 3.[2] At present two features of this function merit notice. First, for small values of either input, the usage of the other input can become so great that output is zero. Second, the production surface rises to a unique maximum at $x = y = 1·125$ and declines thereafter. In point of fact, output is zero when $x = y = 1·50$.

---

[1] Cobb and Douglas [1928] and Arrow, Chenery, Minhas and Solow [1961]. For another derivation of the CES function, see Kendrick and Sato [1963].

[2] I am indebted to Mr Earl Sasser for the programming and calculations upon which the numerical examples are based.

TABLE 3 *Tabular representation of equation (4.2.10)*
with a = 10,000

X \ Y	0·5	0·6	0·7	0·8	0·9	1·00	1·10	1·11	1·125	1·130	1·140	1·150
0·5	1667	2019	2183	2053	1509	417	0	0	0	0	0	0
0·6	2019	2592	2995	3125	2862	2069	595	404	101	0	0	0
0·7	2183	2995	3659	4069	4105	3633	2499	2343	2092	2005	1823	1632
0·8	2053	3125	4069	4779	5135	5003	4229	4110	3916	3847	3702	3549
0·9	1509	2862	4105	5135	5832	6059	5665	5585	5450	5401	5297	5183
1·00	417	2069	3633	5003	6059	6667	6673	6634	6561	6533	6470	6398
1·10	0	595	2499	4229	5665	6673	7099	7103	7095	7088	7069	7042
1·11	0	404	2343	4110	5585	6634	7103	7112	7110	7106	7091	7068
1·125	0	101	2092	3961	5450	6561	7095	7110	7119	7118	7110	7094
1·13	0	0	2005	3847	5401	6533	7088	7106	7118	7118	7113	7099
1·14	0	0	1823	3702	5297	6470	7069	7091	7110	7113	7111	7102
1·15	0	0	1632	3549	5183	6398	7042	7068	7094	7099	7102	7097

4.2.2 Graphical representation

To represent a production function graphically, the number of variables must be restricted so that dimensionality is not a problem. To that end, let the production function be

$$q = f(x, y),$$ (4.2.11)

a specific form of which is given by equation (4.2.10).

A portion of a typical production surface corresponding to equation (4.2.11) is shown in figure 17. The production surface is $OYQX$ (note that only the rising portion of the surface is shown in the figure). If the surface is intersected at $Y = Y_1$, the curve Y_1PF shows a cross-section of the surface in the Q–X plane. Similarly, holding X constant at X_1, X_1PD traces the outputs obtainable for a given input of X and variable usage of Y.

4.2.3 Isoquants

Cross-sections of the production surface in the $Q-X$ and $Q-Y$ planes are useful because they show how total product varies with the variable usage of one input, the other input held constant. Thus these cross-sections illustrate one fundamental property of continuously differentiable production functions: output varies in response to a change in *any one* input, all other inputs held constant. The change in input usage may be in either direction; output always responds unless the point of absolute saturation has been attained (e.g. at the input point (1·5, 1·5) in equation (4.2.10)).

63

This contrasts sharply with the case of fixed-proportion production functions, in which output responds only to a negative variation in a single limitational input.

The single-input variation property is very important; yet there is another property of equal importance: various combinations of inputs may be used to produce the same quantity of output. That is, one input

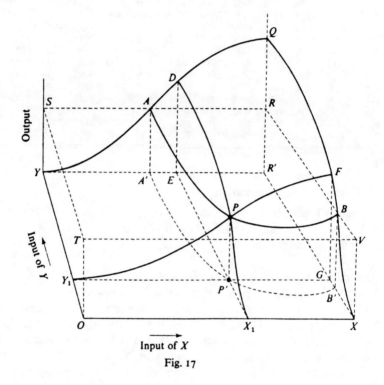

Fig. 17

may be substituted for another while maintaining a constant level of output. Another cross-section, one in the X-Y plane, serves to ilustrate this property.

Again consider figure 17. Intersect the production surface $OYQX$ by a plane $RSTV$, representing the level of output $RR' = PP' = BB' = YS$. The resulting cross-section is the curve APB. Projecting this cross-section onto the X-Y plane yields the curve $A'P'B'$, which shows all combinations of X and Y that may be used to produce RR' units of output. This projection of the cross-section onto the X-Y plane is called an isoquant.

Definition: An isoquant is a locus of input combinations each of which is capable of producing the same level of output.

64

4.2 THE PRODUCTION FUNCTION

Every possible level of output may be represented by an isoquant. Since output is a continuous variable, there are infinitely many isoquants in any isoquant map, i.e. the isoquant map is everywhere dense. Furthermore, the isoquants do not intersect; this property follows immediately from the assumption that the production function is single-valued.

Various isoquant maps are illustrated in figures 18–20. First, consider figure 18, which depicts typical isoquants from production functions such as those in equations (4.2.4) and (4.2.5). Q_0 and Q_1 are isoquants; since Q_1

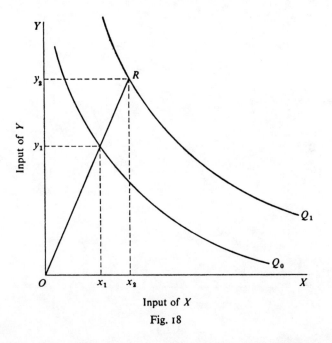

Fig. 18

is located to the northeast of Q_0, the output level associated with Q_1 exceeds the output associated with Q_0.

On an isoquant map any ray from the origin, such as OR in figure 18, represents a constant input ratio, i.e. $(y_1/x_1) = (y_2/x_2)$. Thus an isoquant map enables one simultaneously to observe the way in which the input ratio changes for a given level of output and the way in which output changes for a given input ratio. To reemphasize, output is constant and the input ratio changes for movements along an isoquant, whereas the input ratio is constant and output changes for movements along a ray from the origin.

It is only in special cases that isoquant maps resemble the map in figure 18. Generally, the *full* isoquant map consists of a set of concentric

65

ellipses, as shown in figure 19.[1] The more interior the ellipse, the greater the associated output. Isoquant maps have this elliptical shape when there is a unique maximum output that is physically attainable. The maximum is simply a dot (M) on the map at the point where the ellipses degenerate. For the production function in equation (4.2.10), the maximum is attained at $x = 1.125$, $y = 1.125$. A fair representation of an elliptical isoquant may be obtained by plotting the four input combinations yielding 7,110 units of output according to equation (4.2.10), see table 3.

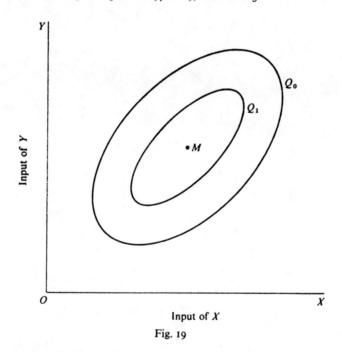

Fig. 19

If the production function does not have a unique maximum, the isoquants are not ellipses. In this case they are hyperbolas or parabolas similar to those shown in figure 20. As we shall later see, when the isoquant map resembles the one in figure 20, it is of great interest to determine the locus of points (OS) along which the slopes of the isoquants are infinite and the locus (OS') along which the slopes are zero.

4.3 Single input variations

In section 4.2 two different types of cross-sections of the production surface were examined: (*a*) the type showing the variation in output associated

[1] Except when the production function is homogeneous. For a numerical illustration, see Cassels [1936].

with a variation of one input (and hence the input ratio), and (*b*) the type showing the variations in the input combination associated with a constant level of output. In this section our attention is directed to the results of single-input variation, while the following section is concerned with input substitution when output is held constant.

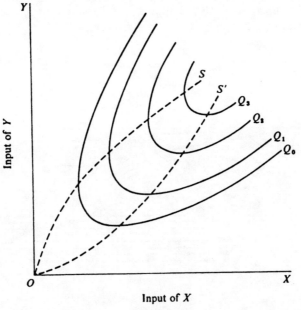

Input of X

Fig. 20

Another view of the cross-section for a single-input variation is shown in figure 21. This graph depicts equation (4.2.11), and the section X_1PS shows the particular form

$$q = f(y | x = x_1).\qquad(4.3.1)$$

This cross-section illustrates the behavior of total output over the entire range from $f(0 | x = x_1) = 0$ to the saturation point $f(y_1 | x = x_1) = 0$.

4.3.1 Marginal product

The concept of marginal product is introduced by the following
Definition: Consider a production function of the form

$$q = f(x_1, x_2, ..., x_n)\qquad(4.3.2)$$

that satisfies the conditions stated in section 4.1. The marginal product of the *i*th input is the partial derivative of the production function with respect to the input under consideration:

$$MP_i = \frac{\partial q}{\partial x_i} = f_i(x_1, x_2, ..., x_n).[1]$$ (4.3.3)

In general, the marginal product of an input is a function of all inputs. This is emphasized in equation (4.3.3) by writing $f_i(x_1, x_2, ..., x_n)$. If f_i is a continuous function of all the inputs at a specified input combination, X_i is said to be a *continuity factor* at that point.[2]

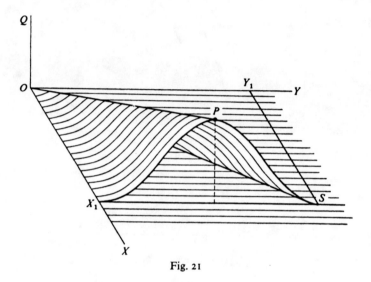

Fig. 21

Now consider the exact increment of equation (4.3.2):

$$\Delta q = df + \sum_{i}^{n} \eta_i dx_i,$$ (4.3.4)

where $\eta_i \to 0$ as $dx_i \to 0$ if all inputs are continuity factors at an input point. In this case the increments dx_i may be chosen so small that $\Delta q - df \to 0$. Hence

$$df = \Sigma f_i dx_i$$ (4.3.5)

is a suitable approximation of the actual increment Δq when all inputs are continuity factors. In other words, the total increment of output is equal to the sum of the input increments each multiplied by its marginal product.

Specific examples of marginal product functions may be obtained from the production functions in equations (4.2.4)–(4.2.10). For example, the

[1] For a detailed discussion of several alternative meanings of 'marginal product', see Machlup [1936b].
[2] Frisch [1965, p. 54] presumably introduced this definition.

marginal products for equations (4.2.4) and (4.2.5) are, respectively,

$$\frac{\partial q}{\partial x} = \frac{\alpha q}{x} \quad \text{and} \quad \frac{\partial q}{\partial y} = \frac{\beta q}{y}, \tag{4.3.6}$$

and $$\frac{\partial q}{\partial x} = \gamma^{-\rho} \delta \left(\frac{q}{x}\right)^{1+\rho} \quad \text{and} \quad \frac{\partial q}{\partial y} = \gamma^{-\rho}(1-\delta)\left(\frac{q}{y}\right)^{1+\rho}. \tag{4.3.7}$$

Similarly, the marginal products from equation (4.2.10) are

$$\frac{\partial q}{\partial x} = a(2xy + y^2 - \tfrac{8}{3}x^3) \quad \text{and} \quad \frac{\partial q}{\partial y} = a(x^2 + 2xy - \tfrac{8}{3}y^3). \tag{4.3.8}$$

Numerical values for the marginal products in equations (4.3.8) are shown in table 4.

4.3.2 Marginal returns and input relations

An examination of the second partial derivatives of equation (4.3.2) enables one to determine a good bit about the behavior of the marginal product function. Denote the second partial derivatives by

$$\frac{\partial^2 q}{\partial x_j \partial x_i} = f_{ij} \quad (i, j = 1, 2, \ldots, n). \tag{4.3.9}$$

The f_{ii} terms are sometimes called the *direct acceleration coefficients* and the f_{ij} terms *cross-acceleration coefficients*.[1]

The direct acceleration coefficient shows whether the marginal product function increases or decreases at any point. That is, if $f_{ii} > 0$ at a point, $f_i = MP_i$ is an increasing function at that point. Similarly, if $f_{ii} < 0$ at a point, $f_i = MP_i$ is a decreasing function at that point. Consequently, at a given input point there are increasing or diminishing marginal returns from the ith input according as $f_{ii} \gtrless 0$.

In certain production functions, such as equations (4.2.4) and (4.2.5), the direct acceleration coefficient is always negative. If this is so, the marginal product function itself must always be a nonnegative function. In other types of production functions, such as equations (4.2.9) and (4.2.10), the direct acceleration coefficient is sometimes positive and sometimes negative. In this case marginal returns increase over certain ranges of inputs and diminish over others. The fact that every acceptable production function is characterized by a range of diminishing marginal returns is usually called the

Law of variable proportions: With a given state of technology, if the quantity of one productive service is increased by equal increments, the quantities of the other productive services remaining fixed, the resulting

[1] Frisch [1965, pp. 58–61].

TABLE 4 *Marginal products of X and Y from equations (4.3.8)*

Inputs	0·5	0·6	0·7	0·8	0·9	1·000	1·100	1·110	1·125	1·130	1·140	1·150
0·5	4167	6267	8567	11067	13767	16667	—	19881	20396	—	—	—
0·6	2740	5040	7540	10240	13140	16240	19540	18714	19260	19442	19809	20178
0·7	353	2853	5553	8453	11553	14853	18353	16428	17003	17196	17583	17972
0·8	-3153	-453	2447	5547	8847	12347	16047	12861	13466	13669	14076	14485
0·9	-7940	-5040	-1940	1360	4860	8560	12460	7854	8490	8702	9129	9558
1·000	-14167	-11067	-7767	-4267	-567	3333	7433	1248	1913	2136	2583	3032
1·100	—	-18693	-15193	-11493	-7593	-3493	807	493	1161	1385	1834	2285
1·110	—	-19550	-16030	-12310	-8390	-4270	50	-673	0	225	677	1131
1·125	—	-20869	-17319	-13569	-9619	-5469	-1119	-1070	-396	-170	283	738
1·130	—	—	-17757	-13997	-10037	-5877	-1517	-1879	-1202	-975	-520	-63
1·140	—	—	-18648	-14868	-10888	-6708	-2328	-2706	-2025	-1798	-1341	-882
1·150	—	—	-19557	-14757	-11757	-7557	-3175	—	—	—	—	—

70

increment of product will decrease after a certain point. That is, $f_{ii} < 0$ $(i = 1, 2, ..., n)$ over some range of inputs.[1]

The direct acceleration coefficient shows how the marginal product of input X_i varies when the usage of X_i varies. The cross-acceleration coefficient f_{ij} shows how the marginal product of X_i varies when the usage of X_j changes. If $f_{ij} > 0$, the marginal product of X_i increases when the input of X_j increases. The inputs are accordingly said to be *complementary* at the input point under consideration. On the other hand, if $f_{ij} < 0$, the marginal product of X_i declines when the usage of X_j increases. In this situation the inputs are said to be *competitive* or *alternative*.[2] The complementarity relation generally prevails. Furthermore, if there is a range of competitiveness (i.e. input points for which $f_{ij} < 0$), there must also exist a range of input complementarity.

4.3.3 Average product

The concept of average product is introduced by the following

Definition: The average product of an input at any factor point is the quantity of output per unit of the input used, i.e. the output–input ratio. Given the production function in equation (4.3.2), the average product of the i-th input is

$$AP_i = \frac{q}{x_i} = \frac{f(x_1, x_2, ..., x_n)}{x_i}, \qquad (4.3.10)$$

where the right-most expression emphasizes that the average product of one input is typically a function of all inputs.

A measure closely related to average product is sometimes called the *fabrication coefficient* of the ith input.[3] The fabrication coefficient shows, on average, the number of units of input X_i used per unit of output. Thus it is the input–output ratio, the inverse of average product. Denoting the fabrication coefficient of the ith input by θ_i, we have

$$\theta_i = \frac{x_i}{q} = \frac{1}{AP_i}. \qquad (4.3.11)$$

4.3.4 Average returns

Changes in the level of output resulting from input variations are often called 'returns to something'. When all inputs are varied in the same proportion, one speaks of 'returns to scale'. When a single input is varied, the

[1] For a historical account of the development of the law of variable proportions, see Stigler [1946]. For an interesting recent contribution, see Tangri [1966].

[2] The complementary-competitive relation should not be confused with the more important *substitution* relation. The latter concerns the *size* of the marginal products at a point, the former concerns the change in the marginal products in a neighborhood of the point.

[3] This is the terminology of Frisch [1965, p. 62].

appropriate concept is 'marginal' or 'average' returns. In subsection 4.3.2 it was shown that there are increasing or diminishing marginal returns according as $f_{ii} \gtrless 0$. The reason for this classification, of course, lies in the fact that f_{ii} is the first derivative of the marginal product function f_i.

In the same way, for a single input variation there exist increasing or diminishing average returns according as

$$\frac{\partial(q/x_i)}{\partial x_i} \gtrless 0. \tag{4.3.12}$$

Performing the differentiation, one obtains

$$\frac{\partial(q/x_i)}{\partial x_i} = \frac{1}{x_i}\left(f_i - \frac{q}{x_i}\right) = \frac{1}{x_i}(MP_i - AP_i). \tag{4.3.13}$$

From the last expression in equation (4.3.13) it follows immediately that there are increasing or diminishing average returns to the ith input at a given input point according as the marginal product is greater than or less than the average product.

Another familiar relation is obtainable from equation (4.3.13). The average product is a maximum when

$$\frac{\partial(q/x_i)}{\partial x_i} = 0 \quad \text{and} \quad \frac{\partial^2(q/x_i)}{\partial x_i^2} < 0. \tag{4.3.14}$$

Equations (4.3.13) and (4.3.14) taken together imply that the average product function attains its maximum at the point where marginal and average products are equal. The sufficient condition for a true maximum is

$$\frac{\partial^2(q/x_i)}{\partial x_i^2} = \frac{1}{x_i}f_{ii} - \frac{2}{x_i^2}\left[f_i - \frac{q}{x_i}\right] = \frac{1}{x_i}f_{ii} < 0. \tag{4.3.15}$$

Since $x_i > 0$ at any factor point, the existence of a true maximum on the average product function requires the marginal product function to be in the stage of diminishing marginal returns.

4.3.5   Relations among the product curves

At this point it is useful to summarize the relations that exist among the total, marginal, and average product curves. The typical cross-section shown in figure 21 is reproduced in figure 22 as the total product curve *OCE*. The corresponding marginal and average product curves are *OA'C'D'E* and *OBE* respectively (at this time, ignore the lower panel of the figure).

By condition (4.2.2) imposed on the production function, the total product curve emanates from the origin. Since the function is zero, its first derivative is too. Hence the marginal product curve begins at the origin. By applying L'Hospital's Rule it may be shown that the average product curve also begins at the origin. Consequently, all three product curves emanate from the origin.

Total and marginal product curves. As previously seen, the marginal product curve may decrease monotonically throughout its entire range,

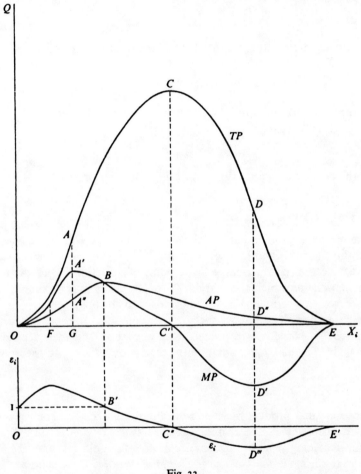

Fig. 22

or it may have rising and falling segments. In the latter case, there may or may not be points of inflection along the marginal product curve. The marginal product function depicted in figure 22 illustrates the more general case in which the marginal product curve both rises and falls and in which it contains points of inflection.

73

It is now convenient to state the following mathematical

Criterion: Consider any function $\eta = \phi(\xi)$. The function is said to have a point of inflection[1] at $\xi = x$ if $\phi_{xx} = 0$. If $\phi_{xxx} < 0$, the function changes from concave from above to concave from below; if $\phi_{xxx} > 0$, concavity changes in the opposite direction.[2]

The total product curve in the cross-section under consideration is

$$q = f(x_i|x_j) \quad \text{for} \quad j \neq i. \tag{4.3.16}$$

Hence marginal product, or the slope of the total product curve, is

$$\frac{\partial q}{\partial x_i} = f_i. \tag{4.3.17}$$

The marginal product function attains an extreme value when

$$\frac{\partial^2 q}{\partial x_i^2} = \frac{\partial f_i}{\partial x_i} = f_{ii} = 0; \tag{4.3.18}$$

and the extremum is a maximum or a minimum according as

$$\frac{\partial^3 q}{\partial x_i^3} = \frac{\partial^2 f_i}{\partial x_i^2} = f_{iii} \lessgtr 0. \tag{4.3.19}$$

If the marginal product curve attains a maximum at a point such as A', conditions (4.3.18) and (4.3.19) must hold. Hence by the criterion stated above, the total product curve has a point of inflection (A) at the input combination for which the marginal product curve is a maximum. The direction of concavity changes from 'above' to 'below'.

In general production laws such as equation (4.2.10), the cross-section total product curve rises from zero to a maximum and then declines to zero again. The maximum point on the total product curve (C) is attained when

$$\frac{\partial q}{\partial x_i} = f_i = 0 \quad \text{and} \quad \frac{\partial^2 q}{\partial x_i^2} = f_{ii} < 0. \tag{4.3.20}$$

Hence marginal product must be zero and declining when total product reaches its maximum. These conditions are satisfied by point C' in figure 22.

The remaining relation of interest concerns the points D and D'. First note that since the marginal product curve must be decreasing at C', it must become negative beyond C'. Next, since total product is zero at E, so is its derivative. Now let us summarize: (*a*) by assumption, the marginal product function is continuous; (*b*) marginal product is zero at C' and E. Hence by Rolle's Theorem, the marginal product function must have at

---

[1] A point of inflection is a point at which the direction of concavity changes.

[2] A function is said to be concave from above (below) at a point if it lies above (below) its tangent in a neighborhood of the point.

least one extreme point between C' and E. By assumption, the production function increases monotonically over the range from A to C and decreases monotonically over the range from C to E. Therefore, the marginal product function has *only one* extreme point over the range; and since the marginal product is negative within the range, the extremum must be a minimum.

Suppose the minimum occurs at D'. Thus at this point $f_{ii} = 0$ and $f_{iii} > 0$. Applying the criterion, the total product curve has a point of inflection at D, where its concavity changes from 'below' to 'above'.

Marginal and average products. The chief relation between the marginal and average product curves was established in section 4.3.4. Specifically, the average product curve attains its maximum at the point (B) where marginal product equals average product. For lower levels of input usage, marginal product exceeds average product; at greater input usages, average product exceeds marginal product. Beyond its maximum point, the average product curve declines monotonically, reaching zero when total product is zero.

The only other relation of interest concerns the concavity of the average product function. The average product curve may or may not have a point of inflection; but if it has one, it will have two. If a point of inflection exists, it will occur at the point where

$$\frac{\partial^2(q/x_i)}{\partial x_i^2} = \frac{1}{x_i} f_{ii} - \frac{2}{x_i^2}\left(f_i - \frac{q}{x_i}\right) = 0. \tag{4.3.21}$$

Since $\qquad f_{ii} = 0$ at A' and $f_i - \dfrac{q}{x_i} \neq 0$ there,

the point of inflection must occur to the left of A'' (and to the left of D'').

Next, observe that if a point of inflection exists to the left of A'', the concavity of the average product curve must change from 'above' to 'below'. Consider the third derivative:

$$\frac{\partial^3(q/x_i)}{\partial x_i^3} = \frac{1}{x_i} f_{iii} - \frac{3}{x_i^2} f_{ii} + \frac{6}{x_i^3}\left(f_i - \frac{q}{x_i}\right). \tag{4.3.22}$$

In light of equation (4.3.21) and the known direction of concavity change if it changes, the existence of a point of inflection corresponding to equation (4.3.21) requires

$$f_{iii} < 0. \tag{4.3.23}$$

Now consider the marginal product curve in the interval from 0 to A'. At A', $f_{iii} < 0$; and f_{iii} may be less than zero throughout the range. Thus the average product curve may have a point of inflection in the range from 0 to A'' whether or not the marginal product curve does. If the latter curve does have a point of inflection, f_{iii} must equal zero at some point between 0 and A'. Further, since $f_{iii} < 0$ at A', f_{iii} must change from positive, to zero, to negative over the range. Hence in light of inequality (4.3.23), if both the marginal and average product curves have a point of inflection in the range from o to $A'(A'')$, the point of inflection on the average product curve corresponds to a greater input usage than does the point of inflection on the marginal product curve. If the point of inflection on the marginal product curve is associated with the input of OF units of X_i, the point of inflection on the average product curve must lie between F and G. Therefore, the point of inflection on the average product curve occurs before the point of inflection on the total product curve. Similar statements apply, *mutatis mutandis*, to the point of inflection that occurs to the left of D''.

4.3.6 Output elasticity and the elasticity of average product

At any given input point, a comparison of marginal and average products permits one to determine the output elasticity of the input in question. Formally, the concept is stated in the following

Definition: The output elasticity of the ith input is the proportional change in output induced by a change in the ith input relative to the given proportional change in this input. For the production function in equation (4.3.2), the output elasticity of the ith input (ϵ_i) is

$$\epsilon_i = \frac{\partial q}{q} \div \frac{\partial x_i}{x_i} = \frac{\partial q}{\partial x_i} \frac{x_i}{q} = f_i \div \frac{\mathrm{I}}{q/x_i} = \frac{MP_i}{AP_i}. \qquad (4.3.24)$$

Thus the output elasticity at an input point is the ratio of the marginal product to the average product at the point in question.

As examples, the output elasticities for equations (4.2.4)–(4.2.6), respectively, are

$$\epsilon_x = \alpha, \qquad\qquad \epsilon_y = \beta; \qquad\qquad (4.3.25)$$

$$\epsilon_x = \gamma^{-\rho}\delta\left(\frac{q}{x}\right)^{\rho}, \qquad \epsilon_y = \gamma^{-\rho}(\mathrm{I}-\delta)\left(\frac{q}{y}\right)^{\rho}; \qquad (4.3.26)$$

$$\epsilon_x = \frac{2x(ay-bx)}{2axy-bx^2-cy^2}, \quad \epsilon_y = \frac{2y(ax-cy)}{2axy-bx^2-cy^2}. \qquad (4.3.27)$$

A point worth noting from these examples and from equation (4.3.24) is that the output elasticity is typically a function of all the inputs. Thus the output elasticity generally depends upon the particular input point at which it is measured. In one special case, however, the output elasticities are constants independent of the factor point. This situation, of course, is represented by the Cobb–Douglas production function [equation (4.2.4); the output elasticities are shown in equation (4.3.25)].

The output elasticity can now be used to define the elasticity of average product. Using the conventional elasticity formula,

$$\frac{\partial(q/x_i)}{\partial x_i} \frac{x_i}{q/x_i} = \frac{x_i f_i - q}{x_i^2} \frac{x_i^2}{q} = \frac{f_i}{q/x_i} - 1 = \frac{MP_i}{AP_i} - 1 = \epsilon_i - 1.$$

$$(4.3.28)$$

The elasticity of the average product curve is equal to the output elasticity minus one. Or, using the concept of average returns introduced in subsection 4.3.4, there exist increasing or decreasing average returns at a given point according as $\epsilon_i \gtrless 1$.

The behavior of the output elasticity is shown graphically in figure 22. At the origin both marginal and average products are zero. Using L'Hospital's Rule, it may be shown that $\epsilon_i = 1$. Moving away from the origin, marginal product exceeds average product, so $\epsilon_i > 1$. At point B, where marginal and average products are equal, ϵ_i becomes one again. Beyond B, ϵ_i diminishes, becoming zero when marginal product is zero and negative when the marginal product is negative. As constructed in figure 22, ϵ_i reaches its minimum when marginal product does; however, this is not necessarily the case. The minimum of ϵ_i does not have to conicide with the minimum marginal product. After attaining its minimum, ϵ_i rises to zero at point E, where all product curves are zero.

4.3.7 The stages of production

Since the appearance of Cassels' noted paper, it has become traditional to classify the 'stages of production' relative to single-input variations.[1] According to Cassels, the stages of production are as shown in figure 23. The tasks are to show that production will occur only in Stage II and that point A divides Stages I and II.

First, we should emphasize that the problem at hand concerns the short run only. All inputs are fixed except one. Changes in output can be accomplished only by changes in this one variable input. It is quite obvious that production will not occur at a point to the right of B, where total product is a maximum and marginal product is zero. In Stage III, any additional usage of the variable input diminishes, rather than augments, output. In older terminology, point B corresponds to the *intensive margin* beyond which production will not take place.

It is clear that the conditions of production undergo a fundamental change at the intensive margin; and it is reasonable to designate the portion of the product graph to the right of B as a separate 'stage of production'. To establish the dividing point between Stages I and II requires somewhat more explanation.

[1] Cassels [1936, esp. pp. 226–8].

To begin, note that the point of division is established at *A*, corresponding to maximum average product or the *extensive margin*. In the case of functions homogeneous of degree one, this is clearly the point of demarcation (because the marginal product of the fixed factor is negative to the left of *A*). Otherwise, it is necessary to use the concept of output elasticity developed in subsection 4.3.6. above.

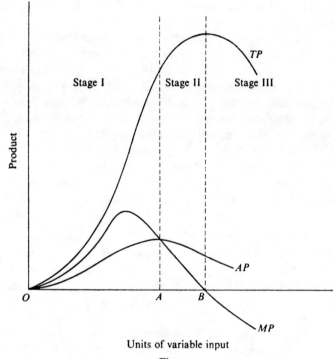

Fig. 23

Output elasticity (ϵ_i) is the proportional change in output relative to a proportional change in input. If $\epsilon_i > 1$, a given increase in usage of the variable input results in a proportionately greater increase in output. The point is that production would never take place over the range of input values for which $\epsilon_i > 1$ because an increase in output could be secured by refusing to utilize all available units of the fixed inputs. Over this range, the entrepreneur has two methods of expanding output: (*a*) expand the usage of the variable input, and (*b*) reduce the utilization of fixed inputs. The latter would always be chosen if a volume of output corresponding to Stage I were to be produced. But in this eventuality, the product curves

78

would have to be redrawn because the effective amount of fixed input has changed.

Relative to the original amount of fixed input, production would never occur over the range for which $\epsilon_i > 1$. It would occur over the range for which $0 \leqq \epsilon_i \leqq 1$. Since $\epsilon_i = 1$ when marginal product equals average product, the division point A is established. There are indeed three distinct stages of production; and a rational entrepreneur will produce only in Stage II, between the extensive and intensive margins.

4.4 The function coefficient[1]

Attention in this chapter has so far been directed to the behavior of output when one input is varied, all other inputs being held constant at some specified level. The same study was undertaken in chapter 2; a comparison of results shows the essential differences between fixed and variable proportions production functions for single input variations. Additionally, in chapter 2 the behavior of output for proportional variations of all inputs was analyzed. It is to a similar task that the present section is devoted.

4.4.1 Proportional input variations and the function coefficient

The concept of the *function coefficient* is introduced by the following

Definition: The function coefficient is the elasticity of output with respect to an equiproportional variation of all inputs. Thus the function coefficient is the proportional change in output relative to the proportional changes in the inputs for movements along a ray from the origin in input space.

Consider any initial input point $x_1^0, x_2^0, ..., x_n^0$. By equation (4.2.1), output is

$$q^0 = f(x_1^0, x_2^0, ..., x_n^0). \qquad (4.4.1)$$

Let each input be increased by the same proportion λ. Thus

$$x_i = \lambda x_i^0 = x_i(\lambda) \quad (i = 1, 2, ..., n), \qquad (4.4.2)$$

and

$$q = f(\lambda x_1^0, \lambda x_2^0, ..., \lambda x_n^0) = g(\lambda). \qquad (4.4.3)$$

Using equation (4.4.3), the definition of the function coefficient (ϵ) may be given more precisely by

$$\epsilon = \frac{dq}{q} \div \frac{d\lambda}{\lambda} = \frac{dg(\lambda)}{d\lambda} \frac{\lambda}{g(\lambda)} = \frac{d \ln q}{d \ln \lambda}, \qquad (4.4.4)$$

where 'ln' denotes the natural logarithm.

[1] The terminology for the concept in question varies. The term 'function coefficient' is used by Carlson [1939]. Schneider [1934] uses 'Ergiebigkeitsgrad der Produktion' for this concept and 'Ertragsfunktion' to refer to equiproportional variation of inputs. Johnson [1913] uses 'elasticity of production' to describe the concept, while Allen [1938] uses 'elasticity of productivity'. Finally, Frisch [1965] uses 'passus coefficient'.

One feature of the function coefficient is immediately apparent from equation (4.4.4). Specifically, λ is a scale factor; hence the function coefficient is the elasticity of output with respect to scale. Thus in a neighborhood of any input point, production is subject to increasing, constant, or decreasing *returns to scale* according as $\epsilon \gtreqless 1$.

As shown in chapter 5, the function coefficient is a constant when the production function is homogeneous; indeed, ϵ is the (constant) degree of homogeneity of the function. If the production function is not homogeneous, however, the function coefficient is a variable that depends upon (a) the specific factor proportion (ray) at which it is measured, and (b) the scale of input usage. Thus for inhomogeneous functions, the magnitude of the function coefficient depends not only upon the ray along which it is measured but also the point at which it is measured. Further, as should be obvious from equation (4.4.4), the function coefficient has a range of negative values if the production surface has a maximum point.

Total output and the function coefficient for equation (4.2.10) are shown in table 5. It is interesting to note that the function coefficient is zero at the input point corresponding to maximum total product. This relation follows immediately from equation (4.4.4) inasmuch as dq must be instantaneously zero at the maximum point.

TABLE 5 *Output and function coefficients from equation (4.2.10)*

$x = y$	Output	Function coefficient
0·500	1667	2·500
0·600	2592	2·333
0·700	3659	2·125
0·800	4779	1·857
0·900	5832	1·500
1·000	6667	1·000
1·100	7099	0·250
1·110	7112	0·154
1·125	7119	0·000
1·130	7118	−0·054
1·140	7111	−0·167
1·150	7097	−0·286
1·500	0	−2·000

4.4.2 Derivation of the function coefficient

The total differential of the production function in equation (4.2.1) is

$$dq = f_1 dx_1 + f_2 dx_2 + \ldots + f_n dx_n, \qquad (4.4.5)$$

or

$$dq = f_1 x_1 \frac{dx_1}{x_1} + f_2 x_2 \frac{dx_2}{x_2} + \ldots + f_n x_n \frac{dx_n}{x_n}. \qquad (4.4.6)$$

When all inputs are varied equiproportionately by the factor λ,

$$\frac{dx_i}{x_i} = \frac{d\lambda}{\lambda} \quad (i = 1, 2, \ldots, n). \qquad (4.4.7)$$

Substituting equation (4.4.7) in equation (4.4.6) yields

$$dq = (\sum_i f_i x_i) \frac{d\lambda}{\lambda}. \qquad (4.4.8)$$

Using definition (4.4.4), one obtains

$$\epsilon = \frac{\sum_i f_i x_i}{q}, \qquad (4.4.9)$$

the desired expression for the function coefficient.

While the derivation given above is the most straightforward, the expression for the function coefficient in equation (4.4.9) may be derived in two alternative ways.[1] To obtain the first alternative, differentiate equation (4.4.3) with respect to λ, obtaining

$$\sum_i \frac{\partial q}{\partial x_i} \frac{dx_i}{d\lambda} = \frac{dg(\lambda)}{d\lambda}. \qquad (4.4.10)$$

From equations (4.4.2) it follows that

$$\frac{dx_i}{d\lambda} = \frac{d(\lambda x_i^0)}{d\lambda} = x_i^0 \quad (i = 1, 2, \ldots .n). \qquad (4.4.11)$$

Using equation (4.4.11) in equation (4.4.10), one obtains

$$\Sigma f_i x_i^0 = \frac{dg(\lambda)}{d\lambda}, \qquad (4.4.12)$$

from which it follows that

$$\Sigma f_i(\lambda x_i^0) = \Sigma f_i x_i = \lambda \frac{dg(\lambda)}{d\lambda} = \left(\frac{dg(\lambda)}{d\lambda} \frac{\lambda}{g(\lambda)} \right) q. \qquad (4.4.13)$$

Finally, using the definition ϵ from equation (4.4.4) reduces equation (4.4.13) to equation (4.4.9).

---

[1] Both these derivations are presumably attributable to Frisch [1965, pp. 75–7].

The final derivation depends upon the fact that the function coefficient is generally dependent upon the particular input point at which it is measured. That is, for any specified ray, the function coefficient depends upon the scale factor. Symbolically,

$$\epsilon = h(x_1, x_2, ..., x_n) = h(\lambda x_1^0, \lambda x_2^0, ..., \lambda x_n^0) = \epsilon(\lambda). \qquad (4.4.14)$$

Substituting equation (4.4.14) into equation (4.4.4), one obtains

$$d \ln g(\lambda) = \epsilon(\lambda) \, d \ln \lambda. \qquad (4.4.15)$$

Next, integrate, equation (4.4.15) between two limits, say $\lambda = 1$ and $\lambda = M$, obtaining

$$\ln g(M) - \ln g(1) = \int_1^M \epsilon(\lambda) \, d \ln \lambda. \qquad (4.4.16)$$

Taking the antilogarithm of equation (4.4.16) yields

$$g(M) = g(1) \exp \left(\int_1^M \epsilon(\lambda) \, d \ln \lambda \right). \qquad (4.4.17)$$

Inserting equation (4.4.3) in equation (4.4.17), one obtains

$$f(Mx_1^0, Mx_2^0, ..., Mx_n^0) = f(x_1^0, x_2^0, ..., x_n^0) \exp \left(\int_1^M \epsilon(\lambda) \, d \ln \lambda \right). \qquad (4.4.18)$$

Next, differentiate equation (4.4.18) with respect to M. This results in

$$\sum_i \frac{\partial f}{\partial (Mx_i^0)} \frac{d(Mx_i^0)}{dM} = q \frac{d \exp \left(\int_1^M \epsilon(\lambda) \, d \ln \lambda \right)}{dM}, \qquad (4.4.19)$$

or since $d \ln \lambda = \frac{1}{\lambda} d\lambda$ and $\frac{d(Mx_i^0)}{dM} = x_i^0,$

$$\sum_i \frac{\partial f}{\partial (Mx_i^0)} x_i^0 = q \exp \left(\int_1^M \frac{1}{\lambda} \epsilon(\lambda) \, d\lambda \right) \frac{\epsilon(M)}{M}. \qquad (4.4.20)$$

Since equation (4.4.18) holds for any M, one may set $M = 1$ in equation (4.4.20). In this case

$$\int_1^{M=1} \frac{1}{\lambda} \epsilon(\lambda) \, d\lambda = 0, \qquad (4.4.21)$$

so equation (4.4.20) becomes

$$\sum \frac{\partial f}{\partial x_i^0} x_i^0 = q\epsilon(1). \qquad (4.4.22)$$

Finally, using equation (4.4.14) in equation (4.4.22), one obtains

$$\sum f_i x_i^0 = q\epsilon(x_1^0, x_2^0, ..., x_n^0). \qquad (4.4.23)$$

In this expression all variables are related to the specific input point $x_1^0, x_2^0, ..., x_n^0$. However, since this point is arbitrary, equation (4.4.9) follows immediately from equation (4.4.23).

4.4.3 Relation of the function coefficient to output elasticities and the elasticity of average product

The general expression for the function coefficient in equation (4.4.9) may be expanded and written as

$$\epsilon = \frac{\partial f}{\partial x_1}\frac{x_1}{q} + \frac{\partial f}{\partial x_2}\frac{x_2}{q} + ... + \frac{\partial f}{\partial x_n}\frac{x_n}{q}. \tag{4.4.24}$$

Using the definition of output elasticity from equation (4.3.24), equation (4.4.24) becomes

$$\epsilon = \epsilon_1 + \epsilon_2 + ... + \epsilon_n. \tag{4.4.25}$$

Thus the function coefficient is the sum of all output elasticities. In a way, this merely reemphasizes a proposition familiar from the calculus: the variation of a function resulting from the simultaneous variation of all arguments equals the sum of the variations in the function ascribable to independent variations of the arguments. Yet it also provides an important connection between simultaneous and independent input variations. In particular, the ultimate proportional change in output is the same whether all inputs are varied simultaneously or one at a time.

An even more meaningful relation may be established between returns to scale and average returns. Consider the expression for the elasticity of the average product of the ith input with respect to the scale factor λ:

$$\frac{d(q/x_i)}{d\lambda}\frac{\lambda x_i}{q} = \frac{dq}{d\lambda}\frac{\lambda}{q} - \frac{dx_i}{d\lambda}\frac{\lambda}{x_i} \quad (i = 1, 2, ..., n). \tag{4.4.26}$$

First, note that the elasticity of any input with respect to the scale factor is unity. Using this information, together with equation (4.4.4), in equation (4.4.26) yields

$$\frac{d(q/x_i)}{d\lambda}\frac{\lambda x_i}{q} = \epsilon - 1 \quad (i = 1, 2, ..., n). \tag{4.4.27}$$

The results contained in equation (4.4.27) are of the first order of importance. For small variations along an input ray, all average products increase, remain unchanged, or decrease according as $\epsilon \gtreqqless 1$. In other words, for proportional input changes, there exist increasing, constant, or diminishing average returns for each input according as production occurs in the region of increasing, constant, or decreasing returns to scale.

4.5 Simultaneous input variations

To this point our attention has been directed exclusively to the variations in output attributable to variations in the use of a single productive input, all other inputs held constant. This study is important because it emphasizes one aspect of production under conditions of variable proportions: output changes in response to a change in factor proportions. Yet this is but one of the essential features of variable proportions production functions. The other is that the same output can be produced by a variety of factor proportions, i.e., one input may be substituted for another without affecting the level of output. To emphasize this important aspect of production, one must analyze the effects of simultaneous input variations.

4.5.1 The marginal rate of technical substitution

As stated above, one input may sometimes be substituted for another without affecting the level of output. In other words, over a certain range inputs may be substituted along an isoquant so that factor proportions vary while output remains unchanged. In effect, one input is substituted for another within this range. It is of considerable interest to measure the rate at which such a substitution can take place.

Definition: The marginal rate of technical substitution of input j for input $i (MRTS_{ji})$ is the number of units by which the usage of j may be reduced when the usage of i is expanded by one unit so as to maintain a constant level of output.

To get at a precise measure of the *marginal* rate, consider the isoquant Q_0 between the points A and B in figure 24. Suppose production is initially organized at point $P(x_1, y_1)$ and subsequently moves to point $S(x_2, y_2)$. In the change X is substituted for Y without affecting the level of output. The rate at which X is substituted for Y is

$$-\frac{Oy_1 - Oy_2}{Ox_1 - Ox_2} = -\frac{PR}{RS}. \qquad (4.5.1)$$

Equation (4.5.1) shows the (positive) rate of substitution for a finite move along Q_0. However, the closer is P to S, the more nearly is the rate of substitution approximated by the tangent to Q_0 at S, i.e. $-\tan TS$. And in the limit, when P is arbitrarily close to S, the *marginal* rate of technical substitution of input Y for input X is given by the negative of the slope of the isoquant at S.

Now consider the production function in equation (4.2.1) and suppose only two inputs change, X_i and X_j. Further, impose the restriction that output does not change. Taking the (relevant) total differential, one obtains

$$dq = f_i dx_i + f_j dx_j = 0. \qquad (4.5.2)$$

Equation (4.5.2) is the differential equation for an isoquant whose slope is, accordingly,

$$\frac{dx_j}{dx_i} = -\frac{f_i}{f_j}. \tag{4.5.3}$$

Using the previous results,

$$MRTS_{ji} = -\frac{dx_j}{dx_i} = \frac{f_i}{f_j}. \tag{4.5.4}$$

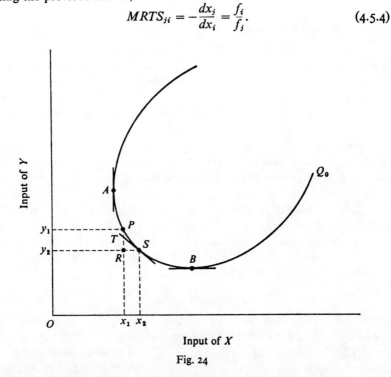

Input of X

Fig. 24

Thus the marginal rate of technical substitution of j for i is the ratio of the marginal product of i to the marginal product of j.

The result (4.5.4) has been obtained under the assumption that input variations are restricted to the arc AB in figure 24. Over this region, inputs are truly substituted one for another inasmuch as the use of additional units of one input permits some units of the other input to be released. The same is not true beyond points A and B. At point A, the marginal product of Y is zero, and it is negative beyond. Thus if the usage of Y is expanded beyond A, the usage of X must also expand to offset the depressive output effect of the negative marginal product. The same statement applies, *mutatis mutandis*, for a movement beyond B, at which point the marginal product of X is zero. Beyond points A and B, the inputs cannot be *substituted* inasmuch as *both* must be increased to maintain a constant level of output. Hence the marginal rate of technical substitution is properly defined only over the range in which both marginal products are non-negative. Thus over the substitution range,

$$MRTS_{ji} = -\frac{dx_j}{dx_i} = \frac{f_i}{f_j} \geq 0. \tag{4.5.5}$$

4.5.2 Production isoclines

Since an isoquant is smoothly continuous by assumption, its slope changes continuously for movements along it. Hence in light of equation (4.5.4), the marginal rate of technical substitution also varies continuously for movements along an isoquant. Indeed, over the substitution range, the marginal rate of technical substitution diminishes from an arbitrarily large number (at A) to zero (at B). Since this is true for one isoquant, it is true for all isoquants.[1] Consequently, given an isoquant map and any stipulated values of the marginal rate of technical substitution, there exists precisely one point on each isoquant at which the marginal rate of technical substitution has the stipulated value.

Definition: A locus of points along which the marginal rate of technical substitution is constant is called an isocline.

On a purely formal level, the isocline corresponding to the marginal rate of technical substitution whose value is $\bar{c}$ (a constant) is given by the following partial differential equation:

$$f_i(x_i, x_j) = \bar{c} f_j(x_i, x_j), \tag{4.5.4}$$

where there are no constants of integration since $f_i(0, 0) = f_j(0, 0) = 0$.

The graphical derivation of an isocline is illustrated in figure 25. Q_0, Q_1, and Q_2 are isoquants and CF, $C'F'$, and $C''F''$ are lines whose slopes are identical. Hence the slopes of Q_0, Q_1, and Q_2 are the same at P, R, and S respectively. Since the (negative) slope of an isoquant is the marginal rate of technical substitution, these rates are the same at P, R, and S. Connecting all points such as P, R, and S generates an isocline such as that shown in figure 25. It is worth noting that since the integral of equation (4.5.6) does not contain a constant term, all isoclines emanate from the origin.

4.5.3 The substitution region

In subsection 4.5.1 it was noted that the marginal rate of technical substitution could only be defined for the negatively sloped portion of an isoquant. In certain cases, such as the production functions shown in

---

[1] As previously noted, certain production functions are such that the marginal products never become zero. However, even in these cases, the marginal products approach zero asymptotically, and the statement in the text holds in the limit.

equations (4.2.4) and (4.2.5), the isoquants are negatively sloped through-out. More generally, however, the isoquant maps resemble those shown in figures 20 and 26. In the former case, the entire map comprises the sub-stitution region; in the latter cases, illustrated by figures 20 and 26, how-ever, the substitition region is only a portion of the entire input space.

Definition: The substitution region is that portion of input space in which all isoquants are negatively sloped. It is thus the region in which one

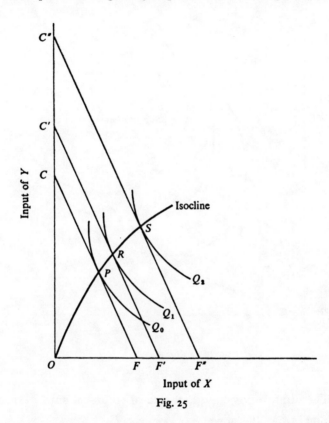

Fig. 25

input may be substituted for another while maintaining a constant level of output.

The substitution region is determined (see figure 26) by finding the two isoclines corresponding to infinite and zero marginal rates of technical substitution. In figure 26 these two isoclines are given by OS and OS' respectively. OS is the locus along which the marginal product of Y is zero; hence the marginal rate of technical substitution is indefinitely large. The opposite characterizes OS', which is the locus along which the marginal product of X is zero. Hence the marginal rate of technical substitution is also zero.

The substitution region lies between these two limiting isoclines, which are sometimes called *ridge lines*. This terminology is presumably based upon the fact that the cross-section total product curves attain maxima in the Q–Y plane for input combinations associated with OS and in the Q–X plane for input combinations associated with OS'.

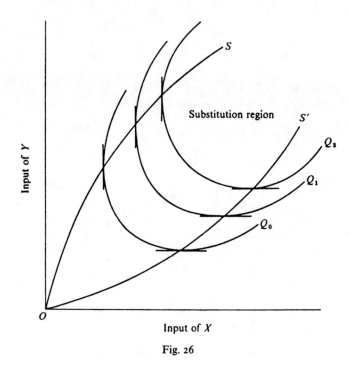

Fig. 26

4.5.4 The diminishing marginal rate of technical substitution

By equation (4.5.3), the slope of an isoquant is

$$\frac{dx_j}{dx_i} = -\frac{f_i}{f_j}. \qquad (4.5.7)$$

Hence the concavity of the isoquant depends upon the second derivative:

$$\frac{d^2x_j}{dx_i^2} = \frac{d\left(-\frac{f_i}{f_j}\right)}{dx_i} = -\frac{f_j\left(f_{ii}+f_{ij}\frac{dx_j}{dx_i}\right)-f_i\left(f_{ij}+f_{jj}\frac{dx_j}{dx_i}\right)}{f_j^2}. \qquad (4.5.8)$$

Substituting from equation (4.5.7) yields

$$\frac{d^2 x_j}{dx_i^2} = -\frac{1}{f_j^3}\,(f_j^2 f_{ii} - 2f_i f_j f_{ij} + f_i^2 f_{jj}). \tag{4.5.9}$$

If the right-hand side of equation (4.5.9) is positive, the isoquant is concave from above; if negative, it is concave from below.

Over the substitution region, all isoquants are concave from above. Within the region, $f_i > 0$ and $f_{ii} < 0$ for all i. In almost all cases, $f_{ii} > 0$ in the substitution region. But regardless of the sign of f_{ij}, the term in parentheses on the right in equation (4.5.9) must be negative; hence the right-hand side is positive, and the isoquant is concave from above in the substitution region.[1]

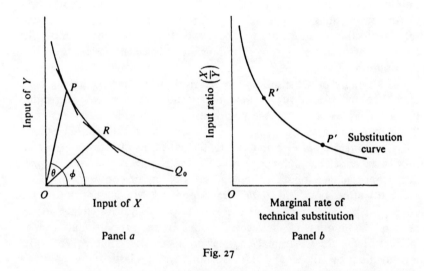

Panel a

Panel b

Fig. 27

The fact that isoquants are concave from above in the substitution region enables one to establish the following

Proposition: as X_i is substituted for X_j so as to maintain a constant level of output, the marginal rate of technical substitution declines. Thus throughout the substitution region, there is a *diminishing marginal rate of technical substitution.*

[1] If the production function is homogeneous of degree one, f_{ij} and f_{ii} necessarily have opposite signs. Otherwise, f_{ij} and f_{ii} may have identical signs. In this case, the concavity of the isoquant cannot be inferred *a priori* from the technical theory of production. However, as shown in chapter 6, economic efficiency can be attained if, and only if, production isoquants are concave from above within the substitution region.

4.5.5 The elasticity of substitution

Consider the isoquant Q_0 in panel a, figure 27, and the $(Y:X)$ input ratio represented by the ray OP, i.e. $y/x = \tan\theta$. At this input ratio and scale of operation, the slope of the isoquant at point P gives the marginal rate of technical substitution. Now transfer to panel b and plot this pair of values, i.e. the $X:Y$ ratio and the associated marginal rate of technical substitution. The point P on Q_0 might, for example, give rise to the point P' in panel b.

Next, select another input ratio, say OR, where $y/x = \tan\phi$. This gives rise to another value of the marginal rate of technical substitution. Plot this point, and many similar points, on Panel b and connect all such points. The resulting curve, called the *substitution curve*, shows how factor proportions change in response to a change in the marginal rate of technical substitution. The elasticity of this curve, called the *elasticity of substitution*, is very important in the neoclassical theory of distribution.[1]

The elasticity of substitution is a relatively new concept, having been introduced by Hicks in 1932.[2] Hicks himself did not give a precise definition in the text of his book: '...the "elasticity of substitution" is a measure of the ease with which the varying factor can be substituted for others' [1932, p. 117]. He did give an exact mathematical formulation of the concept in an appendix [pp. 244–5]; but the mathematical definition applies only to production functions homogeneous of degree one.

Shortly after Hicks' *Theory of Wages* appeared, Mrs Robinson gave the concept a more precise definition: '...the proportionate change in the ratio of the amounts of the factors divided by the proportionate change in the ratio of their marginal physical productivities.'[3] Subsequent to its introduction by Hicks and Mrs Robinson, the elasticity of substitution became the subject of intense investigation, possibly because the concept was initially misunderstood by many economists.[4] However, it would seem that by 1938,[5] the concept was well established and widely understood.

[1] This graphical treatment of the elasticity of substitution is presumably attributable to Lerner [1933a]. It was also used in Ferguson [1964a].

[2] Hicks [1932, p. 117 and pp. 244–5].

[3] Robinson [1933, p. 330, n. 2]. Mrs Robinson also defined the elasticity of substitution in terms of input prices (p. 256). However, she states (p. 330) that the definition given above is the more fundamental one.

[4] For a sampling of this literature, see Champernowne [1935], Friedman [1936], Hicks [1933], Hicks [1936], Kahn [1933], Kahn [1935], Kaldor [1937], Lerner [1933a], Lerner [1934], Lerner [1936], Machlup [1935], Machlup [1936a], Meade [1934a, b], Pigou [1934], Robinson [1936], Sweezy [1933], and Tarshis [1934].

[5] Allen [1938, pp. 340–3].

By equation (4.5.3) the marginal rate of technical substitution (denoted by s below) is

$$s = -\frac{dx_j}{dx_i} = \frac{f_i}{f_j}.$$ (4.5.10)

Further, let y represent the input ratio x_j/x_i. The elasticity of substitution (σ) is given by the following

Definition: The elasticity of substitution of X_j for X_i is

$$\sigma = \frac{dy}{y} \div \frac{ds}{s},$$ (4.5.11)

where the differentials are restricted to variations along an isoquant. Thus the elasticity of substitution refers only to input substitutions associated with a constant level of output.

The formula (4.5.11) may be written directly in terms of the partial derivatives of the production function. First, note that

$$dy = \frac{x_i\,dx_j - x_j\,dx_i}{x_i^2},$$ (4.5.12)

and

$$ds = \frac{\partial s}{\partial x_i}\,dx_i + \frac{\partial s}{\partial x_j}\,dx_j.$$ (4.5.13)

Since

$$dx_j = -\frac{f_i}{f_j}\,dx_i = -s\,dx_i,$$ (4.5.14)

equations (4.5.12) and (4.5.13) may be written

$$dy = -\frac{sx_i + x_j}{x_i^2}\,dx_i,$$ (4.5.15)

and

$$ds = -\left(s\,\frac{\partial s}{\partial x_j} - \frac{\partial s}{\partial x_i}\right)dx_i.$$ (4.5.16)

Next,

$$\frac{\partial s}{\partial x_j} = \frac{\partial(f_i/f_j)}{\partial x_j} = \frac{f_j f_{ij} - f_i f_{jj}}{f_j^2},$$ (4.5.17)

and

$$\frac{\partial s}{\partial x_i} = \frac{\partial(f_i/f_j)}{\partial x_i} = \frac{f_j f_{ii} - f_i f_{ji}}{f_j^2}.$$ (4.5.18)

Substituting equations (4.5.15)–(4.5.18) in formula (4.5.11) yields an expression for the elasticity of substitution based directly upon the production function:

$$\sigma = -\frac{f_i f_j (x_i f_i + x_j f_j)}{x_i x_j (f_{ii} f_j^2 - 2f_{ij} f_i f_j + f_{jj} f_i^2)}.$$ (4.5.19)

In this form it is readily seen that there is no 'problem of symmetry' at all.[1]

---

[1] The 'problem of symmetry' was posed by Tarshis [1934] and Machlup [1935]; the 'problem' was disposed of by Lerner [1936].

The elasticity of substitution of X_i for X_j is precisely the same as the elasticity of substitution of X_j for X_i.

Considering an alternative expression for the elasticity of substitution enables one to obtain additional information. Substituting equations (4.5.15) and (4.5.16) in formula (4.5.11) yields

$$\sigma = \frac{s}{x_i x_j} \frac{x_i s + x_j}{s(\partial s/\partial x_j) - (\partial s/\partial x_i)}. \tag{4.5.20}$$

The change in the slope of an isoquant is given by

$$\frac{d^2 x_j}{dx_i^2} = -\frac{ds}{dx_i} = s\frac{\partial s}{\partial x_j} - \frac{\partial s}{\partial x_i}. \tag{4.5.21}$$

Hence the elasticity of substitution may also be written

$$\sigma = \frac{s}{x_i x_j} \frac{x_i s + x_j}{(d^2 x_j/dx_i^2)}. \tag{4.5.22}$$

Since s, x_i, and x_j are positive, the elasticity of substitution is inversely proportional to the change in the slope of the isoquant. Further, since an isoquant must be concave from above over the substitution region, $d^2 x_j/dx_i^2 > 0$. Thus the elasticity of substitution is a nonnegative magnitude. Two limiting values of the elasticity of substitution may be found by using equation (4.5.22). First, if the two inputs are perfect substitutes, the isoquants are a series of straight lines. The second derivative is accordingly zero, and the elasticity of substitution is infinite. The other extreme occurs when the inputs cannot be substituted for one another while maintaining a constant output. This is the case of fixed proportions between limitational inputs. The isoquants are right angles, the second derivative approaches a limiting value of infinity, and the elasticity of substitution approaches a limiting value of zero. Generally, the inputs must be mutually limitative at a point if the elasticity of substitution is to be a nonzero magnitude.[1]

In summary, the elasticity of substitution is a nonnegative measure of the relative ease with which one input may be substituted for another while maintaining a constant output. Typically, the elasticity is zero when the inputs are mutually limitational and strictly positive when the inputs are mutually limitative.[2] The elasticity is a pure number independent of the units in which inputs and outputs are measured. Finally, it is a symmetrical relation that is typically a function of the input point at which it is measured.

[1] For exceptions, see subsection 2.4.2.
[2] An exception in the case of mutual limitativeness is given by the following production function:
$$q = ax + by \quad (0 < a, 0 < b).$$

92

5

TECHNICAL ASPECTS OF CONTINUOUS
PRODUCTION FUNCTIONS HOMOGENEOUS
OF DEGREE ONE

5.1 Introduction

This chapter is devoted to a systematic and intense investigation of the technical theory of production in the special case of linearly homogeneous production functions. This might seem unnecessary inasmuch as this class of functions is a highly simplified form of the general class considered in chapter 4. Yet such a discussion is worthwhile. First, the assumption of linear homogeneity is so specialized and simplifying that it leads to some significant extensions of the general theory of production. Even more important, perhaps, this assumption seems to be an accurate empirical approximation of production conditions in a wide range of circumstances. Thus these extensions appear to have important empirical applications. Second, the case of linear homogeneity is so important in the analyses of distribution and aggregate production that it merits special attention. Finally, and somewhat surprisingly, there seems to be a widespread misunderstanding of certain aspects of the technical theory of production under conditions of linear homogeneity.

The last point is illustrated by the recent argument concerning 'diminishing returns and linear homogeneity'. The argument was begun, innocently enough, by Nutter.[1] He cited the following textbook statements, one of which is attributable to negligence, the other to error. The first is from Liebhafsky:[2]

Many writers also draw the total product curve with a point of inflection and then 'assume that the production function is linearly homogeneous'. A thorough search of the literature has failed to reveal a single case in which a writer has *specified* a linearly homogeneous production function which produces such a total product curve! The procedure of drawing the curve in this way and then assuming it to be linearly homogeneous is confusing, and those who draw the curve in this way and make the assumptions have the burden of stating the specific function they are employing.

---

[1] Nutter [1963].   [2] Liebhafsky [1963, p. 126, n. 3].

The second quotation is from Stonier and Hague:[1]

If returns to scale (outlay) are *constant*, the marginal productivity of a variable factor used in conjunction with a fixed factor will always diminish as more of the variable factor is used.

Nutter's note was followed by a number of interpretative comments,[2] which seems all the more surprising because several examples were given by Allen in 1938.[3]

5.2 Homogeneous functions

5.2.1 Mathematical properties of functions homogeneous of degree one

At the outset it is useful to list some important properties of linearly homogeneous functions. A proof of properties (i)–(vi) and a statement of criterion (viii) may be found in any standard calculus text or in Allen [1938]. A derivation of property (vii) is provided. Without loss of generality, attention is restricted to a function of two variable inputs. The reader is asked to note that '*A* and *B*' replace '*X* and *Y*' as the inputs. This substitution permits the use of a convenient transformation in subsection 5.2.3 and elsewhere.

Let the production function be

$$q = f(a, b), \tag{5.2.1}$$

where q is output, a and b are the quantities used of inputs A and B, and f is homogeneous of degree one. Then

    (i) $q \equiv af_a + bf_b$ (Euler's Theorem);

    (ii) the first partial derivatives of a function homogeneous of degree one are homogeneous of degree zero;

    (iii) $f_{bb} = \dfrac{a^2}{b^2} f_{aa}$;

    (iv) $af_{aa} = -bf_{ab}$ and $bf_{bb} = -af_{ab}$.

From properties (iii) and (iv) it follows that

    (v) $f_{aa} = f_{bb} = f_{ab} = 0$ when any one of the three is zero and there is a positive level of input.

    (vi) $a^2 f_a^2 + 2abf_af_b + b^2 f_b^2 = q^2$.

---

[1] Stonier and Hague [1955, p. 229].

[2] See, in alphabetical order, Chattopadhyay [1966], Fortenay [1964], Liebhafsky [1964], Moeseke [1965], Nutter [1964] and [1965], Piron [1966], Rowe [1964] and [1965], Sato [1964], and D. Schneider [1964].

[3] Allen [1938, p. 322]. It is also interesting to note that Allen suggested a general form of the function Nutter used (p. 323, exercise 20).

The final property to be listed must be derived. Differentiate property (i) with respect to a, obtaining

$$af_{aa} + bf_{ab} = 0. \tag{5.2.2}$$

Differentiating equation (5.2.2) with respect to a further yields

$$f_{aaa} = -\frac{1}{a}f_{aa} - \frac{b}{a}f_{aab}. \tag{5.2.3}$$

Next differentiate equation (5.2.2) with respect to b, obtaining

$$f_{aab} = -\frac{1}{a}f_{ab} - \frac{b}{a}f_{abb}. \tag{5.2.4}$$

Finally, differentiate property (i) twice with respect to b:

$$f_{abb} = -\frac{1}{a}f_{bb} - \frac{b}{a}f_{bbb}. \tag{5.2.5}$$

By substituting equation (5.2.5) into equation (5.2.4) and the resulting expression for f_{aab} into equation (5.2.3), one obtains

$$f_{aaa} = -\frac{1}{a}f_{aa} + \frac{b}{a^2}f_{ab} - \frac{b^2}{a^3}f_{bb} - \frac{b^3}{a^3}f_{bbb}. \tag{5.2.6}$$

The desired property is obtained by substituting properties (iii) and (v) into equation (5.2.6):

(vii) $f_{aaa} = -\dfrac{1}{a}f_{aa} - \dfrac{b^3}{a^3}f_{bbb}.$

To conclude these mathematical notes, it is convenient to introduce the criterion for determining a point of inflection. Consider any function $\eta = \phi(\xi)$. The function is said to have a point of inflection at $\xi = x$ if the direction of concavity changes at this point.

(viii) *Criterion*: The function $\eta = \phi(\xi)$ has a point of inflection at $\xi = x$ if $\phi_{xx} = 0$. If $\phi_{xxx} < 0$, the function changes from concave from above to concave from below.[1] If $\phi_{xxx} > 0$, the concavity changes in the opposite direction.

5.2.2 The elasticity of substitution

In chapter 4 it was shown that the elasticity of substitution may be written as

$$\sigma = -\frac{f_a f_b (af_a + bf_b)}{ab(f_{aa}f_b^2 - 2f_{ab}f_a f_b + f_{bb}f_a^2)}. \tag{5.2.7}$$

[1] *Definition*: A function is said to be concave from above at a point if the function lies above its tangent in a neighborhood of the point; it is concave from below if it lies beneath its tangent in a neighborhood of the point.

Using the properties listed in subsection 5.2.1 permits a great simplification. By property (i), the numerator may be written

$$f_a f_b(af_a + bf_b) = qf_a f_b. \tag{5.2.8}$$

Next, by property (iv) the denominator may be written

$$ab(f_{aa}f_b^2 - 2f_{ab}f_a f_b + f_{bb}f_a^2) = 2abf_a f_b, \tag{5.2.9}$$

which, by property (vi), becomes

$$2abf_a f_b, = -q^2 f_{ab}. \tag{5.2.10}$$

Substituting equations (5.2.8) and (5.2.10) in the elasticity formula (5.2.7) yields

$$\sigma = \frac{f_a f_b}{qf_{ab}}. \tag{5.2.11}$$

The expression in equation (5.2.11) is a good deal simpler than the one in equation (5.2.7). Nonetheless, it is a partial differential equation whose quadrature causes difficulty. To obtain a more easily integrable form, an alternative expression for σ is desirable. By its assumed homogeneity, the production function (5.2.1) may be written

$$y = g(x) \quad \text{or} \quad z = h(w), \tag{5.2.12}$$

where $\qquad y = \dfrac{q}{b}, \quad x = \dfrac{a}{b}, \quad z = \dfrac{q}{a} \quad \text{and} \quad w = \dfrac{b}{a}.$

Either form shows the average product as a function of the input ratio.

For the moment, consider only the form $y = g(x)$. The marginal product of A is

$$\frac{\partial q}{\partial a} = \frac{\partial(bg(x))}{\partial a} = bg'(x)\frac{dx}{da} = g'(x). \tag{5.2.13}$$

In a similar fashion, the marginal product of B is

$$\frac{\partial q}{\partial b} = \frac{\partial(bg(x))}{\partial b} = g(x) + bg'(x)\frac{dx}{db} = g(x) - xg'(x). \tag{5.2.14}$$

By definition, the elasticity of substitution is

$$\sigma = \frac{dx}{ds}\frac{s}{x}, \tag{5.2.15}$$

where s is the marginal rate of technical substitution (f_b/f_a). First,

$$\frac{ds}{dx} = \frac{d(f_b/f_a)}{dx} = \frac{d\left(\dfrac{g(x) - xg'(x)}{g'(x)}\right)}{dx} = -\frac{g(x)\,g''(x)}{(g'(x))^2}. \tag{5.2.16}$$

Inverting the right-hand side of equation (5.2.16) and multiplying by s/x yields the desired form of the elasticity of substitution:

$$\sigma = -\frac{g'(x)\,(g(x)-xg'(x))}{xg(x)\,g''(x)}. \qquad (5.2.17)$$

By analogy, the elasticity for $z = h(w)$ is

$$\sigma = -\frac{h'(w)\,(h(w)-wh'(w))}{wh(w)\,h''(w)}. \qquad (5.2.18)$$

In equations (5.2.17) and (5.2.18) the elasticity of substitution is written as a nonlinear differential equation; but it is not a *partial* differential equation inasmuch as the input ratio is the only independent variable. If one can specify a value of σ and obtain a quadrature of either (5.2.17) or (5.2.18), the resulting equation will represent the general class of linearly homogeneous production functions possessing the stipulated form of the elasticity of substitution.

One might consider only two broad classes of functions, those with constant and those with variable elasticities of substitution. A fourfold division is more rewarding, however, because the marginal products behave differently when the elasticity is constant at zero or one and constant at any other magnitude.

5.2.3 Classes of linearly homogeneous production functions

Zero elasticity of substitution. Set $\sigma = 0$ in equation (5.2.17). Ignoring the trivial solution, one obtains the following first-order linear differential equation:

$$\frac{dg}{g} - \frac{dx}{x} = 0. \qquad (5.2.19)$$

Letting the constant of integration be $1/\alpha$, the solution is

$$\ln g = \ln x + \ln \frac{1}{\alpha}, \qquad (5.2.20)$$

or
$$g = \frac{1}{\alpha}\, x. \qquad (5.2.21)$$

Substituting for g and x in equation (5.2.21) yields

$$q = \frac{1}{\alpha}\, a. \qquad (5.2.22)$$

A similar integration of equation (5.2.18) yields

$$q = \frac{1}{\beta}\, b, \qquad (5.2.23)$$

where $1/\beta$ is a constant of integration.

97

Two basic forms of zero-elasticity-of-substitution production functions may be obtained from equations (5.2.22) and (5.2.23). Adding the two solutions yields the following form:

$$q = \frac{1}{\alpha} a + \frac{1}{\beta} b. \tag{5.2.24}$$

If one requires that equations (5.2.22) and (5.2.23) both hold or that one be redundant, the special Leontief form of a fixed-proportions production function is obtained:

$$q = \min\left(\frac{1}{\alpha} a, \frac{1}{\beta} b\right). \tag{5.2.25}$$

In equation (5.2.24) the marginal products are positive and constant for all variations in the inputs. The marginal products from equation (5.2.25) are somewhat different. Suppose an initial point of mutual input limitationality, i.e. $q = (1/\alpha) a = (1/\beta) b$. For a decrease in (say) a, its marginal product is $1/\alpha$, a constant. On increase its marginal product is zero. Hence when the elasticity of substitution is zero, the marginal products must either be positive constants or nonnegative and constant at two different levels, with a finite discontinuity at the point of mutual input limitationality.[1]

Unit elasticity of substitution.[2] When the elasticity of substitution is not zero, it is only necessary to use one of the alternative expressions. Equation (5.2.17) is the one selected for integration.

When the elasticity of substitution is set equal to one, equation (5.2.17) becomes, upon rearrangement,

$$g''(x) + \frac{1}{x} g'(x) - \frac{1}{g(x)} g'^2(x) = 0. \tag{5.2.26}$$

Introduce the transformation

$$g(x) = e^{u(x)}, \tag{5.2.27}$$

which reduces equation (5.2.26) to

$$u''(x) + \frac{1}{x} u'(x) = 0. \tag{5.2.28}$$

Finally, let $\quad u'(x) = p(x), \tag{5.2.29}$

thereby obtaining $\quad p'(x) + \frac{1}{x} p(x) = 0. \tag{5.2.30}$

[1] See chapter 2 for a more thorough discussion of the marginal products derived from equation (5.2.25).
[2] The next two derivations are indicated briefly in Ferguson [1965b]. Alternative derivations are given in Arrow, Chenery, Minhas, and Solow [1961], Brown and de Cani [1963], and Brown [1966].

An integrating factor for equation (5.2.30) is $e^{\int (1/x)\,dx}$. Thus the solution is

$$p(x) = \frac{\alpha}{x}, \tag{5.2.31}$$

where α is a constant of integration.

Now substitute the solution (5.2.31) into equation (5.2.29), obtaining

$$du = \frac{\alpha}{x}\,dx, \tag{5.2.32}$$

whose solution is $\qquad u(x) = \alpha \ln x + \ln A, \tag{5.2.33}$

where A is a constant of integration.

Finally, substitute solution (5.2.33) into the transformation (5.2.27), obtaining $\qquad g(x) = e^{\alpha \ln x + \ln A} = Ax^{\alpha}. \tag{5.2.34}$

Using the definitions of g and x transforms equation (5.2.34) into

$$\frac{q}{b} = A\left(\frac{a}{b}\right)^{\alpha}, \tag{5.2.35}$$

or $\qquad q = Aa^{\alpha}b^{1-\alpha}, \tag{5.2.36}$

precisely the Cobb–Douglas function in its linearly homogeneous form. For economic relevance, of course, one must stipulate that $A > 0$ and that $0 < \alpha < 1$.

An essential feature of the integration process should be noted. By setting $\sigma \equiv 1$ in equation (5.2.17), one obtains the basic differential equation of this model, equation (5.2.26). As one may observe, this equation *does not* contain a parameter. Hence the solution equation contains only *two* parameters, the constants of integration associated with the two quadratures. These parameters are A and α, which are called the *efficiency* parameter and the *input intensity* parameter respectively. A is so named because, for every input combination, the greater is A, the greater is the level of output. The reason for the designation given α is explained below.

Characteristics of the Cobb–Douglas function. From equation (5.2.36), the marginal products are

$$\frac{\partial q}{\partial a} = \alpha A \left(\frac{a}{b}\right)^{\alpha - 1} \quad \text{and} \quad \frac{\partial q}{\partial b} = (1 - \alpha) A \left(\frac{a}{b}\right)^{\alpha}. \tag{5.2.37}$$

Since every term in each expression is strictly positive for a positive level of inputs, the marginal products themselves are always positive. Further, they decrease monotonically throughout the range of input values from 0 to ∞. This fact may easily be seen from

$$\left.\begin{aligned}
\frac{\partial^2 q}{\partial a^2} &= \alpha(\alpha - 1) Aa^{\alpha - 2}b^{1-\alpha}, \\[2mm]
\frac{\partial^2 q}{\partial b^2} &= -\alpha(1 - \alpha) Aa^{\alpha}b^{-\alpha - 1}.
\end{aligned}\right\} \tag{5.2.38}$$

From equations (5.2.37), the marginal rate of technical substitution of a for b (denoted s) is[1]

$$s = \frac{\alpha}{1-\alpha} \left(\frac{b}{a}\right)^{1}.$$ (5.2.39)

For any given level of s, the greater is α, the smaller the $b:a$ input ratio. Thus the greater α, the more a-intensive the production process at any production point. This accounts for designating α the 'input intensity' parameter.

The derivative of equation (5.2.39) with respect to the input ratio $(b/a = w)$ is

$$\frac{ds}{dw} = \frac{\alpha}{1-\alpha}.$$ (5.2.40)

Inverting and multiplying by the $s:w$ ratio confirms that the elasticity of substitution is indeed unity:

$$\frac{dw}{ds}\frac{s}{w} = \sigma = \frac{1-\alpha}{\alpha} \cdot \frac{\alpha}{1-\alpha} \left(\frac{b}{a}\right) \cdot \left(\frac{a}{b}\right) \equiv 1.$$ (5.2.41)

A final property of the Cobb–Douglas function should be noted because it represents, in fact, a mildly undesirable characteristic.[2] To introduce this point, suppose the marginal products are always nonnegative, as they are in the Cobb–Douglas case.[3] Then, as the use of one input is expanded indefinitely while the use of the other is held constant, the marginal product of the expanded input should approach zero asymptotically, i.e.

$$\lim_{a\to\infty} \frac{\partial q}{\partial a} = 0 \quad \text{and} \quad \lim_{b\to\infty} \frac{\partial q}{\partial b} = 0.$$ (5.2.42)

If expressions (5.2.42) hold, it must follow that

$$\lim_{a\to\infty} q = m_1 \quad \text{and} \quad \lim_{b\to\infty} q = m_2,$$ (5.2.43)

where m_1 and m_2 are positive, *finite* constants.

Applying this to the Cobb–Douglas function in equation (5.2.36), one finds

$$\lim_{a\to\infty} \frac{\partial q}{\partial a} = \lim_{a\to\infty} \alpha A \left(\frac{a}{b}\right)^{\alpha-1} = 0$$ (5.2.44)

when α satisfies the imposed condition (i.e. $0 < \alpha < 1$). However,

$$\lim_{a\to\infty} q = \lim_{a\to\infty} A a^{\alpha} b^{1-\alpha} = \infty.$$ (5.2.45)

---

[1] For the moment, ignore the exponent '1' placed on the input ratio.
[2] To the best of my knowledge, the following point is attributable to Brown [1966, pp. 34–5].
[3] Brown [1966, p. 34]. Input designation changed from 'capital and labor' to 'a and b' so as to correspond to the text.

The same type of expressions holds for the marginal product of B and for output as B expands indefinitely. Thus the Cobb–Douglas function would seem to contain an internal contradiction. In fact, it does not, as Brown explains:

> the apparent contradiction...is easily resolved as soon as we note that, in the Cobb–Douglas production function, output will become infinite to a higher order than the marginal product vanishes when a grows indefinitely large while b remains constant. In other words the incremental a services contribute to output so as to permit it to diverge before the marginal product converges to zero as a inputs grow very large.

While the function does not contain an internal contradiction, one should nonetheless ideally like to have the function approach a finite limit as one input is increased without bound. Indeed, to conform to the prescriptions of Knight, the function should attain a maximum and then decline.[1,2]

Constant elasticity of substitution. For many years the Cobb–Douglas function, or one of its variants, was used almost exclusively in statistical studies of production functions and in theoretical analyses of a wide variety of problems. Presumably the mathematical simplicity of the function overcame objections to its crucial limitation, i.e. unit elasticity of substitution. In 1961, however, Arrow, Chenery, Minhas, and Solow popularized a new class of production functions that is mathematically simple, often statistically tractable, and characterized by a constant elasticity of substitution.[3] Since that time, the CES function has been dominant in the literature.

The CES function may be derived in the following way. Let σ be a constant in equation (5.2.17). This ordinary, nonlinear differential equation may then be written

$$g''(x) + \frac{1}{\sigma x} g'(x) - \frac{1}{\sigma g(x)} g'^2(x) = 0. \tag{5.2.46}$$

The dependent variable may be eliminated by introducing the following transformation:

$$g(x) = e^{u(x)}. \tag{5.2.47}$$

---

[1] F. H. Knight [1933, p. 100]. Also, see the Appendix to this chapter.

[2] For alternative forms of the Cobb–Douglas function that do not involve unitary elasticity of substitution see Heady and Dillon [1961], Newman and Read [1961], and Ferguson and Pfouts [1962].

[3] The origin of the CES function is not clear. Certainly it was discovered independently by Arrow, Chenery, Minhas, and Solow [1961], by Brown and de Cani [1963b] and by Kendrick and Sato [1963]. It has subsequently become the object of considerable theoretical research. See, in alphabetical order, Gorman [1965], McFadden [1963], Mukerji [1963], Paroush [1964], Scheper [1965], Uzawa [1962], Whitaker [1964], and Yasui [1965].

Using equation (5.2.47) in equation (5.2.46) yields

$$u''(x) + \frac{1}{\sigma x} u'(x) + \left(\frac{\sigma - 1}{\sigma}\right) u'^2(x) = 0. \tag{5.2.48}$$

To reduce equation (5.2.48) to a first-order, nonlinear differential equation, substitute the transformation

$$u'(x) = p(x) \tag{5.2.49}$$

to obtain

$$\frac{p'(x)}{p^2(x)} + \frac{1}{\sigma x} \frac{1}{p(x)} + \left(\frac{\sigma - 1}{\sigma}\right) = 0. \tag{5.2.50}$$

Finally, the reduction process is completed by setting

$$\frac{1}{p(x)} = w(x), \tag{5.2.51}$$

which transforms equation (5.2.50) into a first-order, linear differential equation:

$$w'(x) - \frac{1}{\sigma x} w(x) = \frac{\sigma - 1}{\sigma}. \tag{5.2.52}$$

An integrating factor for equation (5.2.52) is

$$e^{-1/\sigma \int dx/x} = e^{\ln x^{-1/\sigma}} = x^{-1/\sigma}. \tag{5.2.53}$$

Substituting equation (5.2.53) in equation (5.2.52) and performing the integration, one obtains

$$w = x\left[1 + \left(\frac{1 - \delta}{\delta}\right) x^{(1-\sigma)/\sigma}\right], \tag{5.2.54}$$

where $(1 - \delta)/\delta$ is the constant of integration. When the solution (5.2.54) is substituted in equation (5.2.51) and the resultant into equation (5.2.49), one obtains

$$\int du = \int \frac{dx}{x\left[1 + \left(\frac{1 - \delta}{\delta}\right) x^{(1-\sigma)/\sigma}\right]} + \ln \gamma \delta^{\sigma/(\sigma-1)}, \tag{5.2.55}$$

where $\gamma \delta^{\sigma/(\sigma-1)}$ is the chosen constant of integration. After some manipulation,[1] one obtains

$$u = \ln \left[\left(\frac{1 - \delta}{\delta}\right) + x^{(\sigma-1)/\sigma}\right]^{\sigma/(\sigma-1)} + \ln \gamma \delta^{\sigma/(\sigma-1)}. \tag{5.2.56}$$

---

[1] Direct integration yields

$$u = \frac{\sigma}{1 - \sigma} \ln \left| \frac{x^{(1-\sigma)/\sigma}}{1 + \left(\frac{1 - \sigma}{\sigma}\right) x^{(1-\sigma)/\sigma}} \right| + \gamma \delta^{\sigma/(\sigma-1)}.$$

Multiplying the numerator and denominator of the expression in brackets by $x^{-(1-\sigma)/\sigma}$ leads to the results stated in equation (5.2.56).

Substituting equation (5.2.56) into equation (5.2.47), one obtains

$$g(x) = \gamma \delta^{\sigma/(\sigma-1)}\left[\left(\frac{1-\delta}{\delta}\right)+x^{(\sigma-1)/\sigma}\right]^{\sigma/(\sigma-1)}. \qquad (5.2.57)$$

Since $g(x) = q/b$ and $x = a/b$, equation (5.2.57) may be written

$$q = \gamma[\delta a^{(\sigma-1)/\sigma}+(1-\delta)\,b^{(\sigma-1)/\sigma}]^{\sigma/(\sigma-1)}. \qquad (5.2.58)$$

Finally, let
$$\sigma = \frac{1}{1+\rho}. \qquad (5.2.59)$$

Substituting equation (5.2.59) into equation (5.2.58) yields the CES function in its conventional form:

$$q = \gamma[\delta a^{-\rho}+(1-\delta)\,b^{-\rho}]^{-1/\rho}. \qquad (5.2.60)$$

To be economically meaningful, one must further stipulate that $\gamma > 0$, $0 < \delta < 1$, and $\sigma \geqslant 0$. The last inequality, however, does not place a sign restriction upon ρ; however, it does require that ρ lie in the interval $\infty \geqslant \rho \geqslant -1$.

The CES function contains three parameters, two introduced as constants of integration and one attributable to the assumption that the elasticity of substitution is a constant. The constants are γ, δ, and ρ, which are called the *efficiency*, *input intensity*, and *substitution* parameters respectively. The role of γ in the CES function is identical to the role of A in the Cobb–Douglas function. The reasons for the other designations will become apparent below.[1]

Characteristics of the CES function. The marginal products from the CES function are

$$\frac{\partial q}{\partial a} = \delta\gamma^{-\rho}\left(\frac{q}{a}\right)^{1/\sigma} \quad \text{and} \quad \frac{\partial q}{\partial b} = (1-\delta)\,\gamma^{-\rho}\left(\frac{q}{b}\right)^{1/\sigma}. \qquad (5.2.61)$$

Since each term in both expressions is positive, both marginal products are positive for all nonzero values of the inputs. Furthermore, both marginal product functions decrease monotonically throughout their entire range. This fact follows immediately when property (i) is used along with the second derivatives:

$$\left.\begin{aligned}
\frac{\partial^2 q}{\partial a^2} &= \frac{1}{\sigma}\,\delta\gamma^{-\rho}\left(\frac{q}{a}\right)^{(1-\sigma)/\sigma}\left(\frac{a\frac{\partial q}{\partial a}-q}{a^2}\right), \\[2ex]
\frac{\partial^2 q}{\partial b^2} &= \frac{1}{\sigma}\,(1-\delta)\,\gamma^{-\rho}\left(\frac{q}{b}\right)^{(1-\sigma)/\sigma}\left(\frac{b\frac{\partial q}{\partial b}-q}{b^2}\right).
\end{aligned}\right\} \qquad (5.2.62)$$

[1] Both the Cobb–Douglas and the CES functions may be derived so as to contain an additional parameter, called the *returns-to-scale* parameter. In this case, the production function is assumed to be homogeneous, but not necessarily of degree one. For the derivation, see Ferguson [1965b] or Brown [1966].

From equations (5.2.61), the marginal rate of technical substitution of B for A is

$$s = \left(\frac{\delta}{1-\delta}\right)\left(\frac{b}{a}\right)^{1/\sigma}. \tag{5.2.63}$$

For any given values of the elasticity of substitution and the marginal rate of technical substitution, the greater δ, the smaller the $b:a$ input ratio. Hence the greater δ, the more a-intensive the production process at any production point. Thus δ is the 'input intensity' parameter; it is closely related to, but not identically the same as, α in the Cobb–Douglas function.

The derivative of equation (5.2.63) with respect to the $b:a$ input ratio $(= w)$ is

$$\frac{ds}{dw} = \frac{1}{\sigma}\left(\frac{\delta}{1-\delta}\right)\left(\frac{b}{a}\right)^{(1/\sigma)-1}. \tag{5.2.64}$$

Inverting and multiplying by the $s:w$ ratio yields

$$\frac{dw}{ds}\frac{s}{w} = \sigma\left(\frac{1-\delta}{\delta}\right)\left(\frac{b}{a}\right)^{(\sigma-1)/\sigma} \cdot \left(\frac{\delta}{1-\delta}\right)\left(\frac{b}{a}\right)^{1/\sigma} \cdot \left(\frac{b}{a}\right)^{-1} = \sigma = \frac{1}{1+\rho}. \tag{5.2.65}$$

Equation (5.2.65) confirms that the elasticity of substitution is indeed a constant and equal to $1/(1+\rho)$. At this point it is interesting to compare equations (5.2.39) and (5.2.63). In the Cobb–Douglas and CES cases, the elasticity of substitution is merely the reciprocal of the exponent of the input ratio in the expression for the marginal rate of technical substitution.

Two additional features of the CES function merit attention. The first of these is the asymptotic behavior of the function as one input increases without bound, the other input remaining fixed. As shown below, the results depend entirely upon the magnitude of the elasticity of substitution. Let $a \to \infty$ while b is constant and consider the form of the CES function shown in equation (5.2.58):

$$[\lim_{a\to\infty} q = \lim_{a\to\infty} \gamma[\delta a^{(\sigma-1)/\sigma} + (1-\delta)\, b^{(\sigma-1)/\sigma}]^{\sigma/(\sigma-1)} \to ?. \tag{5.2.66}$$

The limit value clearly depends upon the value of σ. Suppose $\sigma > 1$. Then

$$\lim_{\substack{a\to\infty \\ \sigma>1}} q = \lim_{\substack{a\to\infty \\ \sigma>1}} \gamma[\delta a^{(\sigma-1)/\sigma} + (1-\delta)\, b^{(\sigma-1)/\sigma}]^{\sigma/(\sigma-1)} \to \infty. \tag{5.2.67}$$

In this case, the product increases without bound as a increases without bound, b held fixed. No limiting asymptote is attained. On the other hand, if $\sigma < 1$, a finite limit exists. When $\sigma < 1$, the exponents in equation (5.2.66) are negative; hence one may write

$$\lim_{\substack{a\to\infty \\ \sigma<1}} q = \lim_{\substack{a\to\infty \\ \sigma<1}} \frac{\gamma}{\left[\dfrac{\delta}{a^{(1-\sigma)/\sigma}} + \dfrac{1-\delta}{b^{(1-\sigma)/\sigma}}\right]^{\sigma/(1-\sigma)}} = \gamma(1-\delta)^{\sigma/(1-\sigma)}\, b. \tag{5.2.68}$$

5.2 PROPERTIES OF HOMOGENEOUS FUNCTIONS

The behavior of the marginal products is entirely consistent with the behavior of total output. Consider the limiting value of the marginal product of a when $\sigma > 1$:

$$\lim_{\substack{a \to \infty \\ \sigma > 1}} \frac{\partial q}{\partial a} = \lim_{\substack{a \to \infty \\ \sigma > 1}} \frac{\gamma \delta [\delta a^{(\sigma-1)/\sigma} + (1-\delta) b^{(\sigma-1)/\sigma}]^{1/(\sigma-1)}}{a^{1/\sigma}}$$

$$= \gamma \delta \left[\delta + (1-\delta) \left(\frac{b}{a} \right)^{(\sigma-1)/\sigma} \right]^{1/(\sigma-1)}$$

$$= \gamma \delta^{\sigma/(\sigma-1)} > 0. \tag{5.2.69}$$

The marginal product of A does not approach zero as a increases without bound, b held constant. Instead, when the elasticity of substitution exceeds unity, the marginal product asymptotically approaches a positive finite limit. Hence the total product function itself increases without bound, as shown in equation (5.2.67).

When the elasticity of substitution is less than unity, the marginal product of A approaches zero as the usage of A increases without bound. This is immediately apparent from the following limit analysis:

$$\lim_{\substack{a \to \infty \\ \sigma < 1}} \frac{\partial q}{\partial a} = \lim_{\substack{a \to \infty \\ \sigma < 1}} \gamma \delta \left[\delta + (1-\delta) \left(\frac{b}{a} \right)^{(\sigma-1)/\sigma} \right]^{1/(\sigma-1)}$$

$$= \frac{\gamma \delta}{\left[\delta + (1-\delta) \left(\frac{a}{b} \right)^{(\sigma-1)/\sigma} \right]^{1/(1-\sigma)}} = 0, \tag{5.2.70}$$

since

$$\left(\frac{a}{b} \right)^{(1-\sigma)/\sigma} \to \infty \quad \text{as} \quad a \to \infty.$$

The technical rationale of these results is clearly explained by Brown:[1]

when $\sigma > 1$, the factors of production resemble each other from a technological point of view, so that if one increases indefinitely, the other being held constant, the technology permits the expanding factor to be substituted relatively easily for the constant factor. Hence, both factors seem to be increasing indefinitely. If $\sigma < 1$, the technology views the factors as being relatively dissimilar so that it is difficult to substitute the expanding for the constant factor. Even though one factor increases indefinitely, the growth of the product is restrained by the technologically scarce constant factor.

The second additional characteristic of the CES function is implicit in the derivation of the Leontief and Cobb–Douglas functions above. In particular, when $\sigma = 1$, the CES function reduces to the Cobb–

---

[1] Brown [1966, p. 50]. The reader who consults this reference should be warned that there is a typographical error in the first equation in the footnote on p. 50. Using Brown's notation, the limit should be $\gamma^{1/\sigma}(1-\kappa)^{\sigma/(\sigma-1)}$.

Douglas function; and when $\sigma = 0$, it reduces to the Leontief function.[1]
To show this, the limit of equation (5.2.60) is taken for $\rho \to 0$ ($\sigma = 1$) and
$\rho \to \infty$ ($\sigma = 0$). First, consider the limit as $\rho \to 0$:

$$\lim_{\rho \to 0} q = \lim_{\rho \to 0} \gamma[\delta a^{-\rho} + (1-\delta) b^{-\rho}]^{-1/\rho} \tag{5.2.71}$$

$$= \frac{\gamma}{\left[\dfrac{\delta}{a^\rho} + \dfrac{1-\delta}{b^\rho}\right]^{1/\rho}}$$

$$= \frac{\gamma b}{\left[\delta\left(\dfrac{b}{a}\right)^\rho + (1-\delta)\right]^{1/\rho}}.$$

The numerator offers no trouble; but as $\rho \to 0$, the denominator takes the
indeterminate form 1^∞. Denote the denominator in equation (5.2.71) by K.
Thus

$$\ln K = \frac{\ln\left[\delta\left(\dfrac{b}{a}\right)^\rho + (1-\delta)\right]}{\rho}, \tag{5.2.72}$$

which is an indeterminate form of the class $0 \div 0$ as $\rho \to 0$. Applying
L'Hospital's Rule,

$$\lim_{\rho \to 0} \ln K = \lim_{\rho \to 0} \frac{\delta e^{\rho \ln (b/a)} \ln\left(\dfrac{b}{a}\right)}{\left[\delta\left(\dfrac{b}{a}\right)^\rho + (1-\delta)\right]} = \delta \ln\left(\frac{b}{a}\right). \tag{5.2.73}$$

Hence
$$\lim_{\rho \to 0} K = \left(\frac{b}{a}\right)^\delta, \tag{5.2.74}$$

and equation (5.2.71) may be written

$$\lim_{\rho \to 0} q = \frac{\gamma b}{\left(\dfrac{b}{a}\right)^\delta} = \gamma b b^{-\delta} a^\delta = \gamma a^\delta b^{1-\delta}. \tag{5.2.75}$$

The rightmost expression in equation (5.2.75) is precisely the Cobb–
Douglas function, q.e.d.
    Second, consider the limit as $\rho \to \infty$:

$$\lim_{\rho \to \infty} q = \lim_{\rho \to \infty} \gamma[\delta a^{-\rho} + (1-\delta) b^{-\rho}]^{-1/\rho}. \tag{5.2.76}$$

[1] Arrow, Chenery, Minhas, and Solow [1961] stated that these reductions 'could be
shown'. Since the limit analysis is not immediately obvious, it seems worthwhile to
state it explicitly here.

The limit must be evaluated for two cases. Suppose $a < b$. Equation (5.2.76) may be rearranged to read

$$\lim_{\rho \to \infty} q = \lim_{\rho \to \infty} \frac{\gamma}{\left[\dfrac{\delta}{a^\rho} + \dfrac{1-\delta}{b^\rho}\right]^{1/\rho}}$$

$$= \lim_{\rho \to \infty} \frac{\gamma a}{\left[\delta + (1-\delta)\left(\dfrac{a}{b}\right)^\rho\right]^{1/\rho}} = \gamma a \qquad (5.2.77)$$

since $(a/b)^\rho \to 0$ when $a < b$ and $\rho \to \infty$ and $\delta^{1/\rho} = 1$. If $b < a$, a similar reduction yields

$$\lim_{\rho \to \infty} q = \gamma b. \qquad (5.2.78)$$

Consequently, since equation (5.2.77) must hold when $a < b$ and equation (5.2.78) must hold when $b < a$, one obtains

$$\lim_{\rho \to \infty} q = \gamma \min(a, b). \qquad (5.2.79)$$

The right-hand side of equation (5.2.79) is a Leontief function, albeit a very special form. The general form of the Leontief function may be obtained by writing the CES function as

$$q = \gamma[\delta^\rho a^{-\rho} + (1-\delta)^\rho\, b^{-\rho}]^{-1/\rho}. \qquad (5.2.80)$$

The limit analysis then yields

$$\lim_{\rho \to \infty} q = \gamma \min\left[\frac{a}{\delta}, \frac{b}{1-\delta}\right]. \qquad (5.2.81)$$

Finally, letting

$$\frac{\gamma}{\delta} = \frac{1}{\alpha} \quad \text{and} \quad \frac{\gamma}{1-\delta} = \frac{1}{\beta},$$

one obtains

$$\lim_{\rho \to \infty} q = \min\left[\frac{a}{\alpha}, \frac{b}{\beta}\right], \qquad (5.2.82)$$

the form of the Leontief function used throughout chapters 2 and 3.

Partial elasticity of substitution. To this point the Leontief, Cobb–Douglas, and CES functions have been treated as though they could only be functions of two variable inputs. In the first two cases this procedure is justifiable because the general form of the Leontief function was discussed in chapters 2 and 3 and the general form of the Cobb–Douglas function is well known. This is not so in the CES case, however; and, in particular, one must ask precisely what is meant by the elasticity of substitution when there are more than two inputs. To get at an answer, it is necessary to introduce the concept of *partial elasticity of substitution*, which is presumably attributable to Allen.[1]

[1] Allen [1938, pp. 503–5].

Let the production function in n variable inputs be written

$$q = f(a_1, a_2, ..., a_n), \tag{5.2.83}$$

where f is homogeneous of degree one and f_i and f_{ij} denote the first and second partial derivatives. Define[1]

$$\kappa_i = \frac{a_i f_i}{\sum\limits_{j}^{n} a_j f_j}. \tag{5.2.84}$$

Hence, by Euler's theorem, $\quad \sum\limits_{i=1}^{n} \kappa_i = 1. \tag{5.2.85}$

Next, let the bordered Hessian determinant of the production function be

$$F = \begin{vmatrix} 0 & f_1 & f_2 & \cdots & f_n \\ f_1 & f_{11} & f_{12} & \cdots & f_{1n} \\ f_2 & f_{12} & f_{22} & \cdots & f_{2n} \\ \vdots & \vdots & \vdots & & \vdots \\ f_n & f_{1n} & f_{2n} & \cdots & f_{nn} \end{vmatrix}, \tag{5.2.86}$$

and let F_{ij} denote the cofactor of f_{ij} in F. Then the partial elasticity of substitution between A_i and A_j, denoted σ_{ij}, is defined as

$$\sigma_{ij} = \frac{a_1 f_1 + a_2 f_2 + ... + a_n f_n}{a_i a_j} \frac{F_{ij}}{F} = \frac{q}{a_i a_j} \frac{F_{ij}}{F}. \tag{5.2.87}$$

Since F is symmetric, it follows immediately that the partial elasticities are also symmetric, i.e. $\sigma_{ij} = \sigma_{ji}$ for $i \neq j$.

The meaning of the partial elasticity of substitution is not as clear as the meaning of the elasticity of substitution when there are only two inputs. Nonetheless, some insight may be obtained. Suppose there are only two inputs; the production function thus becomes

$$q = f(a_1, a_2). \tag{5.2.88}$$

According to definition (5.2.87), the *partial* elasticity of substitution is

$$\sigma_{12} = \frac{q}{a_1 a_2} \cdot \frac{-f_1 f_2}{f_1^2 f_{22} - 2 f_1 f_2 f_{12} + f_2^2 f_{11}}. \tag{5.2.89}$$

Substituting property (iv) and then property (vi) in the denominator reduces the expression to

$$\sigma_{12} = \frac{f_1 f_2}{q f_{12}} = \sigma \tag{5.2.90}$$

by equation (5.2.11). Thus with two inputs, the partial elasticity of substitution is exactly the same as the elasticity of substitution defined above.

---

[1] As shown below, in equilibrium the marginal products are proportional to input prices. In this case, κ_i is the proportion of the total cost spent on input A_i.

5.2 PROPERTIES OF HOMOGENEOUS FUNCTIONS

To establish another property of the partial elasticity of substitution, expand F by alien cofactors, using (say) row one:

$$f_1 F_{i1} + f_2 F_{i2} + \dots + f_n F_{in} = 0 \quad (i = 1, 2, \dots, n). \tag{5.2.91}$$

From definition (5.2.84), we have

$$\kappa_1 \sigma_{i1} = \frac{f_1 F_{i1}}{a_i F}, \quad \kappa_2 \sigma_{i2} = \frac{f_2 F_{i2}}{a_i F}, \quad \dots, \quad \kappa_n \sigma_{in} = \frac{f_n F_{in}}{a_i F}. \tag{5.2.92}$$

Hence from equation (5.2.91) it follows that

$$\sum_{j=1}^{n} \kappa_j \sigma_{ij} = 0 \quad (i = 1, 2, \dots, n), \tag{5.2.93}$$

or

$$\sum_{j \neq 1}^{n} \kappa_j \sigma_{ij} = -\kappa_i \sigma_{ii} \quad (i = 1, 2, \dots, n). \tag{5.2.94}$$

It will subsequently be shown that F must be associated with a negative definite quadratic form; hence

$$\frac{F_{ii}}{F} < 0 \quad (i = 1, 2, \dots, n). \tag{5.2.95}$$

By equation (5.2.87) and inequality (5.2.95),

$$\sigma_{ii} < 0 \quad (i = 1, 2, \dots, n). \tag{5.2.96}$$

Substituting inequality (5.2.96) in equation (5.2.94), one obtains

$$\sum_{j \neq 1}^{n} \kappa_j \sigma_{ij} > 0. \tag{5.2.97}$$

Recalling that $\kappa_j > 0$ for all j, inequality (5.2.97) implies that some of the partial elasticities may be negative. But some must be positive; and when the weights are considered, the positive elasticities must more than counterbalance the negative ones.

In chapter 4 two inputs, A_i and A_j, were said to be competitive or complementary according as $f_{ij} \lessgtr 0$. While this definition has considerable intuitive appeal, it has one defect. Specifically, output changes as one of the inputs is changed. Thus the output effect may dominate the substitution effect, thereby obscuring the true relation between the inputs. That is, this definition includes an output effect, just as the older definition of complementarity in consumption includes the income effect. This defect may be remedied by defining input complementarity in terms of the partial elasticity of substitution, thereby restricting the definition to substitution along an isoquant. Thus A_i and A_j are competitive or complementary according as $\sigma_{ij} \gtrless 0$. By inequality (5.2.97), any one input must, on

109

balance, be competitive with all other inputs. In other words, the competitive relation must dominate.[1]

Examples of constant partial elasticity of substitution production functions. Uzawa was presumably the first to develop production functions with constant partial elasticities of substitution;[2] however, his work was soon supplemented by others.[3] For our purposes, we only consider the functions proposed by Uzawa.

The simpler of his functions is

$$q = (\alpha_1 a_1^{-\beta} + \alpha_2 a_2^{-\beta} + \ldots + \alpha_n a_n^{-\beta})^{-1/\beta}. \qquad (5.2.98)$$

This function is homogeneous of degree one, yields diminishing returns to all inputs, and exhibits constantly declining marginal rates of technical substitution. Further, each partial elasticity of substitution is

$$\sigma_{ij} = \frac{1}{1+\beta} \qquad (5.2.99)$$

for all $i \neq j$. Consequently, with the function (5.2.98), all pairs of partial elasticities have the same constant value.

The second function developed by Uzawa is, in simplified and reduced form,

$$q = (\alpha_1 a_1^{-\beta_{12}} + \alpha_2 a_2^{-\beta_{12}})^{-\rho_1/\beta_{12}} (\alpha_3 a_3^{-\beta_{34}} + \alpha_4 a_4^{-\beta_{34}})^{-\rho_2/\beta_{34}}, \qquad (5.2.100)$$

where the α_i, β_{ij}, and ρ_i are constants and $\rho_1 + \rho_2 = 1$. The partial elasticities of substitution are

$$\sigma_{12} = \frac{1}{1+\beta_{12}}, \quad \sigma_{34} = \frac{1}{1+\beta_{34}}, \quad \sigma_{13} = \sigma_{14} = \sigma_{23} = \sigma_{24} = 1.$$
$$(5.2.101)$$

[1] For this definition, see Allen [1938, p. 509]. Notice that the change in definition causes a marked change in classification, but this is just what one would expect. Indeed, the difference in this classification is much like the difference between classifying commodities according to 'price cross-elasticity' and according to the substitution effect only.

   According to the definition used in chapter 4, most inputs are complementary, whereas the competitive relation must dominate under the present definition. When the cross-acceleration coefficient is used as the basis of classification, output is allowed to vary. Thus most inputs are complementary in the production of a variable output. When the partial elasticity of substitution is used as the basis of classification, output is held fixed (i.e. the elasticity is defined only for movements along an isoquant). Thus most inputs are competitive, or substitutes, in the production of a constant output.

   In an entirely different context, Hicks touches upon this difference [1939, footnote on pp. 95–6].

[2] Uzawa [1962].

[3] McFadden [1963] extended Uzawa's work by introducing two new definitions of the partial elasticity of substitution. Scheper [1965] contributed three additional types of multi-input production functions in which the conventional partial elasticities of substitution are constant. Mukerji [1963] and Gorman [1965] analyzed cases in which the partial elasticities have constant ratios.

Equation (5.2.100) is again a generalization of the basic CES function. It is homogeneous of degree one, has monotonically diminishing marginal returns to all inputs, and constantly diminishing marginal rates of technical substitution. The function may be written in a more general form, but equation (5.2.100) captures the essential feature of the Uzawa function. The entire set of inputs may be divided into subsets; within each subset, there is a common partial elasticity of substitution that is not necessarily the same for all subsets. The weakness of this function is that the partial elasticity between inputs in different subsets is always unity. Nonetheless, the Uzawa function is as general as any constant elasticity function presently existing.

Variable elasticity of substitution. A variable elasticity of substitution production function is obtained by setting $\sigma = m(x)$ or $\sigma = n(w)$ and solving either equation (5.2.17) or (5.2.18).[1] The resulting production function depends upon the particular choice of (say) $m(x)$. There can be as many separate forms as there are choices of $m(x)$ that lead to integrable equations. Furthermore, the general integral with $m(x)$ unspecified is meaningless. Hence one can only show that the elasticity of substitution is variable if, but not only if, at least one marginal product becomes negative over some range of the input ratio.

Consider equation (5.2.17), recalling that $g' = f_a$, $(g - xg') = f_b$ and $g'' = bf_{aa}$. The elasticity of substitution may thus be written

$$\sigma = -\frac{f_a f_b}{af f_{aa}}. \qquad (5.2.102)$$

Since a and f are positive, the sign of σ depends upon the signs of $f_a, f_b,$ and f_{aa}. Over the 'relevant range' of production, f_a and f_b are positive and f_{aa} is negative; hence $\sigma > 0$. Now suppose f_a is negative. As shown in section 5.3, when $f_a < 0$, f_b is necessarily positive and there is a range of input ratios over which f_{aa} is negative when f_a is. Thus over a certain range, both numerator and denominator are negative; together with the prefixed minus sign, this implies that $\sigma < 0$. Consequently, since the sign of σ changes with the input ratio, σ itself must be a variable.

5.3 Production functions and the isoquant map: the general case

The discussion in section 5.2 covers the characteristics that are unique to the various constant elasticity production functions. From henceforth the discussion concerns the general form of linearly homogeneous production functions, i.e. those functions in which both marginal products have a negative range of values. As shown below, this also means that there is a range of input ratios over which each marginal product rises.

[1] If the elasticity of substitution is not to be constant, it must be a function of the input ratio so long as the production function is homogeneous of degree one.

5.3.1 Marginal and average products[1]

By definition the marginal product of an input is the first partial derivative of the production function with respect to the input in question. Hence it follows from property (ii) that the marginal product functions are homogeneous of degree zero. In other words, the marginal products are functions of the input ratios only. Symbolically,

$$f_a = f_a\left(\frac{a}{b}\right), \quad f_b = f_b\left(\frac{a}{b}\right). \tag{5.3.1}$$

Consequently, the magnitudes of the marginal products depend only upon the ratio in which the inputs are combined; and, in particular, the scale of input usage does not affect the marginal products. Thus

$$f_a\left(\frac{a}{b}\right) = f_a\left(\frac{\lambda a}{\lambda b}\right), \quad f_b\left(\frac{a}{b}\right) = f_b\left(\frac{\lambda a}{\lambda b}\right) \tag{5.3.2}$$

for $\lambda > 0$.

Next, by definition, the average product of an input is the output–input ratio. Thus the average products are

$$AP_a = \frac{q}{a}, \quad AP_b = \frac{q}{b}. \tag{5.3.3}$$

Using property (i), the average products may be written

$$AP_a = \frac{af_a + bf_b}{a}, \quad AP_b = \frac{af_a + bf_b}{b}. \tag{5.3.4}$$

Since the marginal product functions are homogeneous of degree zero, the average product functions are homogeneous of degree zero as well. The magnitudes of the average products depend only upon the input ratio; and, in particular, the magnitudes are not affected by the scale of input usage.

The above result may be interpreted in terms of a cross-section total product curve. Figure 28 contains three of the infinitely many cross-section total product curves in the Q–A plane. First, recall that the slope of any ray from the origin, such as OR or OS, gives the average product. Second, average product is a maximum when the ray from the origin is tangent to the total product curve. Now, since the maximum value of the average product depends only upon the input ratio, the maximum value is the same irrespective of output. Consequently, the ray OR, which is tangent to $f(a|b = b_1)$ at C, must be tangent to each of the total product curves. For a similar reason, the maxima of the various total product curves must

---

[1] A recent interesting article concerning the marginal products from linearly homogeneous functions is Gerakis [1962].

lie on a common ray from the origin, *OS* in figure 28. In the general case, these two requirements impose conditions that must be satisfied by a family of cross-section total product curves.

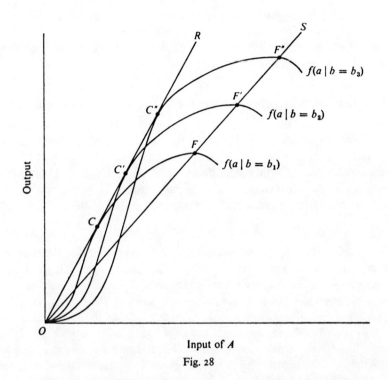

Input of *A*

Fig. 28

5.3.2 Isoclines

An isocline has been defined as the locus of points along which the marginal rate of technical substitution is constant. The marginal rate of technical substitution is the ratio of marginal products. Since each marginal product is homogeneous of degree zero, their ratio is also homogeneous of degree zero. The marginal rate of technical substitution is, accordingly, a function of the input ratio; and, in particular, for any given input ratio, the marginal rate of technical substitution is the same irrespective of the scale of input usage.

In the *A–B* plane, a ray from the origin is a locus along which the input ratio is constant. Since the marginal rate of technical substitution is constant when the input ratio is constant, a ray from the origin is also a locus along which the marginal rate of technical substitution is constant. Hence

113

by definition, an isocline is merely a ray from the origin when the production function is homogeneous of degree one.

The fact that the isoclines are straight lines leads to another important and simplifying feature of linearly homogeneous production functions. Each isoquant in the isoquant map is simply a radial projection of (say) the unit isoquant. Hence the unit isoquant may be used fully to describe the entire isoquant map. This is a useful property in all cases, but it is more particularly so when technological progress is analyzed.

5.3.3 Output elasticities and the economic region of production

In chapter 4, the concepts of output elasticity and function coefficient were introduced and explained. Two features of these concepts should now be recalled. First, the function coefficient (ϵ) is equal to the sum of the output elasticities (ϵ_a and ϵ_b). Second, for homogeneous functions, the function coefficient is precisely equal to the degree of homogeneity. Hence when the production function is homogeneous of degree one,

$$\epsilon = \epsilon_a + \epsilon_b = 1. \tag{5.3.5}$$

Next, recall that the output elasticity of a specified input is the ratio of the marginal product to the average product. Since both marginal and average product functions are homogeneous of degree zero, their ratio is also homogeneous of degree zero. Hence the value of the output elasticity depends only upon the input ratio. In other words, in the A–B plane, the output elasticity of both inputs is constant along a ray from the origin. This is illustrated by the rays OC and OD in figure 29. The ray OC, as constructed, is the locus of input ratios for which the marginal and average products of A are equal. Hence $\epsilon_a = 1$; and by equation (5.3.5), $\epsilon_b = 0$. Similarly, OD is the locus for which $\epsilon_a = 0$ and $\epsilon_b = 1$.

Other rays may be added to figure 29 to display many characteristics of linearly homogeneous functions. First, consider f_a, the marginal product of A. Since f_a is homogeneous of degree zero, it is constant along any ray from the origin. In particular, there is one ray, labelled OE in figure 29, along which f_a is maximum. But a necessary condition for f_a to be a maximum is that $f_{aa} = 0$. By property (v), $f_{bb} = f_{ab} = 0$ when $f_{aa} = 0$. Hence OE is the locus along which all second partials are zero. Similarly, OF is also the locus along which all second partials are zero, this ray being associated with the maximum marginal product of B.

Using these four rays, many features of linearly homogeneous functions may be illustrated. First, start with the ray OC, along which the marginal and average products of A are equal ($\epsilon_a = 1$). To the left of OC, at higher $b:a$ ratios, the marginal product of A exceeds its average product. Hence

114

$\epsilon_a > 1$ and, by equation (5.3.5), $\epsilon_r < 0$. Thus in the cone COB, $\epsilon_a > 1$ and $\epsilon_b < 0$. By analogous reasoning, $\epsilon_a < 0$ and $\epsilon_b > 1$ in the cone DOA.

Next consider the ray OE, along which the marginal product of A is a maximum. To be a maximum, the marginal product of A must be increasing for higher $b:a$ ratios and be decreasing for smaller $b:a$ ratios. Hence $f_{aa} > 0$ to the left of OE and $f_{aa} < 0$ to the right of OE. By properties (iii) and (iv), $f_{bb} > 0$ and $f_{ab} < 0$ to the left of OE. Thus in the cone EOB,

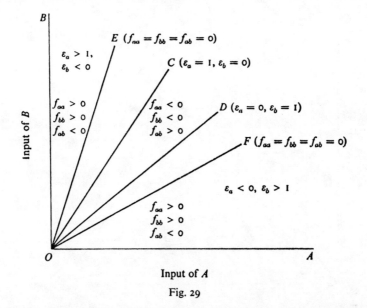

Fig. 29

$f_{aa} > 0$, $f_{bb} > 0$, and $f_{ab} < 0$. As shown in subsection 5, a prescribed concavity condition is not satisfied in this case. That is, the isoquants are concave from below in this region. By a similar argument, it can be shown that $f_{aa} > 0$, $f_{bb} > 0$, and $f_{ab} < 0$ in the cone FOA. Hence the concavity condition is not satisfied in this region.

The concavity condition is satisfied within the cone EOF, where $f_{aa} < 0$, $f_{bb} < 0$, and $f_{ab} > 0$. However, EOF does not represent the economic region of production. Let us use a one-input approach. In the cone EOC the average product of A is rising; it only attains its maximum on the ray OC, where average and marginal products are equal. Similarly, in the cone DOF, the marginal product of A is negative inasmuch as $\epsilon_a < 0$ and the average product of A is positive. Hence the economic region of production is limited to the cone COD, even though the important concavity condition is satisfied within the larger cone EOF. To elaborate, within the cones EOC and DOF the marginal products of B and A respectively are negative.

Hence the concavity condition is met, but the isoquants are positively sloped within these two cones. Thus they are uneconomic regions from a technical standpoint.

5.3.4 Cross-section product curves

For the remainder of this section our attention is directed to a production function of the form

$$q = f(a,b), \tag{5.3.6}$$

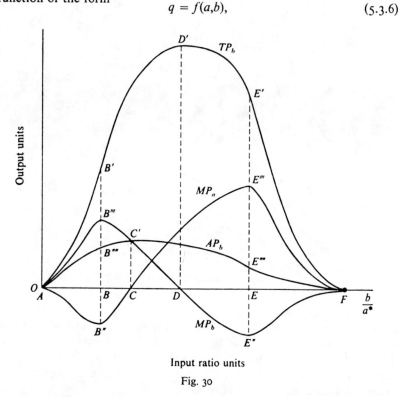

Input ratio units

Fig. 30

where q is physical output and a and b are the physical flows of two variable inputs. The production function is assumed to be homogeneous of degree one and to possess continuous partial derivatives at least to the third order. It is also assumed that

$$f(a, 0) = f(0, b) = f(0, 0) = 0. \tag{5.3.7}$$

The full range of the product curve is shown in figure 30. The graph represents a cross-section of the production surface in the Q–B plane. $TP_b = f(a^*, b)$ is the total product associated with a^* units of A and variable usage of B. $MP_b = f_b$ is the corresponding marginal product

116

curve for B, while $MP_a = f_a$ is the marginal product of A for the various input ratios. It should be noted that the $a^*:b$ ratio increases with movements toward, not away from, the origin. The MP_a curve should properly be viewed as moving from right to left, although in the subsequent discussion its segments are analyzed as though it moved from left to right. Finally, $AP_b = q/b$ is the average product of B.

Many properties of and relations among the curves are very familiar. Almost all of these, however, are either stated or proved for the sake of thoroughness. The basic assumption underlying the analysis is that the marginal product of one input first increases, reaches a unique maximum, and at some point becomes negative. The results of the greatest interest pertain to the shape of MP_b between points D and F and to the shape of MP_a between A and C.

By equation (5.3.7) total product is zero when $b = 0$; hence TP_b begins at the origin. Next, use property (i) to obtain the following expressions for the marginal products:

$$f_b = \frac{q - af_a}{b}, \quad f_a = \frac{q - bf_b}{a}. \tag{5.3.8}$$

Applying L'Hospital's Rule to the first expression shows that MP_b is zero at the origin. Using the result in the second expression, one finds that MP_a is also zero at the origin. Finally, the average product of B is

$$\frac{q}{b} = \frac{a}{b}f_a + f_b. \tag{5.3.9}$$

Substituting the above results in equation (5.3.9) shows that AP_b is zero at the origin. Hence all curves emanate from the origin.

Moving away from the origin, $f_b > 0$ and $f_{bb} > 0$ by assumption. By property (vii), MP_b can be either concave from above or concave from below over a small range of input values. Figure 30 has been constructed under the assumption that MP_b at first increases at an increasing rate, i.e. $f_{bbb} > 0$ in some neighborhood of the origin. Substituting property (iii) in property (vii) and recalling that $f_{bb} > 0$, one finds that $f_{aaa} < 0$, i.e. MP_a must be concave from below over some neighborhood if MP_b is concave from above.

Since MP_b is continuous by assumption, it must pass through a point of inflection before attaining its maximum at B''' because a proper maximum at that point requires $f_{bb} = 0$ and $f_{bbb} < 0$. Since the sign of f_{bbb} changes, and since the third partial derivatives are continuous by assumption, it must equal zero at some point. By criterion (viii) a point of inflection exists at this point. There will also be a point of inflection on MP_a; by property (vii), the points of inflection on the two marginal product curves do not occur at the same input ratio.

117

As stated above, when MP_b attains its maximum at B''', $f_{bb} = 0$ and $f_{bbb} < 0$. By criterion (viii) there is a point of inflection on the total product curve at this input ratio; the total product curve reverses its concavity from 'above' to 'below'. Beyond B''' the marginal product of B declines. As is well known, MP_b intersects AP_b at the latter's maximum and becomes zero at point D, where the cross-section total product curve attains its maximum (D').[1]

Now focus upon the behavior of MP_a from A to E. To begin, let us prove the familiar proposition that the marginal product of A is zero when the average product of B attains its maximum. Differentiating equation (5.3.9) and using property (iv), one obtains

$$\frac{\partial(q/b)}{\partial b} = -\frac{a}{b^2}f_a. \tag{5.3.10}$$

For a maximum, equation (5.3.10) must equal zero. Since the inputs are positive, f_a must equal zero. Next, for a proper maximum, equation (5.3.10) must be positive when the input ratio is less than the critical one, negative when the input ratio is larger. Since the sign of f_a is the opposite, the following proposition is established: the marginal product of A is negative over the range of input ratios that results in an increasing average product of B; the marginal product of A is positive over the input ratio range in which AP_b is declining.

Since $f_a = 0$ at A and C, by Rolle's Theorem there exists *at least* one point between A and C at which $f_{aa} = 0$. By assumption, MP_b has a unique maximum; hence by property (iii) there is *only one* point at which $f_{aa} = 0$. That is, MP_a has an extreme point at the same input ratio for which MP_b attains its maximum. By property (vii), since $f_{bb} = f_{aa} = 0$, f_{aaa} and f_{bbb} have opposite signs. Hence B'' must be a minimum on MP_a.

Finally, MP_a must be decreasing at a decreasing rate at point C. To show this, take the partial derivative of equation (5.3.10), obtaining

$$\frac{\partial^2(q/b)}{\partial b^2} = \frac{a}{b^3}(2f_a + af_{aa}). \tag{5.3.11}$$

Since equation (5.3.11) must be negative for a proper maximum at C', f_{aa} must be negative at this point ($f_a = 0$).

[1] The latter property follows immediately from the fact that $f(a^*, b)$ attains its maximum in the Q–B plane when $f_b = 0$. The former is proved as follows. For a maximum of AP_b,

$$\frac{\partial\left(\frac{q}{b}\right)}{\partial b} = \frac{bf_b - q}{b^2} = 0.$$

Thus at the maximum point,

$$bf_b = q \quad \text{or} \quad f_b = \frac{q}{b}, \quad q.e.d.$$

To summarize: MP_a is zero at the origin; it thereafter declines to a minimum at the point where MP_b is a maximum and then rises to zero at the point where AP_b is a maximum. MP_a has a point of inflection in the range from A to C if MP_b does; but the points of inflection do not occur at the same input ratio.

The shape of AP_b over the range from A to C is not entirely certain. To be sure, it increases over this range and attains its maximum at C'. However, by equation (5.3.11) it may or may not have a point of inflection. If it does, the point must lie to the left of B because at B'''' the average product curve is concave from below (by equation (5.3.11) with $f_{aa} = 0$ and $f_a < 0$).[1]

The range C–D, which corresponds to the cone COD in figure 29, is the so-called 'economic region of production'. From figure 30, it is apparent that the economic region is symmetric when the production function is homogeneous of degree one. That is, Stage I with respect to B is precisely Stage III with respect to A, and vice versa. Stage II, the economic region of production, is the same for both. Accordingly, the intensive margin for the variable input corresponds to the extensive margin for the fixed input, and vice versa. The symmetry brought about by the unique relation between AP_b and MP_a (or AP_a and MP_b) lends added support to the original definition of the economic region as the range from the maximum point on the average product curve to the point at which marginal product is zero.

The behavior of all the curves over the economic region is well known; so our attention is now directed to the range from D to F. First, all curves approach the b/a^* axis asymptotically (theoretically, they all reach zero at infinity). To see this, write equation (5.3.6) as

$$q = \frac{f\left(\dfrac{a^*}{b}, 1\right)}{1/b}. \tag{5.3.12}$$

As b and b/a^* increase without bound, equation (5.3.12) has the indeterminate form $0 \div 0$. Applying L'Hospital's Rule, one has

$$\lim_{\substack{b \\ a^* \to \infty}} q = \lim_{\substack{b \\ a^* \to \infty}} af'\left(\frac{a}{b}, 1\right) = \lim_{a \to 0} af_a = 0. \tag{5.3.13}$$

Hence $q \to 0$ as $b \to \infty$. Therefore $AP_b = q/b \to 0$ as $b \to \infty$. Since AP_b approaches zero, so does its derivative. From equation (5.3.10) it follows

---

[1] This result may seem to contradict the familiar proposition that the average product of the variable input is the same as the total product of the fixed input (because, it might seem, AP_b would have to have points of inflection at B'''' and E''''). However, the derivatives of AP_b, and hence its shape in the Q–B plane, are taken with respect to b. If the derivatives are taken with respect to a, it is seen that AP_b is TP_a in the Q–A space for $b = 1$.

that $f_a \to 0$; and from property (i), $f_b \to 0$. Thus all curves approach the axis asymptotically.

The same argument used above to establish the shape of the curves from A to C may be repeated for the range from D to F. At some point, say F, MP_b is k units less than zero. Since MP_b is continuous, it must also be k units less than zero at some point to the right of D. Hence Rolle's Theorem applies. By our uniqueness assumption, $f_{bb} = 0$ at exactly one point between D and F. Since $f_b < 0$ properly within the range, the point must be a minimum; hence $f_{bbb} > 0$ at E''. Thus by criterion (viii), the total product curve has a point of inflection at E', changing from concave from below to concave from above.

By property (iii), f_a attains an extreme at the same input ratio as f_b. Using $f_{bb} = 0$ in property (vii), the extreme must be a maximum since the sign of f_{aaa} is opposite that of f_{bbb}. Finally, at the input ratio represented by E, AP_b must be concave from above (from equation (5.3.11) with $f_a > 0$ and $f_{aa} = 0$). Since expression (5.3.11) must be negative at C' and positive at E'''', the average product curve has a point of inflection somewhere in the range from C to E. It is interesting to note that whether AP_b has a point of inflection in the A–C range or not, it must have one in the C–E range. Furthermore, such points of inflection as occur cannot occur at the same input ratios that give rise to points of inflection on either the total or marginal product curves.

5.3.5   The isoquant map

Borts and Mishan discussed the economic and uneconomic regions of production in terms of the isoquant map of a linearly homogeneous production function. Using economic arguments, they suggested that the map looks like figure 31, except that the isoquant becomes a horizontal line at point C and thereafter.[1] The object here is not to discuss their economic argument; instead, we wish to determine the shape of a representative isoquant derived from the physical production function. The emphasis is strictly upon technical aspects.

The slope of an isoquant, or the negative of the marginal rate of technical substitution, is

$$\frac{db}{da} = -\frac{f_a}{f_b}. \tag{5.3.14}$$

The second derivative, which determines curvature, is

$$\frac{d^2b}{da^2} = -\frac{f_{aa}f_b^2 - 2f_{ab}f_af_b + f_{bb}f_a^2}{f_b^3}. \tag{5.3.15}$$

[1] Borts and Mishan [1962].

Substituting properties (iii) and (iv) in equation (5.3.15) yields

$$\frac{d^2b}{da^2} = -\frac{f_{aa}}{b^2f_b^3}(a^2f_a^2 + 2abf_af_b + b^2f_b^2). \qquad (5.3.16)$$

Finally, in light of property (vi), equation (5.3.16) reduces to

$$\frac{d^2b}{da^2} = -\frac{q^2f_{aa}}{b^2f_b^3}. \qquad (5.3.17)$$

In what follows it is helpful to refer both to figure 30 and figure 31. Initially consider any point properly within the C–D range. Both marginal

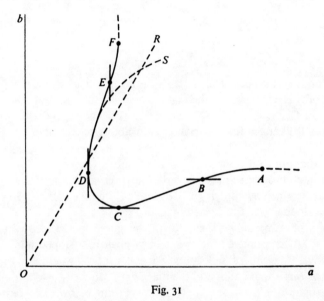

Fig. 31

products are positive; hence by equation (5.3.14), the isoquant has a negative slope. At D, MP_b is instantaneously zero, so the isoquant is vertical at that point. Similarly, at point C, MP_a is zero and the isoquant is horizontal. Outside the C–D range, one marginal product is positive and the other negative. By equation (5.3.14), therefore, the isoquant must have a positive slope. However it cannot have a shape such as DS in figure 31. In that event, the isoquant would be cut by a ray from the origin (OR). It would thereby violate a fundamental property of functions homogeneous of degree one, namely that a proportional expansion of all inputs will result in an expansion of output by the same proportion.

Since the isoquant cannot be concave from above throughout its entire length above D, a point of inflection must exist. As figure 31 is constructed

121

the point of inflection is at E. By criterion (viii), a point of inflection occurs when the second derivative is zero; hence equation (5.3.17) must be zero at this point. Since q^2, b^2, and f_b are not zero, the point of inflection must occur precisely at the point where $f_{aa} = f_{bb} = 0$, i.e. the point of inflection on the isoquant occurs at the point where the marginal product of A attains its maximum and the marginal product of B its minimum.

To determine the direction in which concavity changes, the third derivative must be examined:

$$\frac{d^3b}{da^3} = -\frac{b^2f_b^3(q^2f_{aaa}+2qf_{aa})+q^2f_{aa}(3b^2f_af_b+2bf_af_b^2)}{(b^2f_b^3)^2}. \quad (5.3.18)$$

Since $f_{aa} = 0$ at the point under consideration, equation (5.3.18) reduces to

$$\frac{d^3b}{da^3} = -\frac{b^2f_b^3q^2f_{aaa}}{(b^2f_b^3)^2}. \quad (5.3.19)$$

The denominator is necessarily positive, as are b^2 and q^2. Since the marginal product of B is negative and the marginal product of A is at its maximum, $f_b^3 < 0$ and $f_{aaa} < 0$. Hence the expression is negative; by criterion (viii), the isoquant changes from concave from above to concave from below at E.

When the input ratio increases without bound (i.e. $b \to \infty$ for $a = a^*$), both marginal products approach zero. However, the slope of the isoquant may be determined by applying L'Hospital's Rule.[1] At infinity, represented by F, the slope is positive and infinite.

Exactly the same analysis applies to the shape of the isoquant to the right of C. After point C, the isoquant is positively sloped and concave from above. A point of inflection is reached at B, where the marginal product of B is a maximum and the marginal product of A is a minimum. Beyond this point the isoquant is concave from below. The point A is attained when both marginal products are zero. The slope at this point, by L'Hospital's Rule, is also zero.[2]

5.4 Numerical example

A linearly homogeneous production function satisfying all of the properties discussed in section 5.3 is given by

$$q = 10{,}000\left[\frac{2a^3b^2+a^2b^3}{a^4+b^4}\right]. \quad (5.4.1)$$

[1] F is approached when $b \to \infty$. Hence the slope at F is
$$\lim_{b\to\infty} -\frac{q-bf_b}{af_b} = \lim_{b\to\infty}\frac{bf_{bb}}{af_{bb}} = \lim_{b\to\infty}\frac{b}{a} = \infty.$$

[2] The limit in footnote 1 is taken for $b \to 0$.

5.4 NUMERICAL EXAMPLE

TABLE 6 *Production table*

a \ b	1	2	3	4	5	6	7	8	9	10
1	15000	9412	5488	3735	2796	2221	1836	1562	1358	1200
2	11765	30000	25979	18824	14041	10976	8920	7471	6404	5591
3	7683	29691	45000	42730	35057	28235	23098	19306	16463	14284
4	5603	23529	47003	60000	59024	51959	44260	37647	32319	28081
5	4393	18721	41431	63564	75000	74961	68820	61004	53542	47059
6	3608	15366	35294	59381	79646	90000	90657	85460	77938	70113
7	3060	12975	30205	53113	76917	95429	105000	106191	101860	94831
8	2656	11206	26201	47059	71171	94006	111017	120000	121610	118048
9	2345	9853	23049	41825	64814	89072	110717	126475	135000	136948
10	2100	8786	20534	37441	58824	82861	106685	127128	141839	150000

TABLE 7 *Marginal product of A*

a \ b	1	2	3	4	5	6	7	8	9	10
1	10000	21315	12903	8658	6372	4989	4077	3435	2962	2599
2	−5675	10000	24832	21315	16460	12903	10424	8658	7358	6372
3	−2802	−5841	10000	23339	24382	21315	17947	15129	12903	11155
4	−1535	−5675	−3658	10000	21441	24832	23767	21315	18748	16460
5	−953	−3994	−6396	−1569	10000	19844	24253	24719	23327	21315
6	−646	−2802	−5675	−5841	97	10000	18575	23339	24832	24382
7	−466	−2036	−4513	−6349	−4802	1394	10000	17569	22366	24505
8	−351	−1535	−3538	−5675	−6304	−3658	2413	10000	16761	21441
9	−274	−1194	−2802	−4794	−6262	−5841	−2563	3228	10000	16102
10	−220	−953	−2255	−3994	−5675	−6396	−5172	−1569	3891	10000

TABLE 8 *Marginal product of B*

b \ a	1	2	3	4	5	6	7	8	9	10
1	5000	23114	16089	11742	9157	7483	6319	5465	4813	4299
2	−5952	5000	23607	23114	19346	16089	13614	11742	10297	9157
3	−2472	−7895	5000	20545	24470	23114	20599	18169	16089	14362
4	−1231	−5952	−6822	5000	17852	23607	24390	23114	21243	19346
5	−715	−3776	−7618	−5348	5000	15813	22106	24320	24234	23114
6	−461	−2472	−5952	−7895	−4043	5000	14279	20545	23607	24470
7	−320	−1704	−4392	−7258	−7492	−2970	5000	13102	19112	22629
8	−234	−1231	−3260	−5952	−7824	−6822	−2099	5000	12178	17852
9	−178	−924	−2472	−4741	−7010	−7895	−6078	−1386	5000	11436
10	−140	−715	−1918	−3776	−5952	−7618	−7671	−5348	−797	5000

TABLE 9   *Approximate points on the unit isoquant*

a (exact)	b (approximate)	a (exact)	b (approximate)
2	1·4	5	2·0
2	3·8	6	2·2
3	1·6	7	2·4
3	7·8	8	2·6
4	1·8	9	2·8
4	12·8	10	3·0

Tables 6, 7 and 8 show the total output, the marginal product of A, and the marginal product of B for a–b inputs from 1 to 10. Table 9 shows some approximate points on the unit isoquant.[1]

5.5   Homothetic production functions

To this point the discussion has focused either upon production functions whose elasticity of substitution is always constant or production functions whose elasticity of substitution is a variable that depends upon the input ratio. In the latter case, the elasticity of substitution varies for movements along an isoquant, but it is constant for movements along a ray from the origin. A somewhat broader class of production functions that generally possesses the latter property is called the class of *homothetic* production functions.[2]

Definition: a homothetic function is a monotonically increasing transformation of a homogeneous function.

Thus any homogeneous function is homothetic, but homothetic functions are not necessarily homogeneous.

The literature does not abound with explicit examples of homothetic functions. There are a good many examples of a simple type, namely transcendental functions.[3] The following interesting form has recently been suggested by Miss Clemhout:[4]

$$q = \alpha\, e^{\gamma t} x^{\lambda}, \tag{5.5.1}$$

[1] The a values are exact, the b values approximate. A binary search could have been conducted to determine the exact b values. The game did not seem worth the candle, however. A casual plotting of the points in table 9 shows that the isoquant indeed 'looks like' the one in figure 31.
[2] See Shephard [1953] and Solow [1955].
[3] See Ferguson and Pfouts [1962]; Newman and Read [1961]; Halter, Carter, and Hocking [1957]; Mundlak [1964].
[4] Clemhout [1964].

where α, γ, and λ are positive parameters and

$$x = b \exp\left[\Sigma\beta_n\left(\frac{a}{b}\right)^n\right],\qquad (5.5.2)$$

where the β's are constants, a and b are the inputs, and the sum is extended until the statistical fit is suitable.

APPENDIX TO CHAPTER 5

A NOTE ON PROFESSOR KNIGHT'S PRODUCTION FUNCTION[1]

This chapter has dealt chiefly with a class of linearly homogeneous production functions having two characteristics. First, for the class in question, there èxist input ratios for which each marginal product has negative values.[2] Second, the class of functions considered is 'economically defined' and smoothly continuous from $(0, 0)$ to (∞, ∞).

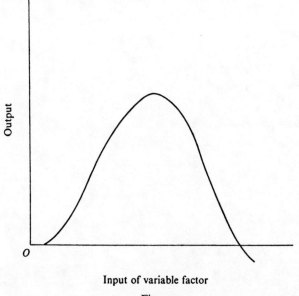

Input of variable factor

Fig. 32

---

[1] See Knight [1933, pp. 98–102, esp. footnote 1, pp. 101–2] and Borts and Mishan [1962].
[2] This class, however, does not include all variable elasticity *functions*. For example, the function $f(a, b) = \sqrt{(a^2 + 4ab)} - a$ has a variable elasticity of substitution but strictly positive marginal products.

The class of functions just described differs significantly from the class of functions used by Knight and by Borts and Mishan, who considered functions defined only over a subset of the positive real numbers.

To illustrate the crucial difference between the two classes of production functions, consider the numerical function used by Borts and Mishan:

$$q = \frac{5a^2}{b} - \frac{a^3}{3b^2}. \qquad (5.\,A.\,1)$$

Output is zero when $a = 15b$, and the function is 'economically defined' only over the range in which $a \leqq 15b$.

Consider figure 32. In the q–a cross-section, the total product curve starts to the *right* of the origin and ultimately *cuts* the a-axis at a finite value of a. To obtain the Knight–Borts–Mishan class of equations, the production function must contain at least two terms, and at least one term must be *subtracted* from the other(s). Since I can find neither a technical nor an economic rationale for subtracting terms in a production function, I prefer the formulation adopted here.

6

ECONOMIC THEORY OF PRODUCTION
WITH FIXED INPUT PRICES

6.1 Introduction

The technical theory of production is that segment of production theory in which *economic magnitudes*, such as input and output prices, are not introduced. A good bit of theory, as illustrated by chapters 4 and 5, can be developed without regard to economic considerations. Yet much the more important part of the theory requires the use of economic magnitudes and economic criteria. It is to the economic theory of production that the following five chapters are devoted.

We shall begin with a special case so as to consider the simpler parts of the theory first. To this end, in chapters 6 and 7 it is assumed that input prices are fixed and constant, or what is the same, that the entrepreneur in question is a perfect competitor in all input markets. This assumption enables us to determine some simple but important rules concerning optimal input combinations, the expansion path, short-run and long-run costs, and the comparative static effects of variations in input prices. It is only after examining these in some detail that our attention is turned to the more general, more difficult, and less precise case in which input prices are freely variable.

6.1.1 Isocost curves

The assumptions introduced and discussed in chapter 4 are retained throughout. In particular, there exists a production function

$$q = f(x_1, x_2, ..., x_n), \qquad (6.1.1)$$

or for graphical treatment, $\quad q = f(x_1, x_2), \qquad (6.1.2)$

that is continuous, has continuous first and second partial derivatives, and yields a unique output corresponding to every nonnegative input combination.

Denote the fixed market price of the ith input by p_i. The total cost of using a particular input combination, and thus the total cost of producing the corresponding unique output, is

$$C = \sum_{i=1}^{n} p_i x_i.$$

(6.1.3)

In the case of two inputs, the total cost function may be written

$$x_2 = \frac{1}{p_2} C - \frac{p_1}{p_2} x_1.$$

(6.1.4)

In the form of equation (6.1.4) or its generalizations, the cost of production may be represented by a series of isocost curves (planes or hyperplanes).

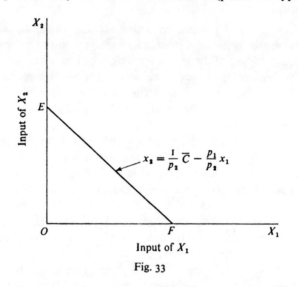

Fig. 33

Suppose C in equation (6.1.4) is set equal to some constant $\overline{C}$. The isocost curve corresponding to $C = \overline{C}$ is shown in figure 33. The line EF is the isocost curve. Its ordinate intercept E shows the number of units of X_2 that may be purchased for $\overline{C}$ dollars at the fixed price p_2 if no units of X_1 are hired. The abscissa intercept F shows the same thing for X_1. The slope of the isocost curve is the negative of the input-price ratio, i.e.

$$\frac{dx_2}{dx_1} = -\frac{p_1}{p_2}.$$

(6.1.5)

The curve EF may thus be given the following

Definition: An isocost curve is the locus of all input combinations that may be purchased or hired for a given expenditure of funds. Its slope at every point is the negative of the input-price ratio. From this it follows that when input prices are fixed, isocost curves are straight lines.

128

6.1.2 Shifting the isocost curve

The changes in the isocost curve associated with changes in expenditure or input prices are easily determinable from equation (6.1.4). The changes are illustrated in figure 34. A comparative static change in C, input prices fixed, shifts the curve outward or toward the origin according as expenditure increases or decreases. The slope of the curve, however, is not affected inasmuch as input prices are constant. For example, an increase in expenditure might shift the isocost curve from EF to $E'F'$.

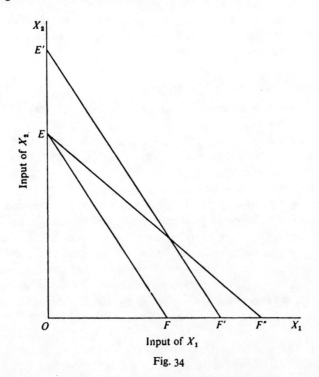

Fig. 34

Proportional changes in *both* input prices lead to similar changes in the isocost curve. In particular, the curve shifts outward or toward the origin according as input prices decrease or increase. The slope of the curve does not change, however, since input prices change proportionately (by assumption).

A change in the price of one input, expenditure and the other input price remaining constant, causes the isocost curve to rotate around one of the intercepts. Suppose the price of X_1 declines. The slope, $-p_1/p_2$, thus declines; the curve rotates counterclockwise around the intercept E (say, from EF

129

to *EF''*). Similarly, an increase in the price of X_1 causes the curve to rotate clockwise around *E*. In like manner, the curve rotates clockwise or counter-clockwise around *F* according as the price of X_2 decreases or increases.

6.2 Optimal input combinations: cost minimization approach[1]

One set of economic magnitudes (input prices) was introduced in section 6.1. The time has now come to introduce an *economic criterion* of efficiency, namely each level of output is produced at the least possible cost. By production functions (6.1.1) or (6.1.2), each level of output may be produced by a variety of input combinations. The problem, therefore, is to determine the *particular* input combination that minimizes the cost of producing a stipulated level of output.

6.2.1 Special case, two variable inputs

When there are only two variable inputs, the problem may be solved graphically, as illustrated in figure 35. It is required to produce the level of output corresponding to the isoquant Q_0 at the least possible cost, given the fixed prices of the inputs. For these given prices, the *I–I'* curves show a portion of the isocost map.

First note that it is impossible to produce Q_0 at the cost represented by $I_1 I'_1$. For that expenditure it is not possible to purchase any combination of resources that is sufficient to produce the Q_0 level of output. One could obtain sufficient resources by spending the amount represented by $I_2 I'_2$; but this amount is unnecessarily large. Least cost is obtained by using the combination of inputs associated with the point of tangency of the isoquant and an isocost curve. This is shown as point *E* in figure 35, where *II'* is tangent to Q_0. At this point of tangency, the slope of the isoquant equals the slope of the isocost curve. Hence the fundamental principle is easily deduced.

Principle: The optimal combination of resources (i.e. the one that minimizes the cost of producing a stipulated level of output) is that combination for which the marginal rate of technical substitution of X_2 for X_1 equals the ratio of the price of X_1 to the price of X_2. Stated alternatively, the marginal product of a dollar's worth of each resource is the same.

Using the principal in the form last stated enables one clearly to see why combinations represented by points such as *F* and *G* are suboptimal. At point *F*, for example, the marginal product of a dollar's worth of X_1 exceeds

[1] The contents of sections 6.2 and 6.3, and most of that of section 6.4, are taken directly from the public domain of economic literature. It seems needless to cite authors at every point. Similar developments may be found, for example, in Carlson [1939], Samuelson [1947], Schneider [1934], and Shephard [1953].

the marginal product of a dollar's worth of X_2. The entrepreneur can reduce cost without affecting output by substituting X_1 for X_2. Similarly, at G the entrepreneur should substitute X_2 for X_1. In general, input substitution is economically desirable unless the combination results in equality between the input-price ratio and the marginal rate of technical substitution.

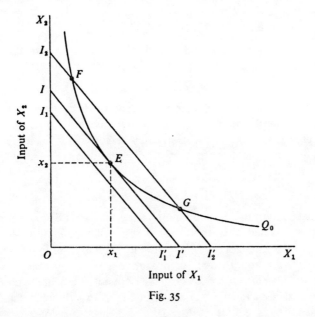

Input of X_1

Fig. 35

6.2.2 General case, multiple inputs

When there are more than two variable inputs, the 'optimal combination' problem does not lend itself to graphical analysis. However, it may be treated quite simply by means of the Lagrange technique for constrained extrema.[1] Specifically, the problem is formulated as follows: minimize

$$C = \sum_{i=1}^{n} p_i x_i, \qquad (6.2.1)$$

subject to

$$f(x_1, x_2, ..., x_n) = \bar{q}, \qquad (6.2.2)$$

where $\bar{q}$ is a stipulated constant.

To arrive at a solution, one first constructs the Lagrange function

$$L \equiv \sum_{i=1}^{n} p_i x_i - \lambda[f(x_1, x_2, ..., x_n) - \bar{q}], \qquad (6.2.3)$$

[1] Just as the economic content of this chapter is well established, so also are the mathematical techniques used. For example, one may consult Hancock [1917], Hotelling [1935], Curtiss [1941], and Samuelson [1947, pp. 357–79].

where λ is the undetermined multiplier. The first-order, or necessary, conditions for the constrained minimum are that all first partial derivatives of equation (6.2.3) equal zero. Performing the differentiation, one obtains

$$\left.\begin{aligned}
\frac{\partial L}{\partial x_i} &= p_i - \lambda f_i = 0 \quad (i = 1, 2, \ldots, n), \\
\frac{\partial L}{\partial \lambda} &= f(x_1, x_2, \ldots, x_n) - \bar{q} = 0.
\end{aligned}\right\} \tag{6.2.4}$$

Expressions (6.2.4) provide $(n+1)$ equations to solve for the $(n+1)$ unknowns $(x_1, x_2, \ldots, x_n, \lambda)$ in terms of the $(n+1)$ parameters

$$(p_1, p_2, \ldots, p_n, \bar{q}).$$

At this point, it is useful to note that equations (6.2.4), the minimizing conditions, implicitly define constant-output demand functions for the n inputs. That is, this set of equations may be solved for the x_i's in terms of the p_i's and the specific output level $\bar{q}$. The resulting expressions, which may be written as

$$x_i = f^i(p_1, p_2, \ldots, p_n, \bar{q}) \quad (i = 1, 2, \ldots, n), \tag{6.2.5}$$

are the constant-output demand functions, i.e. the input demand functions relative to the $\bar{q}$-level of output. Stated somewhat differently, equations (6.2.5) show the changes in quantities demanded resulting from price changes when the equilibrium (comparative static) adjustments are restricted to movements along the original isoquant. Thus only *substitution effects* are shown by these functions. But this is exactly what one would expect inasmuch as equations (6.2.4), and hence equations (6.2.5), are entirely independent of revenue considerations. The *output effect* depends upon the way in which changes in input prices affect the profit-maximizing output of the firm. These more general considerations are deferred until section 6.6.

6.2.3   Interpretation of the first-order conditions

The familiar rules for attaining the optimal input combination may be obtained from the first set of equations in expressions (6.2.4). Eliminating λ among the first n equations, one obtains

$$\frac{f_i}{f_j} = \frac{p_i}{p_j} \quad (i, j = 1, 2, \ldots, n). \tag{6.2.6}$$

Equations (6.2.6) embody one version of the principle stated in subsection 1:

Principle: The optimal input combination is attained at the production point where the marginal rate of technical substitution between every pair of inputs is equal to the price ratio prevailing between that pair of inputs.

6.2 CONSTRAINED COST MINIMIZATION

Alternatively, equations (6.2.4) may be expressed as

$$\frac{f_1}{p_1} = \frac{f_2}{p_2} = \dots = \frac{f_n}{p_n} = \frac{1}{\lambda}. \tag{6.2.7}$$

Equations (6.2.7) embody the other version of the principle stated in subsection 1:

Principle: The optimal input combination is attained at the production point where the marginal productivity of the last dollar spent on resources $(1/\lambda)$ is the same in every use. That is, the marginal productivity of a dollar's worth of any one resource must equal the marginal productivity of a dollar's worth of any other resource.[1]

6.3 Optimal input combinations: output maximization approach

In section 6·2 one criterion of economic efficiency was suggested. Another criterion, equally valid, is that the largest possible output be produced for every stipulated expenditure upon resources. The problem, in other words, involves maximizing output subject to a given level of cost.

Since these are two different approaches to essentially the same problem, the results 'should' be the same. Indeed they are; that the results are identical constitutes one of the many interesting 'duality theorems' in economics:

Duality Theorem: The principle of optimal input combination is the same whether based upon minimizing the cost of producing a given level of output or upon maximizing the output attainable for a given volume of expenditure upon resources.

The remainder of this section is devoted to a proof of this duality theorem.

6.3.1 Special case, two variable inputs

If there are only two variable inputs, the duality theorem may be proved graphically (see figure 36). The given level of expenditure is represented by the isocost curve II'. Q_0, Q_1, and Q_2 comprise a portion of the isoquant map. First note that the output associated with Q_2 is not attainable for the given expenditure. The firm is restricted to input combinations lying in the input-availability space OII'. Since more of one or both resources are available along the boundary II', the optimal input combination lies on this isocost curve.

Points E, F, and G are three of the infinite quantities of output that can be produced with the infinite number of available input combinations.

[1] In chapter 7 it is shown that λ, the factor of proportionality between price and marginal productivity, is in fact the marginal cost of producing an additional unit of the commodity.

It is visually clear, and easily demonstrated, that the maximum output is obtained by using the input combination for which an isoquant is tangent to the given isocost curve. At this point, their slopes are equal; and this equality leads to the principle stated in subsection 1.

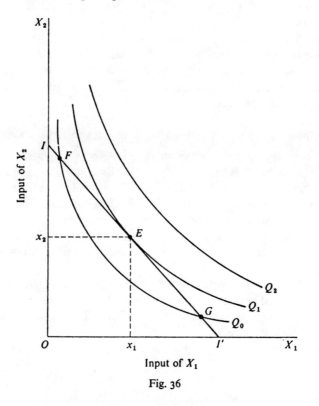

Fig. 36

6.3.2 General case, multiple inputs

As in the previous case, the problem is not amenable to graphical analysis when there are more than two variable inputs. However, it is a simple problem of constrained maximization, which may be formulated as follows:

maximize
$$q = f(x_1, x_2, ..., x_n), \tag{6.3.1}$$

subject to
$$\sum_{i=1}^{n} p_i x_i = \overline{C}, \tag{6.3.2}$$

where $\overline{C}$ is the constant, stipulated level of cost.

First construct the Lagrange function

$$L^* \equiv f(x_1, x_2, ..., x_n) - \lambda^* \left(\sum_{i=1}^{n} p_i x_i - \overline{C} \right). \tag{6.3.3}$$

134

6.3 CONSTRAINED OUTPUT MAXIMIZATION

The first-order, or equilibrium, conditions for a constrained maximum are that all first partial derivatives of equation (6.3.3) equal zero. Performing the differentiation, one obtains

$$\left.\begin{array}{l} \dfrac{\partial L^*}{\partial x_i} = f_i - \lambda^* p_i = 0 \quad (i = 1, 2, ..., n), \\[2mm] \dfrac{\partial L^*}{\partial \lambda^*} = \displaystyle\sum_{i=1}^{n} p_i x_i - \overline{C} = 0. \end{array}\right\} \tag{6.3.4}$$

Expressions (6.3.4) provide $(n+1)$ equations to solve for the $(n+1)$ unknowns $(x_1, x_2, ..., x_n, \lambda^*)$ in terms of the $(n+1)$ parameters

$$(p_1, p_2, ..., p_n, \overline{C}).$$

The proof of the duality theorem follows immediately from equations (6.3.4). First, eliminate λ^* among the first n equations, obtaining

$$\frac{f_i}{f_j} = \frac{p_i}{p_j} \quad (i, j = 1, 2, ..., n). \tag{6.3.5}$$

Conditions (6.3.5) are precisely the same as the conditions shown in equations (6.2.6). Next, write the first n equations as

$$\frac{f_1}{p_1} = \frac{f_2}{p_2} = ... = \frac{f_n}{p_n} = \lambda^*. \tag{6.3.6}$$

Equations (6.2.6), (6.3.5), (6.2.7) and (6.3.6) jointly imply that

$$\frac{1}{\lambda} = \lambda^*, \tag{6.3.7}$$

which completes the proof.

The principle governing optimal input combinations is thus the same however derived. The constant-cost input demand functions implicitly defined by equations (6.3.4), however, are not the same as the constant-output demand functions defined by equation (6.2.4) and shown in equations (6.2.5). From equations (6.3.4), the constant-cost demand functions are

$$x_i = g^i(p_1, p_2, ..., p_n, \overline{C}) \quad (i = 1, 2, ..., n). \tag{6.3.8}$$

The two sets of demand functions are similar in that quantities demanded are functions of the prices. But the final parametric constants in the two sets of equations are different. Equations (6.2.5) are restricted to movements along a given isoquant, while equations (6.3.8) are restricted to movements along an isocost curve. Thus for comparative static changes, equations (6.3.8) contain more than a pure substitution effect because the level of output changes. However, equations (6.3.8) are independent of revenue considerations; thus they cannot reflect the true output effect.

135

6.4 Isoquants and comparative statics

At this point we know the necessary conditions for attaining an optimal input combination: a generalized isoquant must be tangent to an isocost hyperplane. However, such a tangency may not represent a stable equilibrium, i.e. the production point may not be a true constrained maximum or minimum. We shall now show that the second-order, or stability, conditions require the generalized isoquant to be concave from above in all directions.

Since the equilibrium conditions are the same for constrained maximization and constrained minimization, the analysis may be limited to the former.

6.4.1 The second-order conditions

For equations (6.3.4) to represent a proper maximum, any deviation from the input constellation satisfying equations (6.3.5) must lead to a smaller output. Thus the general condition for a proper maximum is

$$d^2f = \sum_i \sum_j f_{ij} dx_i dx_j < 0, \qquad (6.4.1)$$

for
$$df = \sum_i f_i dx_i = 0, \qquad (6.4.2)$$

where not all $dx_i = 0$. For the quadratic form (6.4.1) to be negative definite under the constraint (6.3.2), it is both necessary and sufficient that the latent roots be negative.

Consider the following symmetric bordered Hessian determinant:

$$D = \begin{vmatrix} 0 & p_1 & p_2 & \cdots & p_n \\ p_1 & f_{11} & f_{12} & \cdots & f_{1n} \\ p_2 & f_{12} & f_{22} & \cdots & f_{2n} \\ \vdots & \vdots & \vdots & & \vdots \\ p_n & f_{1n} & f_{2n} & \cdots & f_{nn} \end{vmatrix}. \qquad (6.4.3)$$

For the latent roots of the quadratic form to be negative, it is necessary and sufficient that the successive bordered principal minors of D alternate in sign, the first being positive. The second-order conditions are more meaningful, however, if expressed in another form. From equations (6.3.4):

$$p_i = \frac{1}{\lambda} f_i \quad (i = 1, 2, \ldots, n), \qquad (6.4.4)$$

136

where the asterisk has been dropped from λ. Substituting equations (6.4.4) in equation (6.4.3), one obtains

$$D = \frac{1}{\lambda^2} \begin{vmatrix} 0 & f_1 & f_2 & \cdots & f_n \\ f_1 & f_{11} & f_{12} & \cdots & f_{1n} \\ f_2 & f_{12} & f_{22} & \cdots & f_{2n} \\ \vdots & \vdots & \vdots & & \vdots \\ f_n & f_{1n} & f_{2n} & \cdots & f_{nn} \end{vmatrix} = \frac{1}{\lambda^2} F. \qquad (6.4.5)$$

Since $\lambda > 0$, $1/\lambda^2 > 0$. Thus the signs of D and F, and of their corresponding principal minors, must be identical.

Using this result, the necessary and sufficient conditions for the constrained maximum are that

$$\begin{vmatrix} 0 & f_1 & f_2 \\ f_1 & f_{11} & f_{12} \\ f_2 & f_{12} & f_{22} \end{vmatrix} > 0, \quad \begin{vmatrix} 0 & f_1 & f_2 & f_3 \\ f_1 & f_{11} & f_{12} & f_{13} \\ f_2 & f_{12} & f_{22} & f_{23} \\ f_3 & f_{13} & f_{23} & f_{33} \end{vmatrix} < 0, \text{ etc.,} \qquad (6.4.6)$$

at a production point where equations (6.3.5) are satisfied. Broadly, inequalities (6.4.6) require that generalized isoquants be concave from above in every direction. This condition can be seen precisely for the two-input case. The first inequality in (6.4.6) must be positive, i.e.

$$2f_1 f_2 f_{12} - f_1^2 f_{22} - f_2^2 f_{11} > 0, \qquad (6.4.7)$$

or

$$f_1^2 f_{22} - 2f_1 f_2 f_{12} + f_2^2 f_{11} < 0. \qquad (6.4.8)$$

The slope of an isoquant is $\quad \dfrac{dx_2}{dx_1} = -\dfrac{f_1}{f_2}. \qquad (6.4.9)$

Hence its concavity depends upon the sign of

$$\frac{d^2 x_2}{dx_1^2} = \frac{d\left[-\dfrac{f_1}{f_2} \right]}{dx_1} = -\frac{f_2\left[f_{11} + f_{12}\dfrac{dx_2}{dx_1} \right] - f_1\left[f_{12} + f_{22}\dfrac{dx_2}{dx_1} \right]}{f_2^2}. \qquad (6.4.10)$$

Substituting equation (6.4.9) into expression (6.4.10), one obtains

$$\frac{d^2 x_2}{dx_1^2} = + \frac{1}{f_2^3} [2f_1 f_2 f_{12} - f_1^2 f_{22} - f_2^2 f_{11}]. \qquad (6.4.11)$$

Since $f_2 > 0$, $f_2^3 > 0$. Hence the isoquant is concave from above or below according as the expression in brackets in equation (6.4.11) is positive or negative. By the second-order condition (6.4.7), the bracketed expression must be positive; hence the isoquant must be concave from above. As a consequence, condition (6.4.8) must hold at any equilibrium production point. It is worth noting that inequality (6.4.8) does not necessarily imply diminishing marginal products; it is a definition of diminishing marginal

THEORY OF PRODUCTION

rates of technical substitution. These results may be summarized by the following

Proposition: Over the economically relevant range of production, i.e. the range in which input combinations *may* be optimal, isoquants must be concave from above in every direction; the production surface must be concave from below.

6.4.2 Comparative static changes: constant-output demand curves[1]

Certain properties of constant-output demand functions may be determined from the second-order conditions developed above. First, take the total differential of the equilibrium conditions shown in equations (6.2.4):

$$\sum_j f_{ij} dx_j + \frac{f_i}{\lambda} d\lambda = \frac{1}{\lambda} dp_i \quad (i=1, 2, ..., n),$$
$$\sum_j f_j dx_j = dq. \qquad (6.4.12)$$

Expressions (6.4.12) are $(n+1)$ equations linear in the $(n+1)$ unknown differential elements $(dx_1, dx_2, ..., dx_n, d\lambda)$ and the $(n+1)$ parametric changes $(dp_1, dp_2, ..., dp_n, dq)$. The matrix of coefficients is

$$[G] = \begin{bmatrix} 0 & f_1 & f_2 & \cdots & f_n \\ \frac{f_1}{\lambda} & f_{11} & f_{12} & \cdots & f_{1n} \\ \frac{f_2}{\lambda} & f_{12} & f_{22} & \cdots & f_{2n} \\ \vdots & \vdots & \vdots & & \vdots \\ \frac{f_n}{\lambda} & f_{1n} & f_{2n} & \cdots & f_{nn} \end{bmatrix}, \qquad (6.4.13)$$

whose determinant is denoted by G.

G is $(n+1) \times (n+1)$ in dimension. Number the rows and columns $0, 1, ..., n$. Let G_{0i} be the cofactor of the element in the 0-row and ith column and G_{ij} be the cofactor of the i–j element in the $(n \times n)$ central body of the matrix. Using this notation, equations (6.4.12) may be solved by Cramer's Rule for the differential elements:

$$dx_j = \frac{\sum_{i=1}^n \frac{dp_i}{\lambda} G_{ij} + G_{0j} dq}{G} \quad (j=1, 2, ..., n), \qquad (6.4.14)$$

and

$$d\lambda = \frac{\sum_{i=1}^n \frac{dp_i}{\lambda} G_{i0} + G_{00} dq}{G}. \qquad (6.4.15)$$

[1] Most of the theorems developed in subsections 6.4.2 and 6.4.3 were proved by Samuelson [1947, pp. 63–9].

138

Holding output constant, i.e. setting $dq = 0$, equations (6.4.14) and (6.4.15) may be reduced to the partial derivatives showing the effect of changes in input price:

$$\frac{\partial x_j}{\partial p_i} = \frac{G_{ij}}{\lambda G} \quad (i, j = 1, 2, ..., n), \qquad (6.4.16)$$

$$\frac{\partial x_j}{\partial p_j} = \frac{G_{jj}}{\lambda G} \quad (j = 1, 2, ..., n), \qquad (6.4.17)$$

and
$$\frac{\partial \lambda}{\partial p_i} = \frac{G_{i0}}{\lambda G} \quad (i = 1, 2, ..., n). \qquad (6.4.18)$$

Similarly, by holding input prices fixed, the effect of output changes may be determined:

$$\frac{\partial x_j}{\partial q} = \frac{G_{0j}}{G} \quad (j = 1, 2, ..., n), \qquad (6.4.19)$$

and
$$\frac{\partial \lambda}{\partial q} = \frac{G_{00}}{G}. \qquad (6.4.20)$$

Before proceeding, it is convenient to compare G and F [see equations (6.4.5) and (6.4.13)]. Factoring $1/\lambda$ from the first column of G, it is clear that

$$G = \frac{1}{\lambda} F. \qquad (6.4.21)$$

Since both $[G]$ and $[F]$ are real symmetric matrices, it also follows that

$$G_{ij} = G_{ji} = \frac{1}{\lambda} F_{ij} = \frac{1}{\lambda} F_{ji} \quad (i, j = 1, 2, ..., n), \qquad (6.4.22)$$

$$G_{i0} = \lambda G_{0i} = F_{i0} \quad (i = 1, 2, ..., n), \qquad (6.4.23)$$

and
$$G_{00} = F_{00}. \qquad (6.4.24)$$

From equations (6.4.16) and (6.4.22), one obtains the following result:

$$\frac{\partial x_i}{\partial p_j} = \frac{\partial x_j}{\partial p_i} \quad (i, j = 1, 2, ..., n). \qquad (6.4.25)$$

The following relation is obtained:

Relation: When output is held constant, the change in the usage of the ith input induced by a change in the price of the jth input must be exactly the same as the change in the usage of the jth input resulting from a change in the price of the ith input.

From equations (6.4.21) and (6.4.22) it follows that

$$\frac{G_{ij}}{G} = \frac{F_{ij}}{F}. \qquad (6.4.26)$$

THEORY OF PRODUCTION

From the stability conditions in expressions (6.4.6),

$$\frac{F_{ii}}{F} < 0 \quad (i = 1, 2, ..., n). \tag{6.4.27}$$

Hence from equations (6.4.17), since $\lambda > 0$,

$$\frac{\partial x_j}{\partial p_j} < 0 \quad (j = 1, 2, ..., n). \tag{6.4.28}$$

Inequalities (6.4.28) establish the following

Principle: Output and all *other* prices being held constant, the quantity demanded of any input varies inversely with its price.

Two further relations may be established. Consider equation (6.4.16) written in the following form:

$$\frac{\partial x_i}{\partial p_j} = \frac{1}{\lambda} \frac{G_{ji}}{G} \quad (i = 1, 2, ..., n). \tag{6.4.29}$$

Multiply both sides by $(1/\lambda)f_j$ and sum over j, obtaining

$$\frac{1}{\lambda} \sum_{j=1}^{n} f_j \frac{\partial x_i}{\partial p_j} = \frac{1}{\lambda^2} \sum_{j=1}^{n} f_j \frac{G_{ji}}{G} = 0 \quad (i = 1, 2, ..., n). \tag{6.4.30}$$

The expression must equal zero inasmuch as the sum on the right is the expansion of G by alien cofactors (i.e. the elements of the first column multiplied by the corresponding cofactors of the elements of the ith column). Substituting equation (6.4.4) in the left-hand side of equation (6.4.30), one obtains

$$\sum_{j=1}^{n} p_j \frac{\partial x_i}{\partial p_j} = 0 \quad (i = 1, 2, ..., n). \tag{6.4.31}$$

Multiplying and dividing equation (6.4.31) by x_i yields

$$x_i \sum_{j=1}^{n} \frac{p_j}{x_i} \frac{\partial x_i}{\partial p_j} = x_i \sum_{j=1}^{n} \eta_{ij}^* = 0 \quad (i = 1, 2, ..., n), \tag{6.4.32}$$

where η_{ij}^* is the constant-output price cross-elasticity of input demand and η_{ii}^* is the corresponding direct price elasticity. The following relation is thus obtained:

Relation: The sum of all direct and cross-price elasticities of input demand is zero for constant-output demand curves.

Next, consider the implicit constant-output demand functions shown in equation (6.2.5) and rewritten here as

$$x_i = f^i(p_1, p_2, ..., p_n) \quad (i = 1, 2, ..., n). \tag{6.4.33}$$

It should be noted that the constant output parameter $\bar{q}$ has been suppressed. Equations (6.4.31) and (6.4.32) jointly imply the following

140

Relation: Constant-output demand curves are homogeneous of degree zero in all prices. This relation is also implied by equations (6.3.5).

6.4.3 Comparative statics: changes in output

In order to investigate the comparative static effects of output changes, it is first necessary to determine the meaning of λ in equations (6.2.4). As we shall now see, λ is marginal cost.

From the cost equation (6.1.3), one obtains

$$\frac{\partial C}{\partial q} = \sum_{i=1}^{n} p_i \frac{\partial x_i}{\partial q}. \tag{6.4.34}$$

Substituting equations (6.4.19) and (6.2.4) successively, the following relation is obtained:

$$\frac{\partial C}{\partial q} = \sum_{i=1}^{n} p_i \frac{G_{0i}}{G} = \lambda \sum_{i=1}^{n} \frac{f_i G_{0i}}{G}. \tag{6.4.35}$$

Expanding G by the elements of its first row yields

$$G = 0 . G_{00} + \sum_{i=1}^{n} f_i G_{0i} = \sum_{i=1}^{n} f_i G_{0i}. \tag{6.4.36}$$

Substituting equation (6.4.36) into equation (6.4.35), one finds that

$$\frac{\partial C}{\partial q} = \lambda = \text{marginal cost.} \tag{6.4.37}$$

The first n equations in expression (6.2.4) may be written

$$p_i = \lambda f_i \quad (i = 1, 2, ..., n). \tag{6.4.38}$$

Substitution from equation (6.4.37) yields

$$p_i = \frac{\partial C}{\partial q} f_i \quad (i = 1, 2, ..., n), \tag{6.4.39}$$

which may be stated as the following

Principle: in order to minimize the cost of producing any level of output, the price of each resource must equal its marginal physical product multiplied by the common marginal cost. This result is independent of the revenue conditions confronting any firm.

Next, note that equation (6.4.37) implies that

$$\frac{\partial \lambda}{\partial p_i} = \frac{\partial^2 C}{\partial p_i \partial q} \quad (i = 1, 2, ..., n). \tag{6.4.40}$$

Using equations (6.4.23) in equations (6.4.19) yields

$$\frac{\partial x_i}{\partial q} = \frac{G_{0i}}{G} = \frac{G_{i0}}{\lambda G} \quad (i = 1, 2, ..., n). \tag{6.4.41}$$

Thus from equations (6.4.18) and (6.4.40),

$$\frac{\partial \lambda}{\partial p_i} = \frac{\partial x_i}{\partial q} = \frac{\partial^2 C}{\partial p_i \partial q} = \frac{\partial}{\partial p_i}\left(\frac{\partial q}{\partial C}\right) \quad (i = 1, 2, ..., n). \quad (6.4.42)$$

The implications of equations (6.4.42) may be stated as the following

Principle: for cost to be a minimum for any level of output, the change in usage of an input resulting from a change in output must be the same as the change in marginal cost associated with a change in the price of that input.

6.5 The expansion path

The results of sections 6.2 and 6.3 may be used to establish the expansion path, which is defined as follows:

Definition: The expansion path is the locus of input combinations for which the marginal rate of technical substitution equals the input-price ratio. The expansion path is thus defined by equations (6.2.6) or (6.3.5), where the levels of input usage depend upon the volume of output.

From the definition above, it is obvious that the expansion path is one particular isocline under present assumptions (i.e. fixed input prices). However, the expansion path is not an isocline if relative input prices change with the scale of output.

The expansion path is illustrated in figures 37 and 38. In the former, the line OR represents the expansion path associated with a production function homogeneous of degree one. From chapter 5 we know that the marginal rate of technical substitution is constant along any ray from the origin. Therefore, so long as relative input prices are constant, the expansion path itself must be a ray from the origin.

The more general case is illustrated in figure 38, where the expansion path is constructed with a positive slope and is concave from above. With fixed input prices (or relative prices), the expansion path must generally have a positive slope. The exceptional case is treated briefly in chapter 9. At this point let it suffice to state the following

Relations: if there are no inferior factors of production and if relative input prices remain constant: (i) the expansion path is positively sloped; (ii) it is a ray from the origin if all marginal products are independent of the scale of operation (i.e. the production function is homogeneous of any degree); and (iii) the expansion path is concave from above or below according as the marginal product of X_2 or X_1 declines least rapidly. As figure 38 is constructed, production becomes more X_2-intensive as output expands because the usage of X_2 must be increased relatively more than the usage of X_1 in order to maintain equality between the marginal rate of technical substitution and the fixed input-price ratio.

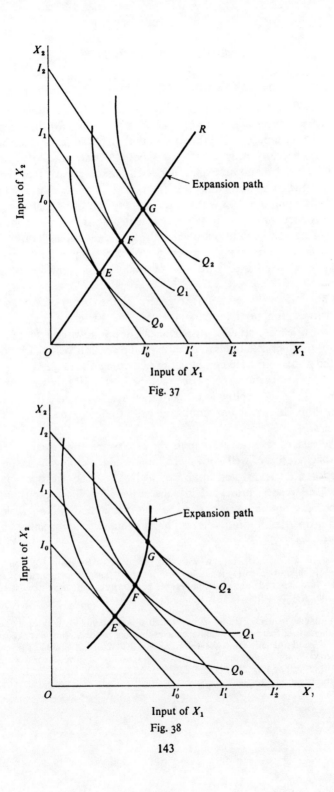

Fig. 37

Fig. 38

143

6.6. Input demand functions[1]

The theory of derived input demand has been examined intensely for the special case in which there is only one variable input. On the other hand, only special instances of the theory of jointly-derived input demand functions have been investigated. In 1938 both Mosak and Allen analyzed related factor demand functions under the assumption of perfect competition in the commodity and factor markets.[2] Somewhat later Samuelson studied the same problem without the assumption of perfect competition in the product market.[3] However, as seen in section 6.4, he imposed a different restrictive condition, namely the firm under consideration is confined to movements along a given production isoquant in response to changes in relative factor prices (i.e. he analyzed constant-output demand functions).

The purpose of this section is to generalize the theory of jointly-derived input demand functions by removing some of the restrictive assumptions contained in earlier studies. In particular, the following assumptions are made: (i) product demand is a function of and varies inversely with product price, the prices of related commodities remaining unchanged throughout;[4] (ii) the firm in question is a perfect competitor in all input markets; and (iii) there is a given production function whose first partial derivatives are positive and decrease monotonically over the relevant range of input quantities.

In the case of two variable inputs the results are quite clear and readily explicable in terms of well-known economic and technological magnitudes. Subsection 6.6.1 is devoted to an exhaustive analysis of this special case. The general case is presented in subsection 6.6.2. The results, in some instances, are not as precise as in the two-factor model. Nonetheless, the general properties of jointly-derived input demand functions may be stated straightforwardly.

[1] The following section is a reprint, with slight changes, of Ferguson [1966b].
[2] Mosak [1938] and Allen [1938]. Allen also assumed linear homogeneity of the production function and long-run competitive equilibrium. For a somewhat different approach, see Puu [1966].
[3] Samuelson [1947, pp. 63–9].
[4] The completely general case involving related product demands may easily be stated in mathematical form. Few definite conclusions are possible, however, because the results depend not only upon the technical substitutability of inputs in producing a specified commodity, but also upon the substitutability of products in consumption and the corresponding inter-commodity substitutability of inputs. This is touched upon, however, in Chapter 8.4.

6.6.1 A two-factor model of input demand

Consider a firm that produces a single commodity under technical conditions given by the production function

$$q = f(x_1, x_2), \tag{6.6.1}$$

where

$$f_1, f_2, f_{12} > 0 \quad \text{and} \quad f_{11}, f_{22} < 0. \tag{6.6.2}$$

In equations (6.6.1) and (6.6.2), q represents the quantity of output, x_1 and x_2 the quantities employed of the two variable inputs, and

$$f_i = \frac{\partial f}{\partial x_i} \quad \text{and} \quad f_{ij} = \frac{\partial^2 f}{\partial x_j \partial x_i}. \tag{6.6.3}$$

The firm markets its product under conditions given by the demand function

$$q = h(p), \quad \frac{dh}{dp} = h' < 0, \tag{6.6.4}$$

where p represents the commodity price. Finally, the firm being a perfect competitor in both input markets, its total cost is

$$C = p_1 x_1 + p_2 x_2, \tag{6.6.5}$$

where p_i is the given market price of the ith input.

The firm selects input quantities x_1 and x_2 so as to maximize profit, which is given by

$$\Pi = r - c = ph(p) - \Sigma p_i x_i. \tag{6.6.6}$$

The marginal, or first-order, conditions for the maximum are given by

$$\frac{\partial \Pi}{\partial x_i} = \left(\frac{h}{h'} + p\right) f_i - p_i = 0 \quad (i = 1, 2). \tag{6.6.7}$$

Equilibrium further requires that the quantity sold be equal to the quantity available for sale, i.e.

$$h(p) = f(x_1, x_2). \tag{6.6.8}$$

Equations (6.6.7) and (6.6.8) provide three equations to solve for the three unknowns (x_1, x_2, and p) in terms of the parametrically given input prices (p_1 and p_2).

Let

$$a = \frac{(h')^2 - hh''}{(h')^3} + \frac{1}{h'} \tag{6.6.9}$$

and

$$b = \left(\frac{h}{h'} + p\right). \tag{6.6.10}$$

The second-order conditions require that the quadratic form associated with

$$d^2 \Pi = \sum_i \sum_j \frac{\partial^2 \Pi}{\partial x_i \partial x_j} dx_i dx_j \tag{6.6.11}$$

be negative definite. This condition, in turn, requires that

$$af_i^2 + bf_{ii} < 0 \quad (i = 1, 2), \tag{6.6.12}$$

and
$$b^2(f_{11}f_{22} - f_{12}^2) + ab(f_1^2 f_{22} - 2f_1 f_2 f_{12} + f_2^2 f_{11}) > 0. \tag{6.6.13}$$

Equations (6.6.7) are the jointly-derived input demand functions in implicit form; quantities demanded are functions of the two input prices and of the commodity price. We are chiefly interested in the comparative static responses of quantities demanded and the commodity price to a change in the parametrically given input price. Without loss of generality, our attention may be confined to a change in p_1, the market price of the first input.

Differentiating equations (6.6.7) and (6.6.8) partially with respect to p_1, the following system of equations is obtained:

$$MV = K, \tag{6.6.14}$$

where
$$[M] = \begin{bmatrix} -h' & f_1 & f_2 \\ ah'f_1 & bf_{11} & bf_{12} \\ ah'f_2 & bf_{12} & bf_{22} \end{bmatrix}, \tag{6.6.15}$$

$$V = \begin{bmatrix} \dfrac{\partial p}{\partial p_1} \\[2mm] \dfrac{\partial x_1}{\partial p_1} \\[2mm] \dfrac{\partial x_2}{\partial p_1} \end{bmatrix}, \tag{6.6.16}$$

$$K = \begin{bmatrix} 0 \\ 1 \\ 0 \end{bmatrix}. \tag{6.6.17}$$

Equations (6.6.14) may be solved by Cramer's Rule to obtain explicit expressions for the variables in V. The denominator in each of these equations is the determinant of $[M]$, specifically

$$M = -h'[b^2(f_{11}f_{22} - f_{12}^2) + ab(f_1^2 f_{22} - 2f_1 f_2 f_{12} + f_2^2 f_{11})]. \tag{6.6.18}$$

The expression in brackets on the right-hand side of equation (6.6.18) is exactly inequality (6.6.13), which is positive. Hence, in light of (6.6.4),

$$M > 0. \tag{6.6.19}$$

Consequently, the sign of each partial derivative in the solution of equations (6.6.14) will depend upon the sign of the numerator.

146

6.6 INPUT DEMAND FUNCTIONS

Commodity price. First, it is easily shown that the commodity price must vary directly with the factor price. Solving equations (6.6.14), one obtains

$$\frac{\partial p}{\partial p_1} = -\frac{\begin{vmatrix} f_1 & f_2 \\ bf_{12} & bf_{22} \end{vmatrix}}{M}. \tag{6.6.20}$$

Observe that
$$b = \frac{h}{h'}+p = \frac{1}{h'}(q+ph') = \frac{q}{h'}(1-\eta), \tag{6.6.21}$$

where
$$\eta = -\frac{p}{q}h' \tag{6.6.22}$$

is the elasticity of commodity demand. Since marginal revenue is

$$\frac{dph(p)}{dq} = p\left(1-\frac{1}{\eta}\right), \tag{6.6.23}$$

$\eta \geqslant 1$, and it is strictly greater than one unless marginal cost is constant or zero.

Using equation (6.6.21), the numerator of equation (6.6.20) may be written

$$\text{sign}\left(\frac{\partial p}{\partial p_1}\right) = \text{sign}\left[\frac{q}{h'}(1-\eta)(f_2 f_{12}-f_1 f_{22})\right]. \tag{6.6.24}$$

From equations (6.6.2) and (6.6.23), the expression in brackets on the right-hand side of equation (6.6.24) must be positive. Hence

$$\frac{\partial p}{\partial p_1} > 0, \tag{6.6.25}$$

which may be stated as the following

Relation: in a two-factor model of a profit-maximizing firm, commodity price varies directly with the price of either input.

Effect upon quantity demanded. Next, consider the effect of a change in factor price upon its own quantity demanded:

$$\frac{\partial x_1}{\partial p_1} = \frac{\begin{vmatrix} -h' & f_2 \\ ah'f_2 & bf_{22} \end{vmatrix}}{M}. \tag{6.6.26}$$

Expanding the numerator, one obtains

$$\text{sign}\left(\frac{\partial x_1}{\partial p_1}\right) = \text{sign}\left[-h'(af_2^2+bf_{22})\right]. \tag{6.6.27}$$

From inequalities (6.6.4) and (6.6.12), this expression must be negative. Hence

$$\frac{\partial x_1}{\partial p_1} < 0, \tag{6.6.28}$$

which may be stated as the following

147

THEORY OF PRODUCTION

Relation: in a two-factor model of a profit-maximizing firm, the quantity of an input demanded varies inversely with its own price.

Relations between inputs. Finally, consider the effect of a change in the price of the first factor upon quantity demanded of the second:

$$\frac{\partial x_2}{\partial p_1} = -\frac{\begin{vmatrix} -h' & f_1 \\ ah'f_2 & bf_{12} \end{vmatrix}}{M}.$$ (6.6.29)

Expanding the numerator and using equation (6.6.22), one obtains

$$\text{sign}\left(\frac{\partial x_2}{\partial p_1}\right) = \text{sign}\left[ff_{12}(1-\eta)+ah'f_1f_2\right].$$ (6.6.30)

Since marginal revenue is negatively sloped, $a < 0$. Hence the rightmost term in equation (6.6.30) is positive (since $h' < 0$; $f_1 > 0, f_2 > 0$). As a consequence

$$\frac{\partial x_2}{\partial p_1} \gtrless 0 \quad \text{according as} \quad \frac{f_1f_2}{ff_{12}} \gtrless (\eta-1)\left[\frac{(h')^2}{2(h')^2-hh''}\right].$$ (6.6.31)

The results in expression (6.6.31) may be summarized in the following

Relation: in a two-factor model of a profit-maximizing firm, the quantity demanded of input two may either be augmented or diminished by a rise in the price of the first factor. The result depends primarily upon the extent of input substitutability and the elasticity of commodity demand. In particular, the greater the substitutability of inputs and the more inelastic the commodity demand over the range of price increases, the more likely is the usage of input two to expand.

The statement above is somewhat vague because of the precise meaning of (f_1f_2/ff_{12}), which was called the 'extent of input substitutability'. In general this expression does not measure the elasticity of substitution. However, it is unequivocally related to input substitutability; and the greater the ease with which one input may be substituted for the other, the more likely is the usage of one input to vary directly with the price of the other.

In a special case, condition (6.6.31) reduces to a very simple expression. If the production function is homogeneous of degree one, we know that the elasticity of substitution (σ) is

$$\sigma = \frac{f_1f_2}{ff_{12}}.$$ (6.6.32)

Furthermore, if the demand function is linear,

$$h'' = 0.$$ (6.6.33)

148

For this special set of circumstances, expression (6.6.31) becomes

$$\frac{\partial x_2}{\partial p_1} \gtrless 0 \quad \text{according as} \quad \sigma \gtrless \frac{(\eta - 1)}{2}. \tag{6.6.34}$$

Let us now summarize the results of the two-factor model: (a) commodity price must vary directly with input price; (b) the quantity demanded of the ith input varies inversely with its own price; (c) the quantity demanded of the jth input may vary either directly or inversely with the price of the ith input. In the last case, the principal determinants are the elasticity of commodity demand and the ease of input substitutability.

In the special case of linear commodity demand and linearly homogeneous production function, the situation is even clearer. For an increase in the price of one input to augment the demand for another, the elasticity of substitution must exceed one-half the elasticity of commodity demand minus one. Since the elasticity of substitution must be nonnegative in a two-factor model, this condition may easily prevail. A boundary case is represented by fixed-proportions technology. In this situation $\sigma = 0$, and the 'less than' sign must hold in expression (6.6.34). If the production function takes the Cobb–Douglas form, $\sigma = 1$; in this case the demand for input two is augmented so long as the elasticity of commodity demand is less than three. Finally, if the production function takes the CES form, σ is a constant whose value is generally believed to be less than unity (although it may, in fact, exceed unity). In that case the critical value of the elasticity of commodity demand becomes smaller. For example, if $\sigma = \frac{2}{3}$, η less than $2\frac{1}{3}$ would cause an increase in the demand for input two in response to an increase in the price of input one.

6.6.2 A multi-factor model of input demand

The multi-factor model of jointly-derived input demand functions is obtained by combining the demand function (6.6.4) with the production function

$$q = f(x_1, x_2, ..., x_n), \tag{6.6.35}$$

in which it is assumed that

$$f_i > 0, f_{ii} < 0 \quad (i = 1, 2, ..., n). \tag{6.6.36}$$

Given market-determined input prices $p_1, p_2, ..., p_n$, the firm selects input quantities $x_1, x_2, ..., x_n$ so as to maximize profit. The first-order conditions are given by

$$bf_i - p_i = 0 \quad (i = 1, 2, ..., n), \tag{6.6.37}$$

where a and b are defined by equations (6.6.9) and (6.6.10). The second-order conditions require negative definiteness of the quadratic form whose

149

determinant is

$$N = \begin{vmatrix} af_1^2+bf_{11} & af_1f_2+bf_{12} & \cdots & af_1f_n+bf_{1n} \\ af_1f_2+bf_{12} & af_2^2+bf_{22} & \cdots & af_2f_n+bf_{2n} \\ \vdots & \vdots & & \vdots \\ af_1f_n+bf_{1n} & af_2f_n+bf_{2n} & \cdots & af_n^2+bf_{nn} \end{vmatrix}. \quad (6.6.38)$$

Without loss of generality in the ensuing analysis, one may assume that there are an even number of inputs. Hence

$$N > 0. \quad (6.6.39)$$

Equations (6.6.37) are the jointly-derived input demand functions whose characteristics we wish to determine. Again it is assumed that the price of the first input changes, the prices of all other inputs remaining constant. The desired information is obtained by adding to equations (6.6.37) the condition
$$h(p) = f(x_1, x_2, \ldots, x_n), \quad (6.6.40)$$
and differentiating the system partially with respect to p_1:

$$\left. \begin{aligned} -h'\frac{\partial p}{\partial p_1} + \sum_j f_j \frac{\partial x_j}{\partial p_1} &= 0, \\ ah'f_1\frac{\partial p}{\partial p_1} + b\sum_j f_{1j}\frac{\partial x_j}{\partial p_1} &= 1, \\ ah'f_2\frac{\partial p}{\partial p_1} + b\sum_j f_{2j}\frac{\partial x_j}{\partial p_1} &= 0, \\ \cdots\cdots\cdots\cdots\cdots\cdots \\ ah'f_n\frac{\partial p}{\partial p_1} + b\sum_j f_{nj}\frac{\partial x_j}{\partial p_1} &= 0. \end{aligned} \right\} \quad (6.6.41)$$

The determinant of equations (6.6.41) is

$$M = \begin{vmatrix} -h' & f_1 & f_2 & \cdots & f_n \\ ah'f_1 & bf_{11} & bf_{12} & \cdots & bf_{1n} \\ ah'f_2 & bf_{12} & bf_{22} & \cdots & bf_{2n} \\ \vdots & \vdots & \vdots & & \vdots \\ ah'f_n & bf_{1n} & bf_{2n} & \cdots & bf_{nn} \end{vmatrix}. \quad (6.6.42)$$

The determinant above has the dimension $(n+1)\times(n+1)$. Number the columns $0, 1, \ldots, n$. Adding $(1/h')f_j$ times the elements of column 0 to the corresponding elements of column j ($j=1, 2, \ldots, n$), one obtains

$$M = \begin{vmatrix} -h' & 0 & 0 & \cdots & 0 \\ ah'f_1 & af_1^2+bf_{11} & af_1f_2+bf_{12} & \cdots & af_1f_n+bf_{1n} \\ ah'f_2 & af_1f_2+bf_{12} & af_2^2+bf_{22} & \cdots & af_2f_n+bf_{2n} \\ \vdots & \vdots & \vdots & & \vdots \\ ah'f_n & af_1f_n+bf_{1n} & af_2f_n+bf_{2n} & \cdots & af_n^2+bf_{nn} \end{vmatrix}. \quad (6.6.43)$$

Expanding the determinant by the first row, it is immediately seen that

$$M = -h'N, \tag{6.6.44}$$

so that

$$\text{sign } M = \text{sign } N > 0. \tag{6.6.45}$$

Solving equations (6.6.41) by Cramer's Rule for $\partial x_1/\partial p_1$, one obtains

$$\frac{\partial x_1}{\partial p_1} = \frac{M_{11}}{M}. \tag{6.6.46}$$

By using the column operations introduced above to prove that the sign of M is the same as the sign of N, one may also show that

$$\text{sign } M_{11} = \text{sign } N_{11}. \tag{6.6.47}$$

Furthermore, since N is negative definite,

$$\text{sign } N_{11} = -\text{sign } N; \tag{6.6.48}$$

thus the same sign relation must hold for M_{11} and M. As a consequence,

$$\frac{\partial x_1}{\partial p_1} < 0, \tag{6.6.49}$$

which may be stated as the following

Relation: in a multi-factor model of a profit-maximizing firm, the quantity of each input demanded must vary inversely with its own price.

To evaluate the remaining partial derivatives, another matrix must be introduced. As shown above, efficient operation requires that each firm, irrespective of its competitive situation, maximize output for any given level of cost. As proved above, this condition requires negative definiteness of the quadratic form whose determinant is

$$F = \begin{vmatrix} 0 & f_1 & f_2 & \cdots & f_n \\ f_1 & f_{11} & f_{12} & \cdots & f_{1n} \\ f_2 & f_{12} & f_{22} & \cdots & f_{2n} \\ \vdots & \vdots & \vdots & & \vdots \\ f_n & f_{1n} & f_{2n} & \cdots & f_{nn} \end{vmatrix}. \tag{6.6.50}$$

Since it has been assumed that n is even, negative definiteness implies

$$F > 0. \tag{6.6.51}$$

Solving equations (6.6.41) for $\partial x_j/\partial p_1$, and recalling that $M > 0$, one obtains

$$\frac{\partial x_j}{\partial p_1} \gtrless 0 \quad \text{according as} \quad M_{1j} \gtrless 0. \tag{6.6.52}$$

In the following, $M_i(F_i)$ represents the cofactor of the ith element in column 0, $M_{ij}(F_{ij})$ the cofactor of the i–j element in the body, and $M_{0ij}(F_{0ij})$ the cofactor of the i–j element in $M_0(F_0)$.

Expanding M_{1j}, one obtains

$$M_{1j} = (-h'b^{n-1}F_{01j} + ah'b^{n-2}F_{1j}). \qquad (6.6.53)$$

Since $F > 0$ by inequality (6.6.51), the sign of M_{1j} is unchanged when each term is divided by F. Factoring out $b^{n-2} > 0$ and recalling that $h' < 0$ and $a < 0$, inequality (6.6.52) may be written

$$\frac{\partial x_j}{\partial p_1} \gtrless 0 \quad \text{according as} \quad \frac{F_{1j}}{F} \gtrless \frac{bF_{01j}}{aF}. \qquad (6.6.54)$$

Finally, multiplying and dividing (F_{1j}/F) by $(\Sigma x_i f_i / x_1 x_j)$, expression (6.6.54) may be written

$$\frac{\partial x_j}{\partial p_1} \gtrless 0 \quad \text{according as} \quad \frac{x_1 x_j}{\Sigma x_i f_i} \sigma_{1j} \gtrless \frac{h(1-\eta)}{ah'} \frac{F_{01j}}{F}, \qquad (6.6.55)$$

where σ_{1j} is the partial elasticity of substitution of input 1 for input j.

The right-most term, F_{01j}/F, is negative;[1] hence the right-hand side is positive. Two conclusions may be stated in the following

Relations: If inputs 1 and j are complementary, $\sigma_{1j} < 0$. Thus quantity demanded of the jth input must vary inversely with the price of the first input. In the more usual case of competitive inputs, quantity demanded of the jth input may vary either directly or inversely with the price of input 1. The direct relation is more likely the greater is the partial elasticity of substitution and the smaller is the elasticity of commodity demand.

If the production function is homogeneous of degree one, it is easy to show that[2]

$$\frac{F_{01j}}{F} = -\frac{x_1 x_j}{q^2}. \qquad (6.6.56)$$

Furthermore, by Euler's theorem,

$$q \equiv \Sigma x_i f_i. \qquad (6.6.57)$$

Hence if the production function is homogeneous of degree one and commodity demand is linear, expression (6.6.55) reduces to

$$\frac{\partial x_j}{\partial p_1} \gtrless 0 \quad \text{according as} \quad \sigma_{1j} \gtrless \frac{\eta - 1}{2}, \qquad (6.6.58)$$

almost the same as the condition obtained in the two-factor model.

Finally,

$$\frac{\partial p}{\partial p_1} = \frac{M_1}{M} = \frac{b^{n-1}F_1}{M}, \qquad (6.6.59)$$

so

$$\frac{\partial p}{\partial p_1} \gtrless 0 \quad \text{according as} \quad F_1 \gtrless 0. \qquad (6.6.60)$$

[1] This statement is true when the production function is homogeneous of degree one and in most other cases as well. It may not hold in case there are inferior inputs (see below, chapter 9). [2] Allen [1938, pp. 481–2].

Generally, $F_1 > 0$ unless there are inferior inputs.[1] However, I can prove $F_1 > 0$ only for the case of linearly homogeneous production functions. By expansion

$$F_1 = -\sum_j f_j F_{01j}.$$

(6.6.61)

Using equation (6.6.56), equation (6.6.61) becomes

$$F_1 = \frac{x_1 F}{q^2} \sum_j x_j f_j = \frac{x_1 F}{h} > 0.$$

(6.6.62)

Hence we have established the following

Relation: If the production function is homogeneous of degree one, commodity price must vary directly with input price. It also varies directly in all cases in which there are no 'inferior' inputs.[2]

6.6.3 Conclusion

The results of this section would seem to complete the analysis of jointly-derived input demand functions begun by Allen, Mosak, and Samuelson (except for the special instance of inferior inputs). Under the most general manageable assumptions, the following results have been obtained: (*a*) the quantity demanded of any input must vary inversely with its own price; (*b*) the commodity price will always vary directly with input price if there are only two inputs, and it will vary directly in almost all other circumstances, and (*c*) the quantity demanded of input *j* may vary either directly or inversely with the price of input *i*. If the inputs are complementary, it must vary inversely. When the inputs are competitive, a direct relation is more likely the greater the (partial) elasticity of input substitution and the smaller the elasticity of commodity demand.

[1] See below, chapter 9.
[2] This proposition is proved in chapter 9.

7

THE THEORY OF COST WITH
FIXED INPUT PRICES

7.1. Introduction

The short-run theory of cost with fixed input prices is perhaps one of the best understood aspects of economic theory. It is correctly, and usually exhaustively, explored in even the most elementary texts. I have nothing new to add to the conventional accounts.[1] For that reason, the short-run theory of cost is entirely ignored.

The long-run theory of cost with fixed input prices is almost as well established as the short-run theory. A graphical analysis of the theory is accordingly omitted, and the mathematical analysis is as restricted as possible.

7.1.1 The expansion path and long-run cost

Assume that the firm under consideration produces a single output under conditions given by the following production function:

$$q = f(x_1, x_2, ..., x_n), \tag{7.1.1}$$

where the x_i's represent the quantities of inputs X_i. The assumptions concerning the production function, which were introduced in chapter 4, are retained throughout. Furthermore, by assumption the firm is a perfect competitor in each input market. Hence the prices of the inputs are given and fixed, i.e.

$$p_i = \bar{p}_i \quad (i = 1, 2, ..., n), \tag{7.1.2}$$

where $\bar{p}_i$ is a constant.

In the 'long run'[2] all inputs are variable. Hence the least cost of producing each level of output is achieved when factor proportions are adjusted so that[3]

$$\frac{f_1}{p_1} = \frac{f_2}{p_2} = ... = \frac{f_n}{p_n}. \tag{7.1.3}$$

---

[1] For example, see Ferguson [1966a].
[2] For the most part, the qualifying term 'long run' is omitted in the ensuing discussion. The reader should remember that all references to cost, unless otherwise explicitly stated, refer to long-run cost.
[3] See chapter 6.

These equations establish the expansion path in input space, a locus such as $OABD$ in figure 39. Mapping the expansion path from input space into cost-output space generates the total cost curve. For example, if r is the price of a unit of capital service, one point is given by Q_0, $[r(OK_1)+w(OL_1)]$; another is given by Q_1, $[r(OK_0)+w(OL_0)]$, etc. Thus the long-run total cost

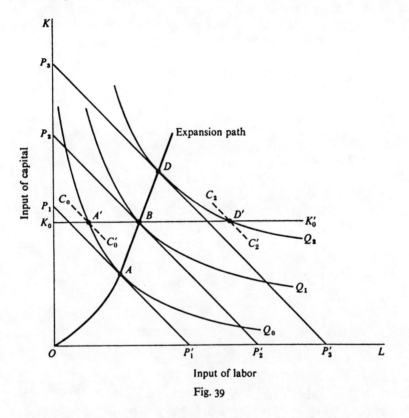

Fig. 39

curve is merely the output-space equivalent of the expansion path. The corresponding average and marginal cost curves are obtained in the usual way.

7.1.2 Viner revisited

Since the seminal paper by Viner,[1] the long-run average cost curve has been portrayed as the envelope of short-run average cost curves. It is indeed the envelope; but explaining why it is sometimes becomes tedious. Yet it may be done quite simply in the two-input case (see figures 39 and 40).

[1] Viner [1931].

155

In figure 39 the Q_i's are isoquants representing successively larger volumes of output, and the P_iP_i''s are isocost curves representing successively larger expenditures at constant input prices. The tangency conditions, equations (7.1.3), generate the expansion path $OABD$, which may be mapped into output space as the total cost curve. LAC in figure 40 is the corresponding long run average cost curve.

Now suppose for the moment that we are in a 'short-run' situation in which the quantity of capital is fixed at K_0K_0'. If production occurs at

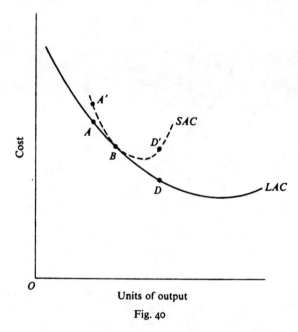

Fig. 40

point B, the short-run and long-run costs are identical. However, any short-run variation of output along K_0K_0' will give rise to higher costs than are entailed when input proportions are optimally adjusted (i.e. equations (7.1.3) hold only at point B on K_0K_0'). For example, if the Q_0-level of output is produced, the firm must operate at A' rather than A. Total cost is represented by $C_0C_0' > P_1P_1'$; hence short-run average cost exceeds long-run, or optimal adjustment, average cost. A similar statement applies to production at D' on Q_2, with short-run cost represented by C_2C_2'.

Since the isoquants Q_0 and Q_2 are arbitrary, the above analysis applies to all levels of output above and below Q_1. Hence the short-run average cost curve lies above the long-run average cost curve at every point other than B, and it is precisely tangent at B. By varying the 'size of plant', i.e. K_0K_0', the 'envelope theorem' is established.

156

7.2 Analysis of long-run cost

Equations (7.1.3) and (7.1.1) together provide n equations in the n input quantities $x_1, x_2, ..., x_n$ and output q, given the input prices. Hence these equations implicitly define input quantities as functions of output along the expansion path:[1]

$$x_i = x_i(q) \quad (i = 1, 2, ..., n). \tag{7.2.1}$$

Thus the production function may be written

$$q = f[x_1(q), x_2(q), ..., x_n(q)]. \tag{7.2.2}$$

Differentiating equation (7.2.2) with respect to q yields

$$\sum_{i=1}^{n} f_i \frac{dx_i}{dq} = 1. \tag{7.2.3}$$

7.2.1 Cost functions

The total cost of production is given by

$$c = \sum_{i=1}^{n} p_i x_i(q) = c(q). \tag{7.2.4}$$

Suppose from some initial point on the expansion path, the inputs are given the arbitrary increments $dx_1, dx_2, ..., dx_n$. From equation (7.2.4) cost expands (or contracts) by

$$dc = \sum_{i=1}^{n} p_i dx_i. \tag{7.2.5}$$

From equations (7.1.1), output expands (or contracts) by

$$dq = \sum_{i=1}^{n} f_i dx_i. \tag{7.2.6}$$

At this point it is convenient to introduce the following

Definition: Marginal cost is the first derivative of the total cost function with respect to output.

From equations (7.2.5) and (7.2.6), marginal cost may *always* be expressed as

$$\frac{dc}{dq} = \frac{\sum_{i=1}^{n} p_i dx_i}{\sum_{i=1}^{n} f_i dx_i}. \tag{7.2.7}$$

However, along the expansion path the expression for marginal cost is simpler. In full, the expansion path is defined by

$$\frac{f_i}{p_i} = \frac{1}{\lambda} \quad (i = 1, 2, ..., n), \tag{7.2.8}$$

[1] Throughout sections 7.2 and 7.3 all equations hold only along the expansion path (or long-run cost curve). Hence this qualifying term is usually omitted.

where λ is the Lagrange multiplier in the constrained cost minimization problem. Thus $p_i = \lambda f_i$ may be substituted in equation (7.2.5), obtaining

$$dc = \sum_{i=1}^{n} p_i dx_i = \lambda \sum_{i=1}^{n} f_i dx_i. \qquad (7.2.9)$$

Thus the ratio in equation (7.2.7) reduces to

$$\frac{dc}{dq} = c' = \lambda, \qquad (7.2.10)$$

a result previously established in chapter 4.

The same result may be obtained by taking the derivative of equation (7.2.4) straightforwardly:

$$\frac{dc}{dq} = c' = \sum_{i=1}^{n} p_i \frac{dx_i}{dq}. \qquad (7.2.11)$$

Substituting $\lambda f_i = p_i$ in equation (7.2.11) yields

$$c' = \lambda \sum_{i=1}^{n} f_i \frac{dx_i}{dq}. \qquad (7.2.12)$$

Substituting equation (7.2.3) in equation (7.2.12) immediately yields equation (7.2.10).

Further information about marginal cost may be obtained by substituting equation (7.2.8) in equation (7.2.10), obtaining

$$c' = \frac{p_i}{f_i} \quad (i = 1, 2, ..., n). \qquad (7.2.13)$$

The result in equation (7.2.13) may be expressed as the following

Relation: Along the expansion path, marginal cost is the ratio of an input's price to its marginal product. Thus on the expansion path, marginal cost is the same irrespective of the input for which it is calculated.

At present there is less to say about average cost, which is merely introduced by the following

Definition: Average cost is the cost per unit of output, or the ratio of total cost to total output. Thus average cost is given by

$$\frac{c}{q} = \frac{c(q)}{q} = \bar{c}(q). \qquad (7.2.14)$$

7.2.2 Elasticities of the cost functions

Let κ denote the elasticity of the total cost function. Thus by definition:

$$\kappa = \frac{dc}{dq}\frac{q}{c} = \frac{c'}{\bar{c}}. \qquad (7.2.15)$$

As customary with elasticities, the elasticity of total cost is the ratio of marginal cost to average cost.[1,2]

Next, the elasticity of average cost is given by

$$\gamma = \frac{d\bar{c}}{dq}\frac{q}{\bar{c}} = \frac{c'}{\bar{c}} - 1 = \kappa - 1. \qquad (7.2.16)$$

Thus the elasticity of average cost is equal to the elasticity of total cost minus one. This relation provides an interesting contrast between elasticities of demand and of cost. The elasticity of demand refers to the average revenue curve. The value of the elasticity of average revenue may be used, in comparison with unity, to infer the behavior of total revenue. The elasticity of cost has the opposite application. Specifically, the value of the elasticity of cost may be used, in comparison with unity, to infer the behavior of the average cost function (and thus the nature of returns to scale along the expansion path).

Finally, we may determine the elasticity of marginal cost. From equation (7.2.15),

$$c' = \bar{c}\kappa. \qquad (7.2.17)$$

From the conventional 'rule of elasticities',[3]

$$\text{El. } c' = \text{El. } \bar{c} + \text{El. } \kappa. \qquad (7.2.18)$$

Setting El. $c' \equiv \rho$ and El. $\kappa = \omega$, equation (7.2.18) may be written as

$$\rho = \kappa - 1 + \omega. \qquad (7.2.19)$$

7.2.3 Cost elasticities and the function coefficient

The cost elasticities may be expressed directly in terms of the function coefficient (ϵ); to do so shows the importance of the reciprocal of the elasticity of cost.[4] Use equations (7.2.8) in equation (7.2.4) to write the cost function as

$$c = \Sigma p_i x_i = \lambda \Sigma f_i x_i. \qquad (7.2.20)$$

From chapter 4 we have the following definition of the function coefficient:

$$\epsilon = \frac{\Sigma f_i x_i}{q}. \qquad (7.2.21)$$

---

[1] The elasticity can also be derived more precisely from equation (7.2.4):

$$\frac{dc}{dq}\frac{q}{c} = \frac{q}{c}\left[\sum_{i=1}^{n} p_i \frac{dx_i}{dq}\right] = \frac{q}{c}\left[\lambda \sum_{i=1}^{n} f_i \frac{dx_i}{dq}\right] = \lambda \frac{q}{c} = \frac{c'}{\bar{c}}.$$

[2] Moore [1929, p. 77] was presumably the first to introduce the elasticity of cost, which he described as '...the coefficient of relative cost of production'. Moore also described the reciprocal of the elasticity of cost as '...the coefficient of relative efficiency of organization'. The reciprocal of the elasticity of cost had previously been used by Johnson [1913, p. 508] and by Bowley [1924, p. 32]. Also see Allen [1938, pp. 260–2]. On the importance of the reciprocal of the elasticity of cost, see subsection 7.2.3 below.

[3] See Allen [1938, pp. 252–4].   [4] See footnote 2 above.

Using equation (7.2.21) and the definition $\lambda = c'$ in equation (7.2.20) yields

$$c = qc'\epsilon. \tag{7.2.22}$$

Thus total cost at any point on the expansion path is the product of quantity produced, marginal cost, and the function coefficient. Needless to say, equation (7.2.22) holds only for positive values of ϵ because the expansion path lies strictly within the economic region of production. i.e. where $\epsilon > 0$.

A similar relation holds for average cost. Dividing both sides of equation (7.2.22) by q yields

$$\bar{c} = c'\epsilon, \tag{7.2.23}$$

or average cost is the product of marginal cost and the function coefficient. Since c' and q are positive, equations (7.2.22) and (7.2.23) may at first seem surprising. Indeed, on the surface these equations seem to indicate that in a given factor point, the greater the instantaneous returns to scale, the greater are total and average cost! This interpretation is not valid, of course, because c, $\bar{c}$ and c' are themselves functions of ϵ.[1]

To get at the proper relation, divide both sides of equation (7.2.23) by c' and take the reciprocal, obtaining

$$\kappa = \frac{1}{\epsilon}. \tag{7.2.24}$$

Equation (7.2.24) provides the correct interpretation, which is summarized by the following

Relation: The smaller is the instantaneous measure of returns to scale, the greater is the proportional increase in cost relative to a given proportional increase in output.

In a regular production function (see chapter 4), ϵ varies inversely with output. For small q, $\epsilon > 1$; as q increases, $\epsilon = 1$ at a point and $\epsilon < 1$ thereafter. Thus equation (7.2.24) also leads to the following

Relation: Given a regular production law, cost first increases at a decreasing rate, passes through a point of inflection, and increases at an increasing rate thereafter.

This relation is illustrated in figure 41. Next, equations (7.2.16) and (7.2.24) may be used to show the relation between the elasticity of average cost and the function coefficient:

$$\gamma = \kappa - 1 = \frac{1}{\epsilon} - 1 = \frac{1-\epsilon}{\epsilon}. \tag{7.2.25}$$

Finally, the relation between the elasticity of marginal cost and the function

[1] Thus, for example, one *cannot* say $dc/d\epsilon = qc'$.

coefficient may be determined from equation (7.2.19):

$$\rho = \kappa - 1 + \omega = \frac{1-\epsilon}{\epsilon} - \theta_\epsilon \qquad (7.2.26)$$

where θ_ϵ is the elasticity of the function coefficient.[1]

Let us now discuss the implications of equations (7.2.25) and (7.2.26), which are illustrated in figure 42. For the moment, assume that the production function follows a regular production law. When $\epsilon > 1$, $\gamma < 0$. Therefore, a given proportional increase in output causes a smaller

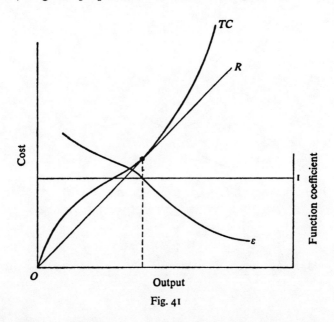

Fig. 41

proportional *reduction* in average cost.[2] On the other hand, when $\epsilon < 1$, $\gamma > 0$. In this case, a given proportional increase in output causes an increase in average cost that is less than proportional or greater than proportional according as $\epsilon \gtrless \frac{1}{2}$. It is obvious from equation (7.2.25) that $\gamma = 0$ when $\epsilon = 1$. Thus there is an extreme point on the average cost curve corresponding to $\epsilon = 1$; in light of the analysis just above, the extremum must be a minimum.

[1] This follows from the 'rule of elasticity', as follows:
$$\text{El. } \kappa = \text{El. } 1 - \text{El. } \epsilon = -\text{El. } \epsilon \quad \text{or} \quad \omega = -\theta_\epsilon.$$

[2] When the elasticity of average cost is negative, it must be inelastically negative, i.e. when $\epsilon > 1$,
$$-\left|\frac{\epsilon-1}{\epsilon}\right| < 1.$$

Turn now to equation (7.2.26). The magnitude of θ_ϵ cannot be determined without specifying a particular production function. However it is known that in a general production law, $d\epsilon/dq < 0$. Hence $\theta_\epsilon < 0$, and $-\theta_\epsilon > 0$ over the relevant range of production. On the other hand, if the production function is homogeneous (see chapter 5), ϵ is a constant and $\theta_\epsilon \equiv 0$.

When $\epsilon > 1$, the elasticity of marginal cost may be negative. This occurs if returns to scale are very strong, so that the negative term $(1-\epsilon)/\epsilon$ dominates the necessarily positive term $-\theta_\epsilon$. However, it must become positive

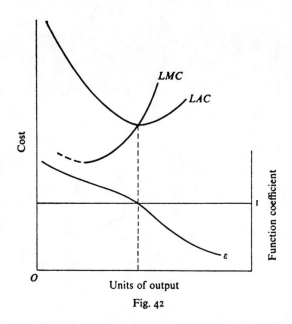

Fig. 42

at some output rate while $\epsilon > 1$ because of the influence of $-\theta_\epsilon > 0$, and *a fortiori* it is positive for $\epsilon < 1$. Further, a comparison of equations (7.2.25) and (7.2.26) reveals that the marginal cost function must always be more elastic than the average cost function, given a regular production law. When $\epsilon = 1$, θ_ϵ is instantaneously zero, marginal cost and average cost are therefore equal.

These results for a regular production law may be summarized as the following

Relations: (i) Average cost diminishes when $\epsilon > 1$, attains its minimum when $\epsilon = 1$, and increases when $\epsilon < 1$; (ii) when the elasticity of average cost is negative, it must be inelastically negative; however it is positively elastic for $\epsilon < \frac{1}{2}$; (iii) marginal cost may have a declining range; however it must turn up before $\epsilon = 1$; (iv) at $\epsilon = 1$, marginal cost equals average cost; and (v) the marginal cost function is always more elastic than the average cost function unless the production function is homogeneous.

As shown in chapter 5, ϵ is a constant when the production function is homogeneous. Indeed, with a homogeneous production function, there exist increasing, constant, or decreasing returns to scale according as $\epsilon \gtreqless 1$. From equations (7.2.25) and (7.2.26), it is apparent that the elasticities of average and marginal cost are identical when ϵ is a constant (i.e. $\theta_\epsilon \equiv 0$). Further, the curves are negatively or positively sloped according as $\epsilon \gtrless 1$; they are horizontal when $\epsilon = 1$.

Let us summarize these results as the following

Relations: (i) when the production function is homogeneous, the elasticities of marginal and average cost are the same; (ii) the functions are negatively or positively sloped according as there are increasing or decreasing returns to scale; (iii) if the production function is homogeneous of degree one, there are constant returns to scale; in this case, average and marginal cost are identical *and* constant.[1]

7.3 Two examples of cost functions

From the discussion above it is apparent that with fixed input prices, total cost is a function of output and of nothing else. But output is determined by the production function. Thus if a specific production function is known, the associated cost function can always be derived. As will be obvious, direct derivation of cost functions can become a messy business even for very simple production functions.

7.3.1 The Cobb–Douglas function

In this subsection the cost function associated with a Cobb–Douglas production function is derived and examined in detail. In the following subsection, the CES function is treated in a cursory manner.

Write the Cobb–Douglas function in the form

$$q = ax_1^\alpha x_2^\beta \quad (0 < a, \alpha, \beta). \tag{7.3.1}$$

Let p_1 and p_2 represent the constant unit prices of the inputs X_1 and X_2. From equation (7.3.1) equality between the marginal rate of technical substitution and the input-price ratio, the condition defining the expansion path, requires that

$$\frac{p_1}{p_2} = \frac{\alpha x_2}{\beta x_1}. \tag{7.3.2}$$

Next, take the logarithms of equations (7.3.1) and (7.3.2) and write them as

[1] On this score, see Samuelson [1947, pp. 78–80].

163

a pair of simultaneous equations:

$$\left.\begin{array}{l} \alpha \ln x_1 + \beta \ln x_2 = \ln q - \ln a, \\ -\ln x_1 + \ln x_2 = \ln \beta - \ln \alpha + \ln p_1 - \ln p_2. \end{array}\right\} \qquad (7.3.3)$$

Solving equations (7.3.3) simultaneously for x_1 and x_2 yields

$$\left.\begin{array}{l} x_1^* = (a^{-1}q\beta^{-\beta}\alpha^{\beta}p_1^{-\beta}p_2^{\beta})^{1/(\alpha+\beta)}, \\ x_2^* = (a^{-1}q\beta^{\alpha}\alpha^{-\alpha}p_1^{\alpha}p_2^{-\alpha})^{1/(\alpha+\beta)}, \end{array}\right\} \qquad (7.3.4)$$

where x_1^* and x_2^* are the quantities of the inputs required to produce q units of output at the cost-minimizing input ratio (given by equation (7.3.2)).

The cost of producing q units of output is

$$c = p_1 x_1^* + p_2 x_2^*. \qquad (7.3.5)$$

Substituting equations (7.3.4) in equation (7.3.5) yields

$$c = p_2 \left[\left(\frac{\beta p_1}{\alpha p_2}\right)^{\alpha} \frac{q}{a} \right]^{1/(\alpha+\beta)} + p_1 \left[\left(\frac{\beta p_1}{\alpha p_2}\right)^{-\beta} \frac{q}{a} \right]^{1/(\alpha+\beta)}. \qquad (7.3.6)$$

Now consider the following reduction of the rightmost term in equation (7.3.6):

$$p_1 \left[\left(\frac{\beta p_1}{\alpha p_2}\right)^{-\beta} \frac{q}{a} \right]^{1/(\alpha+\beta)} = \frac{p_1 \left[\left(\frac{\beta p_1}{\alpha p_2}\right)^{-\beta} \left(\frac{\beta p_1}{\alpha p_2}\right)^{\alpha+\beta} \frac{q}{a} \right]^{1/(\alpha+\beta)}}{\left[\left(\frac{\beta p_1}{\alpha p_2}\right)^{\alpha+\beta} \right]^{1/(\alpha+\beta)}}$$

$$= \frac{p_1 \left[\left(\frac{\beta p_1}{\alpha p_2}\right)^{\alpha} \frac{q}{a} \right]^{1/(\alpha+\beta)}}{\left(\frac{\beta p_1}{\alpha p_2}\right)} = \frac{\alpha p_2}{\beta} \left[\left(\frac{\beta p_1}{\alpha p_2}\right)^{\alpha} \frac{q}{a} \right]^{1/(\alpha+\beta)}. \qquad (7.3.7)$$

Substituting equation (7.3.7) in equation (7.3.6), one obtains

$$c = p_2 \left[\left(\frac{\beta p_1}{\alpha p_2}\right)^{\alpha} \frac{q}{a} \right]^{1/(\alpha+\beta)} + \frac{\alpha p_2}{\beta} \left[\left(\frac{\beta p_1}{\alpha p_2}\right)^{\alpha} \frac{q}{a} \right]^{1/(\alpha+\beta)}, \qquad (7.3.8)$$

or

$$c = p_2 \left(\frac{\alpha+\beta}{\beta}\right) \left[\left(\frac{\beta p_1}{\alpha p_2}\right)^{\alpha} \frac{q}{a} \right]^{1/(\alpha+\beta)}. \qquad (7.3.9)$$

Since the technological parameters a, α, and β are given, as well as the market parameters p_1 and p_2, equation (7.3.9) shows cost as a function of output alone.

Average and marginal cost may be obtained immediately from the cost function (equation (7.3.9)):

$$\bar{c} = \left[p_2 \left(\frac{\alpha+\beta}{\beta}\right) \left(\frac{\beta p_1}{\alpha p_2}\right)^{\frac{\alpha}{\alpha+\beta}} \left(\frac{1}{a}\right)^{\frac{1}{\alpha+\beta}} q^{\frac{1-\alpha-\beta}{\alpha+\beta}} \right] \qquad (7.3.10)$$

and

$$c' = \frac{1}{\alpha+\beta}\left[p_2\left(\frac{\alpha+\beta}{\beta}\right)\left(\frac{\beta p_1}{\alpha p_2}\right)^{\frac{\alpha}{\alpha+\beta}}\left(\frac{1}{a}\right)^{\frac{1}{\alpha+\beta}}q^{\frac{1-\alpha-\beta}{\alpha+\beta}}\right]. \qquad (7.3.11)$$

Similarly, the elasticity of cost is

$$\kappa = \frac{c'}{\bar{c}} = \frac{1}{\alpha+\beta}, \qquad (7.3.12)$$

the exponent of q in the cost function. In like manner, the elasticity of average cost is

$$\gamma = \kappa - 1 = \frac{1-\alpha-\beta}{\alpha+\beta}, \qquad (7.3.13)$$

which is also the exponent of q in the average cost function. Finally, since $\theta_c \equiv 0$ for homogeneous functions (i.e., the function coefficient is a constant), the elasticity of marginal cost is

$$\rho = \gamma = \kappa - 1 = \frac{1-\alpha-\beta}{\alpha+\beta}. \qquad (7.3.14)$$

One readily sees from equations (7.3.12)–(7.3.14) that the degree of homogeneity is of the utmost importance. This fact may also be seen directly from the average and marginal cost functions and their derivatives. For convenience, let

$$b = p_2\left(\frac{\alpha+\beta}{\beta}\right)\left(\frac{\beta p_1}{\alpha p_2}\right)^{\alpha/(\alpha+\beta)}\left(\frac{1}{\alpha}\right)^{1/(\alpha+\beta)} > 0. \qquad (7.3.15)$$

Then

$$c'' = \left[\frac{1-(\alpha+\beta)}{(\alpha+\beta)^2}\right]bq^{\frac{1-2(\alpha+\beta)}{\alpha+\beta}}, \qquad (7.3.16)$$

$$\bar{c}' = \left(\frac{1-(\alpha+\beta)}{\alpha+\beta}\right)bq^{\frac{1-2(\alpha+\beta)}{\alpha+\beta}}, \qquad (7.3.17)$$

$$c''' = \left(\frac{1-3(\alpha+\beta)+2(\alpha+\beta)^2}{(\alpha+\beta)^3}\right)bq^{\frac{1-3(\alpha+\beta)}{\alpha+\beta}}, \qquad (7.3.18)$$

and

$$\bar{c}'' = \left(\frac{1-3(\alpha+\beta)+2(\alpha+\beta)^2}{(\alpha+\beta)^2}\right)bq^{\frac{1-3(\alpha+\beta)}{\alpha+\beta}}. \qquad (7.3.19)$$

Further, let us note that

$$1-3(\alpha+\beta)+2(\alpha+\beta)^2\begin{cases} > 0 & \text{for} \quad (\alpha+\beta) > 1.0, \\ < 0 & \text{for} \quad 0.5 < (\alpha+\beta) < 1.0, \\ > 0 & \text{for} \quad (\alpha+\beta) < 0.5. \end{cases} \qquad (7.3.20)$$

The properties of the average and marginal cost curves may now be determined from equations (7.3.10)–(7.3.20). First, from equations (7.3.10) and (7.3.11), marginal cost is greater than or less than average cost according as there are decreasing or increasing returns to scale (i.e. according as $(\alpha+\beta) \lessgtr 1$). Next, from equations (7.3.16) and (7.3.17), the marginal and average cost curves rise or fall according as there are decreasing or increasing returns to scale. Finally, consider equations (7.3.18)–(7.3.19) and inequality (7.3.20). If increasing returns to scale prevail, both the average and marginal cost curves decline and are concave from above. If there are decreasing returns to scale such that

$$0 \cdot 5 < (\alpha+\beta) < 1,$$

both curves rise and are concave from below. On the other hand, if there are strongly decreasing returns to scale, i.e. $(\alpha+\beta) < 0 \cdot 5$, the curves not only rise but are concave from above.

The very special case of constant returns to scale has not yet been mentioned. If $(\alpha+\beta) = 1$, equation (7.3.9) reduces to

$$c = bq. \tag{7.3.21}$$

Thus cost is a linear function of output, as would be expected. Average and marginal costs are constant and equal, as shown by

$$c' = \bar{c} = b, \tag{7.3.22}$$

and
$$\kappa = 1, \quad \gamma = \rho = 0. \tag{7.3.23}$$

7.3.2 The CES function

The linearly homogeneous form of the CES function may be written

$$q = \gamma[\delta x_1^{-\rho}+(1-\delta)\, x_2^{-\rho}]^{-1/\rho}. \tag{7.3.24}$$

The cost function, in this case, is somewhat more difficult to derive. The expansion path is defined by

$$\left(\frac{x_1}{x_2}\right)^{-(1+\rho)} = \left(\frac{1-\delta}{\delta}\right)\frac{p_1}{p_2}. \tag{7.3.25}$$

Thus, using the notation above,

$$x_1^* = \left(\frac{1-\delta}{\delta}\right)^{-\sigma}\left(\frac{p_1}{p_2}\right)^{-\sigma} x_2^*. \tag{7.3.26}$$

Substitute equation (7.3.26) in equation (7.3.24) to obtain

$$q = \gamma\left[\delta\left(\frac{1-\delta}{\delta}\right)^{1-\sigma}\left(\frac{p_1}{p_2}\right)^{1-\sigma} x_2^{*\,(\sigma-1)/\sigma}+(1-\delta)\, x_2^{*\,(\sigma-1)/\sigma}\right]^{\sigma/(\sigma-1)}.$$

$$\tag{7.3.27}$$

Solving yields

$$x_2^* = \frac{q}{\gamma}\left[\delta\left(\frac{1-\delta}{\delta}\right)^{1-\sigma}\left(\frac{p_1}{p_2}\right)^{1-\sigma}+(1-\delta)\right]^{\sigma/(1-\sigma)}. \qquad (7.3.28)$$

Now substitute equation (7.3.28) in equation (7.3.26), obtaining

$$x_1^* = \frac{q}{\gamma}\left(\frac{1-\delta}{\delta}\right)^{-\sigma}\left(\frac{p_1}{p_2}\right)^{-\sigma}\left[\delta\left(\frac{1-\delta}{\delta}\right)^{1-\sigma}\left(\frac{p_1}{p_2}\right)^{1-\sigma}+(1-\delta)\right]^{\sigma/(1-\sigma)}.$$
$$(7.3.29)$$

Since
$$c = p_1 x_1^* + p_2 x_2^*, \qquad (7.3.30)$$
it follows that

$$c = \frac{q}{\gamma}\left[\left(\frac{1-\delta}{\delta}\right)^{-\sigma}p_1^{1-\sigma}p_2^{\sigma}+p_2\right]\left[\delta\left(\frac{1-\delta}{\delta}\right)^{1-\sigma}\left(\frac{p_1}{p_2}\right)^{1-\sigma}+(1-\delta)\right]^{\sigma/(1-\sigma)}.$$
$$(7.3.31)$$

The first term in brackets on the right-hand side of equation (7.3.31) may be written

$$\left[\left(\frac{1-\delta}{\delta}\right)^{-\sigma}p_1^{1-\sigma}p_2^{\sigma}+p_2\right] = p_1\left(\frac{1-\delta}{\delta}\right)^{-\sigma}\left(\frac{p_2}{p_1}\right)^{\sigma}+p_2. \qquad (7.3.32)$$

After some considerable manipulation, the second term in brackets on the right-hand side of equation (7.3.31) may be written

$$\left[\delta\left(\frac{1-\delta}{\delta}\right)^{1-\sigma}\left(\frac{p_1}{p_2}\right)^{1-\sigma}+(1-\delta)\right]^{\sigma/(1-\sigma)}$$
$$= \left(\frac{1-\delta}{p_2}\right)^{\sigma/(1-\sigma)}\left[p_1\left(\frac{1-\delta}{\delta}\right)^{-\sigma}\left(\frac{p_2}{p_1}\right)^{\sigma}+p_2\right]^{\sigma/(1-\sigma)}. \qquad (7.3.33)$$

Finally, substituting equations (7.3.32) and (7.3.33) in equation (7.3.31) yields the CES cost function:

$$c = \left(\frac{1-\delta}{p_2}\right)^{\sigma/(1-\sigma)}\left[p_1\left(\frac{\delta}{1-\delta}\right)^{\sigma}\left(\frac{p_2}{p_1}\right)^{\sigma}+p_2\right]^{1/(1-\sigma)}\frac{q}{\gamma}. \qquad (7.3.34)$$

As in the linearly homogeneous Cobb–Douglas case, cost is a linear function of output. Thus marginal and average cost are equal and the cost elasticities have the same value (given fixed input prices). The only essential difference between the Cobb–Douglas and CES cost functions lies in the appearance of the elasticity of substitution in the latter.

Since all terms in equation (7.3.34) are positive, one may easily show that

$$\frac{dc}{d\gamma} < 0, \qquad (7.3.35)$$

and
$$\frac{dc}{d\sigma} < 0. \qquad (7.3.36)$$

Inequality (7.3.35) implies that cost varies inversely with the 'efficiency' parameter, as should be expected. Inequality (7.3.36) shows that, all other things equal, the greater the elasticity of substitution, the lower the associated level of cost.[1]

[1] The result $dc/d\sigma < 0$ for static cost functions is closely related to the result that the rate of growth of output, given technical progress, is positively associated with the value of σ. See Ferguson [1965d].

The result $dc/d\gamma < 0$ is logical and virtually compelling. That is, the greater the efficiency of production, the lower the associated level of total cost. In the first draft of this chapter, I used the CES given by Walters [1963]. Professor John Moroney discovered that his function implied $dc/d\gamma > 0$ and insisted that my equation be changed. I am much indebted to him on this point. Direct derivation yielded the equation in the text. Further, limit analysis shows that the CES function reduces to the Cobb–Douglas cost function as $\sigma \to 1$. In Walters' function, as $\sigma \to 1$, $c \to q$. Thus the function in Walters' paper must be misprinted.

8

THE ECONOMIC THEORY OF COST AND
PRODUCTION WITH VARIABLE
INPUT PRICES

8.1 Introduction

The analysis in chapters 6 and 7 was simplified by assuming that input prices are fixed and given. It is now time to relax that assumption in order to generalize some of the results. One simplification is retained, however, for without it the analysis would become intolerably intricate. Specifically, we assume that the quantity supplied of each input is a function of its own price but *no other input price*. At first glance this might seem to be very restrictive because it ignores the effects of interdependence in input preference functions, as might be encountered in the supply of labor functions; upon examination, however, it turns out not to be so.

First, recall that every entrepreneur is a perfect competitor in markets for 'general' inputs; rising supply price[1] is a characteristic of inputs specialized to one or a very few uses. Next, consider two specialized inputs, X_i and X_j, used in the production of a commodity. Assuming that the price of X_i is independent of the price of X_j means that X_j is *not* a specialized input used in the production of X_i. While exceptions might be found, it hardly seems they would be numerous. Consequently, I believe this assumption does not place an important restriction upon the generality of the ensuing analysis.

8.1.1 Demand and supply functions

Let the firm in question produce its output according to the variable proportions production function

$$q = f(x_1, x_2, ..., x_n),\qquad(8.1.1)$$

where q is output and the x_i's are the quantities of the inputs used. Let us

---

[1] Throughout the discussion we ignore the possibility of falling supply price. That is, we assume that the production of specialized inputs is not subject to increasing returns to scale, coupled with fixed and/or falling supply prices of the inputs used to produce the specialized input in question.

further assume that the input supply functions, in inverse form, are given by

$$p_i = p_i(x_i) \quad (i=1, 2, ..., n), \tag{8.1.2}$$

where p_i is the price of the ith input. Following the assumption in footnote 1,

$$p_i' = \frac{dp_i}{dx_i} \geqq 0^1 \quad (i=1, 2, ..., n). \tag{8.1.3}$$

Finally, assume that the firm in question is either a perfect competitor, a monopolist, or a homogeneous oligopolist in the commodity market. Thus the output demand function may be written

$$q = h(p), \quad h'(p) \leqq 0, \tag{8.1.4}$$

where p is commodity price.

Following conventional definitions, the elasticity of input supply is

$$\theta_i = \frac{dx_i}{dp_i}\frac{p_i}{x_i} \geqq 0 \quad (i=1, 2, ..., n), \tag{8.1.5}$$

and the elasticity of commodity demand is

$$\eta = -\frac{p}{q}h' \geqq 1. \tag{8.1.6}$$

8.1.2 Cost and the marginal expense of input

The total cost associated with a particular input combination is

$$c = \sum_{i=1}^{n} x_i p_i(x_i). \tag{8.1.7}$$

Since input prices vary with input usage, explicit account must be taken of the cost effect of an expansion or contraction in the usage of an input. Let us first state the following

Definition: The marginal expense of input (MEI) is the addition to total cost attributable to the addition of one unit of the input to the production process.

According to this definition one obtains

$$\text{MEI}_i = \frac{\partial c}{\partial x_i} = p_i + x_i \frac{dp_i}{dx_i} \quad (i=1, 2, ..., n). \tag{8.1.8}$$

Using equation (8.1.5), the marginal expense of input may be expressed as

$$\text{MEI}_i = p_i\left(1 + \frac{x_i}{p_i}\frac{dp_i}{dx_i}\right) = p_i(1 + (1/\theta_i)) \quad (i=1, 2, ..., n). \tag{8.1.9}$$

[1] If a formal distinction were important, $p_i' > 0$ for specialized inputs and $p_i' = 0$ for general inputs. At the present level of abstraction, nothing is gained by dividing inputs into the two classes. Our analysis proceeds as though $p_i' > 0$. The reader may insert as many zeros as he desires.

8.1.3 Isocost curves

While graphical analysis is not used in this chapter, it would seem to be of some use to set out an exact specification of isocost curves when input prices are variable.[1]

If there are only two inputs, or if only two are allowed to vary, the cost function may be written

$$c = x_1 p_1 + x_2 p_2. \tag{8.1.10}$$

Hence the slope of an isocost curve is given implicitly by

$$dc = \left(p_1 + x_1 \frac{dp_1}{dx_1}\right) dx_1 + \left(p_2 + x_2 \frac{dp_2}{dx_2}\right) dx_2 = 0, \tag{8.1.11}$$

or, using equation (8.1.9),

$$\frac{dx_2}{dx_1} = -\frac{p_1(1 + (1/\theta_1))}{p_2(1 + (1/\theta_2))} < 0. \tag{8.1.12}$$

Since the marginal expenses of inputs are strictly positive, the isocost curve is negatively sloped. Since input prices vary, however, it is not a straight line. To investigate its curvature, one must examine the second derivative. Write

$$\frac{dx_2}{dx_1} = -\frac{p_1 + x_1 p_1'}{p_2 + x_2 p_2'}. \tag{8.1.13}$$

Thus

$$\frac{d^2x_2}{dx_1^2} = -\frac{p_2^2(1 + (1/\theta_2))^2 (2p_1' + x_1 p_1'') + p_1^2(1 + (1/\theta_1))^2 (2p_2' + x_2 p_2'')}{p_2^3(1 + (1/\theta_2))^3}. \tag{8.1.14}$$

The denominator in equation (8.1.14) is positive; hence the sign depends upon the numerator. Within the latter, the only terms that can possibly be negative are $(2p_1' + x_1 p_1'')$ and $(2p_2' + x_2 p_2'')$. Since $p_i' > 0$, the numerator can only be negative if one or both input supply functions are strongly concave from below ($p_i'' < 0$). This seems *a priori* doubtful; but it cannot be excluded as a possibility. Generally, however, the numerator is positive; and it is always positive if the supply functions are linear or approximately so. Thus for small changes in factor proportions,

$$\frac{d^2x_2}{dx_1^2} < 0. \tag{8.1.15}$$

Inequalities (8.1.12) and (8.1.15) together imply that isocost curves are downward sloping and concave from below (inequality (8.1.15) by itself is sufficient for concavity from below).

Relations: Isocost curves are always negatively sloped. When the supply prices of inputs are rising, the isocost curves are typically concave from below.

---

[1] To my knowledge, this has been done only by Frisch [1965, pp. 199–201].

8.2. Economic theory of production

When input prices are variable, the expansion-path ratios derived in chapter 6 no longer describe a path of economic efficiency. There are, as we shall see, marginal equivalences that define an expansion path; the only real difference lies in the fact that rising input supply prices must be taken into account.

In this section the marginal equivalences defining the expansion path are derived, first by minimizing the cost of producing a given level of out-

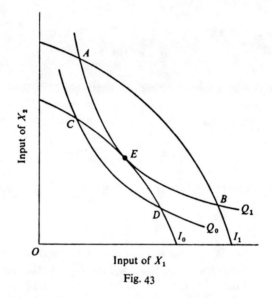

Fig. 43

put, and then by maximizing the output obtainable from a given expenditure upon resources. Both processes are illustrated in figure 43. The isocost-isoquant tangency solution is apparent in the figure, and there is no further discussion of it.

8.2.1 Minimizing the cost of producing a given output

As in chapter 6, the problem of economic efficiency reduces to an exercise in the Lagrange technique for constrained extrema. To minimize cost, equation (8.1.7), subject to a given output, equation (8.1.1), first construct the Lagrange expression

$$L \equiv \sum_{i=1}^{n} x_i p_i(x_i) - \lambda[f(x_1, x_2, ..., x_n) - \bar{q}], \qquad (8.2.1)$$

172

where λ is the undetermined multiplier. The first-order conditions are obtained by setting the first partial derivatives equal to zero:

$$\left.\begin{aligned}\frac{\partial L}{\partial x_i} &= p_i + x_i p_i' - \lambda f_i = 0 \quad (i = 1, 2, \ldots, n), \\ \frac{\partial L}{\partial \lambda} &= f(x_1, x_2, \ldots, x_n) - \bar{q} = 0.\end{aligned}\right\} \tag{8.2.2}$$

The set (8.2.2) contains $(n+1)$ equations that may be solved for the $(n+1)$ unknowns $(x_1, x_2, \ldots, x_n, \lambda)$ in terms of the given input supply functions $p_i(x_i)$ and the parametrically given output. The system may also be solved implicitly to obtain the constant-output demand for input functions:

$$x_i = f^i(p_1, p_2, \ldots, p_n | \bar{q}) \quad (i = 1, 2, \ldots, n). \tag{8.2.3}$$

The first n equations in the set (8.2.2) may be solved so as to state the marginal equivalences in two different ways. First, write the equations

$$\frac{f_1}{p_1(1 + (1/\theta_1))} = \frac{f_2}{p_2(1 + (1/\theta_2))} = \cdots = \frac{f_n}{p_n(1 + (1/\theta_n))} = \frac{1}{\lambda}. \tag{8.2.4}$$

The numerators are the marginal products, the denominators the marginal expenses of the inputs. These marginal equivalences establish the following

Relation: To minimize cost subject to a given output, inputs should be purchased in quantities such that the marginal product per dollar of additional expense is the same for all inputs. These ratios must also equal the reciprocal of marginal cost.

Next, eliminating the Lagrange multiplier from equations (8.2.2) yields the following set of equations:

$$\frac{f_i}{f_j} = \frac{p_i(1 + (1/\theta_i))}{p_j(1 + (1/\theta_j))} \quad (i, j = 1, 2, \ldots, n). \tag{8.2.5}$$

In this form, the first-order conditions establish the following

Relation: To minimize cost subject to a given output, inputs should be purchased in quantities such that the marginal rate of technical substitution between any two inputs equals the incremental input-cost ratio. This equivalence must hold for all pairs of inputs used.

8.2.2 Maximizing output for a given level of cost

The dual efficiency problem is formulated by constructing the following Lagrange function:

$$L^* \equiv f(x_1, x_2, \ldots, x_n) - \lambda^* \left(\sum_{i=1}^{n} x_i p_i(x_i) - \bar{c} \right). \tag{8.2.6}$$

Setting the first partial derivatives equal to zero, one obtains

$$\left.\begin{aligned} \frac{\partial L^*}{\partial x_i} &= f_i - \lambda^*(p_i + x_i p_i') = 0 \quad (i = 1, 2, ..., n), \\ \frac{\partial L^*}{\partial \lambda^*} &= \sum_{i=1}^{n} x_i p_i(x_i) - \bar{c} = 0. \end{aligned}\right\} \quad (8.2.7)$$

The set (8.2.7) provides $(n+1)$ equations that may be solved for the $(n+1)$ unknowns $(x_1, x_2, ..., x_n, \lambda^*)$ in terms of the given input supply functions and the parametrically fixed cost $\bar{c}$. An implicit solution defines the constant-cost demand functions for the inputs.

As in subsection 8.2.1, the first-order conditions may be stated in either of the following ways:

$$\frac{f_1}{p_1(1+(1/\theta_1))} = \frac{f_2}{p_2(1(1/\theta_2))} = \cdots = \frac{f_n}{p_n(1+(1/\theta_n))} = \lambda^*, \quad (8.2.8)$$

or

$$\frac{f_i}{f_j} = \frac{p_i(1+(1/\theta_i))}{p_j(1+(1/\theta_j))} \quad (i, j = 1, 2, ..., n). \quad (8.2.9)$$

Equations (8.2.8) are exactly the same as equations (8.2.4), and equations (8.2.9) are the same as equations (8.2.5). Thus, as in chapter 6, we obtain the following

Duality Theorem: The marginal equivalences defining economic efficiency are the same whether obtained by minimizing the cost of producing a stipulated output or by maximizing the output obtainable from a given expenditure upon resources.

8.2.3 The expansion path

As in chapter 6, either set of marginal equivalences establishes the following

Expansion-path relation: The expansion path is defined either by equations (8.2.4) or (8.2.5). The expansion path is thus the locus along which the marginal rate of technical substitution is equal to the incremental input-cost ratio.

The expansion path for variable input prices differs in one significant respect from the expansion path corresponding to fixed input prices. Specifically, when input prices are variable, the expansion path is *not* an isocline. In all other respects, the expansion paths are identical.

8.2.4 The second-order conditions[1]

Since constrained cost minimization leads to the same conditions as constrained output maximization, the second-order conditions may be

---

[1] This section does not contain an analysis of comparative static changes as did the corresponding section in chapter 6. Generally, if $p_i'' = 0$ and $p_i' > 0$ for all i, the comparative static relations proved in chapter 6 hold. On the other hand, if either

examined for the latter situation only. A proper constrained maximum requires that the latent roots of the quadratic form

$$d^2f = \sum_i \sum_j f_{ij} dx_i dx_j \qquad (8.2.10)$$

be negative subject to $\qquad df = \sum_i f_i dx_i = 0, \qquad (8.2.11)$

not all $dx_i = 0$. This is equivalent to requiring that the successive nested principal minors of the following Hessian determinant alternate in sign, the sign of the first principal minor being positive:

$$D = \begin{vmatrix} 0 & (p_1+x_1p_1') & (p_2+x_2p_2') & \cdots & (p_n+x_np_n') \\ (p_1+x_1p_1') & f_{11} & f_{12} & \cdots & f_{1n} \\ (p_2+x_2p_2') & f_{12} & f_{22} & \cdots & f_{2n} \\ \vdots & \vdots & \vdots & & \vdots \\ (p_n+x_np_n') & f_{1n} & f_{2n} & \cdots & f_{nn} \end{vmatrix} . \qquad (8.2.12)$$

Generally, the second-order conditions impose certain convexity properties upon the production function. But since input prices are variable, the way in which they vary helps to determine the required convexity. To see this, let us examine the first principal minor, which may be written as

$$(p_j+x_jp_j')^2 f_{ii} - 2(p_i+x_ip_i')(p_j+x_jp_j') f_{ij} + (p_i+x_ip_i')^2 f_{jj} < 0. \qquad (8.2.13)$$

By equations (8.2.7),

$$p_i+x_ip_i' = \frac{1}{\lambda^*} f_i \quad (i=1, 2, ..., n). \qquad (8.2.14)$$

Hence inequality (8.2.13) clearly refers to the curvature of the isoquants in the X_i–X_j plane. However, the way in which input prices vary must be taken into account.

In the 'normal' case of rising input supply prices, considered in subsection 8.1.3, the concavity requirement is weak indeed. That is, if the isocost curves are concave from below, the isoquants only have to be 'less' concave than the isocost curves. Thus it is possible to obtain an equilibrium with an *increasing* marginal rate of technical substitution if the firm is an imperfect competitor in the resource markets. As shown previously, however, the marginal rate of technical substitution must be strictly decreasing for non-specialized employment equilibrium for a purely

fails to hold, the comparative static relations do not hold, with one exception. Consider the ith input and suppose $p_i'' > 0$. Then the constant-output demand function for X_i is negatively sloped if all $p_j' > 0$ for $j \neq i$. If some $p_j' < 0$, however, the quantity demanded of the ith input may not vary inversely with its price (along an isoquant). From the equilibrium pictured in figure 44, a decline in the price of X_2 would, over a certain range, reduce the usage of both inputs. The mathematical analysis upon which these statements are based is not reproduced here because of the essentially negative results obtained.

competitive firm. However, if one or both input supply functions is upward sloping but strongly concave downward (cf. equation (8.1.14)), the isocost curves may be concave from above. In this unlikely case, inequality (8.2.13) imposes a very strict concavity requirement: not only must the isoquants be concave from above, they must also be 'more' concave than the isocost curves. Economically, this means that the marginal rate of technical substitution must be diminishing more rapidly than the marginal expenses of input in any employment direction.

In the unlikely case of falling supply price, it is important to note that the expansion path and the 'ridge lines' defining the economic region of production are not isoclines. Consider a situation in which the supply function of the ith input is negatively sloped and the negative p_i' is so large in absolute amount that

$$p_i + x_i p_i' < 0. \tag{8.2.15}$$

Since marginal cost (λ^*) is positive, equations (8.2.7) imply that

$$f_i < 0. \tag{8.2.16}$$

While unlikely, this result is plausible. Inequalities (8.2.15) and (8.2.16) imply that if the price of an input declines quite rapidly when input usage expands, the quantity employed may be so great as to result in a negative marginal product. This is as it should be. It simply means that the reduction in unit cost attributable to the reduction in input price more than offsets the increase in unit cost attributable to the reduction in output. So long as the cost-reducing element dominates, usage of the input will be expanded, even though production occurs in the region of negative marginal returns (from the standpoint of the input in question).

Graphically, this special case would require the type of isocost-isoquant tangency shown in figure 44. The definitions of the economic region and (perhaps) of the expansion path would have to be modified accordingly.

8.3 The theory of cost

As in chapter 7, our attention is restricted to the long-run theory of cost. As we shall see, it does not differ materially from the long-run theory of cost with fixed input prices.

Equations (8.2.5), which define the expansion path, also implicitly define input usage as a function of output. We may accordingly write

$$x_i = x_i(q) \quad (i = 1, 2, \ldots, n). \tag{8.3.1}$$

The production function may thus be expressed as

$$q = f(x_1(q), x_2(q), \ldots, x_n(q)). \tag{8.3.2}$$

Taking the total differential, one obtains

$$\sum_{i=1}^{n} f_i \frac{dx_i}{dq} = 1. \qquad (8.3.3)$$

Hence the aggregation relation introduced in chapter 7 still holds.

8.3.1 Cost functions and their elasticities

Using equations (8.1.7) and (8.3.1), total cost may be expressed as a function of output:

$$c = \sum_{i=1}^{n} x_i p_i(x_i) = \sum_{i=1}^{n} x_i(q) p_i[x_i(q)] = c(q). \qquad (8.3.4)$$

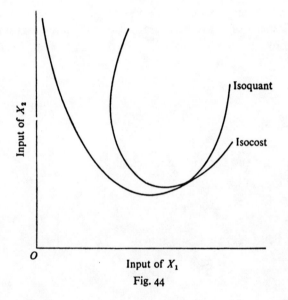

Fig. 44

Average cost is

$$\bar{c} = \frac{c(q)}{q}, \qquad (8.3.5)$$

and marginal cost is

$$c' = \frac{dc(q)}{dq} = \sum_{i=1}^{n} (p_i + x_i p_i') \frac{dx_i}{dq} = \sum_{i=1}^{n} p_i \left(1 + \frac{1}{\theta_i}\right) \frac{dx_i}{dq}. \qquad (8.3.6)$$

From equations (8.2.2),

$$p_i + x_i p_i' = \lambda f_i \quad (i = 1, 2, \ldots, n). \qquad (8.3.7)$$

Substituting equations (8.3.7) into equation (8.3.6) and using equation (8.3.3), one obtains

$$c' = \sum_{i=1}^{n} p_i \left(1 + \frac{1}{\theta_i}\right) \frac{dx_i}{dq} = \lambda \sum_{i=1}^{n} f_i \left(\frac{dx_i}{dq}\right) = \lambda. \qquad (8.3.8)$$

177

Equation (8.3.8) establishes the previously stated, but unproved, proposition that the Lagrange multiplier associated with the constrained cost minimization problem is marginal cost.

Substituting equation (8.3.8) in any equation in the set (8.2.2) allows one to write marginal cost as

$$c' = \frac{p_i(1+(1/\theta_i))}{f_i} \quad (i=1, 2, ..., n). \tag{8.3.9}$$

Thus the common marginal cost equals the common ratio between incremental input cost and marginal product. Stated otherwise, at the margin all inputs are equally dear since all marginal products are proportional to their respective marginal expenses of input.

The elasticity formulae are entirely unaffected by variable input prices. Hence the elasticity of total cost, average cost, and marginal cost are given, respectively, by

$$\kappa = \frac{c'}{\bar{c}}, \tag{8.3.10}$$

$$\gamma = \kappa - 1 \tag{8.3.11}$$

and
$$\rho = \kappa - 1 - \omega, \tag{8.3.12}$$
where ω is the elasticity of κ.

8.3.2 Cost and the function coefficient

Rewrite equations (8.2.4) as

$$\lambda f_i = p_i\left(1+\frac{1}{\theta_i}\right) \quad (i=1, 2, ..., n). \tag{8.3.13}$$

Multiply on both sides by x_i and sum over i, obtaining

$$\lambda \sum_{i=1}^{n} f_i x_i = \sum_{i=1}^{n} x_i p_i\left(1+\frac{1}{\theta_i}\right). \tag{8.3.14}$$

By definition, the function coefficient ϵ is

$$\epsilon = \frac{\sum_{i=1}^{n} f_i x_i}{q}. \tag{8.3.15}$$

Substituting equation (8.3.15) into equation (8.3.14), one finds that

$$\epsilon q \lambda = \sum_{i=1}^{n} p_i x_i + \sum_{i=1}^{n} (p_i x_i)\frac{1}{\theta_i}. \tag{8.3.16}$$

Let us now define θ as the weighted average of the input supply elasticities, i.e.

$$\theta = \frac{\Sigma p_i x_i \theta_i}{\Sigma p_i x_i}. \tag{8.3.17}$$

8.3 THEORY OF COST

Using definition (8.3.17) in quation (8.3.16) leads to

$$\epsilon q \lambda = \Sigma p_i x_i + \frac{1}{\theta} \Sigma p_i x_i = c\left(1 + \frac{1}{\theta}\right), \qquad (8.3.18)$$

by equation (8.1.7). Substituting equation (8.3.8) in equation (8.3.18), the latter may be solved for total and average cost in terms of the function coefficient

$$c = \frac{\epsilon c' q}{(1 + (1/\theta))}, \qquad (8.3.19)$$

and

$$\bar{c} = \frac{\epsilon c'}{(1 + (1/\theta))}. \qquad (8.3.20)$$

It should be clear that $\dfrac{\epsilon}{1 + (1/\theta)}$ plays the same role in the theory of cost with variable input prices as ϵ plays in the theory of cost with fixed input prices. Define

$$\epsilon^* = \frac{\epsilon}{1 + (1/\theta)}, \qquad (8.3.21)$$

where ϵ^* is the function coefficient adjusted for the average elasticity of input supply. Using definition (8.3.21), equations (8.3.19) and (8.3.20) reduce to the analogues of the corresponding equations in chapter 7:

$$c = \epsilon^* c' q, \qquad (8.3.22)$$

and

$$\bar{c} = \epsilon^* c'. \qquad (8.3.23)$$

Hence the elasticities in terms of the adjusted function coefficient are

$$\kappa = \frac{1}{\epsilon^*}, \qquad (8.3.24)$$

$$\gamma = \kappa - 1 = \frac{1}{\epsilon^*} - 1 \qquad (8.3.25)$$

and

$$\rho = \kappa - 1 - \omega = \frac{1}{\epsilon^*} - 1 - \theta_{\epsilon^*}, \qquad (8.3.26)$$

where θ_{ϵ^*} is the elasticity of the adjusted function coefficient.

8.4 Profit maximization and the derived input demand functions

In chapter 6 the input demand functions of an individual firm were derived under the assumption that input prices are constant to the firm. For the most part, the results were quite clear. In this section the characteristics of input demand functions are analyzed without this assumption. As we shall see, the results are much less precise.

179

The framework of analysis is provided by the production function
(8.1.1), the input supply functions (8.1.2), and the commodity demand
function (8.1.4). However, in general, the slope conditions (8.1.3) are not
imposed upon the input supply functions. The definitions of the elasticity
of demand and the marginal expense of input, given in expressions (8.1.6)
and (8.1.8), respectively, are retained. So, too, is the cost function (8.1.7).

From the demand function (8.1.4), total revenue is

$$r = ph(p),\qquad(8.4.1)$$

from which it follows that marginal revenue is

$$\frac{dr}{dq} = h\frac{dp}{dq}+p = \left(\frac{h}{h'}+p\right).\qquad(8.4.2)$$

To simplify future notation, let

$$\left(\frac{h}{h'}+p\right) = b \geqq 0.\,^{1}\qquad(8.4.3)$$

The slope of the marginal revenue curve is given by

$$\frac{d^2r}{dq^2} = \frac{h'^2-hh''}{h'^2}\frac{dp}{dq}+\frac{dp}{dq} = \frac{h'^2-hh''}{h'^3}+\frac{1}{h'}.\qquad(8.4.4)$$

Again, to simplify notation, let

$$\frac{h'^2-hh''}{h'^3}+\frac{1}{h'} = a \leqq 0.\,^{2}\qquad(8.4.5)$$

One final notational simplification is introduced. From definition (8.1.8)
the slope of the marginal expense of input curve is

$$\frac{d(\text{MEI}_i)}{dx_i} = \frac{\partial^2c}{\partial x_i^2} = 2p_i'+x_ip_i''\quad(i=1, 2, ..., n).\qquad(8.4.6)$$

Hence we define

$$2p_i'+x_ip_i'' = c_i \gtreqless 0\quad(i=1, 2, ..., n).\qquad(8.4.7)$$

8.4.1 Profit maximization

Assume that the economic objective of the firm is profit maximization:
inputs are adjusted until the profit-maximizing output is attained. From
equations (8.1.7) and (8.4.1), profit (π) may be written

$$\pi = r-c = ph(p)-\sum_{i=1}^{n} p_ix_i.\qquad(8.4.8)$$

[1] The 'equal to or greater than zero' condition follows from the assumption of profit
maximization. The inequality must hold unless cost is constant.
[2] The 'equal to or less than zero' condition follows from the assumption of profit
maximization. The inequality must hold unless total revenue is a constant, i.e. the
demand curve confronting the firm is a rectangular hyperbola.

The task is to maximize expression (8.4.8), bearing in mind that equilibrium also requires

$$h(p) = f(x_1, x_2, ..., x_n).\qquad(8.4.9)$$

Performing the maximization, one obtains the following first-order conditions:

$$\frac{\partial \pi}{\partial x_i} = bf_i - (p_i + x_i p_i') = 0 \quad (i = 1, 2, ..., n).\qquad(8.4.10)$$

Since b is marginal revenue, bf_i is marginal revenue product. The equilibrium conditions thus require that the marginal revenue product equal the marginal expense of input for each input used.

The second-order conditions require negative definiteness of the quadratic form whose associated determinant is

$$N = \begin{vmatrix} af_1^2 + bf_{11} - c_1 & af_1 f_2 + bf_{12} & \cdots & af_1 f_n + bf_{1n} \\ af_1 f_2 + bf_{12} & af_2^2 + bf_{22} - c_2 & \cdots & af_2 f_n + bf_{2n} \\ \vdots & \vdots & & \vdots \\ af_1 f_n + bf_{12} & af_2 f_n + bf_{2n} & \cdots & af_n^2 + bf_{nn} - c_n \end{vmatrix}.\qquad(8.4.11)$$

Thus
$$af_i^2 + bf_{ii} - c_i < 0,\qquad(8.4.12)$$

$$b^2(f_{ii}f_{jj} - f_{ij}^2) + ab(f_j^2 f_{ii} - 2f_i f_j f_{ij} + f_i^2 f_{jj}) - a(c_i f_j^2 + c_j f_i^2)$$
$$- b(c_i f_{jj} + c_j f_{ii}) + c_i c_j > 0,\qquad(8.4.13)$$

and generally
$$\frac{N_{ii}}{N} < 0,\qquad(8.4.14)$$

where N_{ii} is the cofactor of the element in the ith row and ith column of N.

8.4.2 Input demand functions

Equations (8.4.10) are the implicit, derived input demand functions whose characteristics we wish to determine. As previously indicated, the results are not precise. They cover the majority of cases, i.e. what 'usually' happens; and they hold whenever the production function is homogeneous of degree one. On the other hand, the results are *not* general; the reader should be aware that they are subject to exception whenever the production function is not homogeneous of degree one.

The system of equations with which we begin is as follows:

$$f(x_1, x_2, ..., x_n) = h(p),\qquad(8.4.15)$$

$$bf_i = p_i + x_i p_i' \quad (i = 1, 2, ..., n).\qquad(8.4.16)$$

The comparative static properties of the demand functions may be investigated by taking the partial derivative of the system with respect to p_1. As in chapter 6, there is no loss of generality involved in concentrating upon p_1 and in assuming that n is even.

Performing the partial differentiation leads to the following system of equations, expressed in matrix form.

$$
\begin{bmatrix}
-h' & f_1 & f_2 & \cdots & f_n \\
ah'f_1 & bf_{11} & bf_{12} & \cdots & bf_{1n} \\
ah'f_2 & bf_{12} & bf_{22} & \cdots & bf_{2n} \\
\vdots & \vdots & \vdots & & \vdots \\
ah'f_n & bf_{1n} & bf_{2n} & \cdots & bf_{nn}
\end{bmatrix}
\begin{bmatrix}
\partial p/\partial p_1 \\
\partial x_1/\partial p_1 \\
\partial x_2/\partial p_1 \\
\vdots \\
\partial x_n/\partial p_1
\end{bmatrix}
=
\begin{bmatrix}
0 \\
2+x_1 p_1'' \\
0 \\
\vdots \\
0
\end{bmatrix}.
\qquad (8.4.17)
$$

The matrix above is $(n+1) \times (n+1)$. Number the rows and columns 0, 1, 2, ..., n. Let M denote the determinant, M_i the cofactor of an element in row (column) 0, M_{ij} the cofactor of the i–j element $(i, j \neq 0)$, and M_{0ij} the cofactor of the i–j element in M_0 $(i, j \neq 0)$.

Using Cramer's Rule, the following solutions are obtained for the partial derivatives of interest:

$$
\frac{\partial x_1}{\partial p_1} = (2+x_1 p_1'') \frac{M_{11}}{M}, \qquad (8.4.18)
$$

$$
\frac{\partial x_j}{\partial p_1} = (2+x_1 p_1'') \frac{M_{1j}}{M} \quad (j=2, \ldots, n), \qquad (8.4.19)
$$

$$
\frac{\partial p}{\partial p_1} = (2+x_1 p_1'') \frac{M_1}{M}. \qquad (8.4.20)
$$

In chapter 6 it was possible to determine the signs of M and of its principal minors by relating M to N. This is no longer possible, however, because the c's appear in N but not in M. A much weaker approach is necessary. In subsection 8.2.2 the first-order conditions for maximizing output subject to a given cost were stated. The second-order conditions also require that the quadratic form associated with the following bordered Hessian determinant be negative definite under one constraint:

$$
F = \begin{vmatrix}
0 & f_1 & f_2 & \cdots & f_n \\
f_1 & f_{11} & f_{12} & \cdots & f_{1n} \\
f_2 & f_{12} & f_{22} & \cdots & f_{2n} \\
\vdots & \vdots & \vdots & & \vdots \\
f_n & f_{1n} & f_{2n} & \cdots & f_{nn}
\end{vmatrix}. \qquad (8.4.21)
$$

Negative definiteness requires that the principal minors alternate in sign, the 3×3 minor in the upper left-hand corner being positive. Further, the assumption that n is even implies

$$
F > 0. \qquad (8.4.22)
$$

Expanding M_{11} and M reveals that

$$
\frac{M_{11}}{M} = \frac{bF_{011} - aF_{11}}{b^2 F_0 - abF}. \qquad (8.4.23)
$$

Thus from equation (8.4.18),

$$\frac{\partial x_1}{\partial p_1} \gtrless 0 \quad \text{according as} \quad (2 + x_1 p_1'') \frac{bF_{011} - aF_{11}}{b^2 F_0 - abF} \gtrless 0. \qquad (8.4.24)$$

In its present form, expression (8.4.24) tells us little if anything. However, consider the denominator. $F > 0$, $b > 0$, $b^2 > 0$, $a < 0$. Hence $-abF > 0$. Furthermore, $F_0 = 0$ if the production function is homogeneous of degree one; and it is positive in most other cases. Let us accordingly consider the 'usual' case in which the denominator is positive.

For the moment, completely ignore the term $(2 + x_1 p_1'')$. Hence expression (8.4.24) may be written

$$\frac{\partial x_1}{\partial p_1} \gtrless 0 \quad \text{according as} \quad \frac{x_1^2}{\Sigma x_i f_i} \sigma_{11} \gtrless \frac{b}{a} \frac{F_{011}}{F}, \qquad (8.4.25)$$

where

$$\sigma_{ij} = \frac{\sum_{r=1}^{n} x_r f_r}{x_i x_j} \frac{F_{ij}}{F} \qquad (8.4.26)$$

is the partial elasticity of substitution between X_i and X_j. Since

$$\frac{F_{ii}}{F} < 0, \qquad (8.4.27)$$

$$\sigma_{ii} < 0.$$

Hence

$$\frac{x_1^2}{\Sigma x_i f_i} \sigma_{ii} < 0. \qquad (8.4.28)$$

On the right, $b > 0$, $F > 0$, and $a < 0$. Typically, or 'usually', $F_{011} < 0$. If the production function is homogeneous of degree one, it must be less than zero. Hence in the 'usual' case,

$$\frac{b}{a} \frac{F_{011}}{F} > 0. \qquad (8.4.29)$$

Therefore, taking $(2 + x_1 p_1'')$ into account,

$$\frac{\partial x_1}{\partial p_1} \gtrless 0 \quad \text{according as} \quad (2 + x_1 p_1'') \lessgtr 0. \qquad (8.4.30)$$

Typically, the quantity demanded of an input varies inversely with its price. However, if the input supply curve is '*too* concave from below', the conclusion is reversed.

Two forces are at work. Suppose p_1 declines. First, there is a substitution of X_1 for 'all other inputs'. The substitution effect always augments the quantity of X_1 demanded when its price falls. Second, however, there are forces that may cause the input demand function to shift significantly. As the input of X_1 increases, *ceteris paribus*, its marginal product declines, thus tending to decrease the demand for X_1. But also, marginal cost falls when p_1 declines, output expands and commodity price and marginal revenue decline. A decline in marginal revenue and marginal product tend to diminish the demand for X_1, while the expansion in output tends to augment it. Expression (8.4.30) simply implies that if the input supply function is 'too' concave from below, the depressive tendencies will outweight the expansive ones; quantity demanded will vary directly with price.

The same type of argument must be used in assessing the other partial derivatives. From equations (8.4.19) and (8.4.21), one may write

$$\frac{\partial x_j}{\partial p_1} = (2 + x_1 p_1') \frac{M_{1j}}{M} = (2 + x_1 p_1') \frac{bF_{01j} - aF_{1j}}{b^2 F_0 - abF}. \qquad (8.4.31)$$

Again, assume that $b^2 F_0 - abF > 0$ and ignore $(2 + x_1 p_1')$ for the moment. One may then write

$$\frac{\partial x_j}{\partial p_1} \gtrless 0 \quad \text{according as} \quad bF_{01j} - aF_{1j} \gtrless 0. \qquad (8.4.32)$$

After rearranging and introducing the elasticity of demand [defined by equation (8.1.6)] and the partial elasticity of substitution [defined by equation (8.4.26)], expression (8.4.32) may be written as

$$\frac{\partial x_j}{\partial p_1} \gtrless 0 \quad \text{according as} \quad \frac{x_1 x_j}{\sum\limits_{i=1}^{n} x_r f_r} \sigma_{1j} \gtrless \frac{h(1 - \eta)}{ah'} \frac{F_{01j}}{F}. \qquad (8.4.33)$$

Consider the right-most term. From above, we know that

$$a < 0, \quad h' < 0, \quad h > 0, \quad \eta > 1.$$

Hence
$$\frac{h(1 - \eta)}{ah'} < 0.$$

In most cases, $F_{01j}/F < 0$; and in particular, if the production function is homogeneous of degree one, the expression must be negative. Consequently, we assume that in the 'usual' situation, the right-hand side is positive.

Reintroducing the omitted term, condition (8.4.33) may finally be written

$$\frac{\partial x_j}{\partial p_1} \gtrless 0 \quad \text{according as} \quad \frac{x_1 x_j}{\Sigma x_r f_r} \sigma_{1j} \gtrless \frac{h(1 - \eta)}{ah'} \frac{F_{01j}}{F} \quad \text{if} \quad (2 + x_1 p_1') > 0,$$
$$(8.4.34a)$$

$$\frac{\partial x_j}{\partial p_1} \gtrless 0 \quad \text{according as} \quad \frac{x_1 x_j}{\Sigma x_r f_r} \sigma_{1j} \lessgtr \frac{h(1 - \eta)}{ah'} \frac{F_{01j}}{F} \quad \text{if} \quad (2 + x_1 p_1') < 0.$$
$$(8.4.34b)$$

If the input supply curve is not 'too' concave from below, the 'usual' case gives the results obtained in chapter 6: the quantity of X_j demanded may vary directly or inversely with the price of X_1; it is more likely to vary *directly* the greater the partial elasticity of substitution and the smaller the elasticity of commodity demand. The results for the 'usual' case are reversed when the input supply function is 'too' concave from below.

Finally, using the assumptions introduced above, we can examine the commodity-price effect of a change in the price of X_1. Equation (8.4.20) may be written as[1]

$$\frac{\partial p}{\partial p_1} \gtreqless 0 \quad \text{according as} \quad F_1 \gtreqless 0 \quad \text{if} \quad (2 + x_1 p_1'') > 0, \quad (8.4.35a)$$

$$\frac{\partial p}{\partial p_1} \gtreqless 0 \quad \text{according as} \quad F_1 \lesseqgtr 0 \quad \text{if} \quad (2 + x_1 p_1'') < 0. \quad (8.4.35b)$$

The cofactor F_1 is 'usually' positive, and it must be positive if the production function is homogeneous of degree one. Hence with all our 'usual' conditions, the commodity price varies directly with input price if the input supply function is not 'too' concave from below. The conclusions are reversed if the input supply function is 'too' concave or if F_1 happens to be negative.

8.4.3 Summary

All results obtained in this chapter closely follow those obtained in chapters 6 and 7; however, the results are much weaker and less precise. Nonetheless, two positive statements can be made.

(1) Even when some or all input prices are variable to the firm, there are definite and precise marginal rules for economic efficiency and for profit maximization. The second-order conditions are similarly precise; however, they cannot be interpreted directly in terms of the concavity of the production surface.

(2) Casual empiricism is sufficient to indicate that the 'usual' cases discussed above are, in fact, the ones that usually occur in the real economic world. In almost all cases, the 'produced' inputs purchased by firms are subject to rising supply prices. Thus to an individual firm, the supply price is either constant or rising. It would seem that only various types of 'labor' input could be subject to falling supply price and/or supply functions that are 'too' concave from below. Unionization effectively removes this possibility for those classes of labor and those markets that are organized.

---

[1] Actually, we assume $-h'(bF_0 - aF) > 0$ instead of $b(bF_0 - aF) > 0$. This is not material since $b > 0$ and $h' < 0$.

Following Scitovsky and Leibenstein,[1] one is tempted to conclude that the entrepreneurial supply function is the only one likely to cause trouble; and this possibility seems remote in the United States.

8.5 Conclusion

The formal presentation of the neoclassical, microeconomic theory of production and cost is now completed. Our attention has been focused exclusively upon (*a*) a single firm that (*b*) produces a single commodity at (*c*) a single point in time by the use of (*d*) inputs that are not 'inferior' ones. We have thus analyzed the static theory of the single-product firm. Chapters 9 and 10 contain summary discussions of those parts of the theory of production that have been excluded from the central body of analysis. The reader who is not particularly interested in these refinements may proceed directly to Part II without missing anything that is essential to the subsequent developments.

[1] See Scitovsky [1943] and Leibenstein [1966].

9

'INFERIOR FACTORS' AND THE THEORIES OF PRODUCTION AND INPUT DEMAND

9.1 Introduction

In chapter 6, and to some extent in chapter 8, an extension of the Allen–Mosak theory of jointly-derived input demand functions was presented.[1] The theory was generalized in chapter 6 to cover imperfect competition in the commodity market; in chapter 8 the extension covered imperfect competition in the input markets. One 'peculiar' result emerged and its reason was not explained. Specifically, it could not be shown that commodity price *always* varies directly with input price.

On the face of it, this seems to be perverse price behavior. However, it is possible to extend the analysis of the previous chapters, to explain precisely the conditions under which the peculiar price variation can occur, and to specify some of the characteristics of production functions that give rise to the phenomenon. And, having found the key to this particular puzzle, it is possible to present several interesting extensions of the theories of production and of jointly-derived input demand functions. As the chapter title suggests, it all turns upon the concept of 'inferior factors' of production.

In what follows, a sketch of the model is first presented for the convenience of the reader. The definition of an 'inferior factor' of production is then introduced and analyzed. In the bulk of the chapter, sections 9.4–9.6, the concept of factor inferiority is used to analyze various aspects of the theories of production and input demand. Section 7 contains a numerical example of a production function in which input 1 is inferior, and Section 8 provides a very brief conclusion.

9.2 The model[2]

Consider a firm that produces output according to the production function

$$q = f(x_1, x_2, ..., x_n), \quad f_i > 0 \quad \text{for all } i, \tag{9.2.1}$$

[1] Allen [1938, pp. 369–74 and pp. 502–9]; Mosak [1938, pp. 761–87]. See also Ferguson [1966b].
[2] The remainder of this chapter follows very closely Ferguson [1967] and [1968b]. For a different approach, see Puu [1966].

and markets it subject to the demand function

$$q = h(p), \quad h'(p) < 0. \tag{9.2.2}$$

In the equations above, q denotes physical output, x_i the quantity of the ith input used, p commodity price, and subscripts indicate partial derivatives.

It is assumed that over the relevant range of output and sales, marginal revenue is strictly positive and decreases monotonically. From equation (9.2.2), marginal revenue is

$$b = \left(\frac{h}{h'} + p\right) > 0, \tag{9.2.3}$$

and its slope is

$$a = \left[\frac{(h')^2 - hh''}{(h')^3}\right] + \frac{1}{h'} < 0. \tag{9.2.4}$$

Assume that the firm in question adjusts its inputs so as to maximize profit, which is given by

$$\pi = pq - \sum_i p_i x_i, \tag{9.2.5}$$

where p_i is the given, constant price of the ith input. The first-order conditions are given by[1]

$$bf_i - p_i = 0 \quad (i = 1, 2, ..., n). \tag{9.2.6}$$

Equations (9.2.6) imply the familiar principle that marginal revenue product must equal input price for each input. These equations are also the jointly-derived input demand functions whose characteristics we wish to determine. Without loss of generality, we may concentrate upon input 1 and assume that n is even.

The desired information is obtained by adding to equations (9.2.6) the market-clearing condition

$$h(p) = f(x_1, x_2, ..., x_n), \tag{9.2.7}$$

and differentiating the system partially with respect to p_1:

$$\left.\begin{aligned}
-h'\frac{\partial p}{\partial p_1} + \sum_j f_j \frac{\partial x_j}{\partial p_1} &= 0, \\
ah'f_i \frac{\partial p}{\partial p_1} + b\sum_j f_{ij}\frac{\partial x_j}{\partial p_1} &= \delta_{1i} \quad (i = 1, 2, ..., n),
\end{aligned}\right\} \tag{9.2.8}$$

where δ_{1i} is the Kronecker delta. The determinant of equations (9.2.8) is

$$M = \begin{vmatrix} -h' & f_j \\ ah'f_i & bf_{ij} \end{vmatrix} \quad (i, j = 1, 2, ..., n), \tag{9.2.9}$$

whose columns are numbered 0, 1, ..., n, and whose cofactors are denoted

---

[1] The second-order conditions are of the first importance inasmuch as they permit the sign inferences below. The second-order conditions are omitted here for the sake of brevity; the interested reader may consult chapter 6.

by M_i for the ith element in column o and by M_{ij} for the i–j element in the central body. It is also necessary to utilize a negative definite quadratic form whose bordered determinant is

$$F = \begin{vmatrix} 0 & f_i \\ f_j & f_{ij} \end{vmatrix} \quad (i, j = 1, 2, \ldots, n). \tag{9.2.10}$$

The columns and cofactors of F are numbered and denoted just as those of M.

The chief results of the earlier chapter are as follows:

$$\frac{\partial x_1}{\partial p_1} = \frac{M_{11}}{M} < 0, \tag{9.2.11}$$

$$\frac{\partial x_j}{\partial p_1} \gtrless 0 \quad \text{according as} \quad \frac{x_1 x_j}{\Sigma x_i f_i} \, \sigma_{1j} \gtrless \frac{h(1-\eta)}{ah'} \frac{F_{01j}}{F}, \tag{9.2.12}$$

$$\frac{\partial p}{\partial p_1} \gtrless 0 \quad \text{according as} \quad F_1 = -\sum_j f_j F_{01j} \gtrless 0, \tag{9.2.13}$$

where, in equation (9.2.12), σ_{1j} is the partial elasticity of substitution of input 1 for input j and $\eta \geq 1$ is the elasticity of commodity demand.

Verbally, the results may be summarized as follows. (a) The quantity demanded of a factor must always vary inversely with its price (9.2.11). (b) The quantity demanded of factor j may vary either directly or inversely. If the inputs are complementary, it must vary inversely. When the inputs are competitive, a direct relation is more likely the greater is the partial elasticity of substitution and the smaller is the elasticity of commodity demand (9.2.12). (c) Commodity price must vary directly with factor price if there are only two inputs or if there are many inputs and the production function is homogeneous of degree one. The possibility of an inverse relation cannot be eliminated however (9.2.13).

9.3 'Inferior factors' of production

Without yet relating the discussion to that of section 9.2, let us define an 'inferior factor' of production as follows: *an input is inferior if an increase in its price leads to an increase in the equilibrium output of the firm.*[1] Using equation (9.2.1), factor 1 is inferior if

$$\frac{\partial q}{\partial p_1} = \sum_j f_j \frac{\partial x_j}{\partial p_1} > 0. \tag{9.3.1}$$

---

[1] Hicks hinted at something like factor inferiority when he spoke of a 'regression relation' between a factor and a product. However, the two relations do not seem to be precisely the same. See Hicks [1939], pp. 93–6. Another view of inferiority may be found in Scott [1962]. A version closely related to that developed here, but limited to the case of perfect competition in the output market, may be found in Bear [1965].

Definition (9.3.1) must now be adapted to our present needs. To that end, differentiate the equilibrium system (9.2.6) with respect to commodity price p, obtaining

$$b\sum_j f_{ij}\frac{\partial x_j}{\partial p} = -ah'f_i \quad (i=1, 2, ..., n).$$ (9.3.2)

Define the negative definite determinant of equations (9.3.2) as follows (note that this precludes linear homogeneity of the production function, as demonstrated below):

$$F^* = |f_{ij}| > 0 \quad (i, j=1, 2, ..., n).$$ (9.3.3)

Using definition (9.3.3), the solution of equations (9.3.2) may be written

$$\frac{\partial x_j}{\partial p} = -\frac{ah'}{b}\frac{\sum_k f_k F^*_{jk}}{F^*}.$$ (9.3.4)

Next, differentiate equations (9.2.6) with respect to p_1, obtaining

$$\sum_j f_{ij}\frac{\partial x_j}{\partial p_1} = \frac{1}{b}\delta_{1i} \quad (i=1, 2, ..., n),$$ (9.3.5)

where δ_{1i} is again the Kronecker delta. Thus

$$\frac{\partial x_j}{\partial p_1} = \frac{F^*_{1j}}{bF^*}.$$ (9.3.6)

Substitute equation (9.3.6) into equation (9.3.1) to obtain

$$\frac{\partial q}{\partial p_1} = \sum_j f_j\frac{\partial x_j}{\partial p_1} = \frac{\sum_j f_j F^*_{1j}}{bF^*}.$$ (9.3.7)

Since $b > 0$ and $F^* > 0$, factor 1 is inferior if, and only if,

$$\sum_j f_j F^*_{1j} > 0.$$ (9.3.8)

Further, using equation (9.3.4) in equation (9.3.7), one obtains

$$\frac{\partial q}{\partial p_1} = -\frac{1}{ah'}\frac{\partial x_1}{\partial p}.$$ (9.3.9)

Note that $a < 0$ and $h' < 0$. From equation (9.3.9), it is always true that the change in output with respect to a change in input price is a negative multiple of the change in the quantity of the input demanded in response to a change in commodity price. In the special case of inferior inputs, a demand-led increase in commodity price results in a decrease in input usage. This is the exact mirror-image of the condition for factor inferiority, namely that a supply-led increase in input price results in an expansion of equilibrium output.

Yet while equilibrium output expands, profit diminishes. This fact, in turn, implies that a factor cannot be inferior at all levels of output. To see this, differentiate the profit function (9.2.5) with respect to p_1, obtaining

$$\frac{\partial \pi}{\partial p_1} = \sum_j (bf_j - p_j) \frac{\partial x_j}{\partial p_1} - x_1. \tag{9.3.10}$$

By equations (9.2.6), each term in parentheses on the right is zero. Hence

$$\frac{\partial \pi}{\partial p_1} = -x_1 < 0. \tag{9.3.11}$$

Thus inequality (9.3.11) shows that factor inferiority is limited to a certain range of output (or of input price).

9.4   Inferior inputs and commodity price

Comparing equations (9.2.10) and (9.3.3) enables one to relate inferior inputs to the 'perverse' commodity price behavior noted above. First observe that

$$F_0 \equiv F^*, \tag{9.4.1}$$

and thus

$$F_{01j} = F_{1j}^* \quad (j = 1, 2, \dots, n), \tag{9.4.2}$$

where F_{01j} is the cofactor of the $1-j$ element in F_0. From expression (9.2.13)

$$F_1 = -\sum_j f_j F_{01j} = -\Sigma f_j F_{1j}^*. \tag{9.4.3}$$

Hence if inequality (9.3.8) holds, i.e., input 1 is inferior, the right-hand side of equation (9.4.3) is negative. By expression (9.2.13)

$$\frac{\partial p}{\partial p_1} < 0. \tag{9.4.4}$$

Consequently, commodity price varies inversely with factor price if, and only if, the factor under consideration is inferior.

Equation (9.4.3) also permits one to establish some relations between factor inferiority and the production function. First, if the production function is homogeneous of degree one,

$$F_1 = \frac{x_1 F}{q^2} \Sigma x_j f_j = \frac{x_1 F}{q} > 0. \tag{9.4.5}$$

Hence by equation (9.4.3), $\sum_j f_j F_{1j}^* < 0,$ (9.4.6)

implying that input 1 is not inferior. Consequently, linear homogeneity of the production function, indeed homogeneity of any degree,[1] precludes factor inferiority.

---

[1] This may be shown by an easy extension of equation (9.4.3).

A somewhat stronger statement may be made. Suppose F^* is a Metzler matrix,[1] i.e. all off-diagonal elements are positive. Then, as Metzler has shown, all the elements of F^{*-1} are negative. Denote these elements by F^{*ij}. Solving equations (9.3.2) by matrix methods rather than Cramer's Rule, one obtains

$$\frac{\partial x_j}{\partial p} = -\frac{ah'}{b} \sum_k f_k F^{*jk}. \qquad (9.4.7)$$

When F^* is a Metzler matrix, equation (9.4.7) is necessarily positive. In light of equation (9.3.9)

$$\frac{\partial q}{\partial p_1} < 0, \qquad (9.4.8)$$

implying that factor 1 is not inferior. Thus the input counterpart of 'gross substitutability' for outputs precludes factor inferiority.

9.5 Inferior inputs and the cross-elasticity of derived input demand functions

The cross-elasticities of input demand may be derived from expression (9.2.12) and, interestingly enough, related directly to factor inferiority. Noting that $F_{01j} = F_{1j}^*$ and $f_j = p_j/b$, multiply both sides of inequalities (9.2.12) by f_j and sum over j. One thus obtains

$$\frac{1}{b} \sum p_j \frac{\partial x_j}{\partial p_1} \gtrless 0 \quad \text{according as} \quad \frac{x_1 \Sigma f_j x_j \sigma_{1j}}{\sum_r f_r x_r} \gtrless \frac{h(1-\eta)}{ah'} \frac{\Sigma f_j F_{ij}^*}{F}. \qquad (9.5.1)$$

Next, introduce the following definitions:

$$\kappa_j = \frac{p_j x_j}{\sum_r p_r x_r} \quad \text{and} \quad \theta_{ij} = \frac{\partial x_j}{\partial p_i} \frac{p_i}{x_j}. \qquad (9.5.2)$$

That is, κ_j is the proportion of total cost attributable to input j, and θ_{ij} is the price cross-elasticity of input demand between factors i and j.

Using these definitions, the left-hand inequality in expression (9.5.1) may be written

$$\frac{1}{b} \sum p_j \frac{\partial x_j}{\partial p_1} = \frac{\sum_r p_r x_r}{b p_1} \Sigma \kappa_j \theta_{1j} \gtrless 0 \quad \text{according as} \quad \Sigma \kappa_j \theta_{1j} \gtrless 0. \qquad (9.5.3)$$

Again using definitions (9.5.2) one may write

$$\frac{x_1 \sum_j f_j x_j \sigma_{1j}}{\sum_r f_r x_r} = x_1 \sum_j \kappa_j \sigma_{1j}. \qquad (9.5.4)$$

---

[1] Metzler [1945]. The following point is made by Bear [1965].

192

9.5 CROSS-ELASTICITY

Now a theorem due to Allen may be used to simplify the problem. Specifically, Allen proved that

$$\sum_j \kappa_j \sigma_{1j} = 0.[1] \tag{9.5.5}$$

Finally, note that the previous sign conditions show that

$$\frac{h(1-\eta)}{ah'F} < 0. \tag{9.5.6}$$

In light of expressions (9.5.3), (9.5.5), and (9.5.6), expression (9.5.1) may be simplified to

$$\sum_j \kappa_j \theta_{1j} \gtrless 0 \quad \text{according as} \quad 0 \gtrless -\sum_j f_j F_{1j}^*. \tag{9.5.7}$$

Hence, if input 1 is normal, the usual result is obtained: the weighted sum of cross-elasticities is negative.[2] The relation is reversed if, and only if, input 1 is inferior. But in this special case, the weighted sum of price cross-elasticities is positive.

9.6 Inferior inputs and the output effect of an input price change

The analysis has so far pertained to the derived input demand functions of a profit-maximizing firm. Therefore, product demand has played an important role. It is illuminating, however, to solve a simpler problem based upon a less stringent maximization assumption. In particular, consider the maximization of output for any given level of expenditure upon inputs, the latter being denoted

$$\overline{C} = \Sigma p_i x_i. \tag{9.6.1}$$

The problem is a simple exercise in the Lagrange technique. Construct the function

$$L \equiv f(x_1, x_2, ..., x_n) - \lambda(\Sigma p_i x_i - \overline{C}). \tag{9.6.2}$$

The first-order conditions are

$$\frac{\partial L}{\partial \lambda} = \Sigma p_i x_i - \overline{C} = 0,$$

$$\frac{\partial L}{\partial x_i} = f_i - \lambda p_i = 0 \quad (i = 1, 2, ..., n). \tag{9.6.3}$$

---

[1] Allen [1938], p. 504.

[2] To illustrate, we can use Allen's results under the assumptions of perfect competition in the commodity market and linear homogeneity of the production function. Allen [1938, p. 508] showed that

$$\theta_{1j} = \kappa_1(\sigma_{1j} - \eta),$$

so

$$\sum_j \kappa_j \theta_{1j} = \kappa_1 \sum_j \kappa_j(\sigma_{1j} - \eta) = -\kappa_1 \sum_j \kappa_j \eta < 0,$$

since $\kappa_j > 0$ for all j and $\eta > 0$.

The second-order conditions require that our determinant F be associated with a negative definite quadratic form. Without loss of generality, we retain the assumption that n is even; hence $F > 0$.

Now displace the equilibrium system (9.6.3) by a change in p_1. The resulting system may be written as follows:

$$
\begin{bmatrix}
0 & p_1 & p_2 & \cdots & p_n \\
p_1 & f_{11} & f_{12} & \cdots & f_{1n} \\
p_2 & f_{12} & f_{22} & \cdots & f_{2n} \\
\vdots & \vdots & \vdots & & \vdots \\
p_n & f_{1n} & f_{2n} & \cdots & f_{nn}
\end{bmatrix}
\begin{bmatrix}
-\dfrac{\partial \lambda}{\partial p_1} \\
\partial x_1/\partial p_1 \\
\partial x_2/\partial p_1 \\
\vdots \\
\partial x_n/\partial p_1
\end{bmatrix}
=
\begin{bmatrix}
-x_1 \\
\lambda \\
0 \\
\vdots \\
0
\end{bmatrix}.
\qquad (9.6.4)
$$

Using Cramer's Rule, the general solution terms are, from equations (9.6.3)

$$
-\frac{\partial \lambda}{\partial p_1} = -\frac{\lambda^2 x_1 F_0}{F} + \frac{\lambda^2 F_1}{F}, \qquad (9.6.5)
$$

$$
\frac{\partial x_j}{\partial p_1} = \frac{(-x_1 \lambda F_j + \lambda^2 F_{1j})}{F} \quad (j = 1, 2, \ldots, n). \qquad (9.6.6)
$$

These expressions can easily be rewritten in familiar terms. To this end, some definitions and identities are needed.

First, by definition,[1] the partial elasticity of substitution of input 1 for input j is

$$
\sigma_{1j} \equiv \frac{\Sigma f_i x_i}{x_1 x_j} \frac{F_{1j}}{F}. \qquad (9.6.7)
$$

From equations (9.2.10) and (9.3.3) it follows that

$$
\left.
\begin{aligned}
F_j &= (-1)^j \sum_k f_k F_{0jk}, \\
F_{0jk} &= (-1)^{j+1} F_{jk}^*.
\end{aligned}
\right\}
\qquad (9.6.8)
$$

Substituting equations (9.6.7) and (9.6.8) in equations (9.6.5) and (9.6.6) yields the familiar form:

$$
-\frac{\partial \lambda}{\partial p_1} = -\frac{\lambda^2 \sum_k f_k F_{1k}^*}{F} - \frac{\lambda^2 x_1 F^*}{F}, \qquad (9.6.9)
$$

$$
\frac{\partial x_1}{\partial p_1} = \lambda \left[\frac{-x_1 \sum_k f_k F_{1k}^*}{F} \right] + \frac{\lambda^2 x_1^2}{\Sigma f_i x_i} \sigma_{11}, \qquad (9.6.10)
$$

$$
\frac{\partial x_j}{\partial p_1} = \lambda \left[\frac{-x_1 \sum_k f_k F_{jk}^*}{F} \right] + \frac{\lambda^2 x_1 x_j}{\Sigma f_i x_i} \sigma_{1j}. \qquad (9.6.11)
$$

These three equations are now discussed in the order of their listing.

[1] See Allen [1938, pp. 503–5].

9.6 OUTPUT EFFECT

(i) Equation (9.6.9). From equations (9.6.3), it is evident that λ is the reciprocal of marginal cost. Noting that $\lambda > 0$, $F > 0$, one may write

$$\frac{\partial \lambda}{\partial p_1} \gtreqless 0 \quad \text{according as} \quad \sum_k f_k F_{1k}^* + x_1 F^* \gtreqless 0. \tag{9.6.12}$$

Suppose input 1 is normal. Then λ varies inversely with p_1, and hence, as would usually be the case, the marginal cost of output varies directly with input price. By similar reasoning, if input 1 is inferior, marginal cost varies inversely with its price. This, of course, explains *why* output increases when p_1 increases (input 1 being inferior). An increase in p_1 shifts the marginal cost curve to the right, thereby intersecting marginal revenue at a point corresponding to a larger volume of output.

(ii) Equation (9.6.10). From definition (9.6.7) and the negative definiteness of F, it follows that $\sigma_{11} < 0$. Hence the 'substitution effect', as we shall call the rightmost term in expression (9.6.10) is always negative. The negative substitution effect, it should be noted, works in favor of the input whose price has decreased. For movements along an isoquant, the quantity of an input demanded varies inversely with its price. In the case of a normal input, the negative substitution effect is reinforced by a positive 'output effect', as we shall call the first term on the right in expression (9.6.10).

Suppose p_1 declines. The negative substitution effect tends to cause an increase in the usage of X_1; and the increase in 'efficiency' output ensuing upon the decline in p_1 typically causes an increase in the usage of X_1 as well. The case of a normal input is illustrated by figure 45. The initial input-price ratio is given by the (negative of the) slope of EF. Equilibrium is attained at point A on Q_1, at which point the usage of X_1 is Ox_{11}. Let the price of X_1 fall, the price of 'all other inputs' remaining constant. The new input-price ratio is indicated by EF'. The ultimate equilibrium is reached at point C on Q_2, with Ox_{12} units of X_1 being used.

The movement from A to C may be decomposed into two parts. The substitution effect is represented by the movement from A to B (also on Q_1), or by the increase in X_1-usage from Ox_{11} to Ox'_{11}. The substitution effect, of course, is determined by finding the increase in usage of X_1 that would occur if the old level of output (Q_1) were produced but the new price ratio prevailed (JK parallel to EF'). The positive output effect is shown by the movement from B on Q_1 to C on Q_2, or from Ox'_{11} to Ox_{12}. In this case, both effects tend to augment the quantity of X_1 used.

However, if input 1 is inferior, the output effect will be negative; that is, the increase in output resulting from the decline in p_1 (counter-clockwise rotation of the isocost curve) tends to cause a reduction in the usage of X_1. This is illustrated in figure 46, which is lettered exactly as figure 45. In this

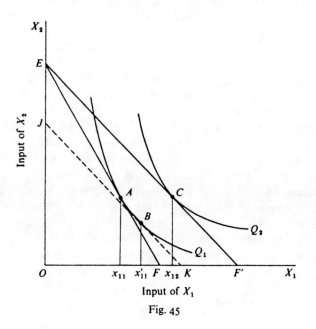

Fig. 45

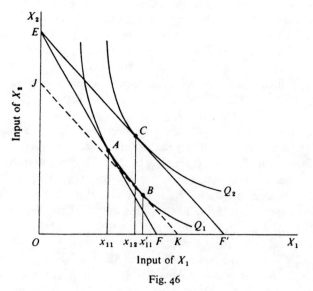

Input of X_1

Fig. 46

case, the output effect, the movement from B on Q_1 to C on Q_2, causes a reduction in the usage of X_1 when its price falls.

It is now useful to state an important

Observation: if input 1 is inferior, the negative output effect may more than offset the negative substitution effect; hence the sign of $\partial x_1/\partial p_1$ may be positive over the range of factor inferiority (but note that the $\partial x_1/\partial p_1$ used here is *not* the slope of the factor demand function).

The situation leading to a positive partial derivative is illustrated in figure 47.

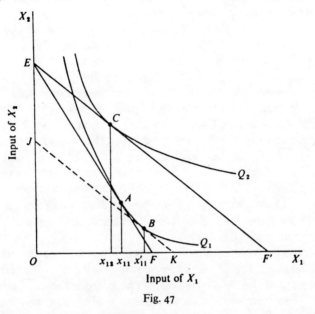

Fig. 47

The implications of the observation and of figure 47 should clear up a matter of some confusion. On a two-dimensional graph it is quite simple to illustrate the output and substitution effects. And it is also easy to construct the graph (as in figure 47) so that there is a range over which a negative output effect more than offsets the negative substitution effect. Conclusion often reached (by analogy with the theory of consumer behavior): there may exist a range of values over which the (individual firm's) demand curve for an input is positively sloped. Comment: not so, because the analogy is false.[1]

[1] It is high time I achnowledge that the paper upon which chapter 6 is based (but, curiously enough, not this chapter) was motivated by Professor John O. Blackburn. He put forth, quite rightly, the argument stated in the text. In answer I produced the proof whose implications are contained in equation (9.2.11) above. My rebuttal, therefore, was that 'you can do anything with graphs; it's safer to use mathematics'.

Individual demand curves, whether for commodities by consumers or for inputs by firms, are based upon the assumption of satisfaction or profit maximization. The indifference curve–budget line graph illustrates the consumer's maximization process; an individual demand curve may accordingly be derived from the graph. The 'economic efficiency' conditions (optimal input combinations) discussed in this section do not incorporate profit maximization. Indeed, these conditions are totally independent of revenue considerations. Hence an input demand function cannot be derived from the corresponding graph, even though it may be used to illustrate factor inferiority graphically.

To summarize: while the $\partial x_1/\partial p_1$ discussed in this section may be positive, it is not the slope of the input demand function derived from the assumption of profit maximization; and the latter is the only true input demand function.

Having got this far with the graphical interpretation of factor inferiority, it is possible heuristically to develop another feature of production functions with inferior inputs. Consider figure 47, in which input X_1 is inferior. In order for the negative output effect more than to offset the negative substitution effect, the successive isoquants must be very close together for high $X_2:X_1$ input ratios and progressively further apart as the $X_2:X_1$ input ratio declines. That is, the marginal rate of technical substitution of X_2 for $X_1(f_1/f_2)$ must diminish for movements along a ray from the origin, or increase for movements along the ray in the direction of the origin.

If the isoquants in figure 47 were not 'labelled', i.e. output levels not indicated, the isoquant map under discussion would 'look just like' or be indistinguishable from an isoquant map representing X_1-using biased technological progress (in the Hicks sense). The interpretations, of course, are opposite; the one applies to movements of a given isoquant toward the origin, the other to outward shifts of successively higher isoquants. Hence inferiority of factor 1 implies an X_2-using *output* bias. In other words, an inferior factor, as Hicks indicated,[1] is one that is more suitable at low levels of output than at high ones.[2]

(iii) Equation (9.6.11). A graphical interpretation of equation (9.6.11) is not necessary since 'all other factors' cannot be inferior in relation to factor 1. However, one may isolate factor j and discuss its relation to factor 1. To this end, let us introduce Allen's classification of input relations: factors 1 and j are *competitive* or *complementary* according as

In general, I think that statement is right, as is the proof. More fundamentally, however, Blackburn was right and I was wrong. His graphical construction was correct; it only required the proper interpretation.
[1] Hicks [1939], p. 96.
[2] It does not seem to follow, however, that this phenomenon is attributable to increasing returns to scale, as Hicks suggested.

$\sigma_{1j} \gtrless 0$.[1] Two polar cases may be described: (a) if inputs 1 and j are competitive and j is inferior, the usage of x_j varies directly with the price of x_1; (b) if the inputs are complementary and j is normal, the usage of j varies inversely with the price of X_1.[2] In mixed cases, e.g. competitive and normal, the sign of the partial cannot be determined *a priori*.

Suppose the price of input 1 declines. In case (a), there is a positive substitution effect for the movement along the original isoquant (since the inputs are competitive). Further, as output expands (jumping to a higher isoquant), there is also a negative output effect attributable to input j's inferiority. Both effects lead to a reduction in the usage of input j as a result of the fall in the price of input 1. Exactly the opposite analysis applies to case (b). Input complementarity causes the usage of input j to increase when the price of input 1 declines. Further, since input j is normal, its usage expands as output expands. Both forces tend to augment the quantity of input j used.

9.7   Numerical example

Consider the production function

$$q = \frac{x_1 - 1}{(x_2 - 2)^2},\tag{9.7.1}$$

defined over the range in which $x_1 > 1$, $x_2 < 2$. The marginal products are

$$\frac{\partial q}{\partial x_1} = \frac{1}{(x_2 - 2)^2} > 0, \quad \frac{\partial q}{\partial x_2} = -\frac{2(x_1 - 1)}{(x_2 - 2)^3} > 0,\tag{9.7.2}$$

and the F^* determinant is

$$F^* = \begin{vmatrix} 0 & -\dfrac{2}{(x_2 - 2)^3} \\ -\dfrac{2}{(x_2 - 2)^3} & +\dfrac{6(x_1 - 1)}{(x_2 - 2)^4} \end{vmatrix}.\tag{9.7.3}$$

By condition (9.3.8), input 1 is inferior if, and only if,

$$\sum_{j=1}^{2} f_j F_{1j}^* > 0.\tag{9.7.4}$$

Using expressions (9.7.2) and equation (9.7.3) in inequality (9.7.4), one obtains

$$\sum_{j=1}^{2} f_j F_{1j}^* = \frac{2(x_1 - 1)}{(x_2 - 2)^6} > 0.\tag{9.7.5}$$

Hence input 1 can be inferior.

[1] Allen [1938, p. 509].
[2] Perhaps we should again emphasize that the partial derivative under consideration is not the derivative of an input demand function.

To see the range of its inferiority, set the constant level of cost $\overline{C}$ at unity and let $p_2 = \frac{1}{3}$. The constrained maximization problem may be put in the Lagrange form

$$L \equiv \frac{x_1 - 1}{(x_2 - 2)^2} - \lambda(p_1 x_1 + \tfrac{1}{3}x_2 - 1). \qquad (9.7.6)$$

The equilibrium conditions are

$$\left. \begin{aligned}
\frac{\partial L}{\partial x_1} &= \frac{1}{(x_2 - 2)^2} - \lambda p_1 = 0, \\
\frac{\partial L}{\partial x_2} &= -\frac{2(x_1 - 1)}{(x_2 - 2)^3} - \tfrac{1}{3}\lambda = 0, \\
\frac{\partial L}{\partial \lambda} &= p_1 x_1 + \tfrac{1}{3}x_2 = 1.
\end{aligned} \right\} \qquad (9.7.7)$$

Collapsing the system (9.7.7) to two equations and solving simultaneously yields the equilibrium values of x_1 and x_2.

In particular, set $p_1 = \frac{2}{3}$. The equilibrium solution for x_1 is $\frac{1}{2}$. Next let $p_1 = \frac{2}{5}$. The corresponding equilibrium value of x_1 is $\frac{7}{6} < \frac{1}{2}$. Over this range, input I is clearly inferior. Extending the example, it is easy to show that input I cannot be inferior over the input price range for which $p_2 = \frac{1}{3}, p_1 \geq \frac{1}{2}$.

9.8 Conclusion

The empirical importance of factor inferiority would be difficult, if not impossible, to assess. On a theoretical level, however, the concept of factor inferiority is important in the theories of production and of derived input demand functions. The concept permits one clearly to explain the theoretical possibility of 'peculiar' commodity price behavior in response to an input price change. Similarly, it leads to a reconciliation of 'graphical observation' in the case of constrained output maximization with the mathematically established theorem that input demand functions are negatively sloped. It would seem that no further arguments are needed to justify an intense analysis of the implications of factor inferiority.

10

THEORY OF THE MULTI-PRODUCT FIRM

10.1 Introduction

Speculation about the selling behavior (revenue side) of multi-product firms may be traced to Pigou and Mrs Robinson and, more recently, to Reder, Coase, Gordon, Clemens, Weldon, Simkin, Edwards, and Bailey.[1] Taking some liberties, one may say that these writers viewed the pricing process in a multi-product firm as an extended application of the Pigou–Robinson theory of price discrimination (Pigou's 'discrimination of the third degree').

Subsequent to this original start, the multi-product firm was given a more thorough and conventional treatment by Hicks, whose approach was later extended by Allen, Samuelson, Dorfman, and Kuenne.[2] Basically, Hicks and his followers used conventional marginal methods to analyze the profit-maximizing behavior of a firm that produces a variety of products by means of a variety of *variable* inputs. Fixed inputs were occasionally introduced; but their important role was not analyzed.

To be sure, it was recognized that the existence of fixed inputs is more significant in the theory of the multi-product firm than in the theory of the single-product firm, even when the latter practices price discrimination.[3] However, it was Pfouts who first realized the *crucial* difference and constructed a model of the multi-product firm that permitted switching of fixed inputs among various outputs.[4] Pfouts' model, and subsequent ones based upon it,[5] cannot be solved by the usual methods of the calculus. The introduction of a variety of fixed inputs leads to a set of linear inequalities as constraints in the maximization process. As a result, the model must be analyzed by means of the Kuhn–Tucker theorems.[6]

---

[1] See Pigou [1932, pp. 275–317]; Robinson [1933, pp. 179–202]; Reder [1941], Coase [1946], Gordon [1948], Clemens [1951], Weldon [1948], Simkin [1947], Edwards [1950], and Bailey [1954].

[2] Hicks [1939, pp. 319–20], Allen [1938, pp. 613–17], Samuelson [1947, pp. 57–89 and pp. 357–79], Dorfman [1951, pp. 6–9], Kuenne [1963, pp. 180–5]. For a very good summary of this approach, see Mauer and Naylor [1964].

[3] See Dorfman [1951, p. 46] and Dorfman, Samuelson, and Solow [1958, p. 202].

[4] Pfouts [1961].   [5] See Dhrymes [1964] and Naylor [1965].

[6] Kuhn and Tucker [1951].

In this chapter the earlier contributions to the theory of the multi-product firm are ignored, only Pfouts' models are analyzed. More specifically, the next section is devoted to a statement of the Kuhn–Tucker theorems. In section 3 the conditions for efficient operation are developed, as in Pfouts' paper, and in section 4 these results are extended to profit maximization.[1]

10.2 The Kuhn–Tucker theorems

The Kuhn–Tucker theorems represent a powerful generalization of the theory of constrained extrema. Not only do the theorems permit the introduction of inequalities as constraints; they also permit the use of non-linear objective functions. Since one cannot plausibly assume linear cost and profit functions for a multi-product firm, the Kuhn–Tucker theorems are a prerequisite for a sophisticated treatment of the problem.

Since both constrained cost minimization (operational efficiency) and profit maximization subject to production function limitations are analyzed, it is necessary to develop both the conditions for constrained minimization and constrained maximization. However, the two sets of conditions are virtually the reverse of each other; thus only one set is examined intensively.

10.2.1 Constrained maximization

The chief result of the Kuhn–Tucker theorems is that a constrained extremum problem can, under fairly weak assumptions, be converted into a saddle-value problem. The conditions that guarantee a saddle point also guarantee the existence of a constrained extremum.

Suppose one wishes to maximize the function

$$g(X) = g(x_1, x_2, ..., x_n) \quad (x_i \geqq 0 \text{ for all } i), \quad (\text{10.2.1})$$

subject to the following m constraints:

$$h_j(X) = h_j(x_1, x_2, ..., x_n) \geqq 0 \quad (j = 1, 2, ..., m). \quad (\text{10.2.2})$$

For the Kuhn–Tucker theorem to hold, three sets of conditions must be satisfied. First, the objective function (10.2.1) and the constraints (10.2.2) must be differentiable. Second, the same $m+1$ functions must be concave, where 'A function is concave if linear interpolation between its values at any two points of definition yields a value not greater than its actual value at the point of interpolation.'[2] Finally, referring to the Lagrange function introduced below [equation (10.2.3)], the possibility of a singular point on

---

[1] Except for minor points, specific citations are not given in the remainder of the chapter. Section 2 is based upon Kuhn and Tucker [1951], section 3 upon Pfouts [1961]. For an approach alternative to that of section 4, see Dhrymes [1964] and Naylor [1965]. [2] Kuhn and Tucker [1951, p. 481].

the frontier is eliminated if $L(X, \lambda^0)$ is a concave function in X and $L(X^0, \lambda)$ is a convex function in λ.

To obtain the constrained maximum, one first constructs a Lagrange function (as in the case of equality constraints):

$$L(X, \lambda) \equiv g(X) + \sum_{j=1}^{m} \lambda_j h_j(X), \tag{10.2.3}$$

$$x_i \geqq 0, \lambda_j \geqq 0 \quad (i = 1, 2, ..., n; j = 1, 2, ..., m).$$

Kuhn and Tucker proved that a necessary and sufficient condition for the existence of a constrained maximum at X^0, λ^0 is the existence of a saddle point at the extreme value. Further, the necessary and sufficient conditions for a saddle point at X^0, λ^0 are as follows:

$$\left.\frac{\partial L}{\partial x_i}\right]_{x_i = x_i^0} \leqq 0 \quad (i = 1, 2, ..., n), \tag{10.2.4}$$

$$\sum_{i=1}^{n} \left.\frac{\partial L}{\partial x_i}\right]_{x_i = x_i^0} x_i^0 = 0, \tag{10.2.5}$$

$$x_i^0 \geqq 0 \quad (i = 1, 2, ..., n), \tag{10.2.6}$$

$$\left.\frac{\partial L}{\partial \lambda_j}\right]_{\lambda_j = \lambda_j^0} \geqq 0 \quad (j = 1, 2, ..., m), \tag{10.2.7}$$

$$\sum_{j=1}^{m} \left.\frac{\partial L}{\partial \lambda_j}\right]_{\lambda_j = \lambda^0} \lambda_j^0 = 0, \tag{10.2.8}$$

$$\lambda_j^0 \geqq 0 \quad (j = 1, 2, ..., m). \tag{10.2.9}$$

In expressions (10.2.4) the strict inequality holds if, and only if, $x_i^0 = 0$; for $x_i^0 > 0$, the equality sign holds. Hence the subsystem (10.2.4)–(10.2.6) is consistent. Similarly, the strict inequality in expression (10.2.7) holds if, and only if, $\lambda_j^0 > 0$; otherwise, the equality holds. Hence the subsystem (10.2.7)–(10.2.9), and therefore the whole system (10.2.4)–(10.2.9), is logically consistent.

10.2.2 Constrained minimization

The conditions for a constrained minimum differ from those of a constrained maximum only in that (i) the objective function and the constraints must be convex functions,[1] and (ii) the concavity–convexity pro-

---

[1] Convexity means that the value of a linear interpolation between any two points of the function is not less than the value of the function at the point of interpolation.

perties of $L(X, \lambda^0)$ and $L(X^0, \lambda)$ are reversed. Accordingly, the necessary and sufficient conditions for a constrained minimum are as follows:

$$\frac{\partial L}{\partial x_i}\bigg]_{x_i = x_i^0} \geqq 0 \quad (i = 1, 2, ..., n), \tag{10.2.10}$$

$$\sum_{i=1}^{n} \frac{\partial L}{\partial x_i}\bigg]_{x_i = x_i^0} x_i^0 = 0, \tag{10.2.11}$$

$$x_i^0 \geqq 0 \quad (i = 1, 2, ..., n), \tag{10.2.12}$$

$$\frac{\partial L}{\partial \lambda_j}\bigg]_{\lambda_j = \lambda_j^0} \leqq 0 \quad (j = 1, 2, ..., m), \tag{10.2.13}$$

$$\sum_{j=1}^{m} \frac{\partial L}{\partial \lambda_j}\bigg]_{\lambda_j = \lambda_j^0} \lambda_j^0 = 0, \tag{10.2.14}$$

$$\lambda_j^0 \geqq 0 \quad (j = 1, 2, ..., m). \tag{10.2.15}$$

The consistency of each subsystem, and hence of the entire system, follows by an argument analogous to that presented at the end of subsection 10.2.1 above.

10.3 Economic efficiency: constrained cost minimization

Fixed factors of production are not important in the analysis of a single-product firm. The funds invested in temporarily fixed inputs are indeed 'sunk'. In the short run, fixed inputs have significance only in that they place some upper limit on production (or what is almost equivalent, they give rise to very rapidly rising marginal cost beyond a certain point).

The same is not true of the multi-product firm because it can use a fixed factor in different lines of production. In this case the fixed inputs become important because of the possibility of transferring units from the production of one product to the production of another. As Pfouts put it, each of the firm's products competes with all its other products for the use of the available fixed factors.

Let the firm produce n products in quantities q_i, using m variable inputs x_j and r fixed inputs y_k. Denote the input of the jth variable factor in producing the ith output by x_{ji}; similarly, y_{ki} represents the kth fixed factor used in producing the ith output. The firm's production function is given by

$$q_i = f_i(x_{1i}, ..., x_{mi}; y_{1i}, ..., y_{ri}) \quad (i = 1, 2, ..., n), \tag{10.3.1}$$

where one or more of the x_{ji} and y_{ki} may have zero values. It is assumed that over the relevant range of production, the production function is continuous and exhibits continuously diminishing marginal rates of technical substitution.

In the production process, the firm incurs three types of cost. First, the cost of the variable inputs is simply the sum of the amounts paid to each of the variable factors:

$$V = \sum_{j=1}^{m} \sum_{i=1}^{n} w_j x_{ji}, \qquad (10.3.2)$$

where w_j is the unit price of the jth variable input. One may either assume that the firm is a perfect competitor in each market or that

$$w_j = g_j \left(\sum_{i=1}^{n} x_{ji} \right) \quad (j = 1, 2, ..., m). \qquad (10.3.3)$$

Generalizing Pfouts' presentation, we assume that input prices are governed by equations (10.3.3).

Second, the money invested in fixed inputs is denoted by F. Finally, a cost is incurred when a fixed input is transferred from one use to another. This cost is referred to as the 'switching cost' and is denoted

$$S = S(y_{11}, ..., y_{r1}, y_{21}, ..., y_{rn}). \qquad (10.3.4)$$

The total cost to be minimized is

$$V + S + F = \sum_{j=1}^{m} \sum_{i=1}^{n} w_j x_{ji} + S(y_{11}, ..., y_{rn}) + F. \qquad (10.3.5)$$

The minimization is to be valid for each level of output; hence it is subject to the constraint

$$\bar{q}_i - f_i(x_{1i}, ..., x_{mi}, y_{1i}, ..., y_{ri}) = 0 \quad (i = 1, 2, ..., n). \qquad (10.3.6)$$

The constrained minimization problem in equations (10.3.5) and (10.3.6) is similar to the constrained minimization problem for the single-product firm. However, the multi-product firm is subject to another set of constraints; namely, the total usage of each fixed input cannot exceed the available amount, although it can fall short of this amount. Let y_k be the available quantity of the kth fixed resource. Then the fixed input utilization constraints may be written

$$\sum_{i=1}^{n} y_{ki} - y_k \leqq 0 \quad (k = 1, 2, ..., r). \qquad (10.3.7)$$

10.3.1 The Kuhn–Tucker conditions

The Lagrange expression corresponding to equation (10.2.3) is

$$L(X, Y, \lambda, \mu) = \sum_{j=1}^{m} \sum_{i=1}^{n} w_j x_{ji} + S(y_{11}, ..., y_{rn})$$

$$+ F + \sum_{i=1}^{n} \lambda_i [\bar{q}_i - f_i(x_{1i}, ..., y_{ri})] + \sum_{k=1}^{r} \mu_k \left(\sum_{i=1}^{n} y_{ki} - y_k \right). \qquad (10.3.8)$$

For the Kuhn–Tucker theorem to be applicable to equation (10.3.8), we must assume that marginal cost is a non-diminishing function of output. This assures that the total cost function is convex. The production functions are concave by assumption; hence when the negative signs in equations (10.3.6) are considered, these functions are also convex. Inequalities (10.3.7) are obviously convex. Hence the requirements of the Kuhn–Tucker theorem are satisfied.

For the constrained minimization problem, the Kuhn–Tucker conditions, analogous to equations (10.2.10)–(10.2.15), are:

$$\frac{\partial L}{\partial x_{ji}} \equiv w_j \left(1 + \frac{1}{\theta_j}\right) - \lambda_i \frac{\partial f_i}{\partial x_{ji}} \geq 0 \quad (i = 1, 2, ..., n; j = 1, 2, ..., m),$$

$$(10.3.9)$$

$$\frac{\partial L}{\partial y_{ki}} \equiv \frac{\partial S}{\partial y_{ki}} - \lambda_i \frac{\partial f_i}{\partial y_{ki}} + \mu_k \geq 0 \quad (i = 1, 2, ..., n; k = 1, 2, ..., r),$$

$$(10.3.10)$$

$$\sum_{i=1}^{n} \sum_{j=1}^{m} \left(\frac{\partial L}{\partial x_{ji}}\right) x_{ji} + \sum_{i=1}^{n} \sum_{k=1}^{r} \left(\frac{\partial L}{\partial y_{ki}}\right) y_{ki} = 0, \quad (10.3.11)$$

$$x_{ji} \geq 0, y_{ki} \geq 0 \quad (i = 1, 2, ..., n; j = 1, 2, ..., m; k = 1, 2, ..., r), \quad (10.3.12)$$

$$\frac{\partial L}{\partial \lambda_i} \equiv \bar{q}_i - f_i(x_{1i}, ..., y_{ri}) \leq 0 \quad (i = 1, 2, ..., n), \quad (10.3.13)$$

$$\frac{\partial L}{\partial \mu_k} \equiv \sum_{i=1}^{n} y_{ki} - y_k \leq 0 \quad (k = 1, 2, ..., r), \quad (10.3.14)$$

$$\sum_{i=1}^{n} \left(\frac{\partial L}{\partial \lambda_i}\right) \lambda_i + \sum_{k=1}^{r} \left(\frac{\partial L}{\partial \mu_k}\right) \mu_k = 0, \quad (10.3.15)$$

$$\lambda_i \geq 0, \mu_k \geq 0 \quad (i = 1, 2, ..., n; k = 1, 2, ..., r). \quad (10.3.16)$$

In expressions (10.3.9), θ_j is the elasticity of supply of the jth variable input. We shall now analyze each of these conditions, noting that the inputs (x_{ji}, y_{ki}) and the shadow prices (λ_i, μ_k) must be nonnegative.

10.3.2 Economic interpretation

Expressions (10.3.9): Rewrite the first condition as

$$w_j \left(1 + \frac{1}{\theta_j}\right) \geq \lambda_i \frac{\partial f_i}{\partial x_{ji}}. \quad (10.3.17)$$

The term on the left is the marginal expense of employing a unit of the jth variable resource. If the firm is a perfect competitor in the jth resource market, of course, $\theta_j \to \infty$ and the marginal expense of input is the same as the resource price. The term on the right-hand side is, in effect, the marginal

206

revenue product of the jth variable input.[1] If the firm is a perfect competitor in the product market, λ_i is the same as the product price; in this case the right-hand side is the value of the marginal product.

Expression (10.3.17) gives rise to two interpretations. If the jth resource is not used in the production of the ith product, the expression explains *why*. Specifically, the imputed marginal value the jth resource would contribute to production is less than the marginal expense its employment would incur. If the jth resource is used in producing the ith output, on the other hand, expression (10.3.17) states the familiar proposition that the marginal expense of input must equal imputed marginal revenue product.

Expressions (10.3.9) must hold for all i and all j. First consider two variable inputs (a and b) used to produce the ith commodity. Familiar conditions are again obtained:

$$\frac{w_a(1+(1/\theta_a))}{w_b(1+(1/\theta_b))} = \frac{\partial f_i/\partial x_{ai}}{\partial f_i/\partial x_{bi}}. \tag{10.3.18}$$

Equation (10.3.18) simply states that the marginal rate of technical substitution between two variable inputs must equal the incremental input-price ratio.

Next, suppose the jth variable input is used in producing outputs i and c. The condition then yields

$$\frac{\lambda_i(\partial f_i/\partial x_{ji})}{\lambda_c(\partial f_c/\partial x_{jc})} = 1. \tag{10.3.19}$$

In other words, the imputed marginal revenue product of a variable input must be the same in each of its uses. Finally, one may generalize equations (10.3.18) and (10.3.19) to obtain

$$\frac{w_a(1+(1/\theta_a))}{w_b(1+(1/\theta_b))} = \frac{\lambda_i(\partial f_i/\partial x_{ai})}{\lambda_c(\partial f_c/\partial x_{bc})}. \tag{10.3.20}$$

Thus the incremental input-price ratio must equal the ratio of imputed marginal revenue products, regardless of the product to which the inputs are allocated.

Expressions (10.3.10): While the quantity of a fixed factor is fixed in total, the quantity allocable to the production of any given product is variable. Hence the term $\lambda_i(\partial f_i/\partial y_{ki})$ is the imputed marginal revenue product of the kth fixed factor used in producing the ith output. Next, $\partial S/\partial y_{ki}$ is the marginal switching cost of the kth fixed input.[2] Finally, μ_k is the 'shadow

---

[1] The partial derivative is, from equation (10.3.1), the marginal product of the jth variable input in the production of the ith product. As shown in chapters 6 and 8, λ_i is the marginal cost of producing the ith product. Since in equilibrium marginal cost and marginal revenue are equal, the right-hand side is definitionally equal to marginal revenue product.

[2] It is appropriate at this point to note that equation (10.3.4), and hence $\partial S/\partial y_{ki}$, embodies an assumption that is undesirable, but nonetheless necessary. The assumption is as follows: the cost of switching a unit of the kth fixed factor to the ith output

price' of the kth fixed factor, or the unit value imputed to that input. Thus μ_k is also the imputed opportunity cost of using the kth fixed input.

Focusing upon output i, write a typical term in expressions (10.3.10) as

$$\frac{\partial S}{\partial y_{ki}} + \mu_k \geq \lambda_i \frac{\partial f_i}{\delta y_{ki}}. \qquad (10.3.21)$$

The left-hand side is the sum of marginal switching cost and unit opportunity cost. Hence it shows the full incremental cost of using the fixed input k in producing the ith output. Thus expression (10.3.21) reflects the customary marginal conditions: (a) if used at all, units of the kth fixed input are allocated to the production of the i-output until the incremental cost of using k in i is equal to the imputed marginal revenue product associated with the use of k in i; (b) if the imputed marginal revenue product is never as great as incremental cost, the kth input will not be used to produce the ith output.[1]

Next, consider two fixed inputs, s and t, used to produce output i. The equilibrium condition in this case is

$$\frac{(\partial S/\partial y_{si}) + \mu_s}{(\partial S/\partial y_{ti}) + \mu_t} = \frac{\partial f_i/\partial y_{si}}{\partial f_i/\partial y_{ti}}. \qquad (10.3.22)$$

Another familiar marginal equivalence is obtained: if two fixed inputs are used in producing a specified commodity, the incremental cost ratio must equal the marginal rate of technical substitution.

Finally, considering the use of the kth fixed input in producing two commodities (a and b), the equilibrium condition becomes

$$\frac{(\partial S/\partial y_{ka}) + \mu_k}{(\partial S/\partial y_{kb}) + \mu_k} = \frac{\lambda_a(\partial f_a/\partial y_{ka})}{\lambda_b(\partial f_b/\partial y_{kb})}. \qquad (10.3.23)$$

is the same irrespective of the usage from which it was transferred. Now it is reasonable to suppose that the cost of switching is less the more closely related are the production processes. For example, the cost of converting a cigarette manufacturing machine from the production of 70 millimeter standard non-filters to 85 millimeter standard non-filters is less than the cost of converting the same machine to the production of 85 millimeter cork-tip cigarettes. Such examples could doubtless be multiplied at will. However, the assumption implicit in equation (10.3.4) precludes this bit of realism. It is to be hoped, however, that it captures enough of reality to be a suitable representation of switching costs.

[1] This interpretation needs some qualification because the model is not flexible enough to handle certain situations. Or, stated differently, the undesirable feature of the switching cost function described in footnote 2, pp. 207–208 comes back to haunt us again. Suppose that at a given instant, machine k is adjusted to produce output a. Now, it might very well be true that $(\partial S/\partial y_{kb}) + \mu_k > \lambda_b(\partial f_b/\partial y_{kb})$ for all $b \neq a$. This condition does not mean that machine k is not used. It simply means that if the machine is used at all, it is only used in the production of output a. There is no switching cost involved; the machine is used in a-production so long as quasi-rent is nonnegative.

The switching cost function postulated is simply not versatile enough to cover the situation described above.

Thus when the same fixed input is used to produce different commodities, the incremental cost ratio must equal the ratio of imputed marginal revenue products.

10.3.3 Conclusion

From the discussion in subsection 10.3.2, it is clear that conditions (10.3.11)–(10.3.16) are satisfied. It seems that the results are also clear. Equations (10.3.18)–(10.3.20) impose the familiar marginal equalities, developed in chapters 6 and 8, upon each variable input employed by a firm. Equations (10.3.21)–(10.3.23) impose an analogous set of marginal equalities upon the fixed inputs used by a firm. But this is exactly what one should expect. The possibility of transferring fixed inputs among different uses makes each fixed input a *variable* from the standpoint of any one commodity. Hence it is quite reasonable that the marginal equivalences associated with the variable inputs should also apply to the quasi-variable inputs whose total usage is limited.

While the mathematical method differs somewhat, the theory of the multi-product firm is a straightforward extension of the theory of the single-product firm. There are no crucial differences in the conclusions. The only distinction is that factors which are fixed to a single-product firm become a separate class of variable factors to the multi-product firm. We shall see that the same conclusion applies to profit-maximizing behavior of a multi-product firm.[1]

10.4 Profit maximization in a multi-product firm

The analytical framework introduced in section 10.3 carries over straightforwardly to the profit maximization model. We have only to introduce the revenue side and define the profit function. Let the inverse demand function for the ith output be

$$p_i = g_i(q_1, q_2, ..., q_n), \qquad (10.4.1)$$

where

$$\frac{\partial q_i}{\partial p_i} < 0 \quad \text{and} \quad \frac{\partial q_i}{\partial p_j} \gtreqless 0 \quad \text{for } i \neq j. \qquad (10.4.2)$$

The total revenue, therefore, is

$$R = \sum_{i=1}^{n} p_i q_i = \sum_{i=1}^{n} g_i(q_1, ..., q_n) f_i(x_{ji}, y_{ki}). \qquad (10.4.3)$$

Finally, using equations (10.4.3) and (10.3.5), profit may be written as

$$\Pi = R - (V + S + F)$$

$$= \sum_{i=1}^{n} g_i f_i - \sum_{j=1}^{m} \sum_{i=1}^{n} w_j x_{ji} - S(y_{11}, ..., y_{rn}) - F. \qquad (10.4.4)$$

---

[1] As stated in footnote 1, p. 202, this section follows the original development attributable to Pfouts [1961]. However, the economic interpretation of expressions (10.3.10) differs from Pfouts' interpretation. Partly for that reason, our overall conclusions differ markedly.

The problem confronting the firm is to maximize the profit function (10.4.4) subject to the constraint imposed by limited availabilities of the fixed inputs. This constraint must now be written

$$y_r - \sum_{i=1}^{n} y_{ki} \geqq 0 \quad (k = 1, 2, \dots, r).$$ (10.4.5)

The associated Lagrange equation is

$$L(X, Y, \nu) \equiv \sum_{i=1}^{n} g_i f_i - \sum_{j=1}^{m} \sum_{i=1}^{n} w_j x_{ji} - S(y_{11}, \dots, y_{rn})$$
$$- F + \sum_{k=1}^{r} \nu_k \left[y_k - \sum_{i=1}^{n} y_{ki} \right].$$ (10.4.6)

10.4.1 The Kuhn–Tucker conditions

The Kuhn–Tucker conditions, analogous to expressions (10.2.4)–(10.2.9) above, are as follows:

$$\frac{\partial L}{\partial x_{ji}} \equiv \left[\sum_{s=1}^{n} p_i \left(1 + \frac{1}{\eta_{is}} \right) \right] \frac{\partial f_i}{\partial x_{ji}} - w_j \left(1 + \frac{1}{\theta_j} \right) \leqq 0$$
$$(i = 1, 2, \dots, n; j = 1, 2, \dots, m), \quad (10.4.7)$$

$$\frac{\partial L}{\partial y_{ki}} \equiv \left[\sum_{s=1}^{n} p_i \left(1 + \frac{1}{\eta_{is}} \right) \right] \frac{\partial f_i}{\partial y_{ki}} - \frac{\partial S}{\partial y_{ki}} - \nu_k \leqq 0$$
$$(i = 1, 2, \dots, n; k = 1, 2, \dots, r), \quad (10.4.8)$$

$$\sum_{i=1}^{n} \sum_{j=1}^{m} \left(\frac{\partial L}{\partial x_{ji}} \right) x_{ji} + \sum_{i=1}^{n} \sum_{k=1}^{r} \left(\frac{\partial L}{\partial y_{ki}} \right) y_{ki} = 0,$$ (10.4.9)

$$x_{ji} \geqq 0, y_{ki} \geqq 0 \quad (i = 1, 2, \dots, n; j = 1, 2, \dots, m; k = 1, 2, \dots, r),$$ (10.4.10)

$$\frac{\partial L}{\partial \nu_k} \equiv y_k - \sum_{i=1}^{n} y_{ki} \geqq 0 \quad (k = 1, 2, \dots, r),$$ (10.4.11)

$$\sum_{k=1}^{r} \left(\frac{\partial L}{\partial \nu_k} \right) \nu_k = 0,$$ (10.4.12)

$$\nu_k \geqq 0 \quad (k = 1, 2, \dots, r).$$ (10.4.13)

In expressions (10.4.7) and (10.4.8),

$$\eta_{is} = \frac{\partial p_s}{\partial q_i} \frac{q_i}{p_s}$$ (10.4.14)

is the price cross-elasticity of commodity demand.

10.4.2 Economic interpretation

In expressions (10.4.7) and (10.4.8), the term

$$\sum_{s=1}^{n} p_i \left(1 + \frac{1}{\eta_{is}} \right)$$

is the aggregate marginal revenue attributable to the addition of one unit of the ith output to sales (i.e. after allowing for the fact that a change in q_i changes the prices of some other outputs). Similarly, v_k is the shadow price or imputed unit opportunity cost of the kth fixed factor. Given these meanings, a casual glance at the system (10.4.7)–(10.4.13) reveals that the economic interpretation is precisely the same as in subsection 10.3.2.

10.4.3 Conclusion

This completes our analysis of the multi-product firm. The overall conclusion to be drawn is precisely the one stated in subsection 10.3.3. Despite a number of apparent differences, the theory of the multi-product firm is entirely analogous to the simpler theory of the single-product firm.

PART II

MACROECONOMIC THEORIES
OF DISTRIBUTION AND
TECHNOLOGICAL PROGRESS

11

TECHNOLOGICAL PROGRESS
AND THE NEOCLASSICAL THEORY
OF PRODUCTION

11.1 Introduction

In passing from microeconomic magnitudes to the corresponding macro-economic values, one must necessarily use some method of aggregation. In the 'Introduction' to this volume, the problem of aggregation was briefly discussed. It was then stated that the rigor of general equilibrium theory would be sacrificed for simplicity: our macroeconomic theory is constructed by analogy with the corresponding microeconomic theory. Thus we assume that the aggregate economic system possesses an aggregate production function; that there are two broad, homogeneous classes of inputs (capital and labor); that the system behaves in a 'purposive' way (i.e., so as to maximize or minimize, possibly subject to constraint); and that the system rewards each input according to competitive imputations. There are, of course, no teleological implications.

In order for the last assumption to be valid from a methodological point of view, one must further assume that 'the' aggregate production function is homogeneous of degree one. Let Y, K, and L denote real output, the real flow of capital services, and the employed labor force. By analogy with the microeconomic theory developed in Part I, chapters 4 and 5, the aggregate production function may be written

$$Y = G(K, L), \tag{11.1.1}$$

where $G(\cdot)$ is homogeneous of degree one in the inputs. Similarly, specific forms of the production function may be developed by analogy. For example, the Cobb–Douglas and the CES functions, respectively, are

$$Y = AK^\alpha L^{1-\alpha} \quad (0 < \alpha < 1), \tag{11.1.2}$$

and

$$Y = \gamma[\delta K^{-\rho} + (1 - \delta) L^{-\rho}]^{-1/\rho}. \tag{11.1.3}$$

The production functions appearing in equations (11.1.1)–(11.1.3) have one very essential feature in common. Specifically, none of them contains a time variable because Part I was concerned only with static and comparative-static analyses of production and distribution. There is a definite reason for this restriction, which reflects my personal view of technological change within a firm. Within an individual firm, technological change is likely to be an erratic process, going forward by fits and starts. Most assuredly, the inventive and innovative processes within a single firm cannot be represented by smooth (exponential) time trends; indeed, it is doubtful that technological change can even be represented by a known probability distribution.[1]

In this situation, it seems that the analysis of technological change must follow the approach developed by Mansfield,[2] or at least one very similar to it. However, this is much too specific and probabilistic for the purposes of this book. Yet when many discrete and almost random influences are aggregated, it is not unreasonable to suppose that aggregate technological change can be represented by a smooth time trend.[3] The macroeconomic analysis becomes correspondingly simpler and fits into the format of this undertaking. Therefore, in the spirit of aggregation by analogy that led to equation (11.1.1), we postulate an aggregate production function of the form

$$Y = F(K, L, t), \tag{11.1.4}$$

where $F(\cdot)$ is homogeneous of degree one in K and L and continuous and differentiable in all arguments. The production function in equation (11.1.4) is, for the most part, used throughout the remainder of the book.

11.2 The classification of technological progress[4]

Since Hicks' pioneering effort,[5] it has become fashionable to classify technological progress according as it is relatively labor or capital saving or neutral in its input-saving effects. But just as an invention may be regarded as relatively saving in the usage of one input, it may also be regarded as relatively 'using' of the other input. In the more recent literature, the latter terminology predominates. Hence we shall uniformly speak of capital-using, labor-using, or neutral technological progress.

The classification of technological progress may be approached from two standpoints, which depend upon the time period under analysis. On the one hand, interest may center on the initial impact of technological pro-

---

[1] See Tintner [1941], [1942 a, b].
[2] See Mansfield [1961], [1962], [1963 a, b, c], [1964], and [1965].
[3] For the same view, see Harrod [1956, p. 23].
[4] Beginning with Mrs Robinson's famous paper [1938], there have been numerous articles expatiating upon the Hicks and Harrod concepts of neutral and biased technological progress. See Asimakopulos [1963], Asimakopulos and Weldon [1963], Kennedy [1962 a, b], Seeber [1962], and Uzawa [1961 a]. The exposition in this section utilizes the graphical devices introduced by Mrs Robinson [1938].
[5] Hicks [1932].

gress. That is, one may chiefly be concerned with the effects of technological progress during a period in which input supplies are relatively fixed. As we shall see, this is Hicks' point of view. On the other hand, one's interest may focus upon the long-run effects of technological progress (i.e. the effects of technological progress when input supplies are allowed to adjust to economic conditions). This is the approach of Harrod.

11.2.1 Short-run effects of technological progress: the Hicks approach

According to Hicks, 'If we concentrate upon two groups of factors, "labour" and "capital", and suppose them to exhaust the list, then we can classify inventions according as their *initial effects* are to increase, leave unchanged, or diminish the ratio of the marginal product of capital to that of labour. We may call these inventions "labour-saving", "neutral", and "capital-saving" respectively.'[1]

Paraphrasing Hicks we may establish the following:

Short-run definition: At a given capital–labor ratio, technological progress is capital using, neutral, or labor using according as the marginal rate of technical substitution of capital for labor decreases, remains unchanged, or increases, where

$$MRTS_{KL} = -\frac{dK}{dL} = \frac{{}^{'}F_L}{F_K}, \qquad (11.2.1)$$

and subscripts denote partial differentiation.

The essence of Hicks' definition is as follows. At any given instant of time, there is a prevailing input-price ratio. Given economically efficient operation, the input-price ratio leads to an equilibrium capital–labor ratio at the point where an isoquant is tangent to an isocost curve. At this point the marginal rate of technical substitution equals the input-price ratio. Now suppose the input-price ratio and the capital–labor ratio are instantaneously fixed. Next, suppose there is technological progress, which is graphically represented by a shift of the isoquant toward the origin. Finally, suppose the technological shift is capital using, implying a decrease in the marginal rate of technical substitution. At the given input-price ratio, there would be an incentive to substitute capital for labor, i.e. to increase the capital–labor ratio. Of course, with fixed input supplies, the capital–labor ratio cannot be changed instantaneously. However, there is an incentive to increase the ratio, and it will be increased in the long run. This is precisely the meaning of Hicks-biased technological progress.

An alternative explanation of the Hicks classification scheme is possible; an examination of this view reveals that technological progress can also be

[1] *Ibid.* p. 121. Italics supplied.

217

classified on the basis of changes in the output elasticities or changes in relative shares.

By definition, the output elasticity of a factor is the ratio of marginal to average product. From equation (11.1.4), the output elasticity of capital (ϵ_K) is

$$\epsilon_K = \frac{F_K}{Y/K} = \frac{KF_K}{Y} = (1-s), \qquad (11.2.2)$$

where s is the relative share of labor, and the third equality follows from the assumption of competitive imputation. By the homogeneity assumption, equation (11.1.4) may be written

$$Y = F(K, L, t) = LF\left(\frac{K}{L}, t\right), \qquad (11.2.3)$$

or
$$y = f(k|t), \qquad (11.2.4)$$

where y and k denote the output–labor and capital–labor ratios respectively. Since the marginal product of capital from equation (11.2.4) is $f'(k|t)$, equation (11.2.2) may also be written as

$$\epsilon_K = \frac{kf'(k|t)}{y} = (1-s). \qquad (11.2.5)$$

Utilizing equations (11.2.4) and (11.2.5) enables one to state the Hicks classification in terms of output elasticities or relative shares.

First, from equation (11.2.4), the marginal product of labor is

$$F_L = \frac{\partial(Ly)}{\partial L} = f(k|t) - kf'(k|t); \qquad (11.2.6)$$

hence from equations (11.2.1) and (11.2.5), the marginal rate of technical substitution of capital for labor is

$$MRTS_{KL} = \frac{f(k|t) - kf'(k|t)}{f'(k|t)}. \qquad (11.2.7)$$

Next, consider two time periods, t_1 and t_2. If technological progress is neutral between t_1 and t_2, Hicks' definition is satisfied if $k_1 = k_2$ and

$$\frac{MRTS_{KL}^{t_2}}{MRTS_{KL}^{t_1}} = 1. \qquad (11.2.8)$$

Finally, using equations (11.2.4) and (11.2.7) in equation (11.2.8) enables one to state the Hicks condition for neutral technological progress as (remembering $k_1 = k_2$):

$$\frac{y_2 - k_1 f'(k_1|t_2)}{y_1 - k_1 f'(k_1|t_1)} \cdot \frac{f'(k_1|t_1)}{f'(k_1|t_2)} = 1. \qquad (11.2.9)$$

If the output elasticity of capital remains constant between t_1 and t_2, we have, from equation (11.2.5) and the assumption that $k_1 = k_2$,

$$\frac{k_1 f'(k_1|t_1)}{y_1} = \frac{k_1 f'(k_1|t_2)}{y_2}. \tag{11.2.10}$$

Using equation (11.2.10) in equation (11.2.9) yields

$$\frac{y_2 \left[1 - \dfrac{k_1 f'(k_1|t_2)}{y_2} \right]}{y_1 \left[1 - \dfrac{k_1 f'(k_1|t_1)}{y_1} \right]} \cdot \frac{y_1}{y_2} = 1. \tag{11.2.11}$$

The equality can obviously hold only if

$$\frac{k_1 f'(k_1|t_2)}{y_2} = \frac{k_1 f'(k_1|t_1)}{y_1}. \tag{11.2.12}$$

Comparing equations (11.2.10) and (11.2.12) establishes the following

Relations: Technological progress is Hicks neutral if, and only if, the output elasticity of capital, and hence the output elasticity of labor, remains constant. By extension, technological progress is capital using or labor using according as the output elasticity of capital increases or decreases. Since the output elasticity of a factor and its relative share are identically the same [equation (11.2.5)], the following statement also holds: technological progress is capital using, neutral, or labor using according as the relative share of capital increases, remains unchanged, or declines. By inversion, all of the above relations may be expressed in terms of the output elasticity or relative share of labor.

The results just obtained are illustrated in figure 48. The initial position is point a, where $y = f(k_1|t_1)$. Suppose technological progress is neutral. Then the curve must shift iso-elastically, so that ϵ_K at points a and b are the same. If the elasticity of $f(k|t_2)$ is greater than the elasticity of $f(k|t_1)$ at $k = k_1$, technological progress is capital using. The same statement holds, *mutatis mutandis*, for labor-using technological progress.

11.2.2 Long-run effects of technological progress: the Harrod approach

The concept of neutrality suggested by Harrod relates to long-run equilibrium. The long-run equilibrium in question has a special character that has come to play an important role in recent theories of 'golden age' growth. Specifically, the long-run equilibrium is defined relative to a given rate of return on capital (rate of interest), which is assumed to be the same before and after (with adjustment of input ratios) technological change.

It seems worthwhile to quote Harrod at some length.

I define a neutral advance as one which, at a constant rate of interest, does not disturb the value of the capital coefficient; it does not alter the length of the production process....It implies, to put it roughly, that the productivity of labour embodied in machines is raised in equal measure with that of those engaged on minding machines; it implies an equal rise of productivity on the part of all labour however far back or forward it may be between the inception and the final stage of production. No one invention is likely, of course, to have this character, but the sum of inventions occuring in a unit period might well have.[1]

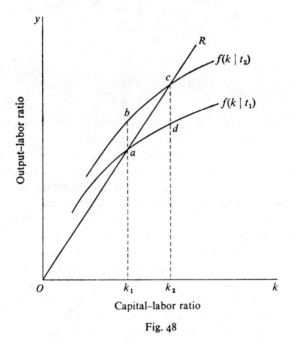

Fig. 48

Further, Harrod commented that

...it has seemed simplest to define a neutral stream of inventions as one which shall require a rate of increase of capital equal to the rate of increase in income engendered by it. If the stream of inventions requires capital to increase at a greater rate, then it is labour-saving or capital-requiring; and conversely....The neutrality of an invention would be determined on my definition by reference to what happens to the capital coefficient, if the rate of interest is constant.[2]

More succinctly, the Harrod classification is as follows: for a given rate of interest, a technological change is capital using, neutral, or labor using according as the capital–output ratio increases, remains unchanged, or diminishes. Obviously, therefore, an invention is capital using, neutral, or

[1] Harrod [1956, p. 23].   [2] *Ibid.* pp. 26–7.

labor using according as the relative share of capital increases, remains constant, or diminishes.

The Harrod concept of neutrality is illustrated graphically by figure 49. As Mrs Robinson pointed out,[1] a Harrod-neutral technological change shifts the average product of capital iso-elastically. This follows immediately, of course, from the definition of the elasticity of average product:

$$\frac{\partial \left(\frac{Y}{K}\right)}{\partial K} \frac{K^2}{Y} = \frac{KF_K - Y}{Y} = \frac{K}{Y} F_K - 1 = \epsilon_K - 1. \qquad (11.2.13)$$

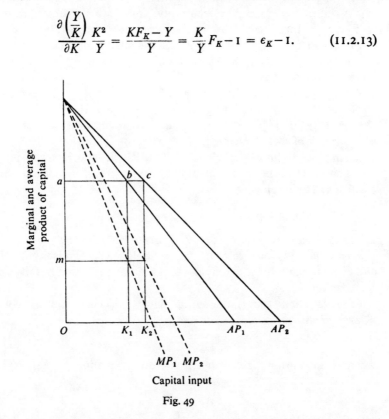

Fig. 49

Harrod neutrality implies constancy of the rate by interest (F_K) and of the capital–output ratio (K/Y). Hence Harrod neutrality implies that ϵ_K, and hence $\epsilon_K - 1$, is constant. Finally, the condition that $\epsilon_K - 1$ is constant implies iso-elastic shifts of the average product curve.

An iso-elastic shift in the average product of capital is shown in figure 49. The average product curve (AP_1) is shifted to the right by a constant percentage (to AP_2). Consider the rate of interest constant at Om. The average product of capital is the same before and after the shift; it is con-

[1] Robinson [1938].

stant at the level Oa. If the technological change were capital using, point c would lie above point b; the reverse holds for labor-using technological progress.

11.2.3 Relation between Hicks- and Harrod-neutrality

For any given production function there is a definite relation between the Hicks and Harrod concepts of neutrality. The relation is shown graphically in figure 48. First, recall that a technological change is Hicks-neutral if $f(k|t)$ shifts iso-elastically for $k = k_1$. On the other hand, Harrod-neutrality implies that the shift of $f(k|t)$ is iso-elastic for a given capital–output ratio, i.e. along the ray OR.

A shift is Hicks-neutral if the elasticity of $f(k|t_1)$ at a is the same as the elasticity of $f(k|t_2)$ at b. Using Harrod's definition, the shift is neutral if the elasticity of $f(k|t_1)$ at a is the same as the elasticity of $f(k|t_2)$ at c. Comparison of these statements establishes the following[1]

Relation: A technological change is both Hicks- and Harrod-neutral if, and only if, the production function is characterized by constant output elasticities at all points.

11.2.4 Two special cases

Using the relation above, it is easy to prove the following

Proposition: In a one sector model, technological progress is both Hicks- and Harrod-neutral if, and only if, the production function has the Cobb–Douglas form.

From equation (11.2.5), the output elasticity of (say) capital is constant if, and only if,

$$\epsilon_K = \frac{kf'(k|t)}{y} = \alpha, \qquad (11.2.14)$$

where α is a constant. Rearranging and using equation (11.2.4) yields

$$\frac{f'(k|t)}{f(k|t)} = \alpha k^{-1}. \qquad (11.2.15)$$

One simple quadrature gives

$$\ln f(k|t) = \alpha \ln k + \ln A, \qquad (11.2.16)$$

or $$f(k|t) = Ak^\alpha, \qquad (11.2.17)$$

where A is a constant of integration. In light of equations (11.2.3) and (11.2.4), equation (11.2.17) becomes

$$Y = F(K, L|t) = AK^\alpha L^{1-\alpha}. \qquad (11.2.18)$$

[1] Extending the argument, it can easily be shown that Hicks- and Harrod-neutrality together imply that the elasticity of $f(k|t_1)$ at d is equal to the elasticity of $f(k|t_2)$ at c.

It is thus seen that t must enter the production independently, i.e. as a multiplicative factor. Hence equation (11.2.18) may be written as

$$Y = F(K, L, t) = A e^{\lambda t} K^\alpha L^{1-\alpha}, \qquad (11.2.19)$$

where λ is a constant. Equation (11.2.19) is precisely the time-series form of the Cobb–Douglas function, thus completing the proof.

From the Proposition above, it is apparent that the Cobb–Douglas function is very special indeed, inasmuch as it reduces the significantly different definitions of neutrality to the same thing. In Part I, chapters 4 and 5 another 'special' feature of the Cobb–Douglas function was noted, namely that the elasticity of substitution is unity at all points. This indicates that there may be a close relation between the value of the elasticity of substitution and the Hicks–Harrod classifications. Indeed, there is, as we shall see in section 11.3 below. Before turning to this, another special case is of interest.

Let us begin by stating the following[1]

Proposition (Uzawa): The production function $F(K, L, t)$ is characterized by Harrod neutrality if, and only if, it may be written

$$F(K, L, t) = G[K, A(t) L],$$

for a positive function $A(t)$.

The form

$$F(K, L, t) = G[K, A(t) L] \qquad (11.2.20)$$

suggests that the CES function is ideally suited to represent Harrod-neutral technological progress.

The Harrod-neutral form of the CES function is[2]

$$Y = A[\delta K^{-\rho} + (1-\delta)(e^{\alpha t}L)^{-\rho}]^{-1/\rho}. \qquad (11.2.21)$$

It immediately follows that equation (11.2.21) represents Hicks' definition of capital-using, neutral, or labor-using technological progress according as

$$\frac{\sigma - 1}{\sigma} \alpha \gtreqless 0. \qquad (11.2.22)$$

The purely labor-augmenting form of the CES function satisfies the conditions for both Hicks- and Harrod-neutrality (for $\sigma \neq 0$) if, and only if, $\sigma = 1$. As shown in chapters 4 and 5, however, when $\sigma = 1$, the CES function reduces to the Cobb–Douglas function, establishing the consistency of the Propositions stated above.

Another relation is worth a passing note. It might seem from the foregoing that Hicks- and Harrod-neutrality are the same if the production

---

[1] The proof is given in Uzawa [1961*a*, pp. 119–20].
[2] See Ferguson [1965*b*, pp. 297–9].

function is separable, i.e., if t enters as a multiplicative factor. It is easy to demonstrate that this is not so.

Write the CES function as

$$Y = A e^{\lambda t} [\delta K^{-\rho} + (1 - \delta) L^{-\rho}]^{-1/\rho}. \qquad (11.2.23)$$

From equation (11.2.23) it follows that

$$MRTS_{KL} = \left(\frac{1-\delta}{\delta}\right) \left(\frac{K}{L}\right)^{1/\sigma}. \qquad (11.2.24)$$

Since the marginal rate of technical substitution is constant for a constant capital–labor ratio, equation (11.2.23) represents Hicks-neutral technological progress.

Now consider the marginal product of capital which, in long-run competitive equilibrium, is the rate of interest (r):

$$F_k = r = A^{-\rho} e^{-\rho \lambda t} \delta \left(\frac{K}{Y}\right)^{-1/\sigma}. \qquad (11.2.25)$$

Writing x for the capital–output ratio, equation (11.2.25) may be expressed more generally as

$$r = r(x, t), \qquad (11.2.26)$$

where, from equation (11.2.25)

$$r(x_1, t_1) \neq r(x_1, t_2).$$

Hence equation (11.2.23) does not depict Harrod-neutral technological progress.

11.3 A general neoclassical model of technological progress[1]

The object now is to develop a model that is applicable to the economy as a whole or to any sector of it. This is important, at present, because it will permit a comparison of Hicks- and Harrod-neutrality in a two-sector model. In chapter 12, the model will be used to analyze the theory of relative shares in one- and two-sector models.

11.3.1 The model

Assume, as above, that the production function is given by

$$Y = F(K, L, t), \qquad (11.3.1)$$

[1] Several writers have advanced more or less similar models. In a sense, the model presented here is an amalgam of these. See Amano [1964], Diamond [1965], Fei and Ranis [1963] and [1965], Drandakis and Phelps [1966], and Bardhan [1965]. This section is a reprint, with some changes, of Ferguson [1968 a].

where $$F_K, F_L > 0 \quad \text{and} \quad F_{KK}, F_{LL} < 0, \tag{11.3.2}$$

and $$r = F_K, \quad w = F_L, \tag{11.3.3}$$

where r and w denote the real rate of interest and the product wage rate.[1]

The *rate* of technological progress, denoted by R, is simply the partial derivative of $F(K, L, t)$ with respect to time reduced to a rate. Hence

$$R = \frac{F_t}{F} = \frac{KF_{Kt} + LF_{Lt}}{KF_K + LF_L}. \tag{11.3.4}$$

Let B represent the *bias* of technological progress. Following Hicks' approach,

$$B = \frac{\partial}{\partial t}\left(\frac{F_K}{F_L}\right) \div \left(\frac{F_K}{F_L}\right) = \frac{F_{Kt}}{F_K} - \frac{F_{Lt}}{F_L}. \tag{11.3.5}$$

From definition (11.3.5), technological progress is (Hicks) capital using, neutral, or labor using according as $B \gtreqless 0$.

Three additional definitional equations are needed:

$$s = \frac{LF_L}{F} = \text{relative share of labor;} \tag{11.3.6}$$

$$(1-s) = \frac{KF_K}{F} = \text{relative share of capital;} \tag{11.3.7}$$

$$\sigma = \frac{F_K F_L}{F F_{KL}} = \text{elasticity of substitution.} \tag{11.3.8}$$

Using definitions (11.3.6) and (11.3.7), equations (11.3.4) and (11.3.5) may be solved so as to express the proportional time changes in the marginal products as functions of the rate and bias of technological progress. To this end, write equations (11.3.4) and (11.3.5) as

$$\frac{R}{F_L} = \frac{KF_{Kt}}{FF_L} + \frac{LF_{Lt}}{FF_L}, \tag{11.3.9}$$

$$\frac{LB}{F} = \frac{LF_{Kt}}{FF_K} - \frac{LF_{Lt}}{FF_L}. \tag{11.3.10}$$

Adding equations (11.3.9) and (11.3.10), one obtains

$$\frac{R}{F_L} + \frac{LB}{F} = \frac{KF_K F_{Kt} + LF_L F_{Kt}}{FF_L F_K}. \tag{11.3.11}$$

[1] In what follows, a subscript denotes partial differentiation. Thus, for example,

$$F_t \equiv \frac{\partial F}{\partial t}.$$

Superior dots denote the total time derivative. Hence

$$\dot{F} = F_K \dot{K} + F_L \dot{L} + F_t.$$

Reducing equation (11.3.11) to a common denominator and clearing yields

$$F_{Kt}(KF_K + LF_L) = FF_K R + LF_L F_K B, \qquad (11.3.12)$$

from whence it follows that

$$\frac{F_{Kt}}{F_K} = R + sB \qquad (11.3.13)$$

since $KF_K + LF_L \equiv F$ by Euler's theorem and $LF_L/F \equiv s$. By a similar reduction process from equations (11.3.9) and (11.3.10), one may easily show that

$$\frac{F_{Lt}}{F_L} = R - (1 - s)\, B. \qquad (11.3.14)$$

Next, observe that

$$F_{Kk} = LF_{KK} \quad \text{and} \quad F_{Lk} = LF_{LK}. \qquad (11.3.15)$$

Thus

$$\frac{F_{Kk}}{F_K} = \frac{LF_{KK}}{F_K} = \frac{LF_L}{F} \cdot \frac{FKF_{KK}}{KF_L F_K}. \qquad (11.3.16)$$

For functions homogeneous of degree one, it is always true that

$$-LF_{LL} \equiv KF_{LK} \quad \text{and} \quad -KF_{KK} \equiv LF_{KL}. \qquad (11.3.17)$$

Using identities (11.3.17) in equation (11.3.16) yields

$$\frac{F_{Kk}}{F_K} = -\frac{LF_L}{F} \cdot \frac{L}{K} \cdot \frac{FF_{LK}}{F_L F_K}. \qquad (11.3.18)$$

Finally using definition (11.3.8) in equation (11.3.18) enables one to write

$$\frac{F_{Kk}}{F_K} = -\frac{s}{\sigma k}. \qquad (11.3.19)$$

By a similar reduction process, it is easy to show that

$$\frac{F_{Lk}}{F_L} = \frac{(1 - s)}{\sigma k}. \qquad (11.3.20)$$

By using equations (11.3.13), (11.3.14), (11.3.19), and (11.3.20), the rates of growth of the marginal products and of real output may be obtained. First, observe that

$$\dot{F}_K = F_{Kt} + F_{KK}\dot{K} + F_{KL}\dot{L}. \qquad (11.3.21)$$

Thus by identities (11.3.17),

$$\frac{\dot{F}_K}{F_K} = \frac{F_{Kt}}{F_K} - \frac{LF_{KL}}{F_K}\frac{k}{k}$$

$$= \frac{F_{Kt}}{F_K} - \frac{LF_L}{F} \cdot \frac{FF_{LK}}{F_L F_K} \cdot \frac{k}{k}. \qquad (11.3.22)$$

Substituting definition (11.3.8) in equation (11.3.22), one may write

$$\frac{\dot{F}_K}{F_K} = \frac{F_{Kt}}{F_K} - \frac{s}{\sigma}\frac{k}{k}. \qquad (11.3.23)$$

Substituting equation (11.3.13) in equation (11.3.23) yields

$$\frac{\dot{F}_K}{F_K} = R + sB - \frac{s}{\sigma}\frac{k}{k}. \tag{11.3.24}$$

In a similar way one may obtain

$$\frac{\dot{F}_L}{F_L} = R - (1-s)B + \frac{(1-s)}{\sigma}\frac{k}{k}. \tag{11.3.25}$$

Finally, we require two additional derivations.

First, by definition $\qquad \dot{F} = F_t + F_K\dot{K} + F_L\dot{L}. \tag{11.3.26}$

Substituting equation (11.3.4) and the definitions of s and k in equation (11.3.26) yields

$$\frac{\dot{F}}{F} = R + (1-s)\frac{k}{k} + \frac{\dot{L}}{L}. \tag{11.3.27}$$

Second, from definition (11.3.7) one obtains

$$\frac{(1\dot{-}s)}{(1-s)} = \frac{\dot{F}_K}{F_K} + \frac{\dot{K}}{K} - \frac{\dot{F}}{F}. \tag{11.3.28}$$

Using equations (11.3.24) and (11.3.27) in equation (11.3.28), one obtains

$$\frac{(1\dot{-}s)}{(1-s)} = sB + s\frac{k}{k} - \frac{s}{\sigma}\frac{k}{k}$$

$$= s\left[B + \left(1 - \frac{1}{\sigma}\right)\frac{k}{k}\right]. \tag{11.3.29}$$

As stated originally, all of these equations hold for single-sector or multi-sector models. To summarize, the basic model of technological progress is as follows:

$$R = \frac{F_t}{F}, \tag{11.3.30}$$

$$B = \frac{F_{Kt}}{F_K} - \frac{F_{Lt}}{F_L}, \tag{11.3.31}$$

$$\frac{F_{Kt}}{F_K} = R + sB, \tag{11.3.32}$$

$$\frac{F_{Lt}}{F_L} = R - (1-s)B, \tag{11.3.33}$$

$$\frac{\dot{F}_K}{F_K} = R + sB - \frac{s}{\sigma}\frac{k}{k}, \tag{11.3.34}$$

$$\frac{\dot{F}_L}{F_L} = R - (1-s)B + \frac{(1-s)}{\sigma}\frac{k}{k}, \tag{11.3.35}$$

$$\frac{\dot{F}}{F} = R + (1-s)\frac{k}{k} + \frac{\dot{L}}{L}, \tag{11.3.36}$$

$$\frac{(1\dot{-}s)}{(1-s)} = s\left[B + \left(1 - \frac{1}{\sigma}\right)\frac{k}{k}\right]. \tag{11.3.37}$$

11.3.2 Hicks- and Harrod-neutrality in a one-sector model

Let us first analyse the Hicks and Harrod concepts of neutrality in a one-sector model, i.e. a model in which Y is real national output and this output is both a consumption and a capital good. We have previously stated that according to Hicks' definition, technological progress is capital using, neutral, or labor using according as $B \gtreqless 0$.

Harrod's concept is somewhat more difficult to express. First, recall that by Harrod's definition, technological change is neutral if the capital–output ratio is constant at a constant rate of interest. In a one-sector model, constancy of the rate of interest implies that

$$\frac{\dot{F}_K}{F_K} = 0. \tag{11.3.38}$$

Substituting equation (11.3.34) in equation (11.3.38) and solving for the rate of change in the capital–labor ratio, the condition for constancy of the interest rate may be written

$$\frac{\dot{k}}{k} = \frac{\sigma R}{s} + \sigma B. \tag{11.3.39}$$

Next, if both the rate of interest and the capital–output ratio are constant, so is the relative share of capital $(1 - s)$. Thus this double condition requires that

$$\frac{(1\dot{-}s)}{(1-s)} = 0. \tag{11.3.40}$$

Substituting equation (11.3.37) in equation (11.3.40) and solving for the rate of change of the capital–labor ratio yields

$$\frac{\dot{k}}{k} = -\frac{B}{(1 - 1/\sigma)}. \tag{11.3.41}$$

Harrod-neutrality occurs when equations (11.3.39) and (11.3.41) are equal. Thus the condition for Harrod-neutrality is expressed by the following equation:

$$\left(1 - \frac{1}{\sigma}\right) R + sB = 0. \tag{11.3.42}$$

Suppose technological progress is Hicks-neutral, so $B = 0$. By equation (11.3.42), technological progress using Harrod's concept is capital using, neutral, or labor using according as $\sigma \gtreqless 1$ (assuming a strictly positive Hicks rate of progress). As shown before, Hicks- and Harrod-neutrality are one and the same if, and only if, the elasticity of substitution is unity, i.e. if, and only if, the production function has the Cobb–Douglas form.

The statement that technological progress is Harrod-capital-using if $\sigma > 1$ (labor using if $\sigma < 1$) may not be so obvious. To see this, recall that

228

technological progress is capital using in Harrod's sense if the capital–output ratio increases at a constant rate of interest. Now, the capital–output ratio increases if

$$\frac{\dot{K}}{K} - \frac{\dot{F}}{F} > 0. \tag{11.3.43}$$

Substitute equation (11.3.36) in the inequality to obtain

$$\frac{\dot{K}}{K} - \frac{\dot{F}}{F} = -R + s\left(\frac{k}{k}\right). \tag{11.3.44}$$

Next, invoke our current assumption that $B = 0$; substitute equation (11.3.39), which states the condition for a constant rate of interest, in equation (11.3.44), obtaining

$$\frac{\dot{K}}{K} - \frac{\dot{F}}{F} = (\sigma - 1) R \gtrless 0 \quad \text{according as} \quad \sigma \gtrless 1. \tag{11.3.45}$$

Expression (1.3.45) establishes the relation stated above.

If technological progress is not Hicks-neutral ($B \neq 0$), the direction of technological progress, using Harrod's concept, depends upon the Hicks rate, the Hicks bias, and the weights given them in equation (11.3.42). For example, if technological progress is Hicks-capital-using and the elasticity of substitution exceeds unity, it is Harrod-capital-using as well. But if the elasticity of substitution is less than one, technological progress could be Harrod-neutral or even labor using.

11.3.3 The model again: two sectors

Now assume that the economy is composed of two sectors, which produce consumption goods (C) and capital goods (M). The production functions, with obvious notation, are

$$C = F(K_C, L_C, t) = L_C f(k_C, t), \tag{11.3.46}$$

$$M = G(K_M, L_M, t) = L_M g(k_M, t). \tag{11.3.47}$$

Since there are now two sectors, it is necessary to introduce relative prices. To that end, let the consumption good be numeraire, and let the price of the capital good in terms of the consumption good be p, i.e.

$$\frac{p_M}{p_C} = p. \tag{11.3.48}$$

The existence of two sectors introduces additional complications as well; specifically, one must pay due heed to equilibrium in the factor market. There are three conditions for factor-market equilibrium: (a) the marginal rates of technical substitution of capital for labor must be the same in both sectors; (b) the wage rate in consumption units must be the same in both sectors; and (c) the rate of interest in consumption units must be the same in both sectors. Since any two of these conditions imply the third, we may, without loss of generality, concentrate upon (a) and (b) above.

The rate of change in the marginal rate of technical substitution in the consumption sector is

$$\frac{\dot{F}_L}{F_L} - \frac{\dot{F}_K}{F_K}. \tag{11.3.49}$$

Substituting equations (11.3.34) and (11.3.35) in expression (11.3.49) yields

$$\frac{\dot{F}_L}{F_L} - \frac{\dot{F}_K}{F_K} = \frac{1}{\sigma_C} \frac{k_C}{k_C} - B_C. \tag{11.3.50}$$

Similarly, in the capital-goods sector,

$$\frac{\dot{G}_L}{G_L} - \frac{\dot{G}_K}{G_K} = \frac{1}{\sigma_M} \frac{k_M}{k_M} - B_M. \tag{11.3.51}$$

Thus condition (a) for factor-market equilibrium requires that

$$\frac{1}{\sigma_C} \frac{k_C}{k_C} - B_C = \frac{1}{\sigma_M} \frac{k_M}{k_M} - B_M. \tag{11.3.52}$$

Equality of the wage rate in the two sectors is established if

$$F_L = pG_L; \tag{11.3.53}$$

and equality is maintained when the rates of change are equal, i.e. when

$$\frac{\dot{p}}{p} = \frac{\dot{F}_L}{F_L} - \frac{\dot{G}_L}{G_L}. \tag{11.3.54}$$

Substitute equation (11.3.35) in equation (11.3.54) to obtain

$$\frac{\dot{p}}{p} = R_C - R_M - (1 - s_C) B_C + (1 - s_M) B_M + \frac{(1 - s_C)}{\sigma_C} \frac{k_C}{k_C} - \frac{(1 - s_M)}{\sigma_M} \frac{k_M}{k_M}. \tag{11.3.55}$$

Finally, substituting equation (11.3.52) in equation (11.3.55) yields condition (b) for factor-market equilibrium:

$$\frac{\dot{p}}{p} = (R_C - R_M) + [(1 - s_M) - (1 - s_C)] B_M - \frac{1}{\sigma_M} [(1 - s_M) - (1 - s_C)] \frac{k_M}{k_M}. \tag{11.3.56}$$

In summary, converting from a one-sector model to a two-sector model requires adding equations (11.3.52) and (11.3.56) to the basic model [equations (11.3.30)–(11.3.37)].

11.3.4 Hicks-neutrality in a two-sector model

Hicks' concept of neutrality may be applied sector-by-sector; thus technological progress is neutral in sector i if $B_i = 0$. The influence of Hicks-neutrality on the factor market equilibrium may be seen from equations (11.3.52) and (11.3.56)

Assume that technological progress is neutral in both sectors, i.e. $B_i = 0$ for $i = C, M$. From equation (11.3.52) it is obvious that the rates of change in the capital–labor ratios must be proportional, the factor of proportionality depending upon the elasticities of substitution. More specifically, the capital–labor ratio must grow more rapidly in the sector in which the elasticity of substitution is the greater. And, of course, the direction of change in the capital–labor ratio must be the same in both sectors.

Continue to assume that technological progress is Hicks-neutral in both sectors. Equation (11.3.56) reduces to

$$\frac{\dot{p}}{p} = (R_C - R_M) - \frac{1}{\sigma_M}[(1 - s_M) - (1 - s_C)]\frac{k_M}{k_M}, \qquad (11.3.57)$$

where $\dfrac{1}{\sigma_C}\dfrac{k_C}{k_C}$ may be substituted for $\dfrac{1}{\sigma_M}\dfrac{k_M}{k_M}$.

First, suppose the rate of technological progress is more rapid in the consumption-good sector. This condition *alone* tends to cause an increase in the relative price of machines. This statement holds, *mutatis mutandis*, if the rate of technological progress is greater in the capital-good sector.

Next, suppose production in the capital-good sector is labor-intensive relative to production in the consumption-good sector.[1] Hence the relative share of capital $(1 - s)$ will be smaller in the capital-good sector than in the consumption sector. As a consequence, an increase in the capital–labor ratio, in either sector and in total, will cause an increase in the relative price of the capital good. This is exactly what one should expect.

As the capital–labor ratio increases, the price of the capital good must fall relative to the wage rate. As this happens, the price of output in the relatively capital-intensive sector must fall relative to the price of output in the labor-intensive sector. Thus wages rise more rapidly than the price of the capital good, and the latter rises more rapidly than the price of the consumption good. In this situation, capital-using technological progress

---

[1] The opposite case is not considered inasmuch as the condition postulated is a stability condition in most two-sector models. See Robinson [1956], Uzawa [1961 b], and Uzawa [1963]. A weaker stability condition has been found; but it does not fit conveniently into this formulation of the neoclassical model. See Amano [1964] and Jones [1965 a].

in the capital-good sector will tend to moderate the increase in the relative price of the capital good, while labor-using technological progress will tend to make the rise more rapid still.

11.3.5   Harrod-neutrality in a two-sector model

Harrod-neutrality within a sector requires constancy of the rate of interest and of the capital–output ratio *in value terms*. This occasions no difficulty in the capital-good sector. The rate of interest is the 'own' rate of return (G_K) and the capital-output ratio is the same in real and value terms. Thus the condition for Harrod-neutrality in the capital-good sector is the same as the condition for Harrod-neutrality in a one-sector model:

$$\left(1 - \frac{1}{\sigma_M}\right) R_M + s_M B_M = 0. \tag{11.3.58}$$

Things are considerably different in the consumption sector. The rate of interest in that sector is F_K/p. Hence constancy of the rate of interest requires that

$$\frac{\dot{F}_K}{F_K} - \frac{\dot{p}}{p} = 0. \tag{11.3.59}$$

Substituting equations (11.3.34), (11.3.52), and (11.3.56) into equation (11.3.59) and simplifying, constancy of the rate of interest in the consumption sector gives rise to the following condition:

$$\frac{\dot{k}_C}{k_C} = \frac{\sigma_C R_M}{s_M} + \sigma_C B_C. \tag{11.3.60}$$

Since p appears in both the numerator and denominator of the capital–output ratio, it may be ignored. Hence from equation (11.3.41), constancy of the capital–output ratio in the consumption sector establishes the following condition:

$$\frac{\dot{k}_C}{k_C} = -\frac{B_C}{(1 - 1/\sigma_C)}. \tag{11.3.61}$$

Equating expressions (11.3.60) and (11.3.61) gives the condition for Harrod-neutrality in the consumption sector:

$$\left(1 - \frac{1}{\sigma_C}\right) R_M + s_M B_C = 0. \tag{11.3.62}$$

11.3.6   Comparison of Hicks- and Harrod-neutrality

Since the capital-good sector is a self-contained entity, as it were, the comparison of Hicks- and Harrod-neutrality follows exactly the comparison in the one-sector model (subsection 11.3.2 above). The nature of technological progress in the consumption sector, under Harrod's classification, depends upon characteristics of both production functions. That is, it is apparent from equation (11.3.62) that the Hicks-rate of technological progress in the capital-good sector, as well as the relative share of labor in that section, influence the Harrod classification in the consumption sector.

Let us begin the comparison by stating[1]

Kennedy's Theorem: Hicks-neutrality in the consumption sector is equivalent to Harrod-neutrality in that sector if there is no technological progress in the capital-good sector.

The proof of this theorem follows immediately from equation (11.3.62). Hicks-neutrality in the consumption sector implies $B_C = 0$. The absence of (Hicks) technological progress in the capital-good sector further implies $R_M = 0$. These two conditions together obviously satisfy the conditions of equation (11.3.62). Of course, if $B_C \neq 0$ and $R_M > 0$, there are a variety of values of σ_C and s_M that could result in Harrod-neutrality.

Two further points, neither of which is *a priori* obvious, deserve mention. First, it is apparent from equation (11.3.62) that only the Hicks-rate, but *not* the Hicks-bias, in the capital-good sector influences the Harrod classification in the consumption sector. At first thought, it might seem that a Hicks-bias in the capital-good sector would tend to influence bias or neutrality in the consumption sector inasmuch as the capital good is an input in the consumption sector. However, equation (11.3.62) clearly shows that this is not the case.

For the second point, continue our original assumption that technological progress is Hicks-neutral in the consumption sector, but assume that the Hicks-rate in the capital-good sector is positive ($R_M > 0$). Under these assumptions, it was shown for the one-sector model [inequalities (11.3.45)] that the Harrod-bias is capital using or labor using according as $\sigma \gtrless 1$. The corresponding relation for the two-sector model is not as simple.

Using equation (11.3.36), note that

$$\frac{\dot{K}_C}{K_C} - \frac{\dot{F}}{F} = s_C \frac{k_C}{k_C} - R_C. \qquad (11.3.63)$$

Equation (11.3.63) must be analyzed for a constant rate of interest. The condition for Harrod-bias is found by substituting equation (11.3.60) into equation (11.3.63), obtaining

$$\frac{\dot{K}_C}{K_C} - \frac{\dot{F}}{F} = \left(\frac{s_C}{s_M} \sigma_C - \frac{R_C}{R_M} \right) R_M. \qquad (11.3.64)$$

Since we have assumed that technological progress is Hicks-neutral in the consumption sector, we must also logically assume that $R_C > 0$. Next,

[1] Kennedy [1962b].

let us reintroduce our assumption that production in the capital-good sector is labor intensive relative to production in the consumption sector. Hence $s_M > s_C$. If $R_C > R_M$, σ_C must clearly exceed unity if there is to be Harrod-capital-using technological progress. But the simple requirement that $\sigma_C > 1$ is not enough. In this case, σ_C may have to exceed unity by a substantial amount to insure capital-using progress. On the other hand, if $R_C < R_M$, σ_C may be less than unity and still be consistent with capital-using technological progress.

In the two-sector model, as in the one-sector model, the elasticity of substitution is an important parameter in determining the Harrod bias. But it is not the *only* magnitude affecting the classification. The ratio of labor's relative shares in the two sectors and the ratio of the Hicks-rates in the two sectors enter the calculation we well. In this situation, no *a priori* statements can be made.[1]

11.4 Conclusion

In this chapter a general neoclassical model of technological progress has been developed. It is used in the next chapter as the basis for analyzing the neoclassical theory of relative factor shares. In this study our attention is directed exclusively to the Hicks classification; however, most of the results may be interpreted in the Harrod framework by using equation (11.3.42) in a one-sector model and equation (11.3.62) in a two-sector model. Thereafter our attention turns to some recently suggested 'alternatives' to the approach developed in this chapter and to some 'alternative' theories of distribution.

---

[1] An excellent and ingenious graphical treatment of the model developed in this section is presented in Jones [1965 b].

12

TECHNOLOGICAL PROGRESS
AND THE NEOCLASSICAL THEORY
OF DISTRIBUTION

12.1 Introduction

The theory of derived input demand, developed in chapters 6, 8, and 9, constitutes the microeconomic theory of distribution. By analogy, the macroeconomic theory of distribution is obtained, together with the conventional 'rules', such as equality of the marginal product and real wage rate under perfect competition. To specialize the theory to two homogeneous inputs, labor and capital, one has only to substitute K and L for the x_i's in chapters 6 and 9. To introduce perfect competition and linear homogeneity of the production function is easy as well. This is done briefly in the following section before turning to the more interesting question concerning the behaviour of relative factor shares.

12.2 Derived demand and the Marshall–Hicks rules[1]

Assume that there exists an 'aggregate' production function

$$q = f(K, L), \qquad (12.2.1)$$

which is homogeneous of degree one in the homogeneous inputs capital (K) and labor (L). Further suppose the economy 'behaves' as though it were a perfectly competitive firm, maximizing profit for parametrically given input and output prices. With obvious notation, the profit equation is

$$\pi = pq - rK - wL. \qquad (12.2.2)$$

The first-order conditions for profit maximization yield the familiar marginal rules:

$$pf_K = r, \qquad (12.2.3)$$

and

$$pf_L = w. \qquad (12.2.4)$$

Equations (12.2.3) and (12.2.4) are the derived input demand equations whose comparative static characteristics we wish to determine. These

---

[1] In this section we follow Allen [1938, pp. 371–4] rather than Hicks [1932, pp. 241–6, and 2nd ed., pp. 373–8].

equations, however, only guarantee equilibrium in the factor markets. To insure equilibrium in the commodity market as well, one must add a market-clearing equation to the system:

$$f(K, L) = h(p), \qquad (12.2.5)$$

where
$$q = h(p), \quad h'(p) < 0 \qquad (12.2.6)$$

is the commodity demand function.

Let us direct our attention to the labor input. Differentiating the system $(12.2.3)$–$(12.2.5)$ partially with respect to w, one obtains

$$\left.\begin{aligned}
f_K \frac{\partial K}{\partial w} + f_L \frac{\partial L}{\partial w} - h'(p) \frac{\partial p}{\partial w} &= 0, \\[2mm]
pf_{KK} \frac{\partial K}{\partial w} + pf_{KL} \frac{\partial L}{\partial w} - f_K \frac{\partial p}{\partial w} &= 0, \\[2mm]
pf_{KL} \frac{\partial K}{\partial w} + pf_{LL} \frac{\partial L}{\partial w} - f_L \frac{\partial p}{\partial w} &= 1.
\end{aligned}\right\} \qquad (12.2.7)$$

It is now convenient to introduce some definitions and identities. The elasticity of substitution is

$$\sigma = \frac{f_K f_L}{q f_{KL}}. \qquad (12.2.8)$$

From the homogeneity of the production function and definition $(12.2.8)$, the second partial derivatives may be written

$$\left.\begin{aligned}
f_{LL} &\equiv -\frac{K}{L} \frac{f_K f_L}{q\sigma}, \\[2mm]
f_{KK} &\equiv -\frac{L}{K} \frac{f_K f_L}{q\sigma}, \\[2mm]
f_{KL} &\equiv \frac{f_K f_L}{q\sigma}.
\end{aligned}\right\} \qquad (12.2.9)$$

Finally, the elasticity of commodity demand is

$$\eta = -\frac{h'}{h} p. \qquad (12.2.10)$$

Substituting these definitions in equations $(12.2.7)$, the system may be written

$$\left.\begin{aligned}
pf_K \frac{\partial K}{\partial w} + pf_L \frac{\partial L}{\partial w} + q\eta \frac{\partial p}{\partial w} &= 0, \\[2mm]
-\frac{wL}{K} \frac{\partial K}{\partial w} + w \frac{\partial L}{\partial w} + q\sigma \frac{\partial p}{\partial w} &= 0, \\[2mm]
r \frac{\partial K}{\partial w} - \frac{rK}{L} \frac{\partial L}{\partial w} + q\sigma \frac{\partial p}{\partial w} &= \frac{qp}{w} \sigma.
\end{aligned}\right\} \qquad (12.2.11)$$

12.2 MARSHALL–HICKS RULES

Solving by Cramer's Rule, one obtains

$$\frac{\partial L}{\partial w} = -\frac{L}{w}\left(\frac{wL}{qp}\,\eta + \frac{rK}{pq}\,\sigma\right),\qquad (12.2.12)$$

$$\frac{\partial K}{\partial w} = -\frac{KL}{qp}\,(\eta - \sigma).\qquad (12.2.13)$$

To simplify these two equations, we need some additional definitions. The elasticity and cross-elasticity of input demands are

$$\theta_{LL} = -\frac{\partial L}{\partial w}\frac{w}{L},\qquad \theta_{KL} = \frac{\partial K}{\partial w}\frac{w}{K}.\qquad (12.2.14)$$

The proportion of total cost expended on each input, which is the input's relative share, is

$$\kappa_L = \frac{wL}{qp},\qquad \kappa_K = \frac{rK}{qp} = (1 - \kappa_L).\qquad (12.2.15)$$

Finally, substituting these definitions in equations (12.2.12) and (12.2.13) yields the following results:

$$\theta_{LL} = (1 - \kappa_L)\,\sigma + \kappa_L\eta,\qquad (12.2.16)$$

$$\theta_{KL} = \kappa_L(\sigma - \eta).\qquad (12.2.17)$$

The interpretation of equations (12.2.16) and (12.2.17) is straightforward. The cross-elasticity of the demand for capital is positive or negative according as $\sigma \lessgtr \eta$. That is, the two inputs are substitutes or complements according as the elasticity of substitution exceeds or falls short of the elasticity of (commodity) demand.

Next, the elasticity of labor demand is a weighted average of the elasticities of substitution and of demand, the weights being the relative factor shares. Going further, we can confirm three of the Marshall–Hicks 'rules' concerning the elasticity of derived input demand.[1] Consider the following partial derivatives obtained from equation (12.2.16):

$$\frac{\partial \theta_{LL}}{\partial \sigma} = (1 - \kappa_L) > 0,\qquad (12.2.18)$$

$$\frac{\partial \theta_{LL}}{\partial \eta} = \kappa_L > 0,\qquad (12.2.19)$$

$$\frac{\partial \theta_{LL}}{\partial \kappa_L} = \eta - \sigma.\qquad (12.2.20)$$

---

[1] The fourth condition, concerning the relation between θ_{LL} and θ_{KK}, cannot be deduced from this model. See Hicks, *op. cit.*

The rules,[1] as Hicks states them,[2] are as follows:

1. 'The demand for anything is likely to be more elastic, the more readily substitutes for that thing can be obtained.'

By expression (12.2.18), this rule clearly holds since $0 < \kappa_L < 1$.

2. 'The demand for anything is likely to be more elastic, the more elastic is the demand for any further thing which it contributes to produce.'

Again, expression (12.2.19) clearly shows that the rule is correct. Finally, we come to the Marshall rule to which Hicks' *caveat* must be added.

3. 'The demand for anything is likely to be less elastic, the less important is the part played by the cost of that thing in the total cost of some other thing, in the production of which it is employed' *providing* the elasticity of commodity demand exceeds the elasticity of substitution.

Consider equation (12.2.20). The validity of that portion of the rule in quotation marks requires $\partial\theta_{LL}/\partial\kappa_L > 0$, which holds if, and only if, $\eta > \sigma$. Thus the qualifying phrase must be added. Thus, as Hicks pointed out, it is 'important to be unimportant' only if commodities can be substituted in consumption more readily than inputs can be substituted in production.

Hicks gave a lengthy explanation of the 'unusual' case, i.e. in which $\sigma > \eta$.[3] However, the explanation can be quickly accomplished by reference to equation (12.2.17). For the 'Marshall rule' to hold, $\eta > \sigma$. By equation (12.2.17), this implies that $\theta_{KL} < 0$, which further implies that capital and labor are complementary in demand. This is normally to be expected in a model in which factor inferiority is excluded. An increase in the wage rate, for example, will cause an increase in commodity price, a decrease in output, and a decrease in the quantities of both inputs used. Thus $\theta_{KL} < 0$ and the 'Marshall rule' holds.

The exception, or Hicks' *caveat*, must be introduced when $\sigma > \eta$, or when the two inputs are substitutes.[4] Suppose the wage rate increases. Commodity price will rise and output will fall; but, if commodity demand in relatively inelastic ($\eta > 1$ by a small amount), the decline in output will be relatively small. The decline in output will itself cause a decrease in both capital and labor inputs. However, relative input price has changed. Capital will be substituted for labor, and if the elasticity of substitution exceeds unity, the increase in capital usage attributable to the change in the input-price ratio may more than offset the decrease in capital usage owing to the decline in output. This describes the 'exceptional case', which

---

[1] Marshall [1920, pp. 384–7, p. 853].

[2] Hicks [1932, p. 242].

[3] Hicks [1932, 2nd ed. pp. 376–8].

[4] It might be well to emphasize that the substitution-complementarity relations now under discussion do not correspond to the similar classification *in production only* (see chapters 4 and 5). Indeed, with two inputs and linear homogeneity, $f_{KL} > 0$ over the relevant range of production. The inputs are *always* complementary in production alone.

is exceptional in that the elasticity of demand must exceed unity and the elasticity of substitution is generally believed to be unity or less.

12.3 Technological progress and relative factor shares

At the macroeconomic level, the distributional questions of greatest interest concern the behavior of aggregate relative shares. The object in this section is to set out the neoclassical theory of relative shares within the framework of the model of technological progress developed in chapter 11. Before doing this, however, a digression is in order.

Writing in 1939, Keynes noted the 'remarkable constancy' of relative shares and called it a 'bit of a miracle'.[1] Subsequently, two controversies have developed. One is whether relative shares have in fact been remarkably constant;[2] the other is whether a special macroeconomic theory of distributive shares is needed to explain constancy (providing it exists). The neoclassical theory of distribution in no way implies constancy of relative shares (although forces that result in constancy may be explained by marginal productivity theory). In light of this, some economists have argued that since aggregate shares have been extraordinarily constant over a long span of time, an acceptable theory of distribution must have constant shares as one of its logical conclusions.[3]

This contention was, in my opinion, convincingly refuted by Bronfenbrenner.[4] Using a conventional neoclassical model, he showed that relative shares are very insensitive to changes in the capital–labor ratio if the elasticity of substitution lies in a plausible range. For example, if the elasticity of substitution lies between 0·75 and 1·50, a five percent change in the relative share of labor would require a change in the capital–labor ratio of 67·5 percent or more. On this basis Bronfenbrenner argued as follows:[5]

We may conclude that conventional marginal distribution theory does in fact imply considerable constancy of relative shares, provided only that the elasticity of substitution between capital and labor is not well below unity. This constancy is perfect only when the elasticity of substitution is unitary, but it is high for other values as well. Conversely, a high degree of constancy in relative shares is consistent with a wide range of elasticities of substitution....

The constancy of relative shares may be complete, as argued by Kaldor, or incomplete, as argued by Kravis. Whether complete or incomplete, this constancy does not argue against marginalist distribution theory. Allegations to the contrary are simply wrong, despite the weight of authority which supports them... whether complete or incomplete, the constancy of relative shares is not a satisfactory 'crucial experiment' for choosing between the marginal theory and its alternatives.

[1] Keynes [1939].
[2] See Kaldor [1955] on the one hand, and Solow [1958] and Kravis [1959] on the other.
[3] See especially Kaldor [1955], [1957], and [1961] and Kaldor and Mirrlees [1962].
[4] Bronfenbrenner [1960].   [5] *Ibid.* p. 287.

Of course, one must also add that constancy of relative shares is not an argument in favor of neoclassical theory against alternatives that imply constancy. If relative shares are constant, another basis for choice must be found.

12.3.1 Neutral technological progress and relative factor shares in a one-sector model[1]

The analysis contained in the remainder of this chapter is based upon the assumptions used in chapter 11. For convenience they are restated here. (1) The output of the economy or of any sector of the economy is given by a production function $F(K, L, t)$, where F is homogeneous of degree one in the two homogeneous inputs K (capital) and L (labor). Over the relevant range of production, both marginal products are strictly positive ($F_K > 0$, $F_L > 0$) and both decrease monotonically ($F_{KK} < 0$, $F_{LL} < 0$). (2) Perfect competition prevails in both the input and output markets, and inputs are rewarded according to competitive imputations. (3) Instantaneous equilibrium prevails at all times in both the input and output markets.

The model of growth and distribution with neutral technological progress is familiar,[2] but it is given here to set the stage for the model of biased progress and relative shares.

With neutral technological progress, the production function may be written

$$Y = e^{\lambda t}F(K, L), \qquad (12.3.1)$$

or

$$y = e^{\lambda t}f(k), \qquad (12.3.2)$$

where $y = Y/L$ and $k = K/L$ are the output–labor and capital–labor ratios respectively. From the homogeneity of equation (12.3.1) it follows that

$$-LF_{LL} \equiv KF_{LK} \quad \text{and} \quad -KF_{KK} \equiv LF_{KL}. \qquad (12.3.3)$$

Further, the elasticity of substitution may be written as

$$\sigma = \frac{F_K F_L}{F F_{KL}}. \qquad (12.3.4)$$

Noting that $e^{\lambda t}f'(k)$ is the marginal product of capital, it follows from equation (12.3.2) that

$$\frac{\dot{y}}{y} = \lambda + (1-s)\frac{\dot{k}}{k}, \qquad (12.3.5)$$

where

$$s = \frac{wL}{Y} = \frac{w}{y} \qquad (12.3.6)$$

---

[1] The remaining portion of this section is based upon Ferguson [1968a].
[2] For example, see Ferguson [1965c, d].

is the relative share of labor. Next, from equation (12.3.1), the real wage rate (w) may be written

$$w = e^{\lambda t}F_L. \tag{12.3.7}$$

Thus

$$\frac{\dot{w}}{w} = \lambda + \frac{KF_{LK}}{F_L}\frac{\dot{K}}{K} + \frac{LF_{LL}}{F_L}\frac{\dot{L}}{L}. \tag{12.3.8}$$

Substituting equations (12.3.3) and (12.3.4) in equation (12.3.8), one obtains

$$\frac{\dot{w}}{w} = \lambda + \frac{(1-s)}{\sigma}\frac{\dot{k}}{k}. \tag{12.3.9}$$

From equation (12.3.6) the rate of change in the relative share of labor is

$$\frac{\dot{s}}{s} = \frac{\dot{w}}{w} + \frac{\dot{L}}{L} - \frac{\dot{Y}}{Y} = \frac{\dot{w}}{w} - \frac{\dot{y}}{y}. \tag{12.3.10}$$

Thus subtracting equation (12.3.5) from equation (12.3.9) gives the desired expression for the rate of change in labor's relative share:

$$\frac{\dot{s}}{s} = \frac{\dot{w}}{w} - \frac{\dot{y}}{y} = -(1-s)\left(1 - \frac{1}{\sigma}\right)\frac{\dot{k}}{k}. \tag{12.3.11}$$

The first result to observe, a well-known one, is that neutral technological progress has no effect whatsoever upon relative shares; the technology parameter λ does not enter equation (12.3.11). Next, note that $(1-s) > 0$ and that casual empiricism leads to the belief that $\dot{k}/k > 0$ (i.e. the rate of capital accumulation exceeds the rate of increase in the employed labor force). Thus the second familiar result is obtained:

$$\frac{\dot{s}}{s} \gtreqless 0 \quad \text{according as} \quad \sigma \lesseqgtr 1. \tag{12.3.12}$$

In summary, we have the following

Relations: If technological progress is neutral, the magnitude of the elasticity of substitution and the direction of change of relative input supplies are the only factors governing the behavior of relative shares. In particular, an increase in the capital–labor ratio will be accompanied by an increase or a decrease in labor's relative share according as $\sigma \lessgtr 1$.

12.3.2   Biased technological progress and relative factor shares in a one-sector model

Let us briefly recall the general model of technological progress developed in chapter 11. The production function is

$$Y = F(K, L, t), \tag{12.3.13}$$

241

from which one obtains the definitions of the rate (R) and bias (B) of technological progress:

$$R = \frac{F_t}{F} = \frac{KF_{Kt}+LF_{Lt}}{F}, \tag{12.3.14}$$

$$B = \frac{F_{Kt}}{F_K}-\frac{F_{Lt}}{F_L}. \tag{12.3.15}$$

Equations (12.3.14) and (12.3.15) may be solved to express the proportional time changes in the marginal products as functions of the rate and bias of technological progress:

$$\frac{F_{Kt}}{F_K} = R+sB, \tag{12.3.16}$$

$$\frac{F_{Lt}}{F_L} = R-(1-s)\,B. \tag{12.3.17}$$

Further, the rates of growth of the marginal product of labor and of national income may be written:

$$\frac{\dot{F}_L}{F_L} = R-(1-s)\,B+\frac{(1-s)}{\sigma}\frac{k}{k}, \tag{12.3.18}$$

$$\frac{\dot{F}}{F} = R+(1-s)\frac{k}{k}+\frac{\dot{L}}{L}. \tag{12.3.19}$$

Now invoke the condition that $w = F_L$. Substituting equations (12.3.18) and (12.3.19) into equation (12.3.10) yields the desired expression for the rate of change in labor's relative share:

$$\frac{\dot{s}}{s} = -(1-s)\left[B+\left(1-\frac{1}{\sigma}\right)\frac{k}{k}\right]. \tag{12.3.20}$$

Noting that when technological progress is Hicks-neutral $B = 0$, equation (12.3.20) reduces precisely to equation (12.3.11).

For the moment assume that $\sigma < 1$ and $k/k > 0$. The term

$$-(1-s)\,(1-(1/\sigma))\,(k/k)$$

thus tends to augment labor's relative share. Similarly, the share is augmented or diminished according as $B \lessgtr 0$, i.e. according as technological progress is labor using or capital using. Indeed, this offers one customary way of defining biased progress, namely to say that technological progress is labor using, neutral, or capital using according as the relative share of labor increases, remains unchanged, or declines. However, this is strictly correct only if (a) the elasticity of substitution is unity, or (b) the rate of capital deepening is zero.

Equations (12.3.11) and (12.3.20) show two ways in which constancy of relative shares may be accounted for within the framework of neoclassical theory.[1] First, from equation (12.3.11), relative shares will be constant if technological progress is neutral and the elasticity of substitution is unity. Second, suppose technological progress is capital using and that $\sigma < 1$ and $k/k > 0$. Then relative shares will remain constant if, and only if, the decrease in the relative demand for labor attributable to capital-using technological progress is exactly offset by the decrease in the relative supply of labor attributable to capital deepening. Alternatively, if the elasticity of substitution exceeds unity, shares will remain constant if, and only if, the increase in the relative demand for labor attributable to labor-using technological progress is precisely offset by the increase in the relative supply of labor attributable to capital deepening and elastic substitutability. Unless these conditions are satisfied exactly, relative shares will change over time.

The effect of Harrod-neutral technological progress may be indicated briefly. In chapter 11 it was shown that technological progress is Harrod-neutral if

$$\left(1 - \frac{1}{\sigma}\right) R + sB = 0, \qquad (12.3.21)$$

or

$$B = -\frac{1}{s}\left(1 - \frac{1}{\sigma}\right) R. \qquad (12.3.22)$$

Substituting equation (12.3.22) in equation (12.3.20) yields

$$\frac{\dot{s}}{s} = -(1-s)\left(1 - \frac{1}{\sigma}\right)\left[\frac{\dot{k}}{k} - \frac{R}{s}\right]. \qquad (12.3.23)$$

One condition for Harrod-neutrality is that the relative share of capital remain constant. Hence the relative share of labor must be constant as well. By equation (12.3.23) this can happen only if (a) the elasticity of substitution is unity, or (b) the precarious balancing of the rate of capital deepening with R/s is somehow achieved.[2]

12.3.3 Biased progress in a purely factor-augmenting model

An interesting special case is provided by the purely factor-augmenting model of technological progress. The form of the model used here has recently become very popular, presumably because it offers a convenient model for statistical testing.[3]

A general CES function with purely factor-augmenting technological

---

[1] Other than the explanation given by Bronfenbrenner.
[2] The simple case of Harrod neutrality in a purely factor augmenting model is presented in the subsection below.
[3] For examples, see David and van de Klundert [1965] and McCarthy [1966].

progress may be written:

$$Y = [(\alpha(t) K)^{-\rho} + (\beta(t) L)^{-\rho}]^{-1/\rho}, \tag{12.3.24}$$

where
$$\sigma = \frac{1}{1+\rho}. \tag{12.3.25}$$

From equation (12.3.24),

$$\frac{F_{Kt}}{F_K} = -\rho \frac{\dot{\alpha}}{\alpha}, \quad \frac{F_{Lt}}{F_L} = -\rho \frac{\dot{\beta}}{\beta}. \tag{12.3.26}$$

Hence from definitions (12.3.15) and (12.3.25)

$$B = \left(1 - \frac{1}{\sigma}\right)\left(\frac{\dot{\alpha}}{\alpha} - \frac{\dot{\beta}}{\beta}\right). \tag{12.3.27}$$

Generally, from equation (12.3.27), it is apparent that technological progress is labor using if: (a) the elasticity of substitution is less than unity and the rate of disembodied capital augmentation exceeds the corresponding rate of disembodied labor augmentation,[1] or (b) if the elasticity of substitution is greater than unity and the rate of labor augmentation exceeds the rate of capital augmentation. Furthermore, the same two statements apply, *mutatis mutandis*, to capital-using technological progress.

Using equations (12.3.20) and (12.3.27), the rate of change in the relative share of labor may be written as follows:

$$\frac{\dot{s}}{s} = -(1-s)\left(1 - \frac{1}{\sigma}\right)\left[\left(\frac{\dot{\alpha}}{\alpha} + \frac{\dot{K}}{K}\right) - \left(\frac{\dot{\beta}}{\beta} + \frac{\dot{L}}{L}\right)\right]. \tag{12.3.28}$$

The term in brackets on the right-hand side of equation (12.3.28) may be regarded as the *effective* gross rate of change in the capital–labor ratio (i.e. the change after allowing for disembodied factor augmentation). Assuming that it is positive,[2] we obtain the following

Relation: The rate of change in labor's relative share is positive or negative according as the elasticity of substitution is less than or greater than unity (i.e. according as $B \lessgtr 0$).

This is precisely the same as the result obtained under the assumption of neutral technological progress because the effect of biased progress is embodied in the rate of change of the 'effective' capital–labor ratio. The result is different, of course, if the rate of labor augmentation exceeds the rate of capital augmentation by an amount sufficient to make the change in the effective capital–labor ratio negative.

[1] This is the statistical result obtained by David and van de Klundert [1965].
[2] Empirically this seems to be the more likely case. Practically everyone will agree that ($\dot{K}/K > \dot{L}/L$). If David and van de Klundert's results ($\dot{\alpha}/\alpha > \dot{\beta}/\beta$) are accepted, the effective change must be positive.

12.3 RELATIVE FACTOR SHARES

Harrod-neutrality may easily be introduced in the purely factor-augmenting model. As Uzawa has shown,[1] technological progress is Harrod-neutral if, and only if,

$$\frac{\dot{\alpha}}{\alpha} = 0 \quad \text{and} \quad \frac{\dot{\beta}}{\beta} > 0. \tag{12.3.29}$$

With this condition, it is convenient to write the CES function as[2]

$$Y = A[\delta K^{-\rho} + (1-\delta)(e^{\gamma t}L)^{-\rho}]^{-1/\rho}. \tag{12.3.30}$$

With this formulation of the production function, equations (12.3.27) and (12.3.28) reduce to

$$B = -\gamma\left(1 - \frac{1}{\sigma}\right), \tag{12.3.31}$$

and

$$\frac{\dot{s}}{s} = -(1-s)\left(1 - \frac{1}{\sigma}\right)\left(\frac{\dot{k}}{k} - \gamma\right). \tag{12.3.32}$$

From equation (12.3.31) and (12.3.32), we obtain the following

Relations: Technological progress is (Hicks) capital using or labor using according as $-\rho\gamma \gtrless 0$. Further, a positive rate of growth of labor's relative share is consistent with an elasticity of substitution greater than unity if, and only if, the rate of labor augmentation exceeds the rate of growth of the nominal capital–labor ratio.[3]

12.3.4 Relative shares in a multi-sector model

The model of technological progress developed in chapter 11 and the model of relative shares developed above apply equally well to a one-sector economy or to one sector of a multi-sector economy. We can now turn to the behavior of aggregate relative shares in a multi-sector economy.

The relative share of labor in the ith sector is

$$s_i = \frac{w_i L_i}{Y_i}, \tag{12.3.33}$$

and its rate of growth is

$$\frac{\dot{s}_i}{s_i} = \frac{\dot{w}_i}{w_i} - \frac{\dot{y}_i}{y_i}. \tag{12.3.34}$$

The right-hand side of equation (12.3.34) may be called the 'within sector' effect inasmuch as it shows the forces that affect the relative share of labor in a given sector. Within any sector, the change in labor's relative share depends exclusively upon the differential in the rates of growth of wages and productivity. In particular, a simple but fundamental fact is stated in

[1] Uzawa [1961 a].   [2] See Ferguson [1965 b].
[3] Comparing equations (12.3.23) and (12.3.32), it is seen that in the purely factor-augmenting case, R/s reduces to γ, the rate of labor augmentation.

equation (12.3.35): the relative share of labor must increase if average wages grow more rapidly than average productivity.

The aggregate share of labor in the economy is a weighted average of the relative shares in the component sectors. Let $\pi_i = Y_i/Y$, the proportion of national income originating in the ith sector. The aggregate relative share of labor may then be written:

$$s = \sum_i \pi_i s_i, \qquad (12.3.35)$$

and its rate of change is

$$\frac{\dot{s}}{s} = \frac{\Sigma(s_i - s)\,\dot{\pi}_i}{s} + \frac{\Sigma\pi_i s_i[(\dot{w}_i/w_i) - (\dot{y}_i/y_i)]}{s}, \qquad (12.3.36)$$

where the first term may be written as it is because $\Sigma\dot{\pi}_i = 0$, so $\Sigma s\dot{\pi}_i = 0$.

The first term on the right-hand side of equation (12.3.36) may be called the 'among sectors' effect. The 'among sectors' effect for any one sector augments the rate of growth of the aggregate relative share if (a) the relative share in the sector exceeds the aggregate share and the sector increases in importance, and (b) if the sector share is less than the aggregate share and the importance of the sector declines. Similarly, the 'among sectors' effect within a sector contributes to a decline in the rate of growth of the aggregate share if (a) the sector share exceeds the aggregate share and the sector declines in importance, and (b) if the sector share is less than the aggregate share and the sector becomes more important. In short, the 'among sectors' effect depends upon the changing composition of aggregate demand and the relation between relative shares in the sector and the economy.

If there are *many* sectors in the multi-sector model,[1] one may reasonably assume that the composition of demand is exogenous to the model of income distribution, i.e. the composition of demand is not influenced by the relative shares of labor and capital. But in a two-sector model such independence cannot generally be assumed since the proportion of output produced in the capital-goods sector must equal the average propensity to save. That is, with obvious notation,

$$\pi_M = \frac{pM}{Y} = \frac{I}{Y} = \frac{S}{Y} = \frac{\alpha Y}{Y} = \alpha, \qquad (12.3.37)$$

where α is the marginal and average propensity to save.

12.3.5 Relative shares in a two-sector model

To analyze the behavior of the aggregate relative share in a two-sector model, it is convenient to examine the two effects separately. Let us first

[1] For example, if sectors are two-digit industries and the aggregate is the manufacturing industry, the condition to be stated should be satisfied.

look at the 'among industries' effect, or the effect of a shift in the composition of demand. The results here depend crucially upon one's assumption concerning the average propensity to save. An extreme case can be disposed of quickly. If the saving propensity is assumed to be constant, it follows from equation (12.3.37) that $\dot{\pi}_M = \dot{\pi}_C = 0$. Hence from equation (12.3.36), the 'among sectors' effect is zero; that is, there can be no change in the composition of demand.

Next, suppose the average (and marginal) propensity to save is given by

$$\alpha = \alpha_L s + \alpha_K (1-s), \qquad (12.3.38)$$

where α_L and α_K are constants. Thus, since $\pi_C = 1 - \pi_M$, one obtains

$$\left.\begin{aligned} \dot{\pi}_M &= \dot{\alpha} = (\alpha_L - \alpha_K)\dot{s}, \\ \dot{\pi}_C &= -\dot{\alpha} = -(\alpha_L - \alpha_K)\dot{s}. \end{aligned}\right\} \qquad (12.3.39)$$

Denote the 'within sector' effect by W. Substituting equations (12.3.39) in equation (12.3.36), one obtains

$$\frac{\dot{s}}{s} = \frac{(s_M - s_C)(\alpha_L - \alpha_K)\dot{s}}{s} + W, \qquad (12.3.40)$$

or solving,

$$\frac{\dot{s}}{s} = \frac{W}{[1 - (s_M - s_C)(\alpha_L - \alpha_K)]}. \qquad (12.3.41)$$

In this case there can be a shift in the composition of demand; but the 'among sectors' effect disappears, its influence being represented by the denominator on the right-hand side of equation (12.3.41).

When the saving propensity shown in equation (12.3.38) is postulated, one normally assumes that

$$1 \geqslant \alpha_K > \alpha_L \geqslant 0. \qquad (12.3.42)$$

Second, as shown by several economists, in order for the model under consideration to be stable, it is necessary for production in the capital-good sector to be labor intensive relative to production in the consumer-good sector. Since the wage rate must be the same in both sectors, labor's share must be greater in the capital-goods sector. Hence

$$s_M > s > s_C. \qquad (12.3.43)$$

Inequalities (12.3.42) and (12.3.43) jointly imply that

$$1 - (s_M - s_C)(\alpha_L - \alpha_K) > 1. \qquad (12.3.44)$$

Thus we have the following

Relation: A change in the composition of demand cannot change the *direction* in which the aggregate relative share shifts, but it does moderate the magnitude of the shift.

TECHNICAL PROGRESS AND DISTRIBUTION

Let us now examine the modified 'within sector' effect. By equations (12.3.37) and (12.3.41),

$$\frac{\dot{s}}{s} = \frac{[(1-\alpha)\, s_C + \alpha s_M]\dfrac{\dot{w}}{w} - \left[(1-\alpha)\, s_C\, \dfrac{\dot{c}}{c} + \alpha s_M\, \dfrac{\dot{m}}{m}\right]}{s[1 - (s_M - s_C)(\alpha_L - \alpha_K)]}, \qquad (12.3.45)$$

since for factor-market equilibrium $w = w_C = w_M$. To avoid a great deal of clutter, let us introduce the simplifying, but somewhat restrictive, assumption that $\alpha_L = 0, \alpha_K = 1$. This, of course, is the von Neumann assumption.

Next, note that

$$\frac{\dot{L}}{L} = \frac{L_C}{L}\frac{\dot{L}_C}{L_C} + \frac{L_M}{L}\frac{\dot{L}_M}{L_M}, \qquad (12.3.46)$$

that

$$s_C = \frac{wL}{C}\frac{L_C}{L} = \frac{L_C}{L}, \qquad (12.3.47)$$

since $\alpha_L = 0$, and that

$$\frac{L_M}{L} = \frac{\alpha s_M}{s} = \frac{1-s}{s}\, s_M. \qquad (12.3.48)$$

After a good bit of manipulation, substituting equations (12.3.47) and (12.3.48) into equation (12.3.45) yields

$$\frac{\dot{s}}{s} = \frac{[ss_C + (1-s)\, s_M]\dfrac{\dot{w}}{w} - s\left[s_C\, \dfrac{\dot{C}}{C} + \dfrac{(1-s)}{s}\, s_M\, \dfrac{\dot{M}}{M} - \dfrac{\dot{L}}{L}\right]}{s[1 + (s_M - s_C)]}. \qquad (12.3.49)$$

Finally, substituting equations (11.3.35), (11.3.36), (11.3.52), (12.3.47), and (12.3.48) into equation (12.3.49), one may express the rate of change in the aggregate relative share as a function of the sectoral relative shares, the sectoral rates and biases of technological progress, the sector elasticities of substitution, and the sectoral rates of change in the capital–labor ratio:

$$\frac{\dot{s}}{s} = \left\{(1-s_C)\left[-B_M + s_C\,\sigma_C(B_M - B_C) - (R_M - R_C)\right. \right.$$
$$\left.\left. + \frac{1}{\sigma_M}\,(1 - s_C\sigma_C - (1-s_M)\,\sigma_M)\,\frac{\dot{k}_M}{k_M}\right]\right\} \div [1 + (s_M - s_C)]. \quad (12.3.50)$$

In the complicated form of equation (12.3.50), there is little definite that can be said about the forces governing the behavior of the aggregate relative share. Indeed, only one *definite* statement can be made: *ceteris paribus*, the aggregate relative share of labor decreases or increases according as the rate of technological progress in the capital-good sector exceeds or falls short of the rate of technological progress in the consumption sector. The reason underlying this relation is easily explained. From the factor-market equilibrium condition [equation (11.3.53)], one obtains

$$\frac{\dot{F}_L}{F_L} = \frac{\dot{p}}{p} + \frac{\dot{G}_L}{G_L}. \qquad (12.3.51)$$

248

12.3 RELATIVE FACTOR SHARES

If $R_M > R_C, \dot{p}/p < 0$ (price must decrease in the more rapidly advancing sector). Hence for equilibrium,

$$\frac{\dot{G}_L}{G_L} > \frac{\dot{F}_L}{F_L}, \qquad (12.3.52)$$

i.e. the marginal product of labor in the capital-goods sector must increase more rapidly (decline more slowly) than the marginal product of labor in the consumption sector. This requires a relative shift of labor from the higher-share sector to the lower-share sector, thereby contributing to a decline in the aggregate relative share.

Two further relations may be established, but both are subject to the same qualification. In most circumstances: (a) the aggregate relative share decreases or increases according as technological progress is capital using or labor using, and (b) the aggregate relative share varies directly with the capital–labor ratio.[1] Statement (a) is *definite* so far as biased technological progress in the consumption sector is concerned. Otherwise, the statements may not hold if the elasticity of substitution in the consumption sector is significantly greater than unity (and significantly greater than the elasticity of substitution in the capital-good sector).

The reasons for the necessary qualification are not difficult to explain. Suppose $B_M > 0$, i.e. there is capital-using technological progress in the capital-good sector. Other things equal, this tends to depress the aggregate relative share. But it also causes a relative shift of labor to the consumption sector. If σ_C is very high, a proportionately greater amount of capital is displaced. The capital–labor ratio in the consumption sector declines; if σ_C is sufficiently high, the increase in the relative share in the consumption sector may more than compensate for the depressive influence of capital-using technological progress in the capital-good sector. The reason for the qualification of statement (b) follows from the customary relation among relative shares, the elasticity of substitution, and the capital–labor ratio.[2]

The interested reader can simplify equation (12.3.50) by assuming Cobb–Douglas production functions in both sectors, by assuming Hicks-neutrality in both sectors ($B_M = B_C = 0$), and by assuming Harrod-neutrality in both sectors ($B_M = B_C = R_M = 0$). The resulting expressions are simpler;

[1] Equation (12.3.50) is expressed in terms of the rate of change in the capital–labor ratio in the capital-good sector. However, from chapter 11, we know that the capital–labor ratio must change in the same direction in both sectors (apart from the influence of biased progress).

[2] It should be emphasized that throughout this analysis I have used Uzawa's strong assumption that the consumption sector is capital intensive relative to the capital-good sector. There is a weaker condition that guarantees stability: the sum of the sectoral elasticities of substitution must exceed unity. See, *inter alia*, Amano [1964] and Jones [1965a]. I used the stronger condition because it is more convenient for this particular formulation of the neoclassical two-stage model.

the same relations hold with the same qualification except in the Cobb–Douglas case.

12.3.6 Conclusion

Chapter 11 and this much of chapter 12 contain a generalized form of the (aggregate) neoclassical theory of production, technological progress, and distribution, or what Samuelson called the 'J. B. Clark neoclassical fairy tale'.[1] So far as production and distribution are concerned, the model seems to be a useful and satisfactory approximation to reality. On this score, let me re-quote the flyleaf passage from Samuelson:[2]

Until the laws of thermodynamics are repealed, I shall continue to relate outputs to inputs—i.e. to believe in production functions. Until factors cease to have their rewards determined by bidding in quasi-competitive markets, I shall adhere to (generalized) neoclassical approximations in which relative factor supplies are important in explaining their market remunerations....a many-sectored neo-classical model with heterogeneous capital goods and somewhat limited factor substitutions can fail to have some of the simple properties of the idealized J. B. Clark neoclassical models. Recognizing these complications does not justify nihilism or refuge in theories that neglect short-term microeconomic pricing.

As previously indicated, it is difficult to separate theories of production and distribution from theories of capital and growth. The essential features of the neoclassical model developed above are the assumptions of continuous, linearly homogeneous production functions and of a single homogeneous capital good. This model, and certain more realistic ones involving heterogeneous capital goods, yield, when applied to capital theory, the following conclusion: there is an inverse relation between the rate of interest and the wage rate; graphically, the relation usually exhibits concavity from above. A further generalization can be stated: if the capital–labor ratio varies directly with the wage-rate of interest ratio, the wage rate, net national product per worker, and the permanently sustainable consumption stream will all vary inversely with the rate of interest.

Some time ago it was discovered that if there is a spectrum of techniques, this inverse relation may not hold. Mrs Robinson was among the first to point out the exceptional case, or one example of it, labelling it the 'Ruth Cohen Curiosum'.[3] Subsequently several other writers explicitly or implicitly recognized this curiosum, if such it be, and most pronounced it to be a 'perverse' relation.[4]

The 'reswitching theorem', as it may be called, attracted little attention until it was erroneously proved to be erroneous by Levhari.[5] His work was followed by a number of papers in which it was conclusively proved that

---

[1] Samuelson [1962].　　　　　　　　　　[2] Samuelson [1966a, pp. 444–5].
[3] Robinson [1956, pp. 109–10].
[4] See Champernowne [1953] and Sraffa [1960].　　　　[5] Levhari [1965].

the 'Ruth Cohen Curiosum' or the 'reswitching of techniques' can exist.[1] This has some definite and potentially damning implications for neoclassical capital theory and possibly for the neoclassical theory of distribution as well. Since our chief object has been a systematic exposition of neoclassical production and distribution theory, it is obligatory upon us to give some consideration to what I shall call the 'Cambridge Criticism'. This is explored in the remaining sections of this chapter before turning to alternative neoclassical models of production, technological progress, and relative factor shares.

12.4 Simple neoclassical theory

The neoclassical theories of distribution and growth are clearly derivative theories, the former depending largely upon the theory of production, the latter upon capital theory. The theories of capital and production are more closely integrated and more fundamental. But in the last analysis neoclassical theory, in its simple and not-so-simple forms, depends upon the basic nature of the 'thing' called *capital*.

12.4.1 Neoclassical views of capital

Capital theory has an ancient, if not entirely honorable, heritage. I think it fair to say, however, that serious theorizing began with Böhm-Bawerk,[2] who formulated the 'period of production' model and grappled with the concept of an 'average period of production'. He was followed in this endeavor by Wicksell who, it should be noted, finally abandoned the notion of an average period of production.[3] Nonetheless, the 'average period' concept was crucial to their theory.

Böhm-Bawerk and Wicksell regarded capital as a 'subsistence fund' that permitted the 'roundabout' use of labor. The larger the fund, the more 'roundabout' the techniques of production could become. More specifically, the size of the fund relative to labor employed depended upon the wage rate and the average period of production; and the average period of production provided an independent criterion for ordering production techniques according to their relative capital intensities. Given this framework, Böhm-Bawerk and Wicksell showed that as the wage rate rises and the rate of interest falls, the techniques brought into use have a longer average period of production. That is, the techniques become more 'roundabout' or more capital intensive and require a larger subsistence

---

[1] See Bruno, Burmeister and Sheshinski [1966], Garegnani [1966], Morishima [1964] and [1966], Pasinetti [1966a], and Samuelson [1966b].

[2] See Böhm-Bawerk [1959]. There were, of course, precursors. For our purposes, the oversimplification in the text is probably acceptable.

[3] Wicksell [1893] and [1901].

fund relative to the quantity of labor employed.[1] This is a result of great importance, even though it depends upon the untenable concept of an average period of production.[2]

The second part of our abbreviated history begins with J. B. Clark and his notion of 'real homogeneous capital'.[3] To use Clark's analogy, capital is like a waterfall. Every second, different water passes over the fall; but the fall itself remains the same. That is, ignoring technological progress (which we are entitled to do at this level of abstraction), there is a *real* substance called capital whose depletion is continuously replaced so that the substance itself remains homogeneous.

Using this simple notion, a succession of economists too numerous to mention have developed the modern version of simple neoclassical theory, the 'J. B. Clark neoclassical fairy tale'. Of course, elaborate versions of the theory may be constructed.[4] But the simple version yields the simple parables upon which we base our understanding of much of the real economic world. In particular, these parables give us a direct relation between the sphere of production and the market and establish the basis for all of microeconomic pricing theory, which is, of course, the heart of neoclassical theory.

To summarize, the important results that emerge are as follows: given competitive markets, (a) the rate of return on capital is the rate of interest (social as well as private), (b) the wage rate varies inversely with the rate of interest, (c) the real capital–labor ratio varies directly with the wage–rate of interest ratio, so (d) distributive shares are well defined; and (e) net national product per worker, or the permanently sustainable consumption stream, varies inversely with the rate of interest.

That is quite a bit to prove; but having proved it, neoclassical theory establishes an orderly relation between the physical realm of production and the commodity and factor markets. In particular, we can say that the lower the rate of interest, the greater the capital intensity of production. All other neoclassical results follow immediately from this simple relation.

[1] Wicksell was careful on this point. See the quotation from his *Lectures*, vol. I, on p. 258 below.
[2] The concept is untenable, of course, because it rests upon the following unacceptable assumptions: (a) simple, rather than compound, interest; (b) absence of fixed capital; and (c) existence of only one factor (labor) other than capital. For an 'old' critique of the concept, see Gaitskell [1936] and [1938]; for more modern ones, see Garegnani [1966] and Samuelson [1966b].
[3] Clark [1888] and [1965].
[4] For example, see Samuelson and Solow [1956].

12.4.2 Real capital and neoclassical theory

Given the necessary assumptions, the neoclassical relations follow from either a period-of-production model or from a real capital model. Most neoclassical theorists, however, have found it considerably easier to work in the context of the real capital model.[1] At this stage it is useful to set out the basic model in its simplest detail. To this end, assume that there exists a production function

$$Q = F(K, L) \tag{12.4.1}$$

that is homogeneous of degree one in the *single homogeneous real* capital good (K) and homogeneous labor (L). By its homogeneity property, the production function may be written so as to relate the average product of labor (y) to the capital–labor ratio (k):

$$y = f(k). \tag{12.4.2}$$

Competitive imputations and linear homogeneity jointly imply that the wage rate (w) and the rate of return on capital or the rate of interest (r) may be written as

$$w = f(k) - kf'(k), \tag{12.4.3}$$

$$r = f'(k). \tag{12.4.4}$$

Thus
$$\frac{dw}{dk} = -kf''(k) > 0, \tag{12.4.5}$$

and
$$\frac{dr}{dk} = f''(k) < 0. \tag{12.4.6}$$

Hence
$$\frac{dw}{dk} \div \frac{dr}{dk} = \frac{dw}{dr} = -k < 0, \tag{12.4.7}$$

and
$$-\frac{r}{w}\frac{dw}{dr} = \frac{r}{w}k = \frac{rK}{wL} = \text{ratio of relative shares.} \tag{12.4.8}$$

Now we have established some of the essential results of neoclassical theory. Let us look at it graphically. Panel a, figure 50, is a graph of inequality (12.4.5). It shows that the wage rate varies directly with the capital–labor ratio. Similarly, panel b illustrates inequality (12.4.6): the rate of interest varies inversely with the capital–labor ratio. The two relations are brought together in panel c, which depicts inequality (12.4.7) and emphasizes that the wage rate must vary inversely with the rate of interest.

The curve in panel c is what Samuelson calls the Surrogate Factor-Price Frontier.[2] By equation (12.4.8) the Marshallian elasticity of this curve is the ratio of aggregate relative shares. Thus with J. B. Clark real homogeneous

---

[1] See Samuelson [1962].   [2] *Ibid.*

capital, the neoclassical production function and the assumption of competitive markets lead to the neoclassical theory of distribution and the neoclassical relations between production and the input and output markets.

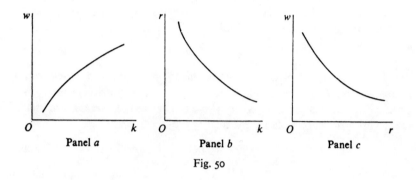

Panel a   Panel b   Panel c

Fig. 50

12.5 The Cambridge Criticism: a first view

The Cambridge Criticism of simple neoclassical theory has been voiced in a number of ways by a number of people for a number of years.[1] For a time it seemed the chief criticisms were that neoclassical theory employs explicit production functions and that it measures capital either in physical units or at current market value instead of in labor time.[2] As it turns out, the critics were groping for something much more fundamental; and after a great deal of misunderstanding, the Achilles heel was found. Indeed, the criticism is more profound than the original critics contemplated.

The whole affair is rather difficult to sort out, chiefly because the critics were searching for their criticism and neoclassical theorists were trying to rebut the criticisms as they arose. To describe this in detail would take us too far into history; however, the interested reader can get a good foretaste by studying the Robinson–Champernowne–Solow discussion of production functions and the theory of capital.[3]

The essential issue may be put this way. If production functions are smoothly continuous and everywhere continuously differentiable, the neoclassical results hold (possibly in a somewhat attenuated form if one allows for heterogeneous capital goods). But if there is no scope for factor substitution except by switching from one fixed-proportions process to

[1] See, especially, Robinson [1953] and [1956], and Kaldor [1955] and [1962].
[2] Mrs Robinson, for example, measures capital (her 'real capital ratio') as the present value of expected net receipts divided by the expenditure on the labor embodied in the piece of equipment. Robinson [1956].
[3] Robinson [1953], Champernowne [1953], and Solow [1955].

another, which implies the existence of heterogeneous capital goods, the simple neoclassical parables may not hold.

This was at first though to involve the 'Ruth Cohen Curiosum', or what is now called the 'reswitching of techniques'. Mrs Robinson enunciated this in 1956:[1]

As a general rule the degree of mechanisation of the technique brought over the frontier by a higher wage rate is higher than that corresponding to a lower wage rate, but it is possible that within certain ranges there may be a perverse relationship. This occurs because of the element of notional interest, which...enters into the price of capital goods....It seems on the whole rather unlikely that cases of this kind should be common, for more mechanised techniques usually require heavier and longer-lived plant, so that the sensitiveness of cost of equipment to differences in the interest rate is likely to be greater for more than for less mechanised techniques, and where this is the case the perverse relationship between wages and mechanisation cannot arise. We may therefore take it as a general rule that a higher degree of mechanisation is associated with a higher, not a lower, level of wages in terms of product.

Here is the germ of the criticism in explicit form. A decrease in the rate of interest may be accompanied by a change from more to less capital-intensive methods of production. If so, there is not an invariant relation between the capital–labor ratio and the wage–rate of interest ratio. And if this invariant relation is missing, all our simple curves in figure 50 have to go, as do most of the theorems of simple neoclassical theory.

Subsequent to Mrs Robinson's discovery, Sraffa, Morishima, Hicks, Pasinetti, Garegnani, Bruno–Burmeister–Sheshinski, and Samuelson definitely proved there can be a 'reswitching of techniques'.[2] Beyond this, Hicks and Brown, *inter alia*, demonstrated that even reswitching is not a necessary condition.[3] It is a simple technological fact that there may exist structures of production for which the neoclassical relation between the sphere of production and the market does not hold. More specifically, there may exist a 'set of blueprints' for which there is no one-to-one correspondence between the capital–labor ratio and the wage–rate of interest ratio. And if so, it is not necessarily true, for example, that productivity increases with the real wage rate or that permanently sustainable net national product increases as the rate of interest declines.

12.6 Professor Samuelson's parable

We can get at an explanation of this by examining Samuelson's 'Parable';[4] and doing so will help us understand the Cambridge Criticism.

[1] Robinson [1956, pp. 109–10].
[2] Sraffa [1960]; Morishima [1964] and [1966]; Hicks [1965], Garegnani [1966]; Bruno, Burmeister and Sheshinski [1966]; and Samuelson [1966b]. The reswitching phenomenon was actually brought out but discarded by Champernowne [1953, pp. 118–19 and pp. 129–30].
[3] Hicks [1965] and Brown [1967].   [4] Samuelson [1962].

TECHNICAL PROGRESS AND DISTRIBUTION

In 1962 Samuelson set out to show that the simple neoclassical theorems are valid in a world of fixed proportions and heterogeneous capital goods. To that end, he assumed that there are many, but not an infinite number, of alternative fixed-proportions processes each of which may be used to produce a common consumption good and the particular capital good used by that process. For example, the alpha process may be used to produce the consumption good (or fixed-proportions basket of goods) or the alpha-capital good. The *crucial* assumption of the model is that the production functions for the capital and consumption goods are the same.

Let M denote machines (the capital good) and C the consumption good. Samuelson's production relations for a typical process may be written as

$$M = C = \min\left(\frac{1}{a_K} K, \frac{1}{a_L} L\right), \qquad (12.6.1)$$

where the a_i's are technological constants. Let us emphasize the implications of equation (12.6.1). Not only are factor proportions the same in both sectors; the a_K's and a_L's are identically the same.

Now it is easy to show that equation (12.6.1) implies the following relation between the wage rate and the rate of interest:[1]

$$w = \frac{1}{a_L} - \frac{a_K}{a_L} r. \qquad (12.6.2)$$

We shall call equation (12.6.2) the process factor-price frontier. It is plotted in panel a, figure 51, as the straight line whose ordinate intercept is $1/a_L$ and whose slope is $-a_K/a_L$. It is important to notice that

$$-\frac{dw}{dr} = \frac{a_K}{a_L} = \frac{K}{M} \div \frac{L}{M} = \frac{K}{C} \div \frac{L}{C} = \frac{K}{L}. \qquad (12.6.3)$$

---

[1] Assume that neither capital nor labor is redundant in either sector (economic efficiency). Thus in the capital-good sector we have

$$M = \frac{1}{a_L} L_M, \quad K_M = \frac{a_K}{a_L} L_M. \qquad (12.1.1)$$

Quasi-rent in the capital-good sector is

$$M - wL_M, \qquad (12.1.2)$$

where w is the wage rate. Using equation (12.1.1) in expression (12.1.2), the rate of return in the capital-good sector, which competition assures us is the same as in the consumption sector and which is also the same as the rate of interest, is

$$r = \frac{M - wL_M}{K_M} = \frac{1}{a_K} - \frac{a_L}{a_K} w. \qquad (12.1.3)$$

Inverting equation (12.1.3) gives equation (12.6.2) in the text.

That is, the slope of each process frontier *is* the aggregate capital–labor ratio associated with that process. Since each frontier is negatively sloped of necessity, the neoclassical relation between production and the market is obtained: the capital–labor ratio varies directly with the wage–rate of interest ratio.

Now add many processes, four of which are shown in panel *b* as $\alpha\alpha'$, $\beta\beta'$, $\gamma\gamma'$, and $\delta\delta'$. The heavily shaded outermost line comprises the grand factor-price frontier. From equation (12.6.3), we see that for each process

$$-\frac{r}{w}\frac{dw}{dr} = \frac{rK}{wL} = \text{ratio of relative shares.} \qquad (12.6.4)$$

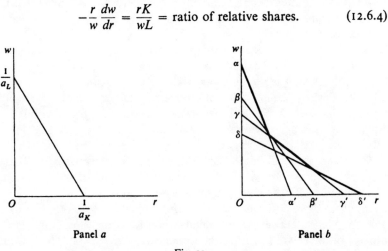

Panel *a*   Panel *b*

Fig. 51

Since this holds for each process frontier, it also holds for the grand factor-price frontier. Hence we obtain *exactly* the same outcome as we did in equation (12.4.8) of the variable-proportions, homogeneous capital model: the elasticity of the factor-price frontier is the ratio of relative shares. All other neoclassical results follow immediately. Hence Samuelson's parable validates the 'neoclassical fairy tale', at least inasmuch as it pertains to the theory of distribution. But the validation is subject to the special assumptions of Samuelson's model.

12.7 The Cambridge Criticism: second view

Commenting on Samuelson's parable, Mrs Robinson asked, 'What is this tale intended to tell us?'[1] It is intended to tell us, as Solow has in a different context,[2] that heterogeneous capital and fixed proportions do not necessarily invalidate simple neoclassical theory. Yet these heterogeneous capital,

[1] Robinson [1962].   [2] See chapter 13 for details.

fixed-proportions models do not validate simple neoclassical theory either; they merely show that it is not invalid in certain situations.

In a very circumspect statement written in 1901, Wicksell said that 'it appears inconceivable *a priori* that an increase of capital could, *ceteris paribus*, coincide with a decrease of both wages and rent—*though the question should be further investigated*'.[1] In 1956, Mrs Robinson enunciated the 'Ruth Cohen Curiosum', as described in section 12.5 above; and subsequently Sraffa, Morishima, Hicks, Pasinetti, Garegnani, Bruno–Burmeister–Sheshinski, and Samuelson definitely proved that there may be a reswitching of techniques that destroys most, if not all, of the theorems of neoclassical theory.[2]

The Cambridge Criticism initially involved only the reswitching case. Actually, the criticism is more profound than the original critics thought. As shown below, it is not necessary to have a reswitching of techniques in order to destroy the parables of simple neoclassical theory. Except for Samuelson's special case, it is generally not possible *a priori* to relate the behavior of the aggregate capital–labor ratio to the wage–rate of interest ratio.

This, then, is the ultimate Cambridge Criticism: there may exist structures of production for which the neoclassical relation between the sphere of production and the market does not hold. Specifically, there may exist a 'set of fixed-proportions blueprints' for which there is not a one-to-one correspondence between the capital–labor ratio and the wage–rate of interest ratio. The full force of the Cambridge Criticism is as follows: it is illegitimate to make an *a priori* specification of the relation between the aggregate capital–labor ratio and the factor-price ratio; but more important still, it is even illegitimate to make such an *a priori* specification for any *sector* of the economy.

In the remainder of this chapter we shall attempt first to explain the Cambridge Criticism and, second, to discuss the conditions under which it is not an empirically important criticism. At the outset we should state that neither neoclassical theory nor the Cambridge Criticism can be assessed *a priori*. Everything depends upon the structure of production and upon the responsiveness of consumers to changes in relative commodity price. If there is 'enough' substitutability in the economy, either between factors of production or between commodities in demand, neoclassical theory emerges unscathed. Otherwise not. The crucial point to emphasize is that the validity of neoclassical theory is an *empirical*, not a *theoretical*, question. At the time of this writing, there have been some, but limited, advances toward the construction of statistical models by means of which the empirical validity of neoclassical theory may be assessed.

[1] Wicksell [1901, p. 183]. Italics supplied. [2] For citations, see footnote 1, p. 251.

Throughout the discussion that follows, we postulate a two-sector economy and a two-process technology. For simplicity, and without loss of generality, we assume that one process corresponds to Samuelson's or Hicks' specifications (i.e. the associated factor-price frontier is a straight line.)

12.7.1 A small deviation from Samuelson's model

First, it is important to analyze the exact nature of Samuelson's assumption concerning the production processes in his model. As shown in section 12.6, Samuelson's technology may be represented by the following production functions:

$$M = C = \min\left(\frac{1}{a_K} K, \frac{1}{a_L} L\right). \tag{12.7.1}$$

As a result, each process has a factor-price frontier of the following form:

$$w = \frac{1}{a_L} - \frac{a_K}{a_L} r. \tag{12.7.2}$$

Thus the slope of the grand factor-price frontier at any point, since each point is on one process frontier, is

$$-\frac{dw}{dr} = \frac{a_K}{a_L} = \frac{K}{M} \div \frac{L}{M} = \frac{K}{C} \div \frac{L}{C} = \frac{K}{L}. \tag{12.7.3}$$

That, is, the slope of the frontier *is* the capital–labor ratio; and since the frontier is negatively sloped, the neoclassical relation between the sphere of production and the market is determined.

Now introduce a small change. Let each process be represented by the following specifications:

$$M = \min\left(\frac{1}{a_{KM}} K_M, \frac{1}{a_{LM}} L_M\right),$$
$$C = \min\left(\frac{1}{a_{KC}} K_C, \frac{1}{a_{LC}} L_C\right), \tag{12.7.4}$$
$$\frac{a_{KM}}{a_{LM}} = \frac{a_{KC}}{a_{LC}}, \quad a_{KM} \neq a_{KC}.$$

That is, *factor proportions* are the same in both sectors, as in Samuelson's model, but the *absolute magnitudes* of the coefficients differ. We shall call this the 'Hicks case', since he emphasized it so strongly.[1] Obviously, it differs only slightly from Samuelson's model; but there is a significant difference in the results.

[1] Hicks [1965, pp. 148–59].

As shown below, each process frontier is given by

$$w = \frac{1}{a_{LC}} - \frac{a_{KM}}{a_{LC}} r. \qquad (12.7.5)$$

Hence

$$-\frac{dw}{dr} = \frac{a_{KM}}{a_{LC}} = \frac{K_M}{L_C} \neq \frac{K}{L}. \qquad (12.7.6)$$

The slope of the frontier does not give the aggregate capital–labor ratio; and hence its elasticity does not give the ratio of aggregate relative shares.

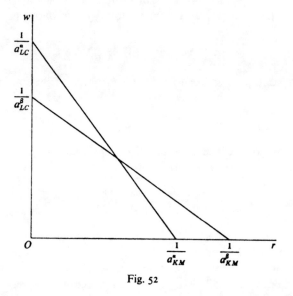

Fig. 52

In sum, the Hicks case alerts one to the possible complications that may arise. Even in the *absence of reswitching*, the factor-price frontier may not yield the neoclassical relation between factor proportions and relative factor prices. The Hicks case also throws light upon the complexities that accompany reswitching.

Consider figure 52 in which two linear processes are shown. The object of the exercise is to show that we can no longer make *absolute* statements about capital intensity as Böhm-Bawerk could with his 'average period of production' and as Samuelson could with his 'grand factor-price frontier'. Visually, $1/a_{LC}^{\alpha} > 1/a_{LC}^{\beta}$. Hence $a_{LC}^{\beta} > a_{LC}^{\alpha}$. Since $a_{LC} = L/C$, we can unequivocally say that beta is labor intensive relative to alpha in the *weak* sense that the labor–output ratio in the consumption sector is greater when beta is used than when alpha is used. *But nothing can be said about the relative capital–output ratios in the consumption sector.*

260

Now since beta is labor intensive relative to alpha, we should very much like to say that alpha is capital intensive relative to beta. As a matter of fact, we can in all cases in which the individual process frontiers are straight lines. Look at the abscissa in figure 52: $1/a_{KM}^{\beta} > 1/a_{KM}^{\alpha}$, which implies that $a_{KM}^{\alpha} > a_{KM}^{\beta}$. The capital–output ratio in the capital-good sector is greater with alpha technique than with beta. So again in a *weak* sense we may say that alpha is capital intensive relative to beta. *But nothing can be said about the relative labor–output ratios in the capital-good sector.*

The Hicks case is certainly not as simple and straightforward as the Samuelson case. But at least we can say the process that is labor intensive in one sector is less capital intensive in the other. Even this must be given up when we get to reswitching.

12.7.2 Parametric representation of the factor-price frontier

In Samuelson's model and in Hicks', the factor-price frontier for each process is a straight line precisely because the factor proportions in each sector are identical. It is interesting to observe what happens when this crucial assumption is relaxed. We concentrate initially upon one process and suppress the superscripts.

Let the production functions be

$$C = \min\left(\frac{1}{a_{KC}} K_C, \frac{1}{a_{LC}} L_C\right), \qquad (12.7.7)$$

$$M = \min\left(\frac{1}{a_{KM}} K_M, \frac{1}{a_{LM}} L_M\right). \qquad (12.7.8)$$

The determinant of the technology matrix is denoted A,[1] and we observe that

$$A = a_{LM} a_{KC} - a_{LC} a_{KM} \qquad (12.7.9)$$

Hence production in the capital-good sector is labor intensive or capital intensive relative to production in the consumption sector according as $A \gtrless 0$.

Since the two sectors are technologically distinct, they are economically distinct as well. Thus let p be the price of machines in terms of consumption goods. Perfect competition requires equality between price and unit cost. Thus we may write

$$p = a_{LM} w + a_{KM} r p, \qquad (12.7.10)$$

$$1 = a_{LC} w + a_{KC} r p. \qquad (12.7.11)$$

[1] That is, the technology matrix is

$$[A] = \begin{bmatrix} a_{LM} & a_{LC} \\ a_{KM} & a_{KC} \end{bmatrix}.$$

Thus the technology matrix is singular in the Samuelson and Hicks cases.

Solving equation (12.7.11) for the price of machines gives

$$p = \frac{1 - a_{LC}w}{a_{KC}r}. \tag{12.7.12}$$

Finally, substituting equation (12.7.12) in equation (12.7.10) and solving for w in terms of r, we find the equation for the factor-price frontier:

$$w = \frac{1 - a_{KM}r}{a_{LC} + Ar}. \tag{12.7.13}$$

There are three features of the factor-price frontier to be noted. First, if factor proportions are the same in both sectors, $A = 0$. In this case, equation (12.7.13) reduces to equation (12.7.5), the factor-price frontier in the Hicks case. Second, the frontier is negatively sloped inasmuch as

$$\frac{dw}{dr} = -\frac{a_{KM}a_{LC} + A}{(a_{LC} + Ar)^2} = -\frac{a_{LM}a_{KC}}{(a_{LC} + Ar)^2} < 0. \tag{12.7.14}$$

The final property concerns the concavity of the frontier. Some preliminaries are first required. Dividing both sides of equation (12.7.10) by p, it is seen that

$$1 - a_{KM}r > 0. \tag{12.7.15}$$

Hence from equation (12.7.13), a positive wage rate implies that

$$a_{LC} + Ar > 0. \tag{12.7.16}$$

From equation (12.7.14), we find that

$$\frac{d^2w}{dr^2} = \frac{2A(a_{LC} + Ar)\, a_{LM}a_{KC}}{(a_{LC} + Ar)^4}. \tag{12.7.17}$$

Every element in this expression is positive with the possible exception of A. Hence

$$\frac{d^2w}{d^2r} \gtrless 0 \quad \text{according as} \quad A \gtrless 0. \tag{12.7.18}$$

In words, the factor-price frontier is concave from above or below according as production in the capital-good sector is labor intensive or capital intensive relative to production in the consumption sector.

12.7.3 A graphical view of reswitching

Quite recently the so-called reswitching theorem (or the Ruth Cohen Curiosum), and some of its implications, have attracted considerable attention. Indeed, as noted above, it is a part of the Cambridge Criticism of simple neoclassical theory. So far as capital theory is concerned, the implications of reswitching may be quite important, especially the impli-

262

cation that a lower permanent consumption stream may be associated with a lower, rather than a higher, rate of interest. As we shall see, the neoclassical theory of distribution may be affected as well because it is generally impossible to specify a unique relation between the aggregate capital–labor ratio and the factor-price ratio.

Let us begin with the Hicks case which, even with its simplicity, illustrates some of the difficulties involved in heterogeneous capital models with or without reswitching. Consider figure 53. From equation (12.7.5) the

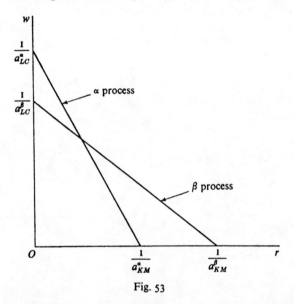

Fig. 53

ordinate and abscissa intercepts are $1/a_{LC}$ and $1/a_{KM}$ respectively. As figure 53 is constructed,

$$\frac{1}{a_{KM}^{\alpha}} < \frac{1}{a_{KM}^{\beta}}. \qquad (12.7.19)$$

Hence $a_{KM}^{\alpha} > a_{KM}^{\beta}$, which implies that $(K/M)^{\alpha} > (K/M)^{\beta}$. Thus the alpha process, as discussed above, is capital intensive relative to the beta process in the weak sense that the capital–output ratio in the capital-good sector is greater when the alpha process is used. In Hicks' terminology, alpha is capital intensive relative to beta because its 'capital-capital' coefficient is greater.

With linear factor-price frontiers, it is obvious that reswitching cannot occur. But even here some caution must be exercised because if alpha is capital intensive relative to beta, beta should be labor intensive relative to alpha. As shown above, in the Hicks case, and all other cases involving linear factor-price frontiers, it is. But beta is labor intensive only in the

263

weak sense that the average product of labor is less when beta technique is used. Or again in Hicks' terminology, beta is labor intensive because its 'labor-consumption' coefficient is greater.

Thus even in the simplest case, excluding Samuelson's model, no definite *a priori* statements can be made about relative capital or labor intensity in terms of the aggregate capital–labor ratio. Again let us point up that this emphasizes an important potential weakness of neoclassical theory: with fixed proportions and heterogeneous capital goods, it may not be possible to establish an invariant relation between the capital–labor ratio and the factor-price ratio. In the case just discussed, there is 'capital intensity

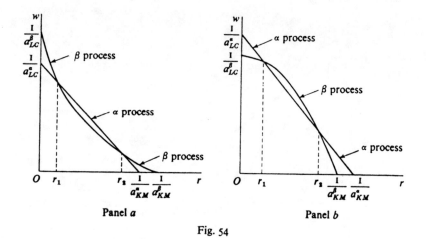

Panel *a*   Panel *b*

Fig. 54

uniqueness', to use Brown's terminology. Fortunately, as he has shown, capital intensity uniqueness is sufficient to establish the neoclassical relation.[1]

Things become more difficult when reswitching occurs, as illustrated in figure 54. Consider panel *a*, whose construction implies that, with beta technique, production in the capital-good sector is labor intensive relative to production in the consumption sector.[2] At very low rates of interest, $o < r < r_1$, the beta technique is chosen. But notice that it is impossible to say that beta is capital intensive relative to alpha. The comparison can only be made in terms of the labor-consumption coefficients; thus one can only say that beta is less labor intensive than alpha.

Now suppose $r_1 < r < r_2$. As a consequence, there is a shift from the less labor-intensive process beta to the more labor-intensive process alpha.

[1] Brown [1967].
[2] In both panels, alpha is a 'straight line' technique, i.e. factor proportions are the same in both sectors.

This, of course, is what one should expect. Finally, suppose $r_2 < r$. There is a shift back to the *less* labor-intensive beta process. This is not at all what one should expect. But notice a difficulty that is inherent in reswitching models. We have said that beta is less labor intensive than alpha; one should like for this to imply that beta is, therefore, capital intensive relative to alpha. But it is not. Comparing the abscissa intercepts, one finds that according to Hicks' classification, alpha is capital intensive relative to beta because its capital-capital coefficient is greater.

In a way this removes a part of the paradox, in another way it compounds it. If one chooses his terminology properly, he can say that as the interest rate rises, there is first a shift from a less to a more labor-intensive process and then a shift from a more to a less capital-intensive process. This makes some sense and helps remove the paradox, especially if one does not pay much attention to what is meant by 'x-intensity'. On the other hand, it compounds the paradox because we simultaneously classify the beta technique as *less labor intensive* and *less capital intensive* than the alpha technique.[1]

The source of difficulty is obvious. One should like to classify processes on the basis of the associated aggregate capital–labor ratios. But this is generally impossible in fixed-proportions, heterogeneous capital models. Following Hicks, about the best one can do is to classify techniques on the basis of the capital-capital coefficient and the labor-consumption coefficient. The *essence* of reswitching is that this scheme of classification always produces the anomalous result just observed.

Without going into details here, the reader may readily see from panel *b*, figure 54, that the same type of analysis applies when production in the capital-good sector is capital intensive relative to production in the consumption sector.

12.7.4 Conclusion

In summarizing to this point, we can say that the Cambridge Criticism is a valid one. If all production processes are characterized by fixed proportions and heterogeneous capital goods, one cannot legitimately postulate *a priori* a unique relation between capital intensity and the factor-price ratio, either within a sector or in the aggregate. Thus the simple neoclassical results concerning the relation between production and input and output markets may not hold. This does not necessarily involve reswitching; but if there is reswitching of techniques, it may further be impossible to give a precise meaning to 'factor intensity'.

The question that confronts us is not whether the Cambridge Criticism

[1] All of this is admirably demonstrated in Brown [1967].

265

is theoretically valid. It is. Rather, the question is an empirical or an econometric one: is there sufficient substitutability within the system to establish the neoclassical results?

12.8 Technical considerations

We shall return to this question briefly after a digression whose purpose is to consider two technical features of reswitching and factor-price frontiers.

12.8.1 Elasticity of a nonlinear frontier

It was stated above that the existence of a nonlinear frontier, with or without reswitching, may impair neoclassical distribution theory because the elasticity of the frontier does not show the ratio of relative shares. It obviously does in Samuelson's model. From equation (12.6.4),

$$-\frac{r}{w}\frac{dw}{dr} = \frac{a_K r}{a_L w} = \text{ratio of relative shares.} \quad (12.8.1)$$

On the other hand, the elasticity of a nonlinear frontier is not at all obvious.

For our use here, the entire model is presented.[1] The basic assumptions are full employment of both factors and perfect competition, the latter requiring that unit cost equal commodity price. Following the notation used in subsection 12.7.2 above, we have

$$\left.\begin{array}{l} a_{LM}M + a_{LC}C = L, \\ a_{KM}M + a_{KC}C = K, \end{array}\right\} \quad (12.8.2)$$

the conditions for full employment. Similarly, equality of price and unit cost gives

$$\left.\begin{array}{l} a_{LM}w + a_{KM}rp = p, \\ a_{LC}w + a_{KC}rp = 1. \end{array}\right\} \quad (12.8.3)$$

The immediate object is to convert equations (12.8.2) and (12.8.3) into equations of change. To this end, define λ_{ij} as the proportion of factor i used in sector j. We can thus define a λ-matrix whose determinant is

$$\lambda = \lambda_{LM} - \lambda_{LC} = \lambda_{KC} - \lambda_{KM}. \quad (12.8.4)$$

Similarly, let θ_{ij} be the relative share of factor i in sector j. Specifically,

$$\left.\begin{array}{ll} \theta_{LM} = \dfrac{a_{LM}w}{p}, & \theta_{KM} = a_{KM}r, \\[2mm] \theta_{LC} = a_{LC}w, & \theta_{KC} = a_{KC}rp. \end{array}\right\} \quad (12.8.5)$$

[1] For a similar model that deals with the rental per unit of capital rather than the rate of interest, see Jones [1965a].

12.8 TECHNICAL CONSIDERATIONS

These terms may be used to define a θ-matrix whose determinant is

$$\theta = \theta_{LM} - \theta_{LC} = \theta_{KC} - \theta_{KM}. \tag{12.8.6}$$

We may note in passing that production in the capital-good sector is labor intensive or capital intensive relative to production in the consumption sector according as either λ or θ is greater than or less than zero. In Samuelson's and Hicks' special cases, λ and θ are zero.[1]

Let $\hat{x}$ denote the proportional change in the variable x, i.e., $\hat{x} = \dfrac{dx}{x}$.

From equations (12.8.2) and (12.8.3) we obtain the following equations of proportional change:

$$\left.\begin{array}{c} \lambda_{LM}\hat{M} + \lambda_{LC}\hat{C} = \hat{L}, \\ \lambda_{KM}\hat{M} + \lambda_{KC}\hat{C} = \hat{K}, \end{array}\right\} \tag{12.8.7}$$

and

$$\left.\begin{array}{c} \theta_{LM}\hat{w} + \theta_{KM}\hat{r} = (1 - \theta_{KM})\hat{p}, \\ \theta_{LC}\hat{w} + \theta_{KC}\hat{r} = -\theta_{KC}\hat{p}. \end{array}\right\} \tag{12.8.8}$$

From equations (12.8.8), one finds that

$$\frac{r}{w}\frac{dw}{dr} = \frac{\hat{w}}{\hat{r}} = 1 + \frac{1+\theta}{\theta}\frac{\hat{p}}{\hat{r}}. \tag{12.8.9}$$

From equation (12.7.12),

$$\hat{p} = \hat{w} + \frac{\theta_{KM}}{\theta_{LM}}\hat{r}. \tag{12.8.10}$$

Using equation (12.8.10) in equation (12.8.9) yields the desired results:

$$-\frac{\hat{w}}{\hat{r}} = \frac{\theta_{KC}}{\theta_{LM}} = \frac{(1-\theta_{LC})}{(1-\theta_{KM})}. \tag{12.8.11}$$

The elasticity of a nonlinear factor-price frontier is not, and cannot be, the ratio of aggregate factor shares.[2] Specifically, it is the ratio of the capital share in the consumption sector to the labor share in the capital-good sector. This alone is certainly not enough to save the simple J. B. Clark parable. Nonetheless, it is important to note that the sectoral relative shares, irrespective of the number of factors, are given by the trace of $[\theta].[\lambda]^T$. Whether this saves the distribution parable or not, however, is a matter of question.

[1] It might be well to note that A, λ, and θ all have identical properties. The A-matrix and its transpose define the static equilibrium conditions. The λ-matrix defines the equations of change for the real variables, and the transpose of the θ-matrix defines the equations of change for the (relative) price variables.

[2] It can be shown that the ratio of aggregate relative shares, θ_K/θ_L, is

$$\frac{\theta_K}{\theta_L} = -\frac{\hat{w}}{\hat{r}} + \frac{1}{\theta_L}(\lambda_{LM}\theta_{LM} - \lambda_{KC}\theta_{KC})\hat{p}.$$

The elasticity would equal the negative of the ratio of aggregate relative shares if relative commodity price did not change. However, $\hat{p}$ cannot be zero by equation (12.8.10).

12.8.2 Conditions for reswitching

It seems worthwhile to set out some conditions for technical reswitching in a two-process model.[1] Reswitching can occur if, and only if, the two process frontiers intersect twice in the positive quadrant. This requires not only common r's for common w's; both r–w pairs must be positive.

First, solve equation (12.7.13) to obtain r in terms of w for the beta process:

$$r = \frac{1 - a_{LC}^\beta w}{a_{KM}^\beta + A^\beta w}. \qquad (12.8.12)$$

Next, equate expressions (12.6.2) and (12.8.12), obtaining the following quadratic in r:

$$r^2 - \frac{1}{a_{KM}^\alpha A^\beta}(A^\beta + a_{LC}^\alpha a_{KM}^\beta - a_{LC}^\beta a_{KM}^\alpha)\, r + \frac{1}{a_{KM}^\alpha A^\beta}(a_{LC}^\alpha - a_{LC}^\beta) = 0. \qquad (12.8.13)$$

Similarly, from equations (12.6.2) and (12.7.13), one obtains

$$w^2 - \frac{1}{a_{LC}^\alpha A^\beta}(A^\beta + a_{LC}^\beta a_{KM}^\alpha - a_{LC}^\alpha a_{KM}^\beta)\, r + \frac{1}{a_{LC}^\alpha A^\beta}(a_{KM}^\alpha - a_{KM}^\beta) = 0. \qquad (12.8.14)$$

Using Descartes' Rule of Sign, one may obtain two sets of conditions. To obtain two positive but not necessarily real roots, the constant terms in the polynomials must be positive. Hence one set of conditions is as follows:

$$\left.\begin{array}{l} a_{LC}^\alpha \gtrless a_{LC}^\beta \quad \text{according as} \quad A^\beta \gtrless 0, \\[4pt] a_{KM}^\alpha \gtrless a_{KM}^\beta \quad \text{according as} \quad A^\beta \gtrless 0. \end{array}\right\} \qquad (12.8.15)$$

The economic interpretation of these conditions is clear. It is given only for the first set of inequalities; the same statement applies, *mutatis mutandis*, to the second set. The reciprocals of the a_{LC}'s are the ordinate intercepts of the individual factor-price frontier lines. Thus if production in the capital-good sector is labor intensive relative to production in the consumption sector with beta technique, alpha technique must be more labor intensive in the consumption sector than beta technique. On the other hand, when production in the capital-good sector is capital intensive relative to production in the consumption sector with beta technique, alpha technique must be less labor intensive in the consumption sector than beta technique. Again, this points up the difficulties encountered above.

The second set of conditions is based upon the r- and w-coefficients in equations (12.8.13) and (12.8.14). From equation (12.8.13), it may be shown that a necessary condition for reswitching is that

$$\frac{a_{KM}^\alpha}{a_{KM}^\beta} \lesseqgtr \frac{a_{LC}^\alpha}{a_{LC}^\beta} \quad \text{according as} \quad A^\beta \gtrless 0. \qquad (12.8.16)$$

[1] For a more elaborate treatment, see Brown [1967].

12.8 TECHNICAL CONSIDERATIONS

This condition implies that the unit capital requirement of alpha technique relative to beta technique must be smaller than the unit labor requirement of alpha technique relative to beta technique when the beta technique itself is relatively labor intensive in the capital-good sector, and *vice versa*.

The corresponding condition based upon equation (12.8.14) is

$$\frac{a^\alpha_{KM}}{a^\beta_{KM}} \gtreqless \frac{a^\alpha_{LC}}{a^\beta_{LC}} \quad \text{according as} \quad A^\beta \gtrless 0. \tag{12.8.17}$$

Here is the striking point: the two conditions are opposites. While these conditions are not both necessary and sufficient, expressions (12.8.16) and (12.8.17) suggest that reswitching is not likely to occur unless the relative unit capital requirements are very nearly equal to the relative unit labor requirements.

12.9 Conclusion

As previously said, there is no doubt that the Cambridge Criticism is valid. Indeed, it is broader than it was first thought to be in that reswitching is not a necessary condition to invalidate the simple 'J. B. Clark neoclassical fairy tale'. If we live in a fixed-proportions world, which may or may not be true, and if capital goods are heterogeneous, which is unquestionably true, there may not exist an invariant relation between factor proportions and the factor-price ratio. At least, one cannot validly *assume a priori* that such an invariant relation exists.

Simple neoclassical theory, with which this book largely deals, would have it so. And if so, simple neoclassical theory is validated. However, the Cambridge Criticism definitely shows that there may be structures of production in which the Clark parables may not hold. It is of no matter that the Robinson-type models of capital and growth are invalidated as well. The crux of the matter is that economists may be unable to make any statements concerning the relation of production to competitive input and output markets.

I believe they can; but that is a statement of faith, as is the flyleaf quotation from Samuelson. The issue is really not that amorphous, however. As Brown has recently shown,[1] it all depends upon the amount of substitutability there is in the system. The existence of a 'sufficient' amount of substitutability establishes capital intensity uniqueness, in the sense that if alpha is capital intensive relative to beta in, say, the consumption sector, beta is labor intensive relative to alpha in the capital-good sector. This is all that is required to establish the neoclassical parables. The significant and unique achievement of Brown is to have shown that

[1] Brown [1967].

269

capital intensity uniqueness is an econometric question susceptible of resolution in a probabilistic sense.

In final summary, the Cambridge Criticism points up a definite potential weakness of simple neoclassical theory. Whether it is an important weakness is a question that cannot be answered *a priori*; but there are developments, mentioned above, which indicate that a *factual* answer may be forthcoming, even if not within the immediate future. Commenting upon this state of affairs, Samuelson wrote: 'If all this causes headaches for those nostalgic for the old time parables of neoclassical writing, we must remind ourselves that scholars are not born to live an easy existence. We must respect, and appraise, the facts of life.'[1] At present, it seems that little can be added to this evaluation.

[1] Samuelson [1966*b*, p. 583].

13

VINTAGE MODELS AND
FIXED PROPORTIONS IN
NEOCLASSICAL THEORY

13.1 Introduction

To some extent, 'technological progress' can occur in the absence of gross investment. In the models treated in chapters 11 and 12, technological progress was strictly of this 'disembodied' type. Other innovations require only small modifications of existing capital equipment and, therefore, negligible capital expenditures. However, certain innovations can be introduced only by scrapping old capital equipment and replacing it by new capital equipment that 'embodies' the new technology. Such changes in technology are brought about only by significant gross investment.

One may add to this 'fact' another 'fact' of some importance: once a piece of capital equipment has been installed, there is often very little scope for factor substitution, certainly not the scope posited in the 'neoclassical fairy tale'. Two questions immediately arise. First, if capital equipment existing at a given moment is in fact heterogeneous, is it possible to define a capital aggregate such as that used in simple neoclassical theory?[1] Second, if machine operation requires fixed or almost-fixed proportions, can one deduce the marginal equivalences upon which neoclassical theory rests?

The first question, while long recognized, was explicitly posed in 1953 by Mrs Robinson and Champernowne.[2] Solow provided the answer.[3] If a production function involves more than one kind of capital good, it can be written in terms of a capital aggregate if the production function satisfies the condition of Leontief's theorem on separable functions.[4] In this context, the Leontief theorem requires that the marginal rate of technical substitution between different types of capital equipment be independent of the amount of labor used. This, of course, is a very restrictive condition.

[1] One approach to this problem was analyzed in chapter 12. One should also point out that neoclassical theory does not have to be 'simple neoclassical theory'. See, for example, Samuelson and Solow [1956].
[2] Robinson [1953] and Champernowne [1953]. Also see Robinson [1955].
[3] Solow [1955].
[4] Leontief [1947b], Proposition I, p. 364. The proposition is proved in Leontief [1947a].

More recently, Fisher has shown that heterogeneous capital may be aggregated if less restrictive conditions are satisfied.[1] More specifically, (a) if there are two factors and constant returns to scale, a necessary and sufficient condition for aggregation is that when labor has been optimally allocated (so that its marginal product is the same in all uses), the average product of labor is the same in all uses (i.e. on all vintages of capital equipment); (b) more generally, if there are constant returns to scale, capital-augmenting technical change is necessary and sufficient to permit aggregation of the heterogeneous capital stock.[2]

In the next sections some heterogeneous capital models of the 'vintage' variety are examined, after which we return to the question of fixed proportions and neoclassical theory.

13.2 Vintage models, or the 'new view' of investment

The 'vintage capital' models presumably originated with Johansen and Solow, but they have subsequently been analyzed by a number of authors.[3] In this section, two models are developed: the Cobb–Douglas model, and a more general factor-augmenting model analogous to that used in subsection 12.3.2 above. The latter reduces to the CES vintage model.

13.2.1 The Cobb–Douglas vintage model[4]

Consider a Cobb–Douglas model in which output produced by labor employed on capital produced in year v (i.e. of vintage v) is

$$q_v(t) = Be^{\lambda v}L_v^\alpha(t)\,[e^{-\delta(t-v)}I(v)]^{1-\alpha}, \qquad (13.2.1)$$

where $q_v(t)$ = output produced at time t on capital equipment of vintage v;

$L_v(t)$ = labor employed at time t on capital equipment of vintage v;

$I(v)$ = gross investment in capital equipment of vintage v;

B = either a constant or $B'e^{\gamma t}$, where γ thus reflects 'disembodied' technical progress;

δ = influence of physical deterioration;

[1] Fisher [1965].
[2] Of course, there can also be 'disembodied' technological progress and/or labor-embodied technological progress inasmuch as these do not affect the capital stock.
[3] Johansen [1959] and Solow [1960]. Also see Solow [1962a, b], Solow [1963a, b], Solow, Tobin, von Weizsacker, and Yaari [1966], Kurz [1963], Phelps [1962], Matthews [1964], Phelps and Yaari [1964], and Phelps [1963]. For other developments, partly or largely empirical, see Berglas [1965], Intriligator [1965], Jorgenson [1966], McCarthy [1966], Phelps and Phelps [1966], Westfield [1966], and Whitaker [1966].
[4] This section, while reflecting the spirit of Solow [1960], incorporates some ideas advanced by McCarthy [1964] and Brown [1966].

$\lambda (> 0)$ = influence of technical improvements embodied in $I(v)$; thus the newer the vintage (i.e. the greater v), the more productive is the labor employed on $I(v)$.

From equation (13.2.1), total output on all employed vintages of capital equipment is

$$q(t) = \int_{-\infty}^{t} q_v(t)\, dv. \tag{13.2.2}$$

The fully employed labor force must be allocated over all utilized vintages of capital equipment. For the allocation to be optimal, the marginal product of labor must be the same irrespective of the vintage of equipment upon which it is employed. From equation (13.2.1), the marginal product at time t of labor used on equipment of vintage $v \leqq t$ is

$$\frac{\partial q_v(t)}{\partial L_v(t)} = \alpha B' e^{\lambda v + \gamma t} [e^{-\delta(t-v)} I(v)]^{1-\alpha} L_v(t)^{\alpha-1}. \tag{13.2.4}$$

Since the marginal product must be the same for all vintages, equation (13.2.4) may be written

$$M(t) = \alpha B' e^{\lambda v + \gamma t} [e^{-\delta(t-v)} I(v)]^{1-\alpha} L_v(t)^{\alpha-1}, \tag{13.2.5}$$

where $M(t)$ is the uniform marginal product of labor.

Next, equation (13.2.5) may be solved to obtain an expression for $L_v(t)$:

$$L_v(t) = M^{-1/(1-\alpha)} (\alpha B')^{1/(1-\alpha)} I(v) \exp\left(\frac{\lambda v + \gamma t}{1-\alpha} - \delta(t-v)\right). \tag{13.2.6}$$

Let

$$a(t) = M^{-1/(1-\alpha)} (\alpha B')^{1/(1-\alpha)}, \quad b = \frac{\lambda}{1-\alpha} + \delta. \tag{13.2.7}$$

Then equation (13.2.6) may be written more compactly as

$$L_v(t) = a(t)\, I(v) \exp\left\{bv + \left(\frac{\gamma}{1-\alpha} - \delta\right)t\right\}. \tag{13.2.8}$$

Next, substitute equation (13.2.8) into equation (13.2.1) to obtain

$$q_v(t) = B' a^{\alpha}(t)\, I(v) \exp\left\{bv + \left(\frac{\gamma}{1-\alpha} - \delta\right)t\right\}. \tag{13.2.9}$$

The final step involves substituting equation (13.2.9) into equation (13.2.2) and integrating. Making the substitution, one obtains

$$q(t) = \int_{-\infty}^{t} B' e^{\lambda v + \gamma t - \delta(t-v)(1-\alpha)} I^{1-\alpha}(v)\, L^{\alpha}(t)\, dv. \tag{13.2.10}$$

Since only v is involved in the integration, equation (13.2.10) may be written

$$q(t) = B' e^{\gamma t} L^{\alpha}(t) \int_{-\infty}^{t} e^{bv(1-\alpha)} I^{1-\alpha}(v)\, dv. \tag{13.2.11}$$

Define

$$J(t) = \int_{-\infty}^{t} e^{bv} I(v)\, dv. \tag{13.2.12}$$

Substituting equation (13.2.12) in equation (13.2.11), Solow's result is obtained:

$$q(t) = B' e^{\gamma t} L^\alpha(t) J^{1-\alpha}(t), \qquad (13.2.13)$$

where $J(t)$ is, by equation (13.2.12), a measure of the aggregate, productivity-adjusted capital stock.

The result is the traditional Cobb–Douglas function in which the productivity-adjusted aggregate of technically heterogeneous capital goods replaces the usual homogeneous capital aggregate. That is to say, the only difference between the usual model and the vintage model lies in $J(t)$. Now consider equation (13.2.12).

Each vintage of capital equipment is weighted by a productivity improvement factor $e^{bv} = e^{\lambda v/(1-\alpha)+\delta v}$. As between two pieces of capital equipment whose vintages differ by one period of time, the newer capital equipment is more productive because: (a) it 'embodies' the technical improvement factor $(\lambda/1-\alpha)$, and (b) it is 'more' capital because the older piece of equipment has suffered 'radioactive decay' at the rate δ.

But now consider the marginal rate of technical substitution of capital goods of vintage u for capital goods of vintage v:

$$\frac{\partial q(t)/\partial I(v)}{\partial q(t)/\partial I(u)} = -\frac{dI(u)}{dI(v)} = e^{b(v-u)}. \qquad (13.2.14)$$

For the moment, set $u = t$, where t is the current period. Thus $e^{b(v-t)}$ is the increase in current capital goods that is required to offset a unit reduction in capital goods of vintage v while maintaining a constant output. Since $b > 0$ and $t > v$, the increase is obviously less than unity, and it is the smaller the greater is the difference between t and v. More generally, $e^{b(v-u)} \gtrless 1$ according as $v \gtrless u$, reflecting the productivity relations between capital goods of different vintages.

To obtain Solow's formulation in equation (13.2.12), set $u = 0$; thus $e^{b(v-u)} = e^{bv}$, the weights of the vintage capital goods. Hence the weights attached to the various vintages of capital goods are simply the marginal rates of technical substitution of vintage zero capital goods for vintage v capital goods.

Finally, notice from equation (13.2.14) that the marginal rate of technical substitution between capital goods of different vintages depends only upon $b = \lambda/(1-\alpha)+\delta$ and the vintage dates. Thus the marginal rate of technical substitution is independent of labor input, thereby satisfying the Leontief condition mentioned in section 13.1. Thus the heterogeneous capital goods can, in fact, be aggregated.

Equation (13.2.13) differs from Solow's original model in that we have introduced neutral, disembodied technological progress as well as embodied progress. However, if one sets $B = $ a constant in (13.2.1), Solow's

274

results are obtained. Also following Solow, an alternative form may be obtained. If assets are valued competitively and if perfect foresight is assumed, the value of assets $A(t)$ is

$$A(t) = e^{-bt}J(t). \tag{13.2.15}$$

Substituting equation (13.2.15) in equation (13.2.13), the following form is obtained:
$$q(t) = B' e^{(\gamma+\lambda)t+\delta(1-\alpha)} L^{\alpha}(t) A^{1-\alpha}(t). \tag{13.2.16}$$

To quote Solow: '...if asset valuations faithfully reflect perfect foresight, the "homogeneous capital model" would be accurate, provided the capital stock were measured not by a count of machines but by the real market value of the stock of capital.'[1]

13.2.2 A factor-augmenting vintage model[2]

Suppose all productivity improvements are embodied in capital equipment. The production function relative to each vintage may be written as

$$q_v(t) = F[\mu(v) K_v(t), L_v(t)], \tag{13.2.17}$$

where F is homogeneous of degree one in the capital and labor inputs, and

$q_v(t) =$ output produced at time t with capital equipment of vintage v;

$L_v(t) =$ labor used on capital equipment of vintage v;

$K_v(t) =$ the stock of capital equipment of vintage v *surviving* at time t;[3]

$\mu(v) =$ productivity factor associated with capital equipment of vintage v; $\mu(v)$ is fixed once investment is made, and $\mu(t) > \mu(v)$ for $t > v$.

As in subsection 13.2.1, we have the following conditions: (a) total output is the sum of the outputs produced on all utilized vintages of capital equipment, and (b) the labor force is fully employed. These conditions are represented mathematically by

$$q(t) = \int_{-\infty}^{t} q_v(t) \, dv, \tag{13.2.18}$$

$$L(t) = \int_{-\infty}^{t} L_v(t) \, dv. \tag{13.2.19}$$

Labor is allocated among the various vintages of capital equipment so that its marginal product is the same wherever used. Assuming perfect

---

[1] Solow [1960], p. 100. For further discussion of this point, see Brown [1966], pp. 81–6.
[2] This section is based on Solow [1964]; also see McCarthy [1965].
[3] In the notation of subsection 13.2.1, $K_v(t) = e^{-\delta(t-v)}I(v)$.

competition and competitive imputations, this means that the marginal product of labor equals the wage rate and that the wage rate is uniform over all utilized vintages of capital equipment. From equation (13.2.17) the wage rate is

$$w(t) = \frac{\partial}{\partial L} F[\mu(v) K_v(t), L_v(t)], \qquad (13.2.20)$$

which, in light of the assumed homogeneity of F, may be written

$$w(t) = \frac{\partial}{\partial L} L_v(t) F\left[\frac{\mu(v) K_v(t)}{L_v(t)}, 1\right]. \qquad (13.2.21)$$

The term $(\mu(v) K_v(t)/L_v(t))$ depends only upon the product wage rate and may accordingly be written

$$\frac{\mu(v) K_v(t)}{L_v(t)} = f_v[w(t)]. \qquad (13.2.22)$$

Also from the homogeneity of F, equation (13.2.18) may be expressed as

$$q(t) = \int_{-\infty}^{t} L_v(t) F\left[\frac{\mu(v) K_v(t)}{L_v(t)}, 1\right] dv. \qquad (13.2.23)$$

Now substitute equation (13.2.22) into equation (13.2.23), obtaining

$$q(t) = \int_{-\infty}^{t} L_v(t) F[f(w(t)), 1] \, dv. \qquad (13.2.24)$$

Since t is not involved in the integration, this becomes

$$q(t) = F[f(w(t)), 1] \int_{-\infty}^{t} L_v(t) \, dv. \qquad (13.2.25)$$

From equation (13.2.19), equation (13.2.25) may be written as

$$q(t) = L(t) F[f(w(t)), 1], \qquad (13.2.26)$$

or

$$q(t) = F[f(w) L, L]. \qquad (13.2.27)$$

Next, using definition (13.2.22) in equation (13.2.19), one obtains the following expression for $L(t)$:

$$L(t) = \int_{-\infty}^{t} L_v(t) \, dv = \frac{1}{f(w)} \int_{-\infty}^{t} \mu(v) K_v(t) \, dv = \frac{1}{f(w)} J(t), \qquad (13.2.28)$$

where

$$J(t) = \int_{-\infty}^{t} \mu(v) K_v(t) \, dv \qquad (13.2.29)$$

is the productivity-adjusted capital stock at time t.[1] Finally, using equation (13.2.28) in equation (13.2.27), one obtains the aggregate production

---

[1] $J(t)$ as used here is entirely analogous to the $J(t)$ used in subsection 13.2.1

function in terms of the productivity-weighted aggregate of the technically heterogeneous capital goods:

$$q(t) = F[fL, L] = F[J(t), L(t)]$$

$$= F\left[\int_{-\infty}^{t} \mu(v) K_v(t) \, dv, \, L(t) \right]. \tag{13.2.30}$$

The weights in this function have the same interpretation as the weights e^{bv} discussed in subsection 13.2.1.

From equation (13.2.30), the special constant elasticity of substitution form follows immediately:

$$q(t) = \gamma[\delta J(t)^{-\rho} + (1-\delta) L(t)^{-\rho}]^{-1/\rho}, \tag{13.2.31}$$

where the elasticity of substitution is given by

$$\sigma = \frac{1}{1+\rho}. \tag{13.2.32}$$

A final point, which emphasizes the special nature of the Cobb–Douglas formulation, merits consideration. The analysis is based upon the CES function (13.2.31) rather than the general form in equation (13.2.30); however, the results apply to the general case. Let S_K and S_L denote the relative shares of capital and labor. From equations (13.2.31) and (13.2.32), one obtains

$$S_K = \frac{J}{q} \frac{\partial q}{\partial J} = \delta \gamma^{1-\rho} \left(\frac{q}{J}\right)^{\rho}, \tag{13.2.33}$$

$$S_L = \frac{L}{q} \frac{\partial q}{\partial L} = (1-\delta) \gamma^{1-\rho} \left(\frac{q}{L}\right)^{\rho}. \tag{13.2.34}$$

Taking the ratio of relative shares, one may write

$$\frac{S_K}{S_L} = \left(\frac{\delta}{1-\delta}\right)\left(\frac{\int_{-\infty}^{t} \mu(v) K_v(t) \, dv}{L}\right)^{(1-1/\sigma)}. \tag{13.2.35}$$

Now suppose μ increases; for example, $\mu(t+1) > \mu(t)$. Other things equal, this increases the numerator relative to the denominator. Thus an increase in μ will cause a change in the ratio of relative shares. In particular, the ratio of relative shares will increase, remain unchanged, or diminish according as the elasticity of substitution is greater than, equal to, or less than unity. Therefore, capital-embodied technical progress is in fact capital using, neutral, or labor using according as the elasticity of substitution is greater than, equal to, or less than unity.[1] As in other situations,

---

[1] For the corresponding situation with purely labor-embodied technological progress, see Ferguson [1965 b]. For the general case, see subsection 12.3.3.

the Cobb–Douglas model is a special case because the elasticity of sub-stitution is unity. In the present formulation, it is a special case because unit elasticity of substitution implies *neutral* embodied technological progress.

13.2.3 The new view and the old

At the empirical level there seems little doubt that most technical advances are embodied in new capital equipment, i.e. technical progress cannot occur in the absence of positive gross investment. At the theoretical level this raises several questions, two of which are discussed here.

First, does the use of old-style capital concepts account for the 'Solow result' that about ninety percent of the observed productivity gain is attributable to neutral technological progress? For a time many writers apparently believed it did. For example, in reviewing Denison's study of economic growth and total factor productivity,[1] Abramovitz wrote: 'The economic model which underlies Denison's calculations stands in sharp contrast to the model with which Robert Solow has been experimenting.... The factual gap between the two views is profound and not really usefully attacked by speculation.'[2] The question was a point of debate until quite recently, when Jorgenson conclusively proved that embodied and disem-bodied technical change have precisely the same factual implications for economic policy.[3]

Second, irrespective of the *factual* implications, do the two views of capital have different model-theoretic implications? This is, in a real sense, much the more important question. If empirical observations convince us that most technical progress is of the embodied variety, and if embodied and disembodied change lead to different model results, all our old models must be scrapped and replaced by new ones, just as old capital equipment is scrapped and replaced by new capital equipment embodying the most recent technical advances. The answer to the question was actually given by Solow in his initial study of embodied technical change. '...if asset valuations faithfully reflect perfect foresight, the "homogeneous capital model" would be accurate, provided the capital stock were measured *not by a count of machines* but by the real market value of the stock of capital.'[4]

This has been most clearly explained by Brown.[5] For the most part, those working with old-style capital models have tried to approximate the flow of capital services by means of the *net* capital stock.[6] The latter is

---

[1] Denison [1962].
[2] Abramovitz [1962, p. 773].
[3] Jorgenson [1966].
[4] Solow [1960, p. 100], italics added.
[5] The remainder of this subsection is based upon Brown [1966, pp. 81–6].
[6] There are exceptions. Denison [1962, pp. 97–8], for example, argues in favor of using gross capital stock.

computed from time-series data on gross investment. Let the present year be t and consider the gross investment made in year $v < t$, $I(v)$. To obtain the present net value of this gross investment, one must allow not only for physical depreciation but also for economic obsolescence that arises because new investment goods embody the technical advances that have been achieved over the period $t-v$.

Brown explained this in the following way:[1]

As new and technically superior capital goods enter the market, the marginal product of vintage capital declines relative to the marginal product of new capital. If the market correctly assesses the relative marginal products, the value of the vintage capital will decline relative to the value of new capital; *the vintage capital suffers obsolescence.* If there is a competitive market for capital, then the decline in the market value of vintage capital relative to the new capital must equal the decline in the marginal product of the vintage capital relative to the marginal product of the new investment good.

Let ω denote the combined rate of depreciation and obsolescence. Since under competition the value of old capital declines relative to new capital in the same proportion as its marginal product declines, ω is clearly equal to Solow's productivity adjustment factor. The current value of the gross investment made at time v is

$$K_v(t) = I(v)\, e^{\omega(v-t)}. \tag{13.2.36}$$

Aggregating equation (13.2.36) over all vintages gives the current value of the net capital stock:

$$K(t) = \int_{-\infty}^{t} I(v)\, e^{\omega(v-t)}\, dv. \tag{13.2.37}$$

From equation (13.2.37), the old-style Cobb–Douglas model would, at first glance, appear to be

$$q(t) = CL^{\alpha}(t) \int_{-\infty}^{t} [I(v)\, e^{\omega(v-t)}\, dv]^{1-\alpha}. \tag{13.2.38}$$

However, a comparison of equations (13.2.11) and (13.2.38) shows that the time paths of output are not the same in the two models. Since the embodied model in equation (13.2.11) is not misspecified, the model in equation (13.2.38) must be. But if a trend term λ, which is the same as Solow's productivity improvement factor, is inserted in the net capital stock model, the two output paths are the same. Hence the correct specification of the net capital stock model is

$$q(t) = Ce^{\lambda t} L^{\alpha}(t)\, K^{1-\alpha}(t). \tag{13.2.39}$$

Thus as both Jorgenson and Brown proved, the rate of growth associated with the two models is the same. Or as Brown put it:[2]

---

[1] Brown [1966, pp. 82–3], italics added.
[2] *Ibid.* pp. 85–6. Notation changed to correspond with that in the text.

...the net stock model and Solow's embodied model are two different ways of conceptualizing the same economic phenomenon...We noted above that if competition were perfect,...the rate at which the productivity of old capital deteriorates relative to new capital—the rate is *b*—would be reflected in the rate of decline of the relative valuations of old and new capital—denoted by ω. In principle, both *b* and ω refer to the same phenomenon—one reflects its physical properties, the other its economic properties...if ω is equal to *b*, the two models yield the same growth rate.

In summary, the results of embodied models and net capital stock models are the same. For theoretical and empirical purposes, the choice between them depends upon the purpose of the investigation and the availability of data.

13.3   Vintage models with fixed proportions

A salient feature of the vintage models discussed above is the assumption that production with each vintage of capital equipment is subject to smooth input substitutability. Since the models discussed also satisfy the Leontief–Solow–Fisher aggregation criterion, it is little wonder that the neoclassical results emerge. More specifically, equation (13.2.30) or equation (13.2.31) could be used in chapter 12 without affecting the results whatsoever. It does not immediately follow, however, that the neoclassical results are obtained if production with technically heterogeneous capital goods is subject to fixed proportions. One approach to the question was developed in chapter 12. The remainder of this chapter is devoted to an alternative approach that establishes the neoclassical results.[1]

13.3.1   Structure of the model

The model to be discussed has many of the characteristics of the two-sector model analyzed in chapters 11 and 12. The chief difference lies in the production functions. The model concerns a two-sector economy. In one sector consumer goods are produced by labor and machines; in the other sector, machines are produced by labor alone. This assumption, of course, is an extreme version of the one found necessary in the two-sector model above, namely production in the capital-good sector is labor intensive relative to production in the consumption sector.

A machine, once produced, has a fixed capacity output of one unit of consumables per year. This holds for all machines, irrespective of vintage. Further, each machine must be operated by a fixed amount of labor; in this case, however, the amount of labor depends upon the vintage of the machine. Finally, each machine is of the 'one-hoss-shay' type with fixed

[1] The remainder of this section, without further citation, is based upon Solow [1962*b*].

life L. That is, each machine operates with unimpaired efficiency and without physical depreciation throughout its life.

A machine that requires λ men to operate all full capacity[1] is said to be a machine of type λ. The basic technological assumption of the model is as follows: the fewer the number of men required to operate a machine at full capacity, the greater the number of men required to construct the machine. More formally, the cost of producing a machine requiring λ men for capacity operation is $c(\lambda) > 0$. By the assumption above, $c'(\lambda) < 0$; as subsequently shown, second-order conditions require $c''(\lambda) > 0$. Thus the cost function is downward sloping, and the marginal cost of reducing λ rises as λ falls.

Finally, $I(v)$ is the number of machines built in year v. A machine built in year v cannot be operated until year $v+1$. It then survives unimpaired through year $v+L$.

13.3.2 Wage determination

Wages are determined so as to provide full employment of the labor force. At any time t there is a maximum stock of L different types of machines: $I(t-L)$ machines of type $\lambda(t-L)$, $I(t-L-1)$ machines of type $\lambda(t-L-1)$, ..., $I(t-1)$ machines of type $\lambda(t-1)$. Thus the maximum number of men that can be employed in the consumption sector is

$$\sum_{t-L}^{t-1} \lambda(v)\, I(v). \tag{13.3.1}$$

Assume that the supply of labor to the consumption sector, $L(t)$, never exceeds this amount. Further, by assumption, the supply of labor to the consumption sector is exogenously given and inelastic with respect to the wage rate.[2]

Let w represent the real wage rate, i.e. the wage rate in terms of consumables. At that real wage, a machine of type λ earns a quasi-rent of $1 - \lambda w$. The demand for labor comes from the set of machines that can profitably be operated, or at least operated without loss. Let $V(t, w)$ denote

---

[1] A machine does not have to operate at full capacity. For example, if a machine requires two men for capacity operation (i.e. to produce one unit of consumables), it may be operated by one man so as to produce one-half unit of consumables. Thus input proportions are not *rigidly* fixed as in the Leontief model; nonetheless, this assumption is far from the smooth substitutability of most neoclassical models.

[2] It is customary to speak of a supply of labor, not of a 'supply of labor to a particular sector'. The model is somewhat incomplete in that employment in the machine sector is not analyzed. Solow assumed that the amount of investment is given exogenously. The type of machine built is determined by the model (see below). Hence the number of workers employed in the machine sector is determined. The supply of labor to the consumption sector may be regarded as the total labor force minus the number employed in the machine sector. Thus in this particular model, the labor force must behave in a permissive way.

the set of vintages between $t-1$ and $t-L$ for which $\lambda w \leqq 1$. The demand for labor at wage w is

$$\sum_{v \in V(t, w)} \lambda(v) \, I(v), \qquad (13.3.2)$$

which is a step-decreasing function of w. Equilibrium in the labor market accordingly requires that

$$L(t) = \sum_{v \in V(t, w)} \lambda(v) \, I(v), \qquad (13.3.3)$$

and w is determined by this full employment relation.

13.3.3 Determining the type of machines built

While the volume of investment per year is, by assumption, exogenously determined, the type of machine built must be determined within the model. Basically, entrepreneurs must determine the value of λ, the number of men required to operate a machine. The smaller the value of λ, the more profitable the machine during its lifetime. However, by the cost function, the smaller the value of λ, the more expensive the machine. Hence rational choice of λ requires balancing the present value of the expected quasi-rents with the cost of machine construction. This involves expected wage rates and interest rates. Solow makes the static assumption that wage and interest rates are expected to remain constant.

Consider an arbitrary value of λ at time t. The expected quasi-rent at time $t+k$ is $1 - \lambda w$ since wages are expected to remain constant. At interest rate ρ, the expected present value of the real flow of net revenues over the life of the machine is

$$\sum_{k=1}^{L} (1 - \lambda w) \, (1 + \rho)^{-k} - c(\lambda) \, w. \qquad (13.3.4)$$

By assumption, entrepreneurs will choose λ so as to maximize this expression. And, under conditions of perfect competition, the interest rate will reach the level at which the maximum value is zero.

Using a simple algebraic relation,[1] expression (13.3.4) may be written as

$$(1 - \lambda w) \frac{1 - (1/(1 + \rho)^L)}{\rho} - c(\lambda) \, w(t). \qquad (13.3.5)$$

Let

$$\phi(\rho) = \frac{1 - (1/(1 + \rho)^L)}{\rho}, \qquad (13.3.6)$$

which is the present value of an annuity of one unit of consumables for L years. The maximization problem may then be written

$$\max_{\lambda} \, (1 - \lambda w) \, \phi(\rho) - c(\lambda) \, w(t). \qquad (13.3.7)$$

---

[1] For $r > 1$,
$$\sum_{k=1}^{L} \frac{1}{r^k} = \frac{1 - (1/r^L)}{r - 1}.$$

The first-order condition is

$$-w\phi(\rho) - wc'(\lambda) = 0, \qquad (13.3.8)$$

or
$$c'(\lambda) = -\phi(\rho). \qquad (13.3.9$$

The second-order condition gives

$$-wc''(\lambda) < 0, \qquad (13.3.10)$$

or
$$c''(\lambda) > 0. \qquad (13.3.11)$$

The economic interpretation of equation (13.3.9) is straightforward: the marginal cost of reducing the labor requirement (λ) of a newly constructed machine must equal the present value of the expected gain in quasi-rents associated with the smaller λ. The second-order condition, inequality (13.3.11), provides that the marginal cost of reducing λ rises as λ falls.

Equation (13.3.9) provides one equilibrium condition. In arriving at this relation, ρ was treated as an exogenous variable. However, it cannot be exogenous for otherwise there would be a pure profit or a pure loss in the machine sector. Thus assume that the interest rate adjusts so as to eliminate profit or loss. This assumption leads to the second equilibrium condition:

$$(1 - \lambda w)\,\phi(\rho) = c(\lambda)\,w. \qquad (13.3.12)$$

Equations (13.3.9) and (13.3.12) together imply that

$$\frac{\lambda w}{1 - \lambda w} = -\frac{\lambda c'}{c}. \qquad (13.3.13)$$

Thus in this model, the equilibrium ratio of relative shares must equal the absolute elasticity of the cost function in the machine sector.[1]

13.3.4 Marginal product of labor

Despite the lack of *ex-post* substitutability between labor and machines, there is *ex-ante* substitutability; and this is enough to insure that the model possesses the usual neoclassical characteristics, which can best be shown by analyzing the marginal products of labor and machines. First consider the marginal product of labor.

Suppose the supply of labor to the consumption sector increases by one man. Assuming non-redundancy of labor, as we have above, there will always be a machine upon which the new man can work.

Suppose the wage rate is given. At this given wage, there exists a set of machines $V(t, w)$ for which quasi-rent is equal to or greater than zero. One way of visualizing the set $V(t, w)$ is as follows: the first machine selected

---

[1] The operation of the model presented in subsections 13.3.1–13.3.3 can only be analyzed by simulation. For such a simulation study, see Solow [1963b].

for use is the one with the least labor requirement; the second machine selected is the one with the next to smallest labor requirement, and so on. Thus machines may be thought of as entering the production process in order of increasing labor intensity. Hence the new worker can most profitably be employed on the least labor-intensive idle machine.

Suppose the supply of labor to the consumer-good sector is such that all machines of vintages $v_1, v_2, ..., v_{k-1}$ are in use and some, but not all, machines of vintage v_k are in use. The vintage v_k machines are thus machines whose quasi-rent is zero. Hence

$$1 - w\lambda(v_k) = 0, \tag{13.3.14}$$

or
$$w = \frac{1}{\lambda(v_k)}, \tag{13.3.15}$$

where $\lambda(v_k)$ is the number of men required for capacity operation of a machine of vintage v_k.

The new worker will be employed on a previously idle machine of vintage v_k. Since it takes $\lambda(v_k)$ men to operate this vintage at capacity, $\lambda(v_k)$ men can produce one unit of output. Hence the (one) marginal man will add $1/\lambda(v_k)$ units to output.[1] Therefore, $1/\lambda(v_k)$ is the marginal product of an additional worker; and by equation (13.3.15), the marginal product is equal to the wage rate.

13.3.5 Marginal product of 'capital'

In determining the marginal product of 'capital', one must first ask what type of machine is to be added to the production process. Suppose that before a machine is added, the marginal machine is of type λ^*. Thus for all machines in use, $\lambda \leqslant \lambda^*$. If a machine of type $\lambda' \geqq \lambda^*$ were added, there would either be no increment to output (if $\lambda' = \lambda^*$) or a negative increment (if $\lambda' > \lambda^*$). This would be true because to man the new machine (recall the assumption of full employment), workers would have to be transferred from more productive to less productive employment. Consequently, only a machine of type $\lambda < \lambda^*$ would be added to the production process.

Suppose such a machine ($\lambda < \lambda^*$) is added. To man it, labor must be transferred from machines of type λ^*. To man one machine of type λ at capacity, so that its output is one unit per period, $\lambda/\lambda^* < 1$ machines of type λ^* must be shut down. Thus the net gain in output, or the marginal product of the additional machine, is

$$\Delta Q = 1 - \frac{\lambda}{\lambda^*}. \tag{13.3.16}$$

[1] See p. 281, footnote 1.

284

Since λ^* is the marginal type, quasi-rent on this type of machine is zero.
Thus
$$1 - \lambda^* w = 0, \tag{13.3.17}$$

or
$$\lambda^* = \frac{1}{w}. \tag{13.3.18}$$

Substituting equation (13.3.18) in equation (13.3.16) yields
$$\Delta Q = 1 - \lambda w. \tag{13.3.19,}$$

Hence, in the neoclassical way, the marginal product of capital is precisely
its quasi-rent.

13.3.6   The interest rate

Since $c(\lambda)$ is the number of men required to build a machine of type λ,
$wc(\lambda)$ is the amount invested in the machine. Hence, from equation
(13.3.19), the marginal product per dollar invested is

$$\frac{1 - \lambda w}{wc(\lambda)}. \tag{13.3.20}$$

Substituting equation (13.3.12) in expression (13.3.20), one obtains

$$\frac{1 - \lambda w}{wc(\lambda)} = \frac{1}{\phi(\rho)} = \frac{\rho}{1 - 1/(1+\rho)^L}. \tag{13.3.21}$$

If machines are infinitely durable, i.e. $L \to \infty$, the term $1/(1+\rho)^L \to 0$.
In this case, equation (13.3.21) becomes

$$\frac{1 - \lambda w}{wc(\lambda)} = \rho. \tag{13.3.22}$$

Thus if machines last forever, the marginal product of machines equals the
interest rate. When a machine does not last foreover, one must allow for
its finite lifetime, represented by L. Then equation (13.3.21) may be written

$$\left[1 - \left(\frac{1}{1+\rho} \right)^L \right] \left[\frac{1 - \lambda w}{wc(\lambda)} \right] = \rho. \tag{13.3.23}$$

In this case, the *net* marginal product of machines equals the interest rate.
The first term on the left in equation (13.3.23) is the 'netting factor', which
becomes smaller and smaller as L increases.

13.3.7   The factor-price frontier

Some further neoclassical properties of the model, including the parametric
form of the factor-price frontier, may be deduced. From equation (13.3.9),

$$c''(\lambda) \, d\lambda = -\phi'(\rho) \, d\rho, \tag{13.3.24}$$

or
$$\frac{d\lambda}{d\rho} = -\frac{\phi'(\rho)}{c''(\lambda)}. \tag{13.3.25}$$

By the second-order condition shown in inequality (13.3.11), $c''(\lambda) > 0$. Next, from equation (13.3.6), one obtains

$$\phi'(\rho) = \frac{\rho L(1/1+\rho)^{L+1}+(1/1+\rho)^L-1}{\rho^2}$$

$$= \frac{-(1+\rho)^{L+1}+(1+\rho)+\rho L}{\rho^2(1+\rho)^{L+1}}. \tag{13.3.26}$$

Since $\rho > 0$, equation (13.3.26) may be written

$$\text{sign}\,[\phi'(\rho)] = \text{sign}\,[1+\rho(L+1)-(1+\rho)^{L+1}]. \tag{13.3.27}$$

The right-hand side of equation (13.3.27) may be expanded to read

$$\text{sign}\,\{1+\rho(L+1)-[1+(L+1)\,\rho+\ldots]\} < 0. \tag{13.3.28}$$

Hence $\phi'(\rho) < 0$, and $\qquad \dfrac{d\lambda}{d\rho} > 0. \tag{13.3.29}$

Inequality (13.3.29) expresses the relation one expects: the labor intensity of production in the consumption sector varies directly with the interest rate. Thus an increase in the interest rate leads to more labor-intensive production or to a reduction in the 'roundaboutness' of production.

To obtain the relation between labor intensity and the wage rate, substitute equation (13.3.9) into equation (13.3.12):

$$-c'(\lambda)\,(1-\lambda w) = c(\lambda)\,w. \tag{13.3.30}$$

Taking the total differential of equation (13.3.30) and solving, one obtains

$$\frac{d\lambda}{dw} = \frac{\lambda c'(\lambda)-c(\lambda)}{c''(\lambda)\,(1-\lambda w)}. \tag{13.3.31}$$

Since the numerator is negative [by the assumption that $c'(\lambda) < 0$] and the denominator is positive it follows that

$$\frac{d\lambda}{dw} < 0. \tag{13.3.32}$$

Thus an increase in the wage rate leads to the construction of new machines of a more mechanized (less labor-intensive) type or to a more 'roundabout' production process.

Finally, dividing inequality (13.3.32) by inequality (13.3.29), one obtains

$$\frac{d\rho}{dw} < 0. \tag{13.3.33}$$

Inequality (13.3.33) is the parametric form of the factor-price frontier, or Samuelson's surrogate production function.[1] Since production in the machine sector is labor intensive relative to production in the consump-

---

[1] For another alternative derivation, see Hicks [1965, p. 140]. Hicks prefers to call this the 'wage equation'.

tion sector, the neoclassical result is obtained: if the wage rate increases, the rate of interest must fall to insure that the most profitable kind of machine that can be built can continue to break even.[1]

13.4 An extension of Solow's model

The basic Solow model developed above can be extended so as to determine the economic life of machines and the division of the labor force between the consumption sector and the capital-good sector. The model presented below accomplishes this, although an analytical solution cannot be determined. Like Solow's model, its operation can only be determined by simulation.

The assumptions of the model differ from Solow's in only two respects: (a) the physical lifetime of a machine is N, its economic lifetime is T, and it is assumed that $N \geq T$; Solow's assumption of actual or potential excess capacity is retained; (b) entrepreneurs determine investment in period t so that the expected present value of the flow of quasi-rents equals the supply price of the machine. This assumption is entirely equivalent to, and leads to the same equation as, Solow's assumption of no-profit equilibrium [equation (13.3.12) above]. It should be noted at this point that the assumption does not provide an independent investment function such as one would find in a complete model. Full employment is determined by equation (13.4.4) below; the interest rate adjusts to validate the investment needed to offset full employment savings. This is far from a genuinely independent investment function that determines aggregate demand and actual employment, which may be substantially different from full employment.

In all essential detail, the model is exactly like Solow's; thus all of Solow's neoclassical results hold and are not repeated. I only add here that the marginal product of labor in the capital-good sector is equal to the wage rate. Suppose an additional worker is added in the capital-good sector. According to the notation of section 13.3, the additional worker can produce $1/c(\lambda)$ part of a machine. The price of machines in consumption units is $wc(\lambda)$; hence the value of the marginal product of a worker in the capital-good sector measured in consumption units is equal to the wage rate.

13.4.1 Notation

The notation in this section follows that introduced above in most cases. For convenience, a glossary is provided here.

---

[1] For a similar model with one sector and technical progress, see Solow, Tobin, von Weizsacker, and Yaari [1966]. For some critical comments, see Thanh [1966].

$c(\lambda) =$ the number of man years required to build a machine whose capacity operation requires λ man years;

$M(t) =$ the number of machines built in year t. It is assumed that: (i) machines are built by labor alone; (ii) all machines built in a given year are of the same type; (iii) each machine, regardless of type, produces one unit of consumables per year when operated at capacity. A machine built at time t enters the production process at time $t+1$ and physically can be operated until time $t+N$, where N is the physical life of the machine;

$w =$ wage rate in consumption units;

$wc(\lambda) =$ price of machines in consumption units; since $wc(\lambda)$ is the unit cost of machines, this implies perfect competition in the capital-good sector;

$\rho =$ rate of interest;

$T =$ economic lifetime of a machine, which is assumed to be equal to or less than its physical lifetime;

$L_c(t) =$ employment in the consumption sector;

$L_m(t) =$ employment in the capital-good sector;

$L(t) =$ available labor force;

$Y(t) =$ output measured in consumption units;

$C(t) =$ consumption;

$S(t) =$ saving;

$s =$ constant marginal and average propensity to save;

$I(t) =$ investment.

13.4.2 Equations of the model

Total output measured in consumption units is, of course, the sum of output in the consumption sector and output in the capital-good sector, the latter measured in consumption units. This is simply the familiar equality of planned saving and investment upon which growth models are built.[1] Since the price of machines in consumption units is $wc(\lambda)$, total output in consumption units is

$$Y(t) = C(t) + w(t)\, c[\lambda(t)]\, M(t). \tag{13.4.1}$$

By assumption, saving is a constant portion of income. Thus

$$S(t) = s\,Y(t). \tag{13.4.2}$$

[1] The fact that the present model is *essentially* a growth model will subsequently become clear.

Since each machine produces one unit of consumption goods and since demand and supply are equal, consumption is simply equal to the number of machines used:

$$C(t) = \sum_{t-T(t)}^{t-1} M(v). \qquad (13.4.3)$$

Next, by assumption, there is full employment of the labor force. Definitionally, this gives

$$L(t) = L_c(t) + L_m(t). \qquad (13.4.4)$$

From the definition of $c(\lambda)$, it follows that

$$L_m(t) = c[\lambda(t)]\, M(t); \qquad (13.4.5)$$

and from the definition of $\lambda(t)$, it follows that

$$L_c(t) = \sum_{t-T(t)}^{t-1} \lambda(v)\, M(v). \qquad (13.4.6)$$

Following Solow, assume that entrepreneurs determine $\lambda(t)$ so as to maximize the expected present value of net revenues over the expected lifetime of the machine. Given static expectations, as in Solow's model,[1] the present value in question is

$$\pi = \sum_{t}^{t+T(t)} (1-\lambda w)(1+\rho)^{-v} - c[\lambda(t)]\, w(t). \qquad (13.4.7)$$

Since $(1-\lambda w)$ is not a variable in the summation under the assumption of static expectations, and since $(1+\rho) > 0$, equation (13.4.7) may be written

$$\pi = (1-\lambda w)\,\phi(\rho) - c(\lambda)\, w, \qquad (13.4.8)$$

where

$$\phi(\rho) = \frac{1-(1/1+\rho)^T}{\rho}. \qquad (13.4.9)$$

Thus for a maximum,

$$\frac{d\pi}{d\lambda} = -w\phi(\rho) - wc'(\lambda) = 0, \qquad (13.4.10)$$

or

$$c'[\lambda(t)] = -\phi(\rho). \qquad (13.4.11)$$

Next, assume that entrepreneurs push investment to the point where the present value of expected quasi-rents is exactly equal to the supply price of machines.[2] Thus

$$wc[\lambda(t)] = \sum_{t}^{t+T(t)} (1-\lambda w)(1+\rho)^{-v}, \qquad (13.4.12)$$

[1] It is not difficult, in principle, to allow for non-static expectations along the lines discussed by Solow [1962b]. However, since this model essentially applies to a path of balanced growth, little is to be gained by introducing non-static expectations (i.e. along a balanced growth path, all expectations must be realized).

[2] As mentioned above, this assumption does not lead to an independent investment function. An alternative assumption that leads to the same result is the one used by Solow: competition eliminates profit in the capital-good sector via adjustments of the rate of interest. In the present version, the interest rate adjusts so that intended investment is exactly consistent with voluntary full-employment saving.

or
$$(1 - \lambda w)\, \phi(\rho) = wc[\lambda(t)], \qquad (13.4.13)$$

which is the same as Solow's no-profit equation.

In this model the economic lifetime of a machine is determined by the fact that the marginal machine yields zero quasi-rent.[1] Thus

$$1 - \lambda[t - T(t)]\, w = 0. \qquad (13.4.14)$$

The model is completed by adding the definitional equations

$$I(t) = wc[\lambda(t)]\, M(t) = wL_m(t), \qquad (13.4.15)$$

and
$$S(t) = I(t). \qquad (13.4.16)$$

There are eleven equations in the model: equations $(13.4.1)$–$(13.4.6)$, $(13.4.11)$, and $(13.4.13)$–$(13.4.16)$. The corresponding eleven variables are total output or income in consumption units $Y(t)$, consumption $C(t)$, saving $S(t)$, investment $I(t)$, the number of machines built $M(t)$, employment in the consumption sector $L_c(t)$ and in the capital-good sector $L_m(t)$, the man years required to operate a machine $\lambda(t)$, the wage rate $w(t)$, the rate of interest $\rho(t)$, and the economic life of machines T. The data and parameters of the model are the savings ratio s, the labor force $L(t)$, the 'cost function' in the capital-good sector $c[\lambda(t)]$, the historical stock of machines $M(v)$ for $v = 0, 1, ..., t-1$ and their historical labor intensities $\lambda(v)$ for $v = 0, 1, ..., t-1$.

13.4.3 Operation of the model

The apparent simultaneity of the model is not real. Indeed, it may be reduced so as to be soluable equation-by-equation. First, substitute equation $(13.4.1)$ in equation $(13.4.2)$, obtaining

$$S(t) = s[C(t) + wc(\lambda)\, M(t)]. \qquad (13.4.17)$$

Then using equations $(13.4.15)$ and $(13.4.16)$ in equation $(13.4.17)$, one may solve for the number of machines built in year t:

$$M(t) = \frac{sC(t)}{wc(\lambda)(1-s)} = \frac{s}{1-s} \cdot \frac{1}{c(\lambda)} \cdot \frac{1}{w} \cdot \sum_{t-T(t)}^{t-1} M(v). \qquad (13.4.18)$$

[1] The reason this model is basically limited to steady-state growth paths is apparent from equations such as $(13.4.3)$, $(13.4.6)$, and $(13.4.14)$. Except in a steady state, there is no guarantee that the wage rate will always rise; hence there is no guarantee that the sequence of values of $\lambda(t)$ will be monotonically decreasing. If $\lambda(t)$ is not monotonically decreasing, there is no guarantee that there will be a critical cut-off age T with all newer machines being used and no older machines being used. Except along a balanced growth path, a vintage of machines can drop out of use for a time (during which wages are rising) and come back into use for a while (during a period of falling wages). In principle this does no damage to the theory; but it makes its analysis much harder and its simulation more complicated.

Next, substitute equations (13.4.14) and (13.4.8) in equation (13.4.5) to obtain

$$L_m(t) = c(\lambda)\, M(t) = \frac{s}{1-s} \cdot \frac{1}{w} \cdot \sum_{t-T(t)}^{t-1} M(v), \qquad (13.4.19)$$

or

$$L_m(t) = \frac{s}{1-s} \cdot \lambda[t-T(t)] \cdot \sum_{t-T(t)}^{t-1} M(v). \qquad (13.4.20)$$

Finally, substituting equations (13.4.20) and (13.4.6) in equation (13.4.4) yields a single equation in the single variable T:

$$L(t) = \frac{s}{1-s} \cdot \lambda[t-T(t)] \sum_{t-T(t)}^{t-1} M(v) + \sum_{t-T(t)}^{t-1} \lambda(v)\, M(v). \qquad (13.4.21)$$

Since $L(t)$, $M(v)$, $\lambda(v)$, and s are data or parameters, equation (13.4.21) may be solved for the economic lifetime of equipment.

The next step is to obtain an expression for labor intensity in the consumption sector. To this end, substitute equations (13.4.11) and (13.4.14) in equation (13.4.13), obtaining

$$-\left(1 - \frac{\lambda(t)}{\lambda[t-T(t)]}\right) c'(\lambda) = \frac{c(\lambda)}{\lambda(t-T(t))}, \qquad (13.4.22)$$

or

$$-\frac{c[\lambda(t)]}{c'[\lambda(t)]} = \lambda[t-T(t)] - \lambda(t). \qquad (13.4.23)$$

Given the solution of T from equation (13.4.21), equation (13.4.23) may be solved for $\lambda(t)$.

The remaining variables follow easily. With $\lambda(t)$ known and the cost function $c[\lambda(t)]$ given, equation (13.4.11) may be solved for $\rho(t)$. Also knowing λ and T, equation (13.4.14) yields $w(t)$, which can then be used in equation (13.4.18) to solve for $M(t)$. Knowing $M(t)$, equation (13.4.5) determines $L_m(t)$, while $L_c(t)$ is determined by the data from equation (13.4.6). With $L_m(t)$ determined, equation (13.4.15) may be solved for $I(t)$, whereupon $S(t)$ follows immediately from equation (13.4.16). Finally, $C(t)$ is determined by the data from equation (13.4.3), and $Y(t)$ follows from equation (13.4.1).

In principle, the system is easily soluble, especially if the data used to obtain the first iteration are generated by exponential growth or decay functions. For example, suppose

$$c[\lambda(t)] = c(0)\, \lambda(t)^{-\gamma} \qquad (\gamma > 0), \qquad\qquad (13.4.24)$$

$$L(t) = L(0)\, (1+n)^t \qquad (n > 0), \qquad\qquad (13.4.25)$$

$$M(v) = M(0)\, (1+g)^v \qquad (v = 0, 1, \ldots, t-1),\, (g > 0), \qquad (13.4.26)$$

$$\lambda(v) = \lambda(0)\, (1-h)^v \qquad (v = 0, 1, \ldots, t-1),\, (h > 0). \qquad (13.4.27)$$

Equation (13.4.24) provides the necessary 'rising marginal cost' condition, while equation (13.4.25) makes balanced growth possible. Equation (13.4.26) provides an historical stock of machines that has steadily increased.

Finally, equation (13.4.27) is the most important of all inasmuch as it establishes a constantly declining labor intensity in the consumption sector. On the one hand, this can reconcile equations (13.4.25) and (13.4.26) when $g > n$; on the other, it insures a critical value of T by inequality (13.3.32). Of course, $T = T(t)$ and it can change over time. One of the interesting questions that could be answered by simulation is whether the model would continue on a balanced growth path along which $T(t)$ and $\rho(t)$ become constants, at least asymptotically. If so, the other interesting question is whether a continuous production function with homogeneous capital would provide an adequate fit to the data generated by simulation of the heterogeneous capital model. That is, will this model validate the 'neoclassical fairy tale' in the same way that Solow's does?[1]

[1] Solow [1963 b].

14

LEARNING BY DOING

14.1 Introduction

As early as 1936, T. P. Wright observed that the number of manhours required to produce an airframe is a decreasing function of the number of airframes of the same type previously produced. Indeed, the connection is very precise; the amount of labor required to produce the nth airframe is proportional to $n^{-\frac{1}{3}}$.[1] This relation has subsequently become basic in the Rand Corporation studies of production and cost planning for the U.S. Air Force.[2]

Other empirical studies have revealed similar results. Hirsch showed the existence of 'learning curves' or 'progress ratios' in the production of various types of machines.[3] Lundberg described the 'Horndal Effect'. The Horndal Iron Works in Sweden had no new investment, and presumably no important change in its methods of production, for a period of fifteen years; yet output per man increased on average by two per cent per year.[4] More recent studies by Sturmey and Rapping have also emphasized the crucial point.[5] Specifically, in observing manufacturing processes, one finds steadily improving performances that can only be attributed to learning from experience on the job.

This conclusion is, indeed, quite commonplace; it is confirmed by casual empiricism as well as statistical studies; it is a technological fact of life that hardly requires explanation. Yet until Arrow's seminal article,[6] this basic relation had not been incorporated into theories of production, distribution, and growth.

14.2 Arrow's model[7]

The fact that a person may learn from experience is, as noted above, commonplace knowledge. How to introduce this fact into an economic

[1] Wright [1936]. [2] Asher [1956] and Alchian [1963].
[3] Hirsch [1952] and [1956]. [4] Lundberg [1961].
[5] Sturmey [1964] and Rapping [1965]. [6] Arrow [1962].
[7] The exposition in this chapter is chiefly based upon Arrow [1962]; however certain aspects and interpretations are believed to be new, others are borrowed from other theoretical studies of 'Learning by Doing'. See Robinson [1962], Robinson [1963], Levhari [1966 a, b].

293

model is not. The examples cited above would seem to suggest that cumulative gross output is a suitable index of experience. Arrow, however, chose to take cumulative gross investment as the appropriate measure. This chapter is based on Arrow's assumption; however, one should note that it (Arrow's assumption) is controversial. Quite different results are obtained if one takes cumulative gross output as the index of experience, for then there is no allocation problem with respect to returns to investment goods as a result of learning by doing (on this score, see below).

The next problem is to determine *where* the 'learning from experience' enters into the conditions of production. Following Solow and Johansen,[1] Arrow assumed that technical change is completely embodied in new capital goods. When a new capital good is produced, it incorporates all the knowledge then available; however, once built, its productive efficiency is not altered by subsequent learning.

To simplify the model mathematically, two further assumptions are introduced: (i) the production process associated with each piece of capital equipment is characterized by fixed coefficients, and (ii) 'new capital goods are better than old ones in the strong sense that, if we compare a unit of capital goods produced at time t_1 with one produced at time $t_2 > t_1$, the first requires the cooperation of at least as much labor as the second, and produces no more product. Under this assumption, a new capital good will always be used in preference to an older one.'[2] In fact, a stronger assumption is used below.

14.2.1 Notation

For convenience, a glossary of the notation to be used is given at the outset:

$G(t)$ = cumulative gross investment at time t or the *serial number* of the machine produced at time t; $G(t)$ is thus the index of 'experience' or 'learning'.

a = output capacity of a machine, which is assumed to be the same for all machines irrespective of serial number.

bG^{-n} = labor requirement per unit of time for operating a machine whose serial number is G; b and n are positive constants, and $0 < n < 1$.[3]

---

[1] Solow [1960] and Johansen [1959].   [2] Arrow [1962, p. 157].

[3] Arrow uses a and bG^{-n} in certain specific situations, but he also uses more general forms, $\gamma(G)$ and $\lambda(G)$ respectively. That is, output per machine and labor requirements are simply specified as functions of the machine's serial number, where $\gamma(G_1) \leqq \gamma(G_2)$ $\lambda(G_1) \geqq \lambda(G_2)$ when $G_2 > G_1$.

   Kaldor has rightly objected to either of these specifications: '...learning takes time, as well as experience (or activity); hence the productivity of the 'machine' with the serial number G will depend not only upon the cumulative total investment G, but on

L = total employment.

w = wage rate.

r = quasi-rent earned on a piece of capital equipment.

x = total gross output.

G^* = serial number of the oldest machine used at a given time.

λ = rate of growth of the labor force, assumed to be an exogenously given constant.

s = savings ratio, assumed to be an exogenously given constant.

14.2.2 Output and the wage rate

Since each machine in operation produces a units of output per period of time, total output is given by

$$x = a(G - G^*), \tag{14.2.1}$$

where $G - G^*$ is the number of machines in use. The value of G^* may be determined by imposing the assumption of full labor-force employment.[1] This permits one to equate the labor supply L with the total labor requirement for operating $G - G^*$ machines:

$$L = b \int_{G^*}^{G} G^{-n} dG = \frac{b}{1-n}(G^{1-n} - G^{*1-n}). \tag{14.2.2}$$

Equation (14.2.2) may be solved for G^*, obtaining

$$G^* = \left(G^{1-n} - \frac{L}{c}\right)^{1/(1-n)}, \tag{14.2.3}$$

where

$$c = \frac{b}{1-n}. \tag{14.2.4}$$

The relation above may now be used to express output as a function of the given parameters, the labor force, and the current serial number of machines. Substituting equation (14.2.3) in equation (14.2.1) yields

$$x = aG\left[1 - \left(1 - \frac{L}{cG^{1-n}}\right)^{1/(1-n)}\right]. \tag{14.2.5}$$

Since output is shown as a function of the labor force and machines, equation (14.2.5) is what Arrow calls a '...production function in a

the time interval over which G is spread. Hence there is no unique function $\lambda(G)$ or $\gamma(G)$...; there is a whole family of such functions, depending on the rate of production of "machines" per unit of time.' Footnote omitted. Kaldor [1962, p. 246].

[1] It might seem that, as in the Solow model presented in chapter 13, the marginal machine should be determined by imposing the condition that it yield zero quasi-rent. It is shown below that this condition is, in fact, satisfied by the marginal machine.

somewhat novel sense',[1] or what we shall call the pseudo-production function.

Since the requirement of zero quasi-rent on the marginal machine was not used to determine the serial number of this machine, it may now be used to derive the wage rate. Measure the wage rate w in units of output. The condition of zero quasi-rent on the marginal machine gives

$$a - wbG^{*-n} = 0. \qquad (14.2.6)$$

Hence, from equations (14.2.6) and (14.2.3), the wage rate may be written as

$$w = \frac{a}{b} \left(G^{1-n} - \frac{L}{c} \right)^{n/(1-n)}. \qquad (14.2.7)$$

As shown below, the wage rate is the marginal product of labor.

14.2.3 Social and private returns

Introducing 'learning by doing' by means of technical progress in the construction of machines causes a basic divergence between private and social returns to an increment in investment. When an entrepreneur invests by purchasing a new machine, i.e. the machine whose serial number is currently greatest, he reaps the benefit of the accumulated knowledge to that point in time. Society as a whole, however, gains more than the individual. The latter, as just said, gets what he gets. Society gets somewhat more because the act of investment *permanently* raises the serial number, and hence the output per man, of all future machines.

That is, if society saves an extra unit of output at time v, then in *all* future time society can enjoy an extra $\partial x/\partial G$ units of output. To get at this, write the pseudo-production function (14.2.5) as

$$x = aG\left[1 - \left(1 - \frac{L}{cG^{1-n}} \right)^{1/(1-n)} \right] = aG\left[1 - \left(G^{1-n} - \frac{L}{c} \right)^{1/(1-n)} G^{-(1-n)/(1-n)} \right]$$

$$= aG\left[1 - \left(G^{1-n} - \frac{L}{c} \right)^{1/(1-n)} \frac{1}{G} \right] = a\left[G - \left(G^{1-n} - \frac{L}{c} \right)^{1/(1-n)} \right]. \qquad (14.2.8)$$

Hence

$$\frac{\partial x}{\partial G} = a\left[1 - \frac{1}{1-n} \left(G^{1-n} - \frac{L}{c} \right)^{1/(1-n)-1} (1-n) G^{-n} \right], \qquad (14.2.9)$$

or,

$$\frac{\partial x}{\partial G} = a\left[1 - \left(G^{1-n} - \frac{L}{c} \right)^{n/(1-n)} G^{-n} \right]. \qquad (14.2.10)$$

Finally, substitute equation (14.2.3) into equation (14.2.10), obtaining

$$\frac{\partial x}{\partial G} = a[1 - G^{*n}G^{-n}] = a\left[1 - \left(\frac{G^*}{G} \right)^n \right]. \qquad (14.2.11)$$

[1] *Op. cit.* p. 158.

14.2 ARROW'S MODEL

This expression is the marginal *social* product of an incremental unit of investment, i.e. the marginal social product attributable to increasing the serial number of all future machines by one digit.

Next, consider the return to a private investor who saves a unit of output at time v and invests it when the serial number of machines is $G(v)$. From this act he will obtain a stream of rentals that may be presented by

$$r(v, t) = a - w(t)\, bG(v)^{-n}. \tag{14.2.12}$$

Substituting equation (14.2.7), the rental stream may be written

$$r(v, t) = a - a\left(G^{1-n} - \frac{L}{c}\right)^{n/(1-n)} G(v)^{-n}. \tag{14.2.13}$$

Next, substitute equation (14.2.3), obtaining

$$r(v, t) = a - aG^{*n}G(v)^{-n} = a\left[1 - \left(\frac{G^*}{G(v)}\right)^n\right]. \tag{14.2.14}$$

From equation (14.2.11), the marginal social product is

$$r(t, t) = \frac{\partial x}{\partial G}. \tag{14.2.15}$$

Finally, comparing equations (14.2.11) and (14.2.14), one sees that

$$a\left[1 - \left(\frac{G^*(t)}{G(t)}\right)^n\right] \geq a\left[1 - \left(\frac{G^*(t)}{G(v)}\right)^n\right], \tag{14.2.16}$$

with the equality holding only at $t = v$, i.e. only instantaneously at the moment the investment is made.

As time passes, $G^*(t)$ increases. As new machines with higher serial numbers are introduced, the serial number of the marginal machine increases. As time goes forward, for some $t > v$, $G^*(t) = G(v)$, i.e. the machine with serial number $G(v)$ becomes the marginal machine $G^*(t)$, yielding zero quasi-rent. Thereafter it is retired as obsolete.

The same explanation may be stated somewhat differently. Suppose a private investor at time v purchases a machine whose serial number is $G(v)$. His return is the discounted sum of the quasi-rents he receives over the life of the machine, until the time t at which $G^*(t) = G(v)$. The value of his investment to society as a whole, however, is greater than the discounted sum. The *act of investment* by the private investor increases the serial number of *all* subsequent machines. Since, in the Arrow model, all technical progress is represented by the serial number of machines, society is *permanently* better off because of the higher serial number of all future machines. Even though the specific machine purchased by the investor is ultimately scrapped because of obsolescence, its social product remains the same because it has permanently raised the serial numbers of all subsequent machines.[1]

[1] An alternative view of the divergence of private and social product is presented in the appendix to this chapter.

14.2.4 Marginal products and relative shares

The pseudo-production function in equation (14.2.5) is characterized
(socially) by increasing returns to scale. To see this, write the function as

$$x = a\left[G-\left(G^{1-n}-\frac{L}{c}\right)^{1/(1-n)}\right]. \tag{14.2.17}$$

Increase G by the proportion λ and L by the proportion $\lambda^{1-n} < \lambda$:

$$a\left[\lambda G-\left(\lambda^{1-n}G^{1-n}-\frac{\lambda^{1-n}L}{c}\right)^{1/(1-n)}\right] = a\left[\lambda G-\lambda\left(G^{1-n}-\frac{L}{c}\right)^{1/(1-n)}\right], \tag{14.2.18}$$

or

$$\lambda a\left[G-\left(G^{1-n}-\frac{L}{c}\right)^{1/(1-n)}\right] = \lambda x. \tag{14.2.19}$$

If there were constant returns to scale, an increase in output from x to λx
would require an increase in *both* inputs by the proportion λ. In this case,
however, if G is increased to λG and L is increased to $\lambda^{1-n}L < \lambda L$, output
increases from x to λx. Hence the pseudo-production function of the
Arrow model exhibits increasing social returns to scale.

The marginal social product of labor is found from equation (14.2.17):

$$\frac{\partial x}{\partial L} = \frac{1}{1-n}\frac{a}{c}\left(G^{1-n}-\frac{L}{c}\right)^{n/(1-n)}. \tag{14.2.20}$$

Using definition (14.2.4), one may write

$$\frac{1}{1-n}\frac{a}{c} = \frac{1}{1-n}.a.\frac{1-n}{b} = \frac{a}{b}. \tag{14.2.21}$$

Hence equation (14.2.20) may be written as

$$\frac{\partial x}{\partial L} = \frac{a}{b}\left(G^{1-n}-\frac{L}{c}\right)^{n/(1-n)}, \tag{14.2.22}$$

which is precisely the same as equation (14.2.7). Thus the wage rate is equal
to the marginal social product of labor. Since it is, and since the production
function displays increasing returns to scale, capital can obviously not
receive its marginal social product. This does not raise a problem so far as
distribution is concerned because capital does receive its marginal private
product or quasi-rent. But, needless to say, the divergence of marginal
social product and marginal private product will, other things equal, cause
a misallocation of resources.

For the moment, suppose capital did receive its marginal social product.
Then, by equations (14.2.10) and (14.2.8), the relative share of capital
would be

$$\frac{G}{x}\frac{\partial x}{\partial G} = \frac{1-\left(G^{1-n}-\frac{L}{c}\right)^{n/(1-n)}G^{-n}}{1-\left(1-\frac{L}{cG^{1-n}}\right)^{1/(1-n)}}. \tag{14.2.23}$$

From equation (14.2.11),

$$1 - \left(G^{1-n} - \frac{L}{c}\right)^{n/(1-n)} G^{-n} = 1 - \left(\frac{G^*}{G}\right)^n. \tag{14.2.24}$$

Next, consider the denominator of equation (14.2.23):

$$1 - \left(1 - \frac{L}{cG^{1-n}}\right)^{1/(1-n)} = 1 - \left(G^{1-n} - \frac{L}{c}\right)^{1/(1-n)} G^{-1}, \tag{14.2.25}$$

which, from equation (14.2.3), may be written as

$$1 - \left(G^{1-n} - \frac{L}{c}\right)^{1/(1-n)} G^{-1} = 1 - \frac{G^*}{G}. \tag{14.2.26}$$

Thus if capital received its marginal social product, its relative share would be

$$\frac{G}{x}\frac{\partial x}{\partial G} = \frac{1 - (G^*/G)^n}{1 - (G^*/G)}. \tag{14.2.27}$$

If equation (14.2.27) held, the *implied* relative share of labor would be

$$1 - \frac{G}{x}\frac{\partial x}{\partial G} = \frac{(G^*/G)^n - (G^*/G)}{1 - (G^*/G)}. \tag{14.2.28}$$

On the other hand, labor *actually* receives, as its relative share,

$$\frac{L}{x}\frac{\partial x}{\partial L} = \frac{\frac{1}{b}\left(G^{1-n} - \frac{L}{c}\right)^{n/(1-n)} L}{\left[G - \left(G^{1-n} - \frac{L}{c}\right)\right]^{1/(1-n)}}. \tag{14.2.29}$$

Substituting equations (14.2.2) and (14.2.3) in equation (14.2.29) and rearranging, the actual relative share of labor is

$$\frac{L}{x}\frac{\partial x}{\partial L} = \frac{1}{1-n}\left[\frac{(G^*/G)^n - (G^*/G)}{1 - (G^*/G)}\right]. \tag{14.2.30}$$

Comparing equations (14.2.28) and (14.2.30), the actual share of labor is greater than what it would be if capital received its marginal social product by the proportion $1/(1-n) > 1$.

After a brief digression it is possible to give a simple explanation of this result. It is difficult to define the *rate* of technological progress in Arrow's model. Ideally, one should like to define technological progress as it is defined in regular neoclassical models, namely as $(1/x)(\partial x/\partial t)$. Unfortunately, this approach leads nowhere. Technological progress occurs in Arrow's model if, and only if, G increases (since n is assumed to be constant). The only way the average product of labor can be increased is to increase G. Thus it seems reasonable to define the rate of technological progress as

$$\left[\frac{1}{bG^{-n}}\frac{d}{dG}(bG^{-n})\right] = \frac{n}{G}. \tag{14.2.31}$$

By equation (14.2.31), the rate of technological progress is a variable rate that decreases monotonically and asymptotically approaches zero.

Now consider the following expansion:

$$\frac{1}{1-n} = 1+n+n^2+\ldots = 1+\sum_{i=1}^{\infty}n^i = 1+G\sum_{i=1}^{\infty}\frac{n^i}{G}. \tag{14.2.32}$$

From equations (14.2.28), (14.2.30), and (14.2.32), it is seen that labor receives the share it would receive if capital were paid its marginal social product, plus a multiple of its 'as-if' share. The multiple is simply the 'present value' of the instantaneous rate of technological progress. That is, the current rate of technological progress is imputed to each year from the present throughout all time, and each year's imputed rate is discounted by the number of years from the present to the year in question.

This explanation of labor's relative share throws the allocation problem into perspective. Labor, at least in its relative share, reaps the entire benefit of permanently higher serial numbers (i.e. over and above the quasi-rent or marginal private product received by investors). Under certain assumptions concerning saving behavior, there will be a misallocation of resources unless investors receive the marginal social product of capital. If this is the case, there is a simple solution. Tax wages at the rate n and distribute the proceeds to all people who have ever invested (regardless of whether the machine in which they invested is still used). For current investors, the total subsidy received will increase throughout the life of the machine. When the machine is scrapped, the total subsidy received will exactly equal the differential between the sum of the marginal private products directly received and the sum of the annual marginal social products of capital.

14.3   The growth path

14.3.1   Stability of the growth path

It would so far seem that the labor force would have to behave permissively as capital accumulates. However, it is not difficult to show that Arrow's model is, in part, a model with a stable exponential growth path.[1] To that end, introduce the customary neoclassical assumption that the labor force grows at the constant exponential rate λ:

$$L(t) = L_0 e^{\lambda t}, \quad \frac{\dot{L}}{L} = \lambda. \tag{14.3.1}$$

[1] For a more detailed treatment, see Levhari [1966a].

The pseudo-production function in equation (14.2.5) thus becomes

$$x = aG\left[1 - \left(1 - \frac{L_0 e^{\lambda t}}{cG^{1-n}} \right)^{1/(1-n)} \right]. \tag{14.3.2}$$

Next, introduce another customary neoclassical assumption, namely that the savings ratio s is a constant. Equating saving (sx) and investment gives the differential equation of the system:

$$\dot{G} = saG\left[1 - \left(1 - \frac{L_0 e^{\lambda t}}{cG^{1-n}} \right)^{1/(1-n)} \right]. \tag{14.3.3}$$

This is a first-order differential equation, for which we may try the following exponential solution:

$$G(t) = G_0 e^{\lambda/(1-n) t}, \tag{14.3.4}$$

and

$$\dot{G}(t) = \frac{\lambda}{1-n} G_0 e^{\lambda/(1-n) t}. \tag{14.3.5}$$

Substituting equations (14.3.4) and (14.3.5) in equation (14.3.3) yields

$$\frac{\lambda}{1-n} = sa\left[1 - \left(1 - \frac{L_0}{cG_0^{1-n}} \right)^{1/(1-n)} \right], \tag{14.3.6}$$

or

$$G_0(s) = \frac{(L_0/c)^{1/(1-n)}}{\left[1 - \left(1 - \frac{\lambda}{as(1-n)} \right)^{1-n} \right]^{1/(1-n)}}, \tag{14.3.7}$$

providing[1]

$$as > \frac{\lambda}{1-n}. \tag{14.3.8}$$

$G_0(s)$ is a monotonically increasing function of s.[2] The problem is to show that the solution of equation (14.3.3) tends asymptotically to the exponential solution. To that end, define

$$Z = \ln G - \frac{\lambda}{1-n} t, \tag{14.3.9}$$

so that

$$\dot{Z} = \frac{\dot{G}}{G} - \frac{\lambda}{1-n}. \tag{14.3.10}$$

[1] Unless the inequality holds, the savings ratio would be too small to sustain steady growth at the rate $\lambda/(1-n)$.

[2] Ignoring the squared denominator,

$$\text{sign} \left[\frac{dG_0(s)}{ds} \right] = \text{sign} \left[\left(\frac{L_0}{c} \right)^{1/(1-n)} \left\{ a\lambda(1-n) \left[1 - \left(1 - \frac{\lambda}{as(1-n)} \right)^{1-n} \right]^{n/(1-n)} \right. \right.$$

$$\left. \left. \times \left(1 - \frac{\lambda}{as(1-n)} \right)^{-n} \div [as(1-n)]^2 \right\} \right].$$

It is readily seen that this expression must be positive when inequality (14.3.8) holds.

Substituting equations (14.3.9) and (14.3.10) in equation (14.3.3) yields

$$\dot{Z} = sa\left[1-\left(1-\frac{L_0}{c}\,e^{-(1-n)Z}\right)^{1/(1-n)}\right]-\frac{\lambda}{1-n}. \qquad (14.3.11)$$

The right-hand side of equation (14.3.11) contains only constants and parameters except for Z; thus it is a function of Z that may be written $f(Z)$. It may be shown that $f(Z)$ is a monotonically decreasing function of Z,[1] so

$$\lim_{Z\to\infty} f(Z) = -\frac{\lambda}{1-n} < 0. \qquad (14.3.12)$$

Further for the positive magnitude $Z = \dfrac{1}{1-n}\ln\dfrac{L_0}{c}$,

$$f\left(\frac{1}{1-n}\ln\frac{L_0}{c}\right) = as - \frac{\lambda}{1-n} > 0 \qquad (14.3.13)$$

by inequality (14.3.8). Therefore, by the monotonicity of $f(Z)$, there exists a unique positive value of Z, say Z^*, for which $f(Z^*) = 0$, and such that $\dot{Z} > 0$ if $Z < Z^*$ and $\dot{Z} < 0$ if $Z > Z^*$. Hence $Z \to Z^*$.

Finally, solving

$$f(Z^*) = 0, \qquad (14.3.14)$$

one obtains

$$Z^* = \frac{1}{1-n}\ln\frac{(L_0/c)}{\left[1-\left(1-\dfrac{\lambda}{as(1-n)}\right)^{1-n}\right]^{1/(1-n)}} = \ln G_0(s) \quad (14.3.15)$$

by equation (14.3.7). Thus $G(t) \to G_0 e^{\lambda/(1-n)\,t}$ asymptotically. The steady growth path exists and is asymptotically stable.

14.3.2 Properties of the growth path

It has just been shown that under certain neoclassical assumptions, Arrow's model is characterized by a stable growth path. It is interesting to observe that this path has certain features that are characteristic of most neoclassical growth models.[2]

From equations (14.3.4) and (14.3.5) the rate of growth of cumulative gross investment is

$$\frac{\dot{G}}{G} = \frac{\lambda}{1-n}. \qquad (14.3.16)$$

[1] Straightforwardly,

$$\frac{df(Z)}{dZ} = -\frac{saL_0}{c}e^{-(1-n)Z}\left(1-\frac{L_0}{c}e^{-(1-n)Z}\right)^{n/(1-n)},$$

which must be negative by equation (14.3.2) and definition (14.3.9).

[2] For a general description of single-sector neoclassical models, see Ferguson [1965c] and [1968a].

Similarly, from equation (14.3.5)

$$\dot{x} = aG\left[\frac{\dot{G}}{G} - \left(G^{1-n} - \frac{L}{c}\right)^{n/(1-n)} \frac{\dot{G}}{G} + \frac{\lambda}{1-n} \frac{L}{cG} \left(G^{1-n} - \frac{L}{c}\right)^{n/(1-n)}\right].$$

(14.3.17)

Substituting equation (14.3.16) in equation (14.3.17) yields

$$\dot{x} = a \frac{\lambda}{1-n}\left[G - \left(G^{1-n} - \frac{L}{c}\right)^{1/(1-n)}\right];$$

(14.3.18)

thus

$$\frac{\dot{x}}{x} = \frac{\lambda}{1-n}.$$

(14.3.19)

By equations (14.3.16) and (14.3.19), output and cumulative gross investment grow at the same rate along the stable growth path. Hence the cumulative investment–output ratio is a constant, i.e.

$$\frac{G}{x} = \text{a constant on the balanced path.}$$

(14.3.20)

This is closely akin to a central result of neoclassical growth theory. In neoclassical theory with technical progress, the balanced growth path, if it exists and is asymptotically stable, is characterized by a constant capital-output ratio. The result in Arrow's model is the same, except that cumulative gross investment is not reduced to a 'capital' stock by subtracting the number of obsolete machines.

A second point of similarity between Arrow's model and the neoclassical model concerns 'capital deepening'. More specifically, the capital–labor ratio increases at a constant rate in the neoclassical model. In the present model, the cumulative gross investment–labor ratio increases at a constant rate since $\lambda/(1-n) - \lambda > 0$. A third similarity between the two models lies in the fact that the rate of growth along the stable path is not affected by the savings ratio although, of course, the levels of output and investment are influenced by this magnitude.

Four additional neoclassical properties of Arrow's model may be easily derived. From equation (14.2.1), the rate of growth of output is

$$\frac{\dot{x}}{x} = \frac{G}{G-G^*} \frac{\dot{G}}{G} - \frac{G^*}{G-G^*} \frac{\dot{G}^*}{G^*}.$$

(14.3.21)

Substituting equations (14.3.16) and (14.3.19) in equation (14.3.21) immediately yields

$$\frac{\dot{G}^*}{G^*} = \frac{\lambda}{1-n},$$

(14.3.22)

or

$$\frac{\dot{G}^*}{G^*} = \frac{\dot{G}}{G} = \frac{\dot{x}}{x}.$$

(14.3.23)

Equation (14.3.23) implies that the economic lifetime of machines is a constant along the stable growth path. This result corresponds exactly to that of Solow in his neoclassical model discussed in chapter 13 above.

Next, it may be shown that the wage rate grows at a positive rate along the equilibrium path. From equation (14.2.7),

$$\dot{w} = \frac{a}{b} \cdot n \cdot \frac{\lambda}{1-n} \left(G^{1-n} - \frac{L}{c} \right)^{n/(1-n)}. \qquad (14.3.24)$$

Hence

$$\frac{\dot{w}}{w} = \frac{n}{1-n} \lambda = \lambda \sum_{i=1}^{\infty} n^i < \lambda, \qquad (14.3.25)$$

the inequality holding for any plausible value of n (i.e. for $n \leqq 0{\cdot}49$). The wage rate thus grows at a positive rate that is somewhat less than the rate of growth of the labor force. The wage rate has a positive rate of growth in the neoclassical one-sector model also, but the precise relation between the rates of growth of the wage rate and the labor force cannot be determined *a priori*.

Third, the rates of growth of the marginal social product of investment and of quasi-rent are zero, as in the neoclassical model. From equation (14.2.11), one obtains

$$\frac{d}{dt} \left(\frac{\partial x}{\partial G} \right) = -an \left(\frac{G^*}{G} \right)^n \left(\frac{\dot{G}^*}{G^*} - \frac{\dot{G}}{G} \right). \qquad (14.3.26)$$

By equation (14.3.23) the expression above is zero, and hence the growth rate itself is zero. The same result for quasi-rent follows immediately from equation (14.2.14).

Finally, as in the neoclassical model, relative shares are constant along the equilibrium path. By definition, the relative share of labor σ is

$$\sigma = \frac{wL}{x}. \qquad (14.3.27)$$

Hence

$$\frac{\dot{\sigma}}{\sigma} = \frac{\dot{w}}{w} + \frac{\dot{L}}{L} - \frac{\dot{x}}{x}. \qquad (14.3.28)$$

Substituting equations (14.3.25), (14.3.1), and (14.3.19) yields

$$\frac{\dot{\sigma}}{\sigma} = 0. \qquad (14.3.29)$$

Since the relative share of labor is constant along the equilibrium path, it follows immediately that the relative share of capital is constant as well. Thus along the stable path, the rate of growth of cumulative gross investment exactly equals the sum of the rates of growth of the labor force and of the wage rate.

14.4 Conclusion

In retrospect, Arrow's 'learning by doing' model of production and technological progress looks very much like the heterogeneous capital models of Samuelson and Solow.[1] Indeed, technological progress comes about in much the same way in the Solow and Arrow models. The chief difference is that the models of Samuelson and Solow are essentially two-sector models, while Arrow's is a one-sector model.

Except for small technicalities, it seems that Arrow's model is subject to reservation on two grounds. First it is difficult, if not impossible, to extend the model to a two-sector model of accumulation and growth. Second, while the process of technological progress is clear, the definition and interpretation of the *rate* of technological progress are not. One definition was suggested above, based upon the fact that investment is the vehicle of technological progress. Other definitions can be put forward, however, and they might fit more conveniently and conventionally into the framework of growth theory.

While these reservations are important, they do not mean that the notion of 'learning by doing' should be ignored. Indeed, 'learning by doing' is a fact of life; and it seems likely that some index of experience, perhaps not Arrow's, will be incorporated in more general models in the future.

APPENDIX TO CHAPTER 14

PROFESSOR FRANKEL'S VARIANT[2]

In a paper also published in 1962, Marvin Frankel suggested a micro-macro structure of production functions that possesses many of the characteristics of Arrow's model. Indeed, one may readily interpret Frankel's aggregate production function as a 'learning by doing' function.

Frankel's model concerns a one-sector economy composed of a large number of firms, each of which produces according to the Cobb–Douglas function:

$$P_i = aHK_i^\alpha L_i^{1-\alpha}. \tag{14.A.1}$$

P_i, K_i, and L_i are output, capital input, and labor input by the ith firm, while, a, H, and α are parameters common to all firms.

Assuming that each firm produces $1/n$th of total output, the corresponding aggregate production function is

$$P = aHK^\alpha L^{1-\alpha}. \tag{14.A.2}$$

[1] See chapters 12 and 13.   [2] Frankel [1962].

Frankel calls the firm parameter H the 'development modifier', and he specifically suggests that one might assume that

$$H = \left(\frac{K}{L}\right)^{\beta}.$$ (14.A.3)

Using equation (14.A.3) in equations (14.A.1), the individual microeconomic production functions become

$$P_i = a\left(\frac{K}{L}\right)^{\beta} K_i^{\alpha} L_i^{1-\alpha},$$ (14.A.4)

which are homogeneous of degree one in the variables that each entrepreneur can *perceptibly* control. The aggregate production function is also homogeneous of degree one, which differs from the pseudo-production function in Arrow's model. However the essential similarity is preserved because of the divergence between marginal private and marginal social product.

The marginal private products are

$$\frac{\partial P_i}{\partial K_i} = a\alpha H K_i^{\alpha-1} L_i^{1-\alpha},$$ (14.A.5)

and

$$\frac{\partial P_i}{\partial L_i} = a(1-\alpha)\, H K_i^{\alpha} L_i^{-\alpha}.$$ (14.A.6)

Rewarding according to competitive imputation, of course, exactly exhausts the expected product.

To determine the marginal social product continue the assumption that each firm accounts of $1/n$th of the economic activity of the society. Thus the microeconomic production functions may be written:

$$P_i = a\left(\frac{K}{L}\right)^{\beta}\left(\frac{K}{n}\right)^{\alpha}\left(\frac{L}{n}\right)^{1-\alpha}.$$ (14.A.7)

The marginal social products are

$$\frac{\partial P_i}{\partial (K/n)} = \alpha(\alpha+\beta)\, K^{\alpha+\beta-1} L^{1-\alpha-\beta},$$ (14.A.8)

and

$$\frac{\partial P_i}{\partial (L/n)} = a(1-\alpha-\beta)\, K^{\alpha+\beta} L^{-(\alpha+\beta)}.$$ (14.A.9)

The marginal private product of capital is less than the marginal social product. Hence in the investment planning stage, each entrepreneur decides to use too little capital because he does not anticipate the extra return that results from a general expansion of the capital–labor ratio. In like manner, the marginal private product of labor exceeds its marginal social product.

Thus too much labor is used in the social sense because entrepreneurs do not realize that they contribute to a decline in the aggregate capital–labor ratio by employing an additional worker. Furthermore, the wage rate is too high relative to the social contribution of labor.

Given any set of investment plans, a certain amount is produced. The P_i actually produced in each establishment exceeds the P_i anticipated by the entrepreneur. Since wage payments may be viewed as contractual, the rate of return on capital is greater than anticipated; yet it is not as great as the marginal social product of capital. As in the Arrow model, a portion of wages should be taxed and distributed to entrepreneurs in order to induce the socially optimum amount of investment.

In summary, as in Arrow's model, the act of additional investment pays an unexpected dividend, almost in the form of a 'permanently greater serial number'. In this case, it is a greater capital–labor ratio. But it seems clear that Frankel's 'development modifier' may readily be interpreted as a 'learning by doing' mechanism.

15

MONOPOLY AND AGGREGATE
DEMAND AS DETERMINANTS OF
RELATIVE FACTOR SHARES

15.1 Introduction

As previously noted, some economists have come to believe that a separate *macroeconomic* theory of distribution is needed. To quote a proponent and gentle critic of macroeconomic theories:

...there is a definite demand for a macro-economic distribution theory. The almost complete neglect of macro-economic aggregates and inter-relationships in the neoclassical marginal productivity theory is felt as a serious shortcoming... [but] while the demand for a macro-economic approach to distribution problems is obvious, the lack of a sure foundation for the new theories is similarly evident.[1]

It might be useful to dwell briefly upon the two reasons usually given to justify the 'need' for a macroeconomic theory. The chief reason, although vacuous as Bronfenbrenner has shown,[2] is to explain the constancy of relative factor shares. To quote the most voluable, if not the most persuasive, proponent of this view:

...no hypothesis regarding the forces determining distributive shares could be intellectually satisfying unless it succeeded in accounting for the relative stability of these shares in the advanced capitalist economies over the last 100 years or so, despite the phenomenal changes in the techniques of production, in the accumulation of capital relative to labour and in real income per head.[3]

A potentially more important reason has been stated by Rothschild:

The Keynesian employment theory shattered the belief that total employment could be deduced from an addition of all sectional marginal productivity schedules. In *aggregate* analysis these schedules are no longer independent of the prices paid to factors and can, therefore, not be treated as independent variables...For aggregate demand determines factor employment and incomes and the distribution of these incomes in turn influences the level and structure of aggregate demand. The Keynesian theory thus provided a challenge for a reconsideration of the distribution problem.[4]

---

[1] Rothschild [1961, p. 197].   [2] Bronfenbrenner [1960].
[3] Kaldor [1957, p. 95].   [4] Rothschild [1961, pp. 173-4].

In a certain sense, Rothschild's point is well taken. If distribution theory is to explain relative shares in underemployment disequilibria, due heed must be paid to aggregate demand. Indeed, this is one of the unique features of Schneider's macroeconomic theory.[1] But this is not generally regarded as the *function* of distribution theory. Rather, the object of distribution theory is to explain the division of the social product under conditions of full-employment equilibrium. In this case, aggregate demand and its composition can affect the distributive shares. But as shown in subsection 12.3.4, these effects may easily be incorporated in the neoclassical model and explained by neoclassical analysis.

It therefore seems that a special macroeconomic theory is not so much needed as some apparently believe. But whether needed or not, there has been no shortage of alternative distribution theories. Indeed the list of theories and theorists is so long as to preclude complete coverage. In this chapter the monopoly-based theories of Kalecki and Mitra are discussed, as well as the aggregate demand theories associated with such writers as Kaldor, Boulding, Mrs Robinson, Schneider, and Pasinetti. Chapter 16 is devoted to the new-old theory of induced innovations as the determinant of relative factor shares. For other theories, the reader is referred to some excellent surveys.[2]

15.2   The degree of monopoly and labor's relative share

All explicitly macroeconomic models of distribution have one feature in common. Specifically, some economic aggregate, usually national income, is divided into component parts. This is a matter of definition and, of course, does not yield any new information about the economic world. Kaldor, for example, divides income into capitalists' income and workers' income;[3] Pasenetti divides the same aggregate into income from capital and income from labor;[4] Keynes' division is between consumption and investment;[5] and Kalecki's is among profits, wages, and raw material costs.[6] These divisions are mathematical *identities* and cannot be judged 'right' or 'wrong'. The best the division process can do is to establish empirically useful subaggregates whose magnitudes can be explained by behavioral equations.

Just as there is one pervasive similarity, there is one notable difference

---

[1] Schneider [1957].

[2] Davidson [1960] contains a survey of most theories. Notably missing from this volume are discussions of induced innovations, the recent German work by Bombach, Schneider, and Krelle, and the French school that centers around Marchal. Rothschild [1961] contains brief discussions of the German and French contributions. The theory of Phelps-Brown and Weber, among others, is discussed in Scitovsky [1964].

[3] Kaldor [1955].   [4] Pasinetti [1962].

[5] Keynes [1936].   [6] Kalecki [1938].

among the various theories. Some writers begin with microeconomic units and relations and obtain the corresponding macroeconomic concepts by aggregation. Foremost in this category are Kalecki and Mitra, whose work is examined in this section. The more numerous group, whose work is discussed in section 15.3, begins with macroeconomic aggregates and does not consider the microeconomic pricing policies upon which the aggregates are based.[1] Despite this difference, however, both sets of theorists are concerned with the determinants of aggregate relative shares, and both sets obtain theories that contain neither the marginal nor the technological relations of neoclassical theory.

15.2.1 Kalecki

Historically, the first of the modern 'alternative' theories of distribution is Kalecki's, dating from 1938.[2] And, it might be added, his theory is strongly influenced by the economic milieu of the 1930's. The theory in question, that is to say, gets its special character from Kalecki's observations of the industrial pricing process during the depression years.

Kalecki begins with the assumption that all firms always have excess plant capacity. In this situation, it is further assumed, output may be expanded by using additional units of labor and raw materials in about the same proportions as before. Thus marginal and average 'prime costs' per unit of output are approximately constant and, therefore, the marginal productivity curve is horizontal. Employment is determined by the level of output alone. At this point another distinctive feature of Kalecki's theory appears. He assumes a world of imperfect competition. Thus the output of each firm depends upon its own pricing policy, which Kalecki assumes to be a mark-up of prime costs. This assumed pricing policy, together with the assumptions that the number of workers and the wage bill are proportional to output, leads to Kalecki's chief conclusion: the share of wages in each firm's output is equal to the share of wage cost in the price of output.

Following Kalecki, the theory may be stated more precisely by using a bit of algebra. Let W denote the total wages paid to *production* workers[3]

---

[1] In Kaldor's more recent work, for example Kaldor and Mirrlees [1962], it might seem that microeconomic pricing plays some role inasmuch as Kaldor speaks of entrepreneurial policies. However, there is no true disaggregation. Kaldor discusses a 'representative firm'. In principle, aggregation is accomplished by multiplying by the number of firms. For some reservations concerning Mrs Robinson's model, see subsection 15.3.3 below.

[2] Kalecki [1938], [1939], [1942], [1943], and [1954]. In the earlier versions, Kalecki specifically introduced Lerner's index of monopoly power (Lerner [1933b]). In this section, the 1954 version contained in *Theory of Economic Dynamics* is used.

[3] Kalecki's theory relates essentially to manual laborers. Gross profit in Kalecki's model is composed, *inter alia*, of salaries of non-production workers, interest, and depreciation. Net profit is gross profit minus these three items.

310

and R be the amount spent on raw and processed material. Kalecki assumes that price is determined by applying a uniform mark-up to prime costs. Let $k > 1$ be the uniform amount by which prime costs are increased to obtain price. The gross value of the firm's output is accordingly $k(W+R)$. The margin over prime costs will of course be the greater the larger is k; and k is a measure of monopoly power.[1]

Gross profit is $(k-1)(W+R)$ and gross value added, which is the sum of wages and gross profit, is $W+(k-1)(W+R)$. Hence the production worker share, denoted s, is

$$s = \frac{W}{W+(k-1)(W+R)}, \qquad (15.2.1)$$

or writing j for R/W, $$s = \frac{1}{1+(k-1)(j+1)}. \qquad (15.2.2)$$

Kalecki's simple theory of the behavior of labor's relative share follows immediately from equation (15.2.2). The greater the degree of monopoly (k) and the higher are the terms of trade between raw materials and labor (j), the smaller is the relative share of production workers.

Kalecki's theory is entirely tautological, and has justifiably been criticized on this ground.[2] There is one technological assumption (excess plant capacity) and one postulated behavioral relation (mark-up pricing). Beyond this, Kalecki's theory follows entirely from the *defined* breakdown of income. Further, it seems reasonable to suggest that the theory rests upon very shaky empirical grounds. More particularly, over substantial portions of the postwar years, the American manufacturing sector has operated at full or nearly full capacity. Second, even if mark-up pricing is a suitable approximation of the pricing process in manufacturing industry, it is not a suitable description in other sectors, notably agriculture, government, finance, and services. For these reasons, Kalecki's theory can be dismissed as an explanatory hypothesis of the behavior of relative factor shares.

15.2.2 Mitra

A second model based upon monopoly power, that of Ashok Mitra,[3] actually grew out of an attempt to provide statistical corroboration of Kalecki's model. Mitra constructed a complicated but crude test of

[1] Let p, m, and a represent price, marginal cost, and average cost respectively. Lerner's measure of monopoly power is $(p-m/p)$ [1933b, pp. 157–9]. In Kalecki's theory, the margin created by k is $p-a$. But since Kalecki assumes that $a = m$, his k is directly related to Lerner's measure. More precisely, if Lerner's measure is denoted by L,

$$k = \frac{pL}{m}+1.$$

[2] Bauer [1941, p. 201], Kaldor [1955, pp. 92–4], and Mitra [1954, pp. 29–31].
[3] Mitra [1954].

Kalecki's degree of monopoly hypothesis; the empirical results led Mitra to reject Kalecki's theory and to propose a modification of his own based upon Cournot's model of business behavior.

Mitra's basic assumption, just as Kalecki's, is that all markets are imperfectly competitive. The ith entrepreneur can sell q_i units of output at the market price p. His costs are a strictly increasing function of output. Thus $c_i = c_i(q_i)$. Profit may thus be defined as

$$\pi_i = pq_i - c_i(q_i). \tag{15.2.3}$$

Mitra now adopts the Cournot assumption that each entrepreneur attempts to maximize profit under the belief that his competitors will not react to his quantity changes. Under this assumption, the first-order condition for profit maximization is

$$\frac{d\pi_i}{dq_i} = p + q_i \frac{dp}{dq_i} - c_i'(q_i). = 0, \tag{15.2.4}$$

the familiar equality of marginal revenue and marginal cost.

Mitra next assumes that the uniform demand and total cost functions are linear. More precisely,

$$p = b_0 - b_1 q_i, \tag{15.2.5}$$

and
$$c_i(q_i) = c_0 + c_1 q_i \quad (i = 1, 2, ..., n), \tag{15.2.6}$$

where n is the number of imperfect competitors in the market in question. Taking the appropriate derivatives, substituting in equation (15.2.4), and summing over all firms gives

$$np - b_1 q - nc_1 = 0, \tag{15.2.7}$$

or
$$n(p - c_1) = b_1 q, \tag{15.2.8}$$

where $q = \sum_i q_i$. Substituting for $b_1 q$ from equation (15.2.5) and rearranging gives

$$p\left(1 + \frac{1}{n}\right) = c_1 + \frac{b_0}{n}. \tag{15.2.9}$$

To this point, especially from equation (15.2.6), it would seem that Mitra has assumed constant marginal cost. However, quite independently, he assumes that c_1, the marginal cost function, may be written as

$$c_1 = g_1 L + g_2 r + kp. \tag{15.2.10}$$

In the equation above, L is the average money wage rate, r is the price level of imports,[1] and g_1 and g_2 are what Mitra calls the 'labor quota' and the 'import quota'. Finally, Mitra assumes that depreciation allowances are a part of prime costs and that the same rate of depreciation (k) is applicable for all firms. Hence the term kp represents depreciation per unit of output.

[1] Imports in Mitra's model play the same role as raw materials in Kalecki's model.

Now denote the real wage rate by $s = L/p$. Using this in equation (15.2.10) and substituting the resultant in equation (15.2.9) yields

$$p = \frac{g_2 r + (b_0/n)}{1 + (1/n) - g_1 s - k}. \tag{15.2.11}$$

By definition, the total wage bill is $g_1 Lq$ and *net* national income is

$$[(1-k)p - g_2 r] q.$$

The relative share of wages in national income is

$$w = \frac{g_1 L}{(1-k)p - g_2 r} = \frac{g_1 sp}{(1-k)p - g_2 r}. \tag{15.2.12}$$

Substituting equation (15.2.11) and rearranging gives Mitra's final expression for the relative share of labor:

$$w = \frac{sg_1 g_2 r + \dfrac{sg_1 b_0}{n}}{sg_1 g_2 r + \dfrac{(1-k) b_0 - g_2 r}{n}}. \tag{15.2.13}$$

According to Mitra, equation (15.2.13) contains all of the elements of distribution theory. Specifically, (*a*) the number of sellers (*n*) and the 'zero demand price' (b_0) reflect the market structure; (*b*) the 'labor quota' (g_1) and the 'import quota' (g_2) reflect the structure of production; and (*c*) the wage-price ratio (*s*) connects the input and output markets.

Mitra draws three conclusions from equation (15.2.13). First, an increase in the wage–price ratio will increase the relative share of labor. This result, given Mitra's assumptions, can be obtained independently of equation (15.2.13), however. With the level of output and employment given, an increase in the relative wage must obviously lead to an increase in labor's relative share. Second, an increase in the 'labor quota' will increase labor's relative share. This result is also independent of equation (15.2.13). Of arithmetical necessity, if output and the real wage are constant, an increase in employment will increase the relative share of labor. Finally, an increase in the rate of depreciation or in the 'import' quota will cause an increase in the relative share of labor. This result is also independent of Mitra's equation. With constant price and output, the greater are depreciation and/or imports, the smaller is net national income; and the smaller is this denominator, the greater is the fraction.

In light of the tedious and stringent assumptions underlying Mitra's analysis, it hardly seems necessary to criticize his model. This is emphasized all the more because, while the model is designed to reflect the influence of monopoly on labor's relative share, the effect of a change in the degree of monopoly is indeterminate. That is, a change in n reflects a change in the extent of monopoly. Yet from equation (15.2.13) the sign of $\partial w/\partial n$ cannot be determined *a priori*.[1] One further point deserves notice. Equation (15.2.13) is intended to be an empirical statement holding for the aggregate economy. Thus for the United States, n is in excess of five million. For all practical purposes, equation (15.2.13) shows $w \approx 1\cdot 0$.

15.3 Theories based upon aggregate demand

So far as I can determine, the first 'alternative' theories of distribution based upon aggregate demand are attributable to Boulding and Hahn.[2] The distribution theories of these two writers did not achieve widespread recognition, probably because their distribution models were merely parts of larger works directed toward major reforms in economic theory. There have subsequently appeared contributions by, *inter alia*, Preiser, Schneider, Krelle, Bombach, Findlay, Stobbe, Pasinetti, Sen, Kemp, Soper, and Eisner.[3] However, by far the most prominent of the aggregate demand theorists are Kaldor and Mrs Robinson.[4] To treat all of these models would take us far beyond either the intended scope or object of this book. In the remainder of this chapter, our attention is limited to the models of Kaldor and Mrs Robinson.

15.3.1 Kaldor's model[5,6]

Let P and W represent gross quasi-rent and aggregate wages respectively. Thus national income at factor cost is

$$Y \equiv P + W. \tag{15.3.1}$$

Kaldor assumes that the marginal (and average) propensities to save of capitalists (s_p) and workers (s_w) are given and constant and, in particular, that $s_p > s_w$. Total desired saving is

$$S = s_p P + s_w W, \tag{15.3.2}$$

[1] The sign of $\partial w/\partial n$ depends upon the sign of $g_1 rn(1-k-sg_1)-(1-k)b_0$. If the relative wage and the 'labor quota' are sufficiently small, this expression may be positive.

[2] Boulding [1953] and Hahn [1951].

[3] See Preiser [1953] and [1961], Schneider [1957], Krelle [1957], Bombach [1959a, b], Findlay [1960], Stobbe [1960], Pasinetti [1962], Sen [1963], Kemp [1963], Soper [1964a], and Eisner [1964].

[4] Kaldor [1955], [1957], [1959], [1961]; Kaldor and Mirrlees [1962]; Robinson [1956]. For some objections to the Kaldor–Robinson theory, see Witte [1958], Atsumi [1960], Findlay [1960], Tobin [1960], Ferguson [1964a]. Also see Kaldor [1960a, b].

[5] Subsections 15.3.1 and 15.3.2 are a slight adaptation of Ferguson [1964a, pp. 26–34].

[6] The model is chiefly that of Kaldor [1955]. His subsequent work has been more directly related to the theory of growth. Essentially the same distribution theory emerges.

and the aggregate desired saving ratio (s) is

$$s = \frac{S}{Y} = s_p\left(\frac{P}{Y}\right) + s_w\left(\frac{W}{Y}\right) = (s_p - s_w)\frac{P}{Y} + s_w. \qquad (15.3.3)$$

Since saving must equal investment *ex post*, and since an equilibrium growth path requires *ex-ante* equality as well, Kaldor writes equation (15.3.3) as

$$s \equiv \frac{I}{Y} = (s_p - s_w)\frac{P}{Y} + s_w. \qquad (15.3.4)$$

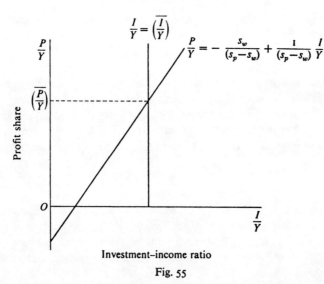

Fig. 55

Solving equation (15.3.4) for the profit share, one obtains

$$\frac{P}{Y} = \frac{1}{(s_p - s_w)}\frac{I}{Y} - \frac{s_w}{(s_p - s_w)}. \qquad (15.3.5)$$

Equation (15.3.5) shows the profit share, and hence the share of labor, as depending upon the investment–income ratio only, given the constant saving propensities. This relation is depicted in figure 55. Since equation (15.3.5) is linear, its graphical counterpart is a straight line. The intercept is negative; and the slope is greater than unity since $0 < s_p - s_w < 1$ by hypothesis. *Given* the independently determined investment–income ratio (I/Y),[1] the relative shares are automatically determined by mapping onto the ordinate.

[1] For the model represented by equation (15.3.5) to be *complete*, the investment–income ratio must be independently determined. In his 1955 paper, Kaldor noted that the profit–wage relation might influence the capital–output ratio via the choice among alternative techniques of production. If such were so, I/Y would not be independent

MONOPOLY, DEMAND, AND DISTRIBUTION

The investment–income theory of distribution is *static*, as may be seen from this formulation. However, to study the role of distribution in economic growth, Kaldor made a legitimate definitional substitution of terms; but after the substitution, the model has a misleadingly dynamic appearance. Note first that investment, by definition, is equal to the change in capital stock. Thus the investment–income ratio may be written

$$\frac{I}{Y} = \frac{\Delta K}{Y}. \tag{15.3.6}$$

Multiplying and dividing the right-hand side of equation (15.3.6) by ΔY, one obtains

$$s = \frac{S}{Y} = \frac{I}{Y} = \frac{\Delta Y}{Y} \cdot \frac{\Delta K}{\Delta Y}. \tag{15.3.7}$$

Let us now consider equation (15.3.7). The first term on the right-most side, $\Delta Y/Y$, is the rate of growth of national income, denoted G. The second term, $\Delta K/\Delta Y$, is the marginal capital–output ratio or, in Harrod's terminology, the required capital–output ratio (C_r). Consequently, equation (15.3.7) reduces to Harrod's famous equation for the warranted rate of growth:

$$G = \frac{s}{C_r}. \tag{15.3.8}$$

Using equations (15.3.5) and (15.3.8), Kaldor argues that relative factor shares tend to be constant. Let G^w represent the warranted rate of growth and G^n the natural rate. Kaldor maintains that relative factor shares adjust so that $G^w = G^n$.[1] But once so adjusted, there is no endogenous economic force to change them.

The adjustment mechanism may be explained as follows. Rewrite equation (15.3.8) as

$$G^w = \frac{s}{C_r} = \frac{(s_p - s_w)(P/Y) + s_w}{C_r}. \tag{15.3.9}$$

In the absence of technological change, or if technological progress is Harrod-neutral, C_r is a constant. Thus any change in G^w must come about

of P/Y, and model (15.3.5) would be underdetermined. In the 1955 paper, Kaldor dismissed this problem simply by assuming that the capital–output ratio is a constant. In the 1957 paper, the independently-determined 'technical progress function' determines a stable long-run capital–output ratio. Similarly, in the 1962 paper, the long-run equality between the rates of growth of productivity per worker and investment per worker determines the capital–output ratio. Thus in his later work, Kaldor does not assume an independently given capital–output ratio. Nonetheless, the ratio is assumed to be independent of economic magnitudes such as relative prices. This is sufficient to establish model (15.3.5).

[1] That is, Kaldor assumes that savings adjust to the *given* level of investment, i.e. to the *given* investment–income ratio at a *given* level of income. Adjustment is achieved by shifting income from low-propensity savers to high-propensity savers or vice versa.

through a change in the numerator. With given savings propensities, the change must come in P/Y.[1]

Now suppose the prevailing situation is such that the warranted rate is less than the natural rate at a full-employment point. Investment is thus encouraged, thereby increasing I/Y. But by equation (15.3.5), an increase in I/Y leads to an increase in P/Y. Hence the profit share increases, and there are forces to cause a continued increase until $G^w = G^n$. The reverse analysis applies when $G^w > G^n$ at a full-employment point. Consequently, distribution changes until $G^w = G^n$ and remains constant thereafter, except for the influence of exogenous forces.

It is worthwhile to emphasize two aspects of the foregoing paragraph. First, this is a full-employment model, not a 'Keynesian' model of *The General Theory* variety. In Keynes' analysis, when saving does not equal investment *ex ante*, income and employment change to establish the equality. In Kaldor's model, on the other hand, income is given at the full-employment level and investment is somehow exogenously given so as to be consistent with full employment. With the assumption of given but different saving propensities, the only way adjustment can be achieved is through a change in relative factor shares. But this is not an *analytical* conclusion. It merely follows for the accounting identities, given the assumptions of the model.

Second, Kaldor's model is somewhat like the 'Keynesian' model of the *Treatise* variety[2] in that it displays the 'widow's cruse' effect: entrepreneurs earn what they spend, and workers spend what they earn. To see this, suppose a moving equilibrium has long been established. $G^w = G^n$ and P/Y is a constant. Now let capitalists suddenly become less thrifty; that is, there is a parametric downward shift of s_p. At the prevailing distribution, desired saving is less than full-employment desired investment. Thus saving must increase; the only way this can be accomplished in Kaldor's model is by a shift of income from workers to capitalists.[3]

15.3.2 A two-sector variant of Kaldor's model

Several characteristics of Kaldor's model may be isolated from the discussion above. In particular, the theory is static, it deals with only one good, it ignores relative commodity prices, and it ignores relative factor prices.

---

[1] That is, the change must ultimately come through a change in the aggregate propensity to save. While s_p and s_w are given constants, s is a weighted average of them, the weights being the relative shares of capital and labor respectively. Hence, for example, if s must increase to maintain *ex-ante* equality of saving and investment, there must be a shift of income from workers to capitalists.

[2] Keynes [1930, vol. I, pp. 123–9].

[3] This is always true so long as $s_p > s_w$; and a solution does not exist if $s_w \geqslant s_p$. The aspect just discussed is treated rather humorously in Tobin [1960].

The explicit recognition of two classes of goods, consumption goods G and investment goods I, leads to a more general model that points up the necessity of introducing some kind of technological relation.

Let us begin with two assumptions: (a) the full-employment labor–capital ratio (L/K) is given, and (b) the average (= marginal) propensities to save of capitalists (s_p) and of workers (s_w) are given constants that satisfy $0 \leqq s_w < s_p \leqq 1$.

The model contains two goods and two generalized homogeneous factors of production. Hence the commodity-price ratio (P_G/P_I) and the factor-price ratio (P_L/P_K) must be determined, as well as the outputs of the two classes of goods. Since only relative magnitudes are determined in general static equilibrium, attention may be focused upon the output *ratio* only. Furthermore, since departures from equilibrium are ignored, demand and supply are always equal for each commodity. Hence relative demand (D_G/D_I) may be used to represent the output ratio in value terms. Notice that (say) D_I is not a microeconomic function relating quantity demanded to price. Instead, D_I is the dollar magnitude of expenditures on investment goods. Consequently, it is a function of income and the distribution of income. Thus income distribution, represented by the ratio of relative shares (W/P), must enter the model. Finally, the saving–income (S/Y) and the investment–income (I/Y) ratios must be determined.

Accounting identities. From national income accounting relations, one obtains

$$Y \equiv P + W. \tag{15.3.10}$$

Furthermore, using Kaldor's saving function,

$$S = s_p P + s_w W. \tag{15.3.11}$$

The Kaldor equation relating the investment–income ratio to the distribution of income may be derived from equations (15.3.10) and (15.3.11):

$$\frac{I}{Y} = (s_p - s_w)\,\frac{1}{1 + (W/P)} + s_w \tag{15.3.12}$$

(see panel c, figure 56). Also from accounting identities, an equation relating the distribution of income to the factor-price ratio for any given labor–capital ratio may be obtained (see panel b, figure 56):

$$\frac{W}{P} = \frac{P_L}{P_K}\frac{L}{K}. \tag{15.3.13}$$

Equations (15.3.12) and (15.3.13) provide two equations in three unknowns, and no additional information can be obtained from accounting relations. Behavioral equations, therefore, must supply the missing elements.

Behavioral relations. Let us turn first to an equation explaining the demand-composition ratio. Given s_p and s_w, the average propensity to consume is $1 - s_p(P/Y) - s_w(W/Y)$. Thus consumption $(= D_G)$ is $Y - s_p P - s_w W$. Similarly, investment (D_I) is $s_p P + s_w W$. The ratio of consumption to investment (the demand-composition ratio) is, accordingly,

$$\frac{D_G}{D_I} = \frac{(W/P) + 1}{s_w(W/P) + s_p} - 1. \qquad (15.3.14)$$

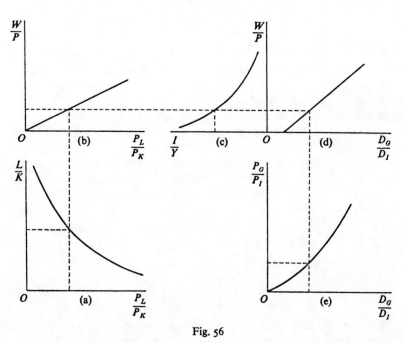

Fig. 56

Since $s_p > s_w$ by assumption, equation (15.3.14) may be written more simply as[1] (panel *d*, figure 56):

$$\frac{D_G}{D_I} = f\left(\frac{W}{P}\right), \quad \frac{df}{d(W/P)} > 0. \qquad (15.3.15)$$

Equation (15.3.15) states that the demand-composition ratio depends upon the distribution of income and that an increase in wages relative to profit

[1] From equation (15.3.14) it is easily seen that $\dfrac{d(D_G/D_I)}{d(W/P)} > 0$ and that the curve has a negative intercept. In panel *d*, figure 56, the relation is shown as a straight line. Actually the curve would be concave from above or below according as

$$s_p \lessgtr s_w[(W/P) + 2].$$

causes an increase in the demand for consumer goods relative to investment goods.

Next assume that the supply of neither good is completely elastic; hence a relative increase in demand for one class of goods must cause an increase in its relative price. In other words, the commodity-price ratio (P_G/P_I) depends upon and varies directly with the demand-composition ratio (D_G/D_I) (panel e, figure 56):

$$\frac{P_G}{P_I} = g\left(\frac{D_G}{D_I}\right), \quad \frac{dg}{d(D_G/D_I)} > 0. \qquad (15.3.16)$$

All five of the basic ratio variables (I/Y, W/P, D_G/D_I, P_G/P_I and P_L/P_K) have now been introduced; but there are only four equations to explain them. An equation involving the factor-price ratio must be added without introducing an additional variable. Explicit reference to the conditions of production has so far been avoided; and it may still be avoided, although most neoclassical economists are likely to read an implicit productivity concept into the equation now to be introduced.

At the outset, it was assumed that the supply of labor L and the supply of capital K are given. To meet the conditions of general equilibrium, the demands for labor and for capital must equal their given supplies. Without specifying *why*, it is plausible to assume that factor prices adjust to maintain these necessary equalities. In other words, relative factor price depends upon the endowed labor–capital ratio. Writing this assumption in inverse functional form (panel a, figure 56):

$$\frac{P_L}{P_K} = h\left(\frac{L}{K}\right), \quad \frac{dh}{d(L/K)} < 0. \qquad (15.3.17)$$

Without necessarily specifying the reasons, it is plausible to assume that relative factor price varies inversely with relative factor availability.

Equilibrium of the model. Equations (15.3.12), (15.3.13), (15.3.15)–(15.3.17) give a complete model of static equilibrium, as indicated graphically in figure 56. Panel a is a graphic representation of equation (15.3.17). The given labor–capital ratio determines the equilibrium factor-price ratio. Moving up to panel b, the distribution of income is determined. Panel b is a graph of equation (15.3.13), where the slope of the line represents the constant (endowed) labor–capital ratio.

Next move across to panels c and d. Panel c is a graphic representation of equation (15.3.12). Given the distribution of income, the investment–income ratio is determined. So also is the demand-composition ratio from panel d, the graphical counterpart of equation (15.3.15). Finally, moving downward to panel e, the equilibrium demand-composition ratio determines the equilibrium commodity-price ratio by means of equation (15.3.16) or its graphical counterpart.

The equilibrium of the model is complete, but it looks as though causality were traceable. The appearance is there because the 'endowed' labor–capital ratio is the parameter of the model. This gives a convenient starting place, but it does not imply causality in the model. For example, relative factor supply might have been regarded as a function of relative factor price (after all, labor and capital are not manna). It would then have been necessary to specify some other given condition, such as I/Y, or add another equation relating one of the endogenous variables to a new parameter.

We have got this far with a model that looks a good deal more like Kaldor's than Hicks'. In particular, technological conditions have been touched upon only tangentially by assuming that relative factor demand is a function of, and varies inversely with, relative factor price. If the model is pushed to a more interesting stage, however, the conditions of production must be stipulated in considerably more detail.

Thus far it has merely been shown that if a solution of the model exists, it is a static equilibrium solution. More interesting questions, however, require analysis of either the comparative-static or the dynamic behavior of the system. In this section the latter is omitted entirely and only a few comments are addressed to the former.

Comparative statics. Since the model contains only one parameter, the given labor–capital ratio, the comparative-static behavior of the system may be studied by shifting this parameter. A positive level of net investment in one period increases the quantity of capital available in the next. Similarly, both population growth and changes in the labor-force participation rate affect the available supply of labor. In the American economy the result has been an increase in both L and K; but according to Fabricant,[1] K has increased more rapidly than L. Let us begin, therefore, by postulating a downward shift in the labor–capital ratio.

As seen in panel *a*, a downward shift in L/K causes an increase in P_L/P_K. The new value of P_L/P_K may be extended upward to panel *b*, and a new line, representing the new L/K ratio, constructed. The intersection of the new P_L/P_K value and the new L/K line in panel *b* determines the new distribution of income, indicated by a new value of W/P. Primary interest lies in determining whether the relative share of labor increases, remains constant, or diminishes. For the specific curve drawn in panel *a*, this information is easily obtainable. But notice that W/P changes in different ways according to the position and shape of the curve in panel *a*. Unless the position of this curve is specified in detail, there is only one comparative-

---

[1] Fabricant [1959].

static conclusion to be drawn: a decrease in the relative availability of labor causes an increase in its relative price, a conclusion that requires nothing like the framework constructed here.

The crux of the matter is the curve in panel a. To specify this curve in detail requires a detailed specification of the conditions of production. When this is done, the model is indistinguishable from the two-sector neoclassical model developed in chapter 12 above.

Conclusions. What are the lessons to be learned from this? They are, I suspect, ones we already know.

(*a*) This is a multi-commodity world in which different commodities require different factor combinations. Hence relative commodity demand must play some role in determining relative factor shares.

(*b*) At the same time, as should be clear from the above model, useful analysis of the behavior of relative factor shares entails reference to the conditions of production. Hence production functions must also play an important role in the determination of relative factor shares.

At this stage it seems appropriate to indicate what the above model is and what it is not. It emphatically is not a theory of distributive shares. I hope that it is a vehicle for exposing the weaknesses of Kaldor's model.

In Kaldor's theory, investment is a completely exogenous variable whose behavior is not determined by the model. In fact, the Kaldor model simply determines the profit share that is consistent with full employment, given an exogenous level of investment and the unequal propensities to save. This is far from a theory of distribution. The force of this criticism is shown by an examination of Kaldor's solution in equation (15.3.5), which is obtained from (15.3.1) and (15.3.2) by simple algebraic operations. Equation (15.3.1) is an ex-post accounting identity, and equation (15.3.2) gives desired or ex-ante saving. A basic condition of the model is that I must equal S, ex-ante and ex-post. There is no behavioral equation to explain investment; it simply must equal desired saving. Since P/Y depends upon the investment–income ratio, there is also nothing in the model to explain distributive shares. P/Y is what it is because in equilibrium it is related to I/Y, and I/Y is what it is because it can be nothing else. Just as relative shares are technologically determined in neoclassical theory, so they are psychologically determined in Kaldor's theory, being ultimately determined by the propensities to save. As emphasized above, this is indeed a 'widow's cruse' model of distribution and relative factor shares.

15.3.3 Mrs Robinson's model

Since her beautifully simple *Economics of Imperfect Competition*,[1] Mrs Robinson has raised more problems than she has solved, not only in economic theory as such but also for economists who try to describe her theory. Working in areas that cry out for mathematical simplicity,[2] she has refused to make the assumptions necessary for mathematical tractability. In a way this is admirable, in a way frustrating because her 'verbal' model yields few conclusions that are not subject to modification and/or change.

While these statements apply to every element of her model of accumulation, they apply more especially to her theory of distribution. In the first place, distribution is not her central concern; her remarks pertaining to distribution appear almost randomly throughout the chief theoretical portion of her book.[3] Second, her discussion is always limited to the very special case in which workers consume their entire income. One should like to remove this assumption so as to make her theory comparable to others. Finally, Mrs Robinson is difficult to understand and describe simply because she cannot be categorized. Her models are 'Keynesian' in that she places emphasis upon aggregate saving and investment. At the same time, her models are uncompromisingly 'neoclassical' in that she emphasizes relative prices and capital–labor substitution. Thus while a simple version of her model 'looks like' Kaldor's model, its interpretation and interior working are quite different.[4]

The following exposition of Mrs Robinson's model contains some drastic simplifications and some changes of her assumptions. In particular, I shall generally use Kaldor's assumption concerning saving propensities rather than Mrs Robinson's. That is, I shall assume that $0 < s_w < s_p < 1$ rather than $s_w = 0$, $s_p = 1$.

Assumptions. Ignoring Mrs Robinson's rentier class, the economy is composed of workers and entrepreneurs, who receive wages and profits respectively. Output is composed of consumption goods and investment goods. The economy is closed; the degree of mechanization is given, and there is no technical progress. Finally, the stock of capital and the labor force grow, if at all, at a steady and harmonious rate.

Given these assumptions, a 'golden age' growth path is attained along which output, investment, capital, and labor all grow at the same rate; wages, the rate of interest, and relative shares are constant. Mrs Robinson's

[1] Robinson [1933].
[2] For some efforts to describe *The Accumulation of Capital* mathematically, see Findlay [1963], Lancaster [1960], and Worswick [1959].
[3] Robinson [1956, pp. 63–176].
[4] In particular, Mrs Robinson does not assume that the investment–income ratio is independent of relative factor shares.

technique is to compare various economies each of which satisfies the conditions of 'golden age' growth, but which differ in such characteristics as wages and degree of mechanization. The same technique is used to analyze once-for-all technical changes.

The basic model. Mrs Robinson's model of income distribution may be given an algebraic form. Let Y, W, and P represent income, the total wage bill, and total profits respectively. One thus has the income accounting identity

$$Y \equiv W + P. \qquad (15.3.18)$$

With the more general saving assumption (see above), consumption (C) may be written as

$$C = (1 - s_w)\, W + (1 - s_p)\, P. \qquad (15.3.19)$$

Substituting equation (15.3.18) and solving for the wage bill yields

$$W = \frac{1}{s_p - s_w}\, C - \frac{1 - s_p}{s_p - s_w}\, Y. \qquad (15.3.20)$$

In like manner, investment expenditure is

$$I = s_w W + s_p P, \qquad (15.3.21)$$

which may be solved for P:

$$P = \frac{1}{s_p - s_w}\, I - \frac{s_w}{s_p - s_w}\, Y. \qquad (15.3.22)$$

Thus the ratio of relative shares, from equations (15.3.20) and (15.3.22), is

$$\frac{P}{W} = \frac{I - s_w Y}{C - (1 - s_p) Y}; \qquad (15.3.23)$$

and the profit share itself is

$$\frac{P}{Y} = \frac{1}{s_p - s_w}\, \frac{I}{Y} - \frac{s_w}{s_p - s_w}. \qquad (15.3.24)$$

Equation (15.3.24) is identically the same as the distribution equation in Kaldor's model, equation (15.3.5). But while the *equations* are the same, the two theories are different. As the reader will recall, Kaldor assumes that the investment–income ratio is entirely independent of the distribution of income. Hence to him, equation (15.3.5) independently determines relative factor shares. This is not true in Mrs Robinson's model. She incorporates the relations among capital, the investment–income ratio, and the rate of profit in her model; and in particular, she does not assume that the technique of production or the degree of mechanization is independent of the rate of profit. Hence equation (15.3.24) is not a single equation showing a one-way causal relation between the profit-share and the investment–income ratio. To get at the other determinants of relative shares requires the introduction of Mrs Robinson's concepts of the capital stock.

The valuation of capital. Mrs Robinson arrives at her crucial concept of capital by stages. First, the *value* of the stock of capital is defined as (*a*) the future profit expected from a unit of capital discounted to the present at the appropriate notional interest rate, or (*b*) the cost incurred in constructing the unit of capital, accumulated to the present at the appropriate notional interest rate, after allowing for the profit the machine has already yielded. In a 'golden age', the two measures turn out to be the same, and the 'notional' interest rate is equal to the rate of profit.

The value of capital so computed is the value of capital in terms of commodities. To convert this to the value of capital in terms of labor time, one divides the value of capital in terms of commodities by the wage per man hour. Finally, what Mrs Robinson calls the *real-capital ratio* is obtained by dividing the value of capital in terms of labor time by the amount of labor employed when the capital equipment is operated at normal capacity. Denote the value of capital in terms of commodities by K. Then the value in terms of labor time is K/w and the real-capital ratio is $K/wL = k$, where w is the real wage rate and L is labor employed at normal capacity operation.

The real-capital ratio and the rate of profit can be incorporated in the algebraic form of the model. Let r denote the rate of return on capital (value in terms of commodities). Thus definitionally,

$$r = \frac{P}{K} = \frac{P}{W}\frac{W}{K} = \frac{P}{W}\frac{wL}{K} = \frac{1}{k}\frac{P}{W}, \qquad (15.3.25)$$

or the ratio of relative shares is simply the product of the rate of return and the real-capital ratio:

$$\frac{P}{W} = kr. \qquad (15.3.26)$$

Rearranging equation (15.3.26) and using definition (15.3.18), one obtains

$$P = rk(Y-P). \qquad (15.3.27)$$

Finally, equation (15.3.27) may be solved to show the relation among the profit share, the rate of return, and the real-capital ratio:[1]

$$\frac{P}{Y} = \frac{1}{1+(1/rk)}. \qquad (15.3.28)$$

Thus the greater the rate of return or the real-capital ratio, the greater is the profit share.

However, not too much can be made of this directly because the rate of return and the real-capital ratio are related. First, in a 'golden age', the notional rate of interest used in calculating the value of capital must equal the rate of return. Second, the rate of return, in relation to the wage rate,

[1] To the best of my knowledge, this relation was first suggested by Sosin [1967].

determines the choice of technique and hence the degree of mechanization. Therefore, while equation (15.3.28) may be used to determine what happens to relative shares when the rate of return and the real-capital ratio change, the behavior of the latter two must be determined jointly. Unfortunately, there is no convenient way to reduce the relation between the rate of return and the real-capital ratio to a mathematical equation. The argument must be verbal.

A digression. It is convenient at this point to introduce Mrs Robinson's diagrams, beginning with what she calls the technical frontier. Given the state of technology, Mrs Robinson conceives a *finite* spectrum of techniques (or 'book of blueprints'), each of which can be used to produce the *same* output with a *different* capital–labor ratio. Each entrepreneur is assumed to select the technique that yields the greatest rate of return given the prevailing wage rate. Thus the 'degree of mechanization' at any moment is governed by the wage rate, and changes in the degree of mechanization are the result of changes in relative factor supplies.[1]

We begin with Wicksell's graph,[2] shown in figure 57. The real-capital ratio is plotted along the abscissa and output per man along the ordinate. The locus $\delta\gamma\beta\alpha$ is what Mrs Robinson calls the 'productivity curve' inasmuch as it shows the output per man associated with each capital–labor ratio expressed in labor time. As the figure is constructed, there are four techniques available. Following Mrs Robinson, these are called the Delta, Gamma, Beta, and Alpha techniques. Suppose technique Gamma is used exclusively. Output per man is OC and real capital per man is Oc. Similarly, with technique Beta, output per man is OB and the real-capital ratio is Ob. Thus CB is the difference in output per man attributable to using Beta technique rather than Gamma, and cb is the increase in real capital per man that is required to increase output per man by CB.

The four techniques, represented by the points δ, γ, β, and α, are technologically given. Since two techniques may be used simultaneously, the points have been connected by straight line segments $\delta\gamma$, $\gamma\beta$, and $\beta\alpha$. Thus, for example, if the existing organization of production lies on the segment $\beta\alpha$, the closer it lies to α, the greater is the proportion of Alpha equipment in the mix.

Suppose the real wage rate is exogenously given at the level OW. The task of the entrepreneur is to select the technique and, therefore, the real-capital ratio that maximizes his rate of profit. As Wicksell has shown,[3] this

---

[1] It is sometimes helpful to think of the 'degree of mechanization' as synonymous with Wicksell's 'length of the period of production'. Mrs Robinson indicates that the two concepts are equivalent. [1956, p. 396].

[2] Wicksell [1893, p. 122] and [1901, p. 180].

[3] Wicksell [1893, pp. 123–4].

is accomplished by drawing a line from W that is tangent to the productivity curve.[1] The corresponding real-capital ratio is the one that maximizes the rate of profit, which is given by $1/ON$. To see this last point, suppose the Gamma technique is chosen. Output per man is OC, so profit per man is WC. The value of capital per man in terms of commodities is $Oc \cdot OW$, so the rate of profit is $WC \div Oc \cdot OW$. Now $OW \div ON$ is equal to $WC \div Oc$. Hence $WC \div Oc \cdot OW = 1/ON$.

In figure 57 the postulated wage rate is compatible with either the Gamma or Beta techniques; and following Mrs Robinson, it is called the Gamma-Beta wage. Each technique is equally profitable. While output per man is

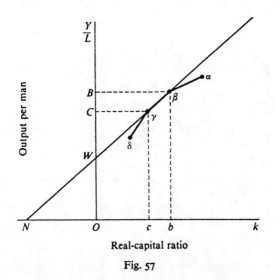

Fig. 57

higher when the Beta technique is used, the real-capital ratio is higher in the same proportion; thus the rate of profit on invested capital is the same.

The possible static equilibria consistent with the wage rate OW are indicated in figure 57. It is possible to show what happens when wage rates are different. Technically, the capital goods and output per man do not change when the wage rate changes. However, when the wage rate changes, the rate of profit changes; and thus the notional interest rate used in calculating the value of capital in terms of commodities changes. Consequently, the productivity curve has to be redrawn for each rate of profit so as to show the difference in the real-capital ratio attributable to the

[1] Of course, with a multi-facet curve such as that in figure 57, the line may be tangent along a facet so that no unique answer is obtained. This point is treated below.

different notional interest rate used in calculating the value of capital in terms of commodities.[1]

Such a manipulation is shown in figure 58. Suppose the wage rate is the Delta-Gamma rate. Production is organized somewhere in the $\delta_3\gamma_3$ stretch, say precisely at γ_3 with real-capital ratio Oc_3. Now suppose the Gamma-Beta wage rate prevails and has long prevailed. The higher wage rate means a lower rate of profit and a smaller value of capital in terms of labor. Thus with the same technical labor requirements, the real-capital ratio is less.[2]

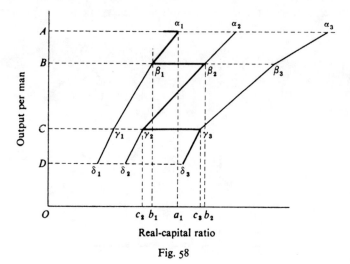

Fig. 58

As constructed, the real-capital ratio falls from Oc_3 to Oc_2, or by the amount $\gamma_2\gamma_3$. At the Gamma-Beta wage, the greater the proportion of Beta equipment in the mix, the greater the real-capital ratio; the productivity curve is positively sloped over the $\gamma_2\beta_2$ range. But if the wage rate were to rise to the Beta-Alpha level, the productivity curve would shift to the left, and the relevant range would be $\beta_1\alpha_1$. Mrs Robinson calls the locus $\delta_3\gamma_3\gamma_2\beta_2\beta_1\alpha_1$ the 'real-capital-ratio curve'.

Finally, we may illustrate the relation between the real-capital ratio and the value of capital per man in terms of commodities. In figure 59, the

---

[1] The valuation problem has been touched upon by Hicks [1932, 2nd ed., pp. 343–8] and explained clearly and ingeniously by Samuelson [1962, pp. 203–5].

[2] Of course, the lower rate of profit means a lower notional interest rate. Therefore, the interest cost that goes into the value of capital in terms either of commodities or labor time is less. At a higher wage rate, the wage cost is greater; and the value of capital in terms of commodities would normally be greater. But the value of capital in terms of labor, and thus the real-capital ratio, must decline because the wage rate in numerator and denominator 'factors out'. This is discussed in greater detail below.

upper panel shows the real-capital ratio curve which, for all practical purposes, is a reproduction of figure 58. The lower panel shows the wage rate and the value of capital per man in terms of commodities.

Suppose the Gamma-Beta wage prevails. Productive equipment may be of the Gamma type, the Beta type, or a mixture of the two. But it is clear that at the Gamma-Beta wage, the greater the proportion of Beta equip-

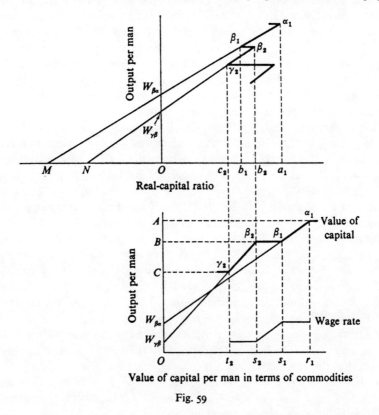

Fig. 59

ment, the greater is the real-capital ratio and the value of capital in terms of commodities.[1] Hence as the real-capital ratio increases from Oc_2 to Ob_2, the value of capital in terms of commodities increases from Ot_2 to Os_2.

Now suppose that the Beta-Alpha wage prevails and has long prevailed. As explained above, the real-capital ratio for Beta equipment would normally fall from Ob_2 to (say) Ob_1. But the value of capital per man in

---

[1] Since the wage rate is the same and output per man greater with Beta equipment, profit per man is greater with Beta equipment. By definition of the Gamma-Beta wage, the *rate* of profit is the same at Gamma and Beta; hence the value of capital in terms of commodities must be greater at Beta.

terms of commodities rises from Os_2 to Os_1 because of the greater wage rate coupled with a lower notional interest rate.[1] Parallel explanations apply to the $\beta_1\alpha_1$ range and to the range beyond α_1.

The degree of mechanization and relative shares. The results of the above digression may now be used, together with equation (15.3.28), to infer some characteristics of the behavior of relative factor shares. In the case of one economy, nothing can be said about the response of relative shares to a change in wage rates except in the Ruth Cohen case. Normally, an increase in the wage rate lowers the rate of return and increases the real-capital ratio. No conclusion can be drawn *a priori.* If the Ruth Cohen Curiosum (i.e. reswitching) prevails, an increase in the wage rate lowers both the rate of return and the real-capital ratio. In this case, there is an unequivocal increase in labor's relative share.

A comparison of economies, both of which are assumed to be in a 'golden age', permits some further inferences. First consider two economies, Beth and Alaph. Only Beta machines are used in Beth, only Alpha machines in Alaph. The wage rate, namely the Beta-Alpha rate, is the same in both economies. The real-capital ratio is greater in Alaph; and hence the relative share of profits is higher in Alaph. Thus all other things equal, the greater the degree of mechanization, the greater the relative profit share.

Next, consider two economies in which the same technique is used. Suppose it is the Beta technique. In one economy, Lower Beth, the wage rate is lower than it is in the other economy, Upper Beth. Since the technique is the same, output per head is the same in both economies. Hence quasi-rent per man, and therefore the profit share, is greater in Lower Beth, the economy with the lower wage rate.

As in the one economy case, it is not possible to compare Alaph at the Alpha wage rate with Beth at the Beta rate. The rate of profit is lower in Alaph, but the real-capital ratio is greater. No conclusion can be drawn *a priori.* Yet it is interesting to note that a fall in the profit share attributable to a higher wage rate can always be prevented if it is possible to shift to a sufficiently higher degree of mechanization.

Technical progress and relative shares. It is now time to introduce technological progress into Mrs Robinson's model. Over time inventions occur that lower the labor required per unit both of consumption and of equipment output. These changes, in their turn, affect the relative factor shares.

First let us introduce the definition of neutral technological progress. According to Mrs Robinson,

A neutral relationship between the two spectra [of techniques] means that, with the superior technique, labour per unit of output and capital in terms of labour

[1] For more discussion of this point, see the Appendix to this chapter.

330

time per unit of output are reduced in the same proportion over the whole range of techniques, so that the real-capital ratio is the same with Beta-plus as with Beta technique, the same with Alpha-plus as with Alpha, and with Gamma-plus as with Gamma.[1]

Suppose there are two economies with the same spectrum of techniques; and the wage rates are such that the Beta technique is chosen in both economies. Next, let there be technological improvement in one economy that brings in an entirely new spectrum of techniques, while the other economy remains technologically stagnant. If the rate of profit remains the same, the Beta-plus technique is selected in the new situation. Then if the real-capital ratio is the same with the Beta-plus technique as with the Beta technique, technological progress is neutral. Similarly, technological progress is capital using or capital saving according as the real-capital ratio is greater or smaller with the Beta-plus technique, the rate of profit being the same with Beta and Beta-plus techniques. For all practical purposes, Mrs Robinson's definition and classification of technological progress are exactly the same as Harrod's.

Armed with these definitions, we can draw some conclusions about the effect of technological progress on relative factor shares. First, suppose there is neutral technological progress as between two economies and the rate of profit is the same. Since, by definition, the real-capital ratio is the same, relative shares are the same in both economies. In the progressive economy, wages are greater in the same proportion as output per man; and the value of capital per man is greater in this same proportion. With the rate of profit the same, total profit in the superior economy expands proportionately with the value of output; relative shares therefore remain constant.

When technological progress is neutral, there is no reason to suppose that the rates of profit are the same as between the two economies. Suppose the rate of profit in the superior economy is lower than in the inferior economy. If the Beta technique is chosen in the latter, the (say) Alpha-plus technique is chosen in the former. Wages relative to output per head are greater in the superior economy, which is just another way of saying that the profit rate is lower. But no *a priori* statement can be made about the real-capital ratios. It is true that the real-capital ratio corresponding to the Alpha-plus technique is the same as *would have been* required for the Alpha technique in the inferior economy. But because of the different rates of notional interest in the two economies, one cannot say whether the real-capital ratio is greater or less in the superior economy. Hence no conclusion about relative shares can be drawn.

If profit rates are equal in the two economies, the relative share of labor

[1] Robinson [1956, p. 133].

in the superior economy is greater or less than the corresponding share in the inferior economy according as technological progress is capital-saving or capital using. This follows immediately from the definitions and equation (15.3.28). The profit rates are equal by assumption; if technological progress is capital saving, the real-capital ratio is smaller in the superior economy. Hence the relative share of labor is greater, and *vice versa*.

If profit rates are not equal in the two economies, definite conclusions cannot be drawn because the notional rate of interest, which enters in the valuation of capital, is different.

Conclusion. Commenting on neoclassical theory, Mrs Robinson wrote as follows:

The traditional 'production function' shows output as a function of labour and 'capital' without specifying the units in which 'capital' is measured. It purports to exhibit the purely technical relations between labour, capital and output. Technical relations are shown by any one of our productivity curves. But the 'production function' also purports to show the relation between wages and profits which gives equilibrium in a given state of technical knowledge. This cannot be deduced from a productivity curve, for each curve is drawn for a particular rate of interest. Given the technical conditions, *we have to know the real-wage rate (or the rate of profit) as a separate datum* (dependent in a static state on the thriftiness of rentiers) in order to determine within what range of real-capital ratios the possible positions of equilibrium lie...the basic fallacy on which the 'production function' is erected is the idea that the marginal product of labour determines the wage rate.[1]

At times it seems that Mrs Robinson's chief criticism of neoclassical theory involves the concept of capital.[2] However, I believe the last sentence quoted above gets at the essence of her objections to neoclassical theory and also at the essence of the difference between the two theories. As shown in chapters 12–14, neoclassical theory does not depend upon *smooth* capital–labor substitutability. All the essential results may be obtained from fixed coefficient production models. Indeed, Mrs Robinson's technical specifications can form the basis of a neoclassical theory, so long as the value of capital is reckoned in terms of commodities. *The* difference between the two theories lies in the fact that Mrs Robinson rejects the notion that marginal productivity is related to the wage rate.

In a way, this is curious. Her model involves profit-maximizing entrepreneurs, more-or-less-pure competition, and perpetual full employment. In light of these three conditions, the marginal value product of labor must *equal* the wage rate (irrespective of whether it *determines* the wage rate).

[1] Robinson [1956, p. 414, footnote 1]. Italics supplied.
[2] See Robinson [1953] and [1955].

This perhaps explains why Mrs Robinson's results are so close to those of neoclassical theory.

Mrs Robinson's theory of distribution has been criticized on many grounds; among others (*a*) for ignoring the possibility of insufficient demand and unemployment; (*b*) the assumption of constant and fixed input coefficients; (*c*) the assumption that the different consumer items are produced in fixed proportions, so that 'consumption' may be treated as one aggregate good; and (*d*) the assumption that workers spend only on consumption goods. I think all of these are rather trivial and quibbling. In my own opinion, the only relevant issue is the following: given the postulate of 'golden age' growth, which is common both to Mrs Robinson's theory and to neoclassical theory, what is the more reasonable postulate concerning wage determination? If one is interested in business cycles or underemployment equilibria or disequilibria, perhaps the 'Keynesian' assumption is more appropriate. On the other hand, the neoclassical assumption seems to be the appropriate one for 'golden age' models.[1]

APPENDIX TO CHAPTER 15

CAPITAL VALUATION IN
MRS ROBINSON'S MODEL

The problem of capital valuation deserves somewhat more comment on two accounts. The first concerns the change in the value of capital in terms of commodities in response to a change in the wage rate. Suppose a wage rate has long prevailed and that competition has brought about equality between the supply price of a piece of capital and the present value of its expected earnings. Thus the value of capital in terms of commodities is the same whether reckoned in terms of cost of construction or expected earnings.

Now let a higher wage prevail. It is clear that under 'normal' circumstances the supply price of capital will increase. While the rate of profit, and thus the notional interest rate, is lower, the greater wage bill will generally cause an increase in the supply price of capital. On the other hand, it might seem that the present value of expected earnings would decrease. To be sure, the decrease in the notional interest rate tends to increase the present value. But quasi-rent per machine in real terms declines because output per head is unchanged. However, the *price* of

---

[1] If one wishes to make quibbling criticism, I think he should concentrate upon the lack of specification of technical conditions in the investment sector.

commodities usually increases in the same proportion as real quasi-rent declines, thus leaving quasi-rent in money terms the same.

This is easily explained. Under the 'golden age' assumptions, employment is not affected by the increase in the wage rate. Hence commodity output is unchanged. But the wage bill is greater, and the entire increase is spent on consumption (by the assumption that $s_w = 0$). Hence the price of commodities must increase with the wage rate. Quasi-rent per machine in money terms remains (approximately) unchanged, the discount rate is less; hence the value of capital per man in terms of commodities is usually greater.

The second item is the now-famous Ruth Cohen Curiosum or the reswitching of techniques. Suppose the Gamma-Beta wage has long prevailed. Since the two techniques yield the same rate of profit, we may assume that entrepreneurs hold a mixture of Gamma and Beta equipment. Now let the wage rate increase slightly. The cost of Gamma and Beta equipment will *normally* increase in the same proportion. Since quasi-rent per machine is greater with Beta equipment, the rate of profit with Beta equipment will normally be greater than with Gamma equipment. Entrepreneurs will accordingly switch from Gamma to Beta technique as their Gamma plants wear out (or become economically obsolete). Since the beta technique requires a higher real-capital ratio, a central proposition is established: an increase in the wage rate leads to an increase in the degree of mechanization, or what Wicksell called the 'height' of investment,[1] or what neoclassical economists would call a substitution of capital for labor.

There is an exception, however, whose importance is at best an empirical question and at worst a moot one. In the Gamma-Beta equilibrium, Beta equipment must cost more than Gamma equipment because its quasi-rent per man is greater. And, as we have seen above, *other things equal*, the cost of both types of equipment will increase proportionately when the wage rate increases, thereby causing a switch to the Beta technique. But it may happen that the gestation period (or period of production) of Gamma equipment is very long relative to that of Beta equipment. The supply price of Gamma equipment would accordingly be more sensitive to the notional interest rate used to accumulate cost. Thus when the notional interest rate falls, the price of Gamma equipment may increase proportionately less than Beta equipment. The effect may be so strong that the Gamma equipment becomes cheaper relative to Beta equipment in a greater proportion than its output per head is less. In this special case, entrepreneurs would have an incentive to switch to the Gamma technique. Thus an increase in the wage rate would cause a decrease in the degree of mechani-

[1] See especially Wicksell [1901, pp. 163–4].

zation or a decrease in the 'height' of investment. This is, of course, nothing more than the reswitching problem encountered in chapter 12.

To quote Mrs Robinson:

It seems on the whole rather unlikely that cases of this kind should be common, for more mechanised techniques usually require heavier and longer-lived plant, so that the sensitiveness of the cost of equipment to differences in the interest rate is likely to be greater for more than for less mechanised techniques, and where this is the case the perverse relationship between wages and mechanisation cannot arise. We may therefore take it as a general rule that a higher degree of mechanisation is associated with a higher, not a lower, level of wages in terms of product.[1]

[1] Robinson [1956, p. 110].

16

INDUCED BIAS OF INVENTION
AND THE THEORY OF DISTRIBUTIVE
SHARES

16.1 Introduction

The classification of inventions is straightforward. Further, determining the capital-using or labor-using character of any particular invention would also be straightforward if one could accurately observe the proper variables, i.e. the change in the marginal rate of technical substitution at a given capital–labor ratio or the change in the capital–output ratio at a given rate of interest. But, unfortunately, these changes cannot be accurately observed. At best, one can only determine, within statistical probability limits, the biased or neutral character of a stream of inventions over time.

Yet one can observe particular inventions and draw non-statistical inferences concerning their factor-saving effects. This, I would suggest, has been the cause of great mischief. The inventions typically observed are those that cause smaller machines and human labor to be replaced by larger machines: locomotives replaced wagon trains, and digital computers have more recently replaced desk calculators and file clerks. Even Pigou was presumably misled, for he wrote: 'Probably, however, the majority of inventions in the narrower sense would have to be reckoned as "labour-saving", because as Cassel has observed, "almost all the efforts of inventors are directed toward finding durable instruments to do work which has hitherto been done by hand."'[1]

Hicks agreed: '...there is no reason to question his [Pigou's] view that inventions have a decided bias in the labour-saving direction. It is indeed difficult to find cases of important capital-saving inventions—wireless is, of course, the standard case, but beyond that, although there can be little doubt that capital-saving inventions occur, they are not easily identified....'[2]

Despite the weight of authority supporting these inferences, they are totally without foundation. Human labor is organized with machinery of one kind; after an invention, it is organized with a different type. Regardless

---

[1] Pigou [1932, p. 675].

[2] Hicks [1932, p. 123]. Professor Hicks, one must observe, has seldom reasoned and written so poorly.

336

of appearances, one simply cannot tell *a priori* what effect this reorganization will have upon the ratio of relative factor shares. Consequently, *a priori* inferences concerning the factor-saving effects of an invention are simply not possible.

16.1.1 Hicks on induced bias

Hicks not only endorsed Pigou's casual empiricism; he tried to give an explanation of it. In doing so, he laid the foundations for the many theories of induced bias that followed. 'The real reason for the predominance of labour-saving inventions,' Hicks wrote, 'is surely that which was hinted at in our discussion of substitution. A change in the relative prices of the factors of production is itself a spur to invention and to invention of a particular kind—directed to economizing the use of a factor which has become relatively expensive. The general tendency to a more rapid increase of capital than labour...has naturally provided a stimulus to labour-saving invention.'[1]

Hicks' view, in other words, is that if labor becomes dear relative to capital, the search for labor-saving inventions is stimulated. In general, this argument is not valid. All imputs are equally dear and equally productive at the margin, providing a 'margin' exists.[2] A change in relative prices leads to factor substitution that re-establishes the margin. So long as technical substitution is possible, one input will never become 'dear' relative to another.

This seems to be what Salter had in mind when he commented upon Hicks' theory as follows:

If one takes this to mean that new labour-saving designs are derived within the fold of existing knowledge, then the process is equivalent to substitution within the designing process...It is simply a matter of words whether one terms new techniques of this character inventions or a form of factor substitution. If, however, the theory implies that dearer labour stimulates the search for new knowledge aimed specifically at saving labour, then it is open to serious objections. The entrepreneur is interested in reducing costs in total, not particular costs such as labour costs or capital costs. When labour costs rise any advance that reduces total cost is welcome, and whether this is achieved by saving labour or capital is irrelevant. There is no reason to assume that attention should be concentrated on labour-saving techniques, unless, because of some inherent characteristic of technology, labour-saving knowledge is easier to acquire than capital-saving knowledge.[3]

In my opinion, this convincingly refutes the Hicks thesis.

[1] Hicks [1932, pp. 124–5].
[2] Of course, Hicks' argument is valid if the production function takes the Leontief form.
[3] Salter [1960, pp. 43–4].

16.1.2 Fellner's rehabilitation[1]

Hicks' theory may be rehabilitated, however, if expectations and/or learning are introduced in the model. More specifically, a preference may develop for inventions that are particularly factor saving in the resource that is becoming more scarce. A *learning process* may induce atomistic firms to behave as though they were large enough to notice the macroeconomic fact that factors of production do not have infinitely elastic supply curves.

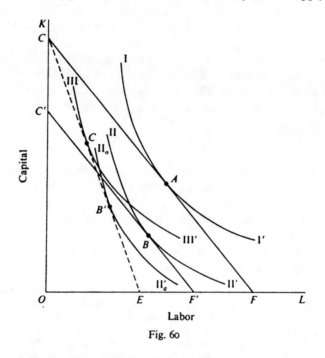

Fig. 60

That is, entrepreneurs may *expect* the wage rate to rise relative to capital rentals even though they realize that their individual actions do not appreciably affect relative factor prices. This expectations hypothesis forms the basis for one of Fellner's models of induced bias, which is illustrated in figure 60.

The graph depicts a typical isoquant-isocost equilibrium at point A on the isoquant I-I' and the isocost CF. Now suppose the entrepreneur must choose between expending research effort to develop innovations described by isoquants II-II' and III-III'. Given the *prevailing* factor-price ratio ($C'F'$ parallel to CF), technology II-II', with equilibrium at B, is superior

[1] See Fellner [1956], [1961 a, b], [1962] and [1966], especially [1961 a].

to the technology *III–III'*. However, if entrepreneurs expect wages to rise relative to the rate of return on capital, *II–II'* will no longer be superior.

Suppose, in particular, that wages are expected to rise so that the dashed line *CE* becomes the relevant expected isocost curve. Then technology *III–III'*, with equilibrium at point *C*, is clearly superior to technology *II–II'*. And most important of all, the organization at *C* is capital intensive relative to the organization at *B*. Thus in a sense one may say that the expectation of a rise in wages relative to the rate of return induced a labor-saving bias in technological change.

This model may be generalized somewhat. At a given moment of time, suppose the firm has attained an isoquant-isocost (optimum combination of resources) equilibrium. Further suppose there are a finite number of technological changes the firm can hope to bring about; it must select one of these. The various technologies that result in the *I–I'* level of output at lower cost are represented in figure 60 by *II–II'* and *III–III'*. The expectation of a rise in the relative wage rate will always lead to the selection of a more capital-intensive technology and, hence, to an induced labor-saving bias.

In terms of the figure, the *III–III'* level of output, with optimal input combination, could be achieved by *IIₐ–IIₐ'*, which is an inward extension of *II–II'*. However, the level of inventive activity, and consequently the cost of invention, would be greater. Hence the rational entrepreneur will choose the labor-saving technology *III–III'*.

Fellner's first model is based upon the assumption of atomistic competition. His second model, illustrated in figure 61, is based upon a monopsony–oligopsony assumption. If relative labor scarcity is increasing rapidly,[1] it may be impossible for firms to employ additional units of labor at a constant price. The firm should then recognize its monopsonistic position and act accordingly. 'Acting accordingly', as will be shown, leads to an induced labor-saving bias in technological change.

In figure 61, *CC'* is a constant input-price isocost curve, and *A* and *B* are two technologies capable of producing the same level of output. With constant input prices, an entrepreneur would be indifferent between the two technologies because the *F-* and *E*-equilibria are both marginally efficient at the same output level.

On the other hand, suppose at the labor usage level represented by *G*, the entrepreneur expects the supply of labor to become less than perfectly elastic, i.e. he expects to become a monopsonist or an oligopsonist. The isocost curve then becomes *CGC''*.[2] In this case, an enterpreneur would

---

[1] The reader is warned that he must put a very loose interpretation on 'relative labor scarcity'. To repeat, at the margin all resources are equally scarce, dear, and productive. All of this may be obviated by the straight-forward assumption of monopsony.

[2] See chapter 8 for the shape of the isocost curve when factor prices are variable.

definitely prefer technology A to technology B because with the latter, output would be $B' < B = A$. Since the equilibrium at F with technology A is capital intensive relative to the equilibrium at E' with technology B, there is, in a certain sense, an induced labor-saving bias in the selection between (more generally, among) technologies.

In summary: Fellner's models are based upon the assumption that entrepreneurs expect the relative price of labor to increase. Therefore an

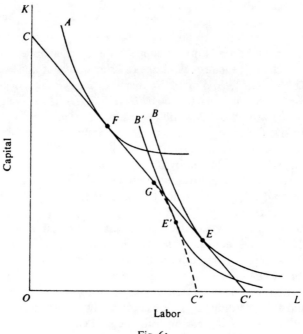

Fig. 61

entrepreneur, in choosing among alternative technologies to which research effort is to be devoted, is led to select the relatively capital-intensive ones. Thus in a sense[1] one may say that the expectation of a rise in the relative wage rate induces entrepreneurs to concentrate inventive activity on relatively labor-saving technological changes. As a consequence, one may also say that the introduction of expectations in a sense rehabilitates Hicks' theory of induced labor-saving bias.

[1] The qualifying phrase 'in a sense' has been used several times; by this expression I generally mean that while there is an appearance of labor-saving change, it is not strictly a labor-saving change in the Hicks sense. In Fellner's model one compares equilibria characterized by different capital–labor ratios.

16.1.3 Ahmad's rehabilitation[1]

Ahmad has taken an approach much different from that of Fellner in an attempt to resurrect Hicks' theory of induced bias. In particular, instead of assuming a finite number of potential technologies to which research effort may be devoted, Ahmad assumes the existence of an historical Innovation Possibility Curve (I.P.C.). This locus he defines as '...simply an envelope of all the alternative isoquants (representing a given output on various production functions) which the businessman expects to develop with the use of the available amount of innovating skill and time (assumed constant throughout the analysis).'[2]

The I.P.C. is, in Ahmad's words, 'a purely technological or laboratory question'. Economic considerations only come into play when a particular isoquant on an I.P.C. is selected.[3] The economic consideration used by Ahmad is minimization of the cost of producing a stipulated level of output.

Finally, Ahmad assumes that there is *no* technological bias in innovating, i.e. that historical innovation possibilities are neutral. Definitionally, I.P.C.'s are neutral

...if the innovation in response to any given relative factor price at time n (the time when the nth innovation is contemplated) is neutral to the innovation in response to the same relative factor price at time $(n-1)$. In terms of the curves the neutrality of the innovation possibility would require that the I.P.C.'s themselves possess the characteristics of two neutral isoquants, while the representative isoquants for each factor-price ratio are also neutral to each other.[4]

Ahmad's theory is illustrated by means of figure 62, where

C_{n-1}, C_n are I.P.C.'s for times $n-1$ and n;
I_{n-1}, I'_{n-1} are two isoquants on C_{n-1};
I_n, I'_n are two isoquants on C_n;
P_{n-1}, P'_{n-1} is the factor-price ratio at time $n-1$;
P_n, P'_n is the factor-price ratio at time n.

The original input-price ratio is represented by P_{n-1}. Given the I.P.C. denoted C_{n-1}, the isoquant I_{n-1} is chosen, and equilibrium is attained at point A. Now suppose the input-price ratio changes to P_n, i.e., the relative price of labor increases. In the short run the best the entrepreneur can do

---

[1] Ahmad [1966]. [2] Ahmad [1966, p. 347].
[3] The question of whether economic considerations should affect the I.P.C. has arisen. Kennedy [1964] made Ahmad's assumption; and Samuelson [1965] questioned it, suggesting that the ratio of relative shares might have a bearing. Kennedy [1966] rebutted Samuelson's argument and partially convinced him (Samuelson [1966a]) that the I.P.C. is a purely technological relation. But see section 16.4.
[4] Ahmad [1966, p. 348].

is to substitute capital for labor, moving from equilibrium at A to equilibrium at B, which is also on I_{n-1}. In contemplating innovation for period n, however, the entrepreneur will select isoquant I'_n rather than I_n because it is compatible with the new price ratio.[1] Now I'_n is capital intensive relative to I_n; so in a sense,[2] I'_n is labor saving relative to I_n. Since I_n is neutral relative to I_{n-1} by hypothesis, I'_n is also labor saving relative to I_{n-1}.

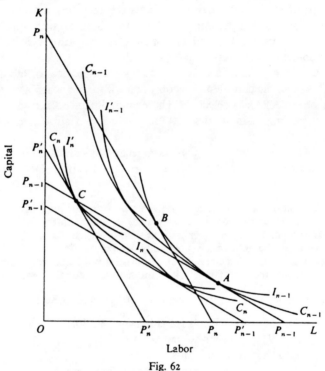

Fig. 62

In summary: Ahmad has built a model of induced labor-saving bias based upon actual, rather than expected, changes in the relative wage. From an initial situation, let wages rise relative to the rate of return on capital. In the short run the entrepreneur can only compensate by substituting capital for labor, given the technology. In the long run, however, he may choose the innovations upon which to concentrate. The point of Ahmad's model, just as that of Fellner's, is simply this: the existence of a relatively higher wage rate makes a relatively capital-intensive invention

[1] In other words, if the technology described by I_n were selected, equilibrium output would be less than that shown by I'_n, while the cost of production would be the same.
[2] See footnote 1, p. 340 above.

more attractive than a relatively labor-intensive invention. In the restricted sense discussed above, this may be called an induced labor-saving bias in technological progress.

16.2 Induced bias and the theory of distribution

The discussion in section 16.1 above relates to theories of induced bias based upon actual or expected changes in relative factor prices. And, in particular, these theories have no implications for the theory of distribution. The signal achievement of Kennedy, if such it be, is his development of a theory of induced bias that (a) is independent of changing relative factor prices, and (b) implies a theory of distributive shares.

Indeed, Kennedy attributes the lack of development of Hicks' theory to its reliance upon changing factor prices. 'One of the reasons why Professor Hicks' theory of induced invention has not been developed as far as it might have been is that it was tied to changes in relative factor prices. This at once brought the theory up against the difficulty of drawing a sharp distinction between the substitution of capital for labour and labour-saving innovation.'[1] That is to say, Hicks' theory is tied to the concept of a production function; Kennedy felt this association should be removed. To this end, he introduced the concept of an 'innovation-possibility frontier', stating, 'Following Kaldor, and recognizing the very great difficulty in principle and impossibility in practice of distinguishing factor substitution from bias in innovation, I had hoped that the innovation-possibility frontier might be able, so to speak, to swallow up the traditional production function and replace it altogether.'[2]

Kennedy succeeded in that his theory represents a logically consistent alternative theory of distribution. Whether one likes the theory and/or its implications is another matter altogether; Kennedy's theory is a genuine alternative.

16.2.1 Kennedy's basic model[3]

Assume that technical progress takes place only in the consumption sector, that the rate of interest is constant, that labor is homogeneous, that production functions are homogeneous of degree one, and that there is perfect competition in both output and input markets. This set of assumptions guarantees the constancy of relative factor prices, so attention may be directed exclusively to technical progress in the consumption sector.[4]

---

[1] Kennedy [1964, p. 542].   [2] Kennedy [1966, p. 442].   [3] Kennedy [1964].
[4] Thus Kennedy divorces his theory of induced bias from changes in relative factor prices. '...there is a good deal to be gained by presenting the theory in the first instance in a model in which relative factor prices do not change. Such a model is, of course, not to be regarded as realistic, since there is no doubt that technical progress in the

Denote the proportion of total cost attributable to labor by λ and the proportion attributable to capital by γ. Hence $\lambda + \gamma \equiv 1$; and by the competitive assumptions above, λ and γ are also the relative shares of labor and capital respectively. Generally, a technical improvement reduces the amount of both labor and capital required to produce a unit of output. Let p and q represent the proportional reductions in labor and capital respectively.[1] Thus a technical change may be defined as labor saving, neutral, or capital saving according as $p \gtreqless q$.

Next, assume entrepreneurs choose, or at least search for, improvements that reduce *unit* cost by the greatest proportion. With constant factor prices, the proportionate reduction in unit cost is

$$r = \lambda p + \gamma q. \qquad (16.2.1)$$

Thus the entrepreneurial choice is not merely a *technological* matter; it is influenced by the economic weights λ and γ, i.e. by the relative shares of the factors.

Finally, assume that the proportional factor reductions are related by an innovation-possibility, transformation, or trade-off curve. This assumption may be written implicitly as

$$\phi(p, q) = 0, \qquad (16.2.2)$$

or explicitly as
$$p = f(q). \qquad (16.2.3)$$

Either form of the innovation-possibility frontier is based upon the assumption that innovation possibilities are governed by purely technological relations and, in particular, are not affected by economic magnitudes.[2]

Given these assumptions, the object of the entrepreneur is to maximize equation (16.2.1) subject to the constraint (16.2.3). To this end, construct the Lagrange function
$$L \equiv \lambda p + \gamma q - \beta[p - f(q)], \qquad (16.2.4)$$

capital-goods industries does lead to a secular fall in the price of capital goods relative to labour.' Kennedy [1964, p. 542]. As shown below, when relative factor prices are variable, some very peculiar results emerge.

[1] Both proportional reductions do not have to be positive. For example, a very high p may require a negative q. That is, a technical improvement may reduce the labor requirement per unit of output so much that the corresponding capital requirement increases. Figures 63 to 65 are constructed so that the innovation possibility frontier lies in both the northwest and southeast quadrants.

[2] See footnote 3, p. 341 above. Referring to the constraint $\phi(p, q) = 0$, Kennedy wrote: 'But there is no reason why this restraint should be the particular one

$$\lambda p + \gamma q = \text{constant}$$

as is implied by Salter's treatment of r as being independently given. Indeed, there is a very good reason why it should not be. In principle, the restraint on the innovation possibilities should be a purely technological one, and the introduction of the economic weights λ and γ into the restraint is therefore improper.' Kennedy [1964, pp. 543-4].

where β is the undetermined multiplier. The first-order conditions give

$$\left.\begin{aligned}\frac{\partial L}{\partial p} &= \lambda - \beta = 0, \\[4pt]\frac{\partial L}{\partial q} &= \gamma + \beta f'(q) = 0, \\[4pt]\frac{\partial L}{\partial \beta} &= p - f(q) = 0.\end{aligned}\right\} \qquad (16.2.5)$$

Eliminating the multiplier and recalling that $f'(q) = dp/dq$, the equilibrium solution may be written

$$\frac{dp}{dq} = -\frac{\gamma}{\lambda}. \qquad (16.2.6)$$

16.2.2 Interpretation

Since λ and γ are necessarily positive, it follows from equation (16.2.6) that

$$\frac{dp}{dq} < 0. \qquad (16.2.7)$$

This is exactly what one should expect. As Kennedy put it, '...the greater the reduction in the labour required to produce a unit of output, the smaller will be the possible reduction in capital required'.[1]

Second, Kennedy argues that

$$\frac{d^2 p}{dq^2} < 0 \qquad (16.2.8)$$

because, 'It is clear that for p to approach its upper limit of 1, even if this were at all possible, very large increases in the amount of capital would be required. Similarly, for q to approach 1, very large increases in labour would be required.'[2] Hence the innovation-possibility frontier $p = f(q)$ has the curvature shown in figure 63 [by inequalities (16.2.7) and (16.2.8)].

As a digression, we may note that it is not necessary to *assume* that inequality (16.2.8) holds, as Kennedy does. From equations (16.2.5), the second-order condition for a constrained maximum requires that

$$\begin{vmatrix} 0 & 1 & 0 \\ 1 & 0 & 0 \\ 0 & 0 & \beta f''(q) \end{vmatrix} = -\beta f''(q) > 0. \qquad (16.2.9)$$

Since $\beta > 0$, inequality (16.2.9) implies the condition (16.2.8).

Let us return to the diagram. The proportionate cost reduction that is to be maximized may be written, from equation (16.2.1), as

$$p = \frac{1}{\lambda} r - \frac{\gamma}{\lambda} q. \qquad (16.2.10)$$

---

[1] Kennedy [1964, p. 544].   [2] *Ibid.*

Hence its slope is
$$\frac{dp}{dq} = -\frac{\gamma}{\lambda}.$$
(16.2.11)

Equations (16.2.6) and (16.2.11) jointly imply a tangency solution such as those illustrated in figure 63.

If λ is large relative to γ, i.e. if the relative share of labor is large in comparison with the relative share of capital, the slope at the point of tangency will be very gentle. Thus the equilibrium $p-q$ values will have

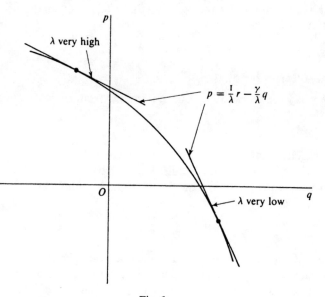

Fig. 63

p large relative to q; indeed, q may even be negative. Since $p > q$ implies a labor-saving bias in technological progress, one concludes that if the relative share of labor exceeds the relative share of capital, there will be an induced labor-saving bias in technological progress.

16.2.3 The theory of distribution

There is a theory of distribution, indeed of constant relative shares, embodied in Kennedy's theory of induced bias. The theory is illustrated in figure 64. A bias in innovation in any one period will change the weights or shares (λ and γ) in the next period. For example, suppose a temporary equilibrium is attained at a point where $p > q$. There is accordingly labor-saving technological progress, which reduces labor's relative share. As a consequence, λ falls and γ rises, thereby increasing the equilibrium slope in the next period. The opposite forces work from an initial temporary equilibrium in which $q > p$.

Now assume that the characteristics of the innovation-possibility frontiers are the same in all periods. The above analysis implies that equilibrium values of the weights, or relative shares, will be established when $p = q$. When $p = q$, there is neutral technological progress, accompanied by constancy of shares. When shares are constant, the weights do not change; and since the innovation-possibility frontier is invariant by assumption, these equilibrium values of the weights persist.[1]

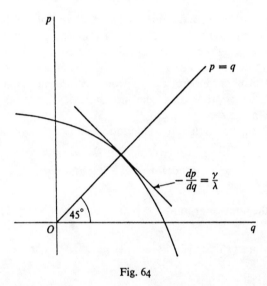

Fig. 64

Thus a stable equilibrium is established in which technological progress is neutral and relative shares are constant. The ratio of relative shares in this equilibrium is given by the slope of the (strictly technologically determined) innovation-possibility frontier. In particular, if $-(dp/dq) < 1$, the relative share of labor will exceed the relative share of capital.[2]

---

[1] The equilibrium is stable since when $p \neq q$, there will be an induced bias in innovation that will tend to restore the equilibrium value.

[2] Kennedy refers to this as an innovational bias; but this terminology can easily lead to confusion since there is neutral technological progress in equilibrium. For the record, Kennedy says that, 'This particular value of dp/dq may be taken as a indicator of the fundamental technological bias in innovation possibilities. If, for $p = q$, dp/dq is greater than one, we may say that there is a labour-saving technological bias, which will result in a higher equilibrium value of γ than of λ.' Kennedy [1964, p. 545]. Let me repeat: there is neutral technological progress. According to Kennedy, the innovational bias is labor-saving or capital saving according as the relative share of capital exceeds or falls short of the relative share of labor.

347

16.2.4 Technical progress in the capital sector

It is now possible to relax the assumption that technical progress is restricted to the consumption sector, or what is the same, to restrict the analysis to a one-sector model. To this end, suppose there is technical progress in the capital sector. The $p = q$ condition will no longer be an equilibrium solution because the share of capital cost in total cost is continuously reduced by the fall in the unit cost of producing capital goods, which is brought about by technological progress in the capital-goods sector.

Let the proportionate reduction in the unit cost of producing capital goods be s. Then in the consumption sector, the equilibrium condition for the weights, following the analysis in subsection 16.2.3 above, is $p = q+s$. Since $-dp/dq$ must be lower when $p > q$ than when $p = q$, it follows that technological progress in the capital-goods sector will result in a higher equilibrium share of labor than when technological progress is restricted to the consumption sector alone.

In general, the proportionate reduction in unit cost is given by

$$r = \lambda p + \gamma(q+s). \tag{16 2.12}$$

However, in a one-sector model, $r = s$. Thus in this case,

$$r = \lambda p + \gamma(q+r). \tag{16.2.13}$$

Similarly, in the one-sector model, constant-share equilibrium requires that

$$p = q+r. \tag{16.2.14}$$

Solving equations (16.2.13) and (16.2.14) simultaneously yields

$$\left.\begin{array}{l} p = r, \\ q = 0, \end{array}\right\} \tag{16.2.15}$$

which is illustrated in figure 65.

As equations (16.2.15) show, equilibrium in a one-sector model ultimately requires that the rate of reduction in capital per unit of output equal zero. This condition, in turn, implies a constant capital–output ratio. Now recall the assumption that the rate of interest is constant. Constancy of the capital–output ratio and the rate of interest jointly imply the existence of Harrod-neutral technological progress; and Harrod-neutrality, as shown in chapter 12, implies constancy of relative shares.

Shifting from a two-sector model in which technical progress occurs only in the consumption sector to a one-sector model involves some changes. In particular, the equilibrium nature of technological progress changes from Hicks-neutrality to Harrod-neutrality.[1] But in both cases,

---

[1] Hicks- and Harrod-neutrality are the same, of course, if the production function (s) is Cobb–Douglas. For the peculiarities of this special case, see section 16.3 below.

relative shares are constant, their ratio being determined by the slope of the technologically determined innovation-possibility curve.

Thus Kennedy's theory of distribution is established. And given the assumptions involved, especially the assumption that the production function need not be specified, Kennedy's theory is a logically valid alternative to the neoclassical theory.

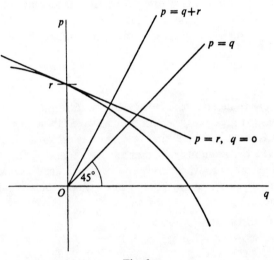

Fig. 65

16.2.5 Ahmad's criticism[1]

Changing assumptions almost always involves changing conclusions. Since Ahmad's criticism essentially amounts to a change in assumptions, it may be regarded as no criticism at all. Nonetheless, it does highlight one important question. The innovation-possibility frontier is a new concept. *What properties* should be imputed to it? Kennedy suggested that the frontier should relate the *proportion* of one factor that could be saved to the *proportion* saved of the other factor. Ahmad, on the other hand, suggests that the frontier should relate the *amount* of one factor saved per unit of output to the *amount* of the other factor saved. Hence the difference simply involves proportions versus absolute amounts. At the present state of knowledge, it is impossible to say which is the more plausible assumption. This section simply underscores the fact that the inferences drawn from the models are not invariant to the assumptions made.

[1] Ahmad [1966].

349

INDUCED BIAS AND DISTRIBUTION

Let u and v denote the amounts of labor and capital saved per unit of output respectively, and let w and r be the wage and rental rates. Thus the amount saved per unit of output is

$$z = uw + vr, \qquad (16.2.16)$$

where
$$u = u(v) \qquad (16.2.17)$$

is a transformation function whose properties are exactly like Kennedy's $p = f(q)$, i.e. $u' < 0$ and $u'' < 0$.

Maximizing equation (16.2.16) subject to constraint (16.2.17) yields

$$\frac{du}{dv} = -\frac{r}{w}. \qquad (16.2.18)$$

Thus factor prices determine factor saving; and in particular, the higher the wage rate, the greater is the tendency to save labor.

Following Kennedy, assume that factor prices are given, Thus equation (16.2.18) shows the amounts of factor savings, u and v. But the induced bias, according to Kennedy, depends upon p and q. Let L and K denote the initial usages of labour and capital. Thus induced bias is labor saving, neutral, or capital saving according as

$$p \equiv \frac{u}{L} \gtreqless q \equiv \frac{v}{K}. \qquad (16.2.19)$$

Expression (16.2.19) embodies a conclusion that is directly opposite to that of Kennedy's model. The greater the initial usage of labor relative to capital, the greater will be labor's relative share for given factor prices. But by expression (16.2.19), the greater is L, the less likely is the induced innovation to be labor saving.

Ahmad's evaluation is worth citing: 'The special nature of Kennedy's case consists in his assumption that the proportion of a factor saved by an invention is independent of the amount of the factor used.... The above clearly shows that Kennedy's assumption is not general, and very different results may be obtained regarding the influence of the same factors on the nature of invention if we make assumptions different from his.'[1]

As noted above, when assumptions are changed, we expect the conclusions to change as well. Ahmad has illustrated this. But he has not shed light upon the interesting question: If one is to deal with the concept of an innovation-possibility frontier, which is the more plausible assumption?

[1] *Ibid.* pp. 352–3.

16.3 Induced innovations and production functions: the Samuelson model[1,2]

As noted above, the model of induced bias *as presented by Kennedy* is a genuinely alternative theory of distribution. Economists of neoclassical persuasion, however, may well ask whether the explicit use of production functions in the model of induced bias will result in a theory of distribution appreciably different from neoclassical theory. To settle this issue is the object of Professor Samuelson's exercise. In one case, Kennedy's exact results are obtained; but even then, one must require that the neoclassical elasticity of substitution be less than unity.

16.3.1 Basic model

Suppose the neoclassical production function, which is assumed to be homogeneous of degree one, takes the purely factor-augmenting form

$$Y = F\left(\frac{L}{\lambda_1(t)}, \frac{K}{\lambda_2(t)}\right). \tag{16.3.1}$$

Thus a reduction in (say) λ_1 reduces the amount of labor (in natural units) needed to produce any given level of output. From equation (16.3.1), the rates of improvement or of factor augmentation are

$$-\frac{1}{\lambda_i}\frac{d\lambda_i}{dt} = \frac{\dot{\lambda_i}}{\lambda_i} = q_i \quad (i=L, K). \tag{16.3.2}$$

Following Kennedy, Samuelson assumes that a greater decrease in λ_1 can be achieved only at the expense of a lesser decrease, or perhaps even an increase, in λ_2.[3] One may accordingly write the Kennedy innovation-possibility frontier as

$$q_2 = f(q_1), \tag{16.3.3}$$

where

$$f'(q_1) < 0, \quad f''(q_1) < 0. \tag{16.3.4}$$

Samuelson's frontier is, in all respects, the same as Kennedy's.

Consider any given set of factor prices (w, r). This set of prices, together with the production function, determines the minimum unit cost of pro-

---

[1] See Samuelson [1965] and [1966a]. For comment, see Kennedy [1966]. For closely related models, see Drandakis and Phelps [1966] and K. Sato [1965].

[2] The mathematical notation in this chapter is regrettable. There was a choice of developing a uniform notation, of following each author discussed, or of following but modifying the notation of each author. With some apologies, I have elected the final option. A similar model, using the notation of chapters 11 and 12, is presented in section 16.4 below.

[3] This is not exactly Samuelson's assumption. In Samuelson [1965], the innovation-possibility frontier is restricted to the positive quadrant. In [1966a], Samuelson points out that this restriction is not necessary, but using it does not affect the results.

duction, which may be written implicitly as

$$M = M[w\lambda_1(t), r\lambda_2(t)] \tag{16.3.5}$$

or explicitly as

$$M = \min [wL + rK] \quad \text{subject to} \quad F(L, K) = 1. \tag{16.3.6}$$

Holding factor prices constant, as Kennedy does, the instantaneous rate of reduction in unit cost is

$$\frac{\dot{M}}{M} = \frac{w\lambda_1}{w\lambda_1 + r\lambda_2}\frac{\dot{\lambda}_1}{\lambda_1} + \frac{r\lambda_2}{w\lambda_1 + r\lambda_2}\frac{\dot{\lambda}_2}{\lambda_2}, \tag{16.3.7}$$

or

$$-\frac{\dot{M}}{M} = \alpha_1 q_1 + \alpha_2 q_2, \tag{16.3.8}$$

where the α_i's are the relative factor shares, i.e.

$$\alpha_1 = \frac{w\lambda_1}{w_1\lambda_1 + w_2\lambda_2} = \frac{wL}{MF}, \quad \alpha_2 = 1 - \alpha_1. \tag{16.3.9}$$

Still following Kennedy, assume that the object is to maximize the instantaneous rate of cost reduction, which is the same as minimizing equation (16.3.8), subject to the constraint imposed by the innovation-possibility frontier. Construct the Lagrange function

$$L \equiv \alpha_1 q_1 + \alpha_2 q_2 - \nu[f(q_1) - q_2], \tag{16.3.10}$$

where ν is the undetermined multiplier. The first-order conditions give

$$\left.\begin{aligned}\frac{\partial L}{\partial \nu} &= f(q_1) - q_2 = 0,\\[4pt]\frac{\partial L}{\partial q_1} &= \alpha_1 - \nu f'(q_1) = 0,\\[4pt]\frac{\partial L}{\partial q_2} &= \alpha_2 + \nu = 0,\end{aligned}\right\} \tag{16.3.11}$$

while the second-order condition requires that

$$\begin{vmatrix} 0 & 0 & 1 \\ 0 & -\nu f''(q_1) & 0 \\ 1 & 0 & 0 \end{vmatrix} = \nu f''(q_1) < 0. \tag{16.3.12}$$

The first-order conditions may be solved to obtain the familiar results:

$$-f'(q_1) = \frac{\alpha_1}{\alpha_2}. \tag{16.3.13}$$

Equation (16.3.13) represents the tangency condition. In equilibrium, the slope of the technologically determined innovation-possibility frontier must equal the ratio of labor's share to capital's share.[1] The second-order condition shows that the innovation-possibility frontier must be concave from below.

Now consider the following definition:

$$\frac{\alpha_1}{\alpha_2} = \frac{(wL/F)}{(rK/F)} = \frac{wL}{rK} = \frac{w\lambda_1}{r\lambda_2}. \tag{16.3.14}$$

Using equation (16.3.14) in the inversion of equation (16.3.13) and appending condition (16.3.3) gives the two differential equations of the model:

$$\left.\begin{aligned} -\frac{\dot{\lambda}_1}{\lambda_1} &= g\left(\frac{\lambda_1}{\lambda_2}\frac{w}{r}\right), \\ -\frac{\dot{\lambda}_2}{\lambda_2} &= f\left(-\frac{\dot{\lambda}_1}{\lambda_1}\right). \end{aligned}\right\} \tag{16.3.15}$$

The sign of $f'(\cdot)$ is known from inequalities (16.3.4). The sign of $g'(\cdot)$ depends upon the elasticity of substitution (σ). Suppose it is less than one. Then an increase in the effective capital–labor ratio will increase the relative share of labor and thereby increase the rate of induced labor-productivity augmentation. The opposite applies when $\sigma > 1$. Hence we have

$$g'\left(\frac{\lambda_1}{\lambda_2}\frac{w}{r}\right) \gtreqless 0 \quad \text{according as} \quad \sigma \lesseqgtr 1. \tag{16.3.16}$$

16.3.2 Stability with Hicks-neutral progress

Suppose, as in Kennedy's first model, that capital and labor in natural units are constant or that they grow at the same rate. Further, suppose there is an initial tangency equilibrium at a point such as A in figure 66, where the rate of labor augmentation exceeds the rate of capital augmentation. If the elasticity of substitution is less than unity,[2] technological progress has a capital-using or labor-saving bias. The relative share of capital increases and that of labor declines; the cost reduction line rotates to the left, becoming less steep. This must continue so long as $q_1 > q_2$, and the reverse movement occurs when $q_2 > q_1$. Graphically, therefore, permanent equilibrium is attained at B, where $q_2^* = q_1^* = q^*$ and $\alpha_1 = \alpha_1^*$ and $\alpha_2 = \alpha_2^*$. But this is a stable equilibrium, with the implied factor shares, if and only if $\sigma < 1$.

---

[1] This is actually Kennedy's result. The verbal difference lies in the fact that Kennedy assumes that the rate of labor improvement is a function of the rate of capital improvement, while Samuelson assumes the opposite. Graphically, the axes are reversed.

[2] See chapter 11 for the relation between the value of the elasticity of substitution and the factor-saving character of technological change.

Mathematically, Hicks-neutrality requires that there exist a root q^* of equations (16.3.15) such that

$$-\frac{\dot{\lambda}_1}{\lambda_1} = -\frac{\dot{\lambda}_2}{\lambda_2} = q^* = f(q^*). \qquad (16.3.17)$$

If such a root exists, and if

$$\lambda_i(t)_{\cdot} = \lambda_i(t_0)\, e^{-q^* t}, \qquad (16.3.18)$$

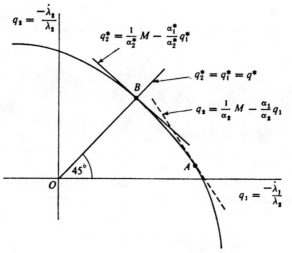

Fig. 66

either initially or asymptotically, then equation (16.3.13) gives the asymptotic equilibrium values of the relative shares:

$$\frac{\alpha_1^*}{\alpha_2^*} = -f'(q^*). \qquad (16.3.19)$$

To quote Samuelson: 'Equations (16.3.17) and (16.3.19) constitute a "theory of relative shares", but the marginal productivity equation... warns us that this is in no genuine sense an "alternative theory" of distribution to the neoclassical one.'[1]

16.3.3 Dynamic properties of the Hicks-neutral model; the Cobb–Douglas case

From inequalities (16.3.16) one gets a hint that the dynamic process is likely to be stable only if $\sigma < 1$. This is reinforced by the verbal-graphical argument presented above. It is now time to turn to a more systematic exposition of the dynamic properties of the model.

[1] Samuelson [1965, p. 344]. Equation numbers changed so as to correspond to the equation numbers in this chapter.

Let us begin with a special case, which might not be so special from a statistical standpoint. Let the production function take the Cobb–Douglas form:

$$f(L, K; t) = A(t) \left(\frac{L}{\lambda_1}\right)^{\frac{3}{4}} \left(\frac{K}{\lambda_2}\right)^{\frac{1}{4}}. \qquad (16.3.20)$$

Thus $\sigma \equiv 1$, $\alpha_1 = \frac{3}{4}$, $\alpha_2 = \frac{1}{4}$. From inequalities (16.3.16), $g'(\cdot) \equiv 0$, so

$$g\left(\frac{\lambda_1}{\lambda_2} \frac{w}{r}\right) = \beta_1, \qquad (16.3.21)$$

where β_1 is a constant. Then, from equations (16.3.15), one has

$$\left.\begin{aligned} -\frac{\dot{\lambda}_1}{\lambda_1} &= \beta_1; & \lambda_1 &= \beta e^{-\beta_1 t}, \\ -\frac{\dot{\lambda}_2}{\lambda_2} &= f(\beta_1) = \beta_2; & \lambda_2 &= \beta' e^{-\beta_2 t}, \end{aligned}\right\} \qquad (16.3.22)$$

where β, β' and β_2 are constants. Thus

$$\frac{\lambda_2}{\lambda_1} = \beta'' e^{(\beta_1 - \beta_2)t}, \qquad (16.3.23)$$

where $\beta'' = \beta'/\beta$. Consequently, the factor-improvement ratio goes to zero or infinity according as $\beta_2 \gtrless \beta_1$.

Since there is no *a priori* reason to suppose that β_1 is either greater than or less than β_2, one might make what Samuelson calls the 'equal ignorance' assumption that $f(q_1)$ is a symmetric function, i.e.

$$q_2 = f(q_1) \quad \text{implies} \quad q_1 = f(q_2). \qquad (16.3.24)$$

In this case, $\qquad q^* = f(q^*) \quad \text{implies} \quad -f'(q^*) = 1, \qquad (16.3.25)$

from whence it follows that the solution of equation (16.3.19) is

$$\alpha_1^* = \alpha_2^* = \tfrac{1}{2}. \qquad (16.3.26)$$

The Cobb–Douglas case is indeed special since $\sigma \equiv 1$. Yet it is of some significance. To obtain Kennedy's Hicks-neutral solution, one must assume that the innovation-possibility frontier is a symmetric function. In this case, the implication of Kennedy's theory is equal relative shares [see equation (16.3.26)]. From equation (16.3.20), the marginal productivity implication is $\alpha_1 = \frac{3}{4}$, $\alpha_2 = \frac{1}{4}$. To quote Samuelson again: 'The C–D case is significant because in it the Kennedy distribution-of-income condition... has no relevance to actual income distibution. Except by fluke, the actual $(\frac{3}{4}, \frac{1}{4})$ income distribution dictated by C–D marginal productivity will differ from the Kennedy distribution of $(\frac{1}{2}, \frac{1}{2})$....'[1]

[1] *Ibid.* p. 345.

16.3.4 Dynamic properties; general case

Now drop the assumption that the production function has the Cobb–Douglas form, but retain Kennedy's assumption that the factor-price ratio is a constant. To investigate the possibility of dynamic stability with Hicks-neutrality, subtract the second equation in expressions (16.3.15) from the first, obtaining

$$-\frac{\dot{\lambda}_1}{\lambda_1}+\frac{\dot{\lambda}_2}{\lambda_2} = -\frac{\dot{\lambda}_1}{\lambda_1}-f\left(\frac{\dot{\lambda}_1}{\lambda_1}\right) = \phi\left(-\frac{\dot{\lambda}_1}{\lambda_1}\right)$$

$$= \phi\left[g\left(\frac{\lambda_1}{\lambda_2}\frac{w}{r}\right)\right] = \phi\left[h\left(\frac{\lambda_2}{\lambda_1}\frac{w}{r}\right)\right] = \psi\left(\frac{\lambda_2}{\lambda_1}\right). \quad (16.3.27)$$

More simply, the differential equation in the factor-improvement ratio may be written

$$\frac{1}{(\lambda_2/\lambda_1)}\frac{d(\lambda_2/\lambda_1)}{dt} = \psi\left(\frac{\lambda_2}{\lambda_1}\right), \quad (16.3.28)$$

where

$$\text{sign } \psi' = -\text{sign } g' = \text{sign } h' = \text{sign } (\sigma-1). \quad (16.3.29)$$

From equations (16.3.28) and (16.3.29), a stable solution of the form

$$\psi\left(\frac{\lambda_2}{\lambda_1}\right)^* = 0 \quad (16.3.30)$$

will exist if, and only if, $\psi' < 0$, which implies that σ must lie in the unit interval.

If these conditions are satisfied, there will be a state of Hicks-neutral technological progress in which the proportional rate of augmentation is the same for both factors. This may be stated as

Samuelson's Theorem I: Given a fixed factor-price ratio, if a Kennedy-neutral-change state exists, it will be stable or unstable according as the elasticity of substitution is less than or greater than unity.

Perhaps more important than the theorem, however, are the reservations implicit in it. First, there may be no stable equilibrium configuration that is compatible with Kennedy's model. Second, even if a stable equilibrium exists, the configuration with the Kennedy condition may not be compatible with the configuration dictated by competitive market imputations.

16.3.5 The model with changing factor prices

In the model as developed to this point, both relative factor prices and relative factor supplies have been held constant. Only the factor-augmentation ratio has been allowed to vary; it is thus not surprising to find that the constancy of this ratio is a necessary condition for a stable equilibrium. But this alone is not enough (see the Cobb–Douglas example above). The elasticity of substitution must lie properly within the unit interval. If so, a position of stable growth equilibrium is attainable and sustainable; in this equilibrium the ratio of relative shares as determined by the model of induced bias corresponds to the ratio determined by marginal productivities. In other cases, the ratios are not the same (except by accident). Given the conditions of the model, marginal productivities determine the *actual* relative shares. Relative shares as *predicted* from the innovation-trade-off model will, in general, not be the same.

It is now time to relax the assumptions. First suppose that factor prices are variable but that relative factor supplies remain constant. The marginal productivity conditions lead to the following ratio of relative shares:

$$\frac{\alpha_1}{\alpha_2} = \frac{wL}{\lambda_1}\frac{\lambda_2}{rK}.$$ (16.3.31)

The ratio of factor prices, being variable, is determined by the relative effective factor supplies, just as is the ratio of relative shares. Hence, equation (16.3.31) may be written

$$\frac{\alpha_1}{\alpha_2} = m\left(\frac{\lambda_2}{\lambda_1}\frac{L}{K}\right).$$ (16.3.32)

Using equation (16.3.32) in the inversion of equilibrium condition (16.3.13), the differential equations of the model are

$$-\frac{\dot\lambda_1}{\lambda_1} = n\left(\frac{\lambda_2}{\lambda_1}\frac{L}{K}\right),$$
$$-\frac{\dot\lambda_2}{\lambda_2} = f\left(-\frac{\dot\lambda_1}{\lambda_1}\right).$$ (16.3.33)

Thus we may write the proportional change in the factor-augmentation ratio as

$$-\frac{\dot\lambda_1}{\lambda_1}+\frac{\dot\lambda_2}{\lambda_2} = \frac{1}{(\lambda_2/\lambda_1)}\frac{d(\lambda_2/\lambda_1)}{dt} = n\left(\frac{\lambda_2}{\lambda_1}\frac{L}{K}\right)-f\left[n\left(\frac{\lambda_2}{\lambda_1}\frac{L}{K}\right)\right] = G\left(\frac{\lambda_2}{\lambda_1}\frac{L}{K}\right).$$ (16.3.34)

Suppose the effective capital–labor ratio increases. If the elasticity of substitution is less than unity, the relative share of labor will increase. Entrepreneurs will thus be induced to seek inventions that increase the rate of labor augmentation relative to the rate of capital augmentation. The opposite holds if the elasticity of substitution is greater than unity. The above argument therefore shows that

$$\text{sign } G'\left(\frac{\lambda_2}{\lambda_1}\frac{L}{K}\right) = \text{sign }(\sigma-1).$$ (16.3.35)

If relative factor supplies in natural units are constant, the system (16.3.33) will have a stable equilibrium state where

$$G\left(\frac{\lambda_2}{\lambda_1}\frac{L}{K}\right) = 0 \qquad (16.3.36)$$

if, and only if, $\qquad G'\left(\frac{\lambda_2}{\lambda_1}\frac{L}{K}\right) < 0. \qquad (16.3.37)$

Thus we may state

Samuelson's Theorem II: Suppose the capital–labor ratio in natural units is constant and entrepreneurs select the combination of factor augmentations that minimizes instantaneous unit cost reduction (subject to the innovation-possibility frontier). If σ is sufficiently bounded away from unity, $G\left(\frac{\lambda_2}{\lambda_1}\frac{L}{K}\right) = 0$ *may have one or more roots* at which the system undergoes Hicks-neutral technological progress. In such states,

$$q^* = f(q^*) \quad \text{and} \quad \frac{\alpha_1^*}{\alpha_2^*} = -f'(q^*).$$

Each equilibrium state will be stable or unstable according as the elasticity of substitution is less than or greater than unity. Further, if the innovation-possibility frontier is symmetric, stable equilibrium implies that $\alpha_1 = \alpha_2 = \frac{1}{2}$.

It may now be well to recount the reservations implicit in the italicized phrase above. First, $G(\cdot) = 0$ may have no real roots even though σ is bounded away from unity. Second, it may have multiple roots, each of which corresponds to a different steady state. However, a multiplicity of roots does not imply a multiplicity of relative shares since q^* is unique. Finally, if $\sigma > 1$, the system will diverge from the (α_1^*, α_2^*) equilibrium toward a single-factor augmenting state where one factor receives the entire product and the other has a zero price.

16.3.6 Variable factor supplies

Let us now relax the assumption that relative factor supplies are constant in favor of the more realistic assumption that capital in natural units grows relative to labor. In particular, assume that the capital–labor ratio in natural units grows at a constant exponential rate. Suppose the elasticity of substitution lies properly within the unit interval. Other things equal, the relative share of labor would approach unity asymptotically. Thus it is intuitively clear that a constant-share equilibrium with $\alpha_2 \neq 0$ requires λ_2/λ_1 to vary inversely and proportionately with K/L, thus preserving a constant capital–labor ratio in effective units.[1] That is to say, if the capital–

---

[1] See chapter 12 and Ferguson [1968a] and [1968c].

labor ratio in natural units increases at a constant rate, the ratio of labor's productivity improvement factor to capital's productivity improvement factor must increase at the same rate. Technological progress must, on balance, be relatively labor augmenting or labor saving. To be more precise, the bias of induced factor augmentation must exactly offset the bias toward capital–labor accumulation.

The general case is illustrated by panel a, figure 67, in which the steady-state equilibrium values (q_1^{**}, q_2^{**}) must satisfy

$$-\frac{\dot{\lambda}_1}{\lambda_1}+\frac{\dot{\lambda}_2}{\lambda_2} = q_1^{**}-q_2^{**} = \gamma = \frac{1}{(K/L)}\frac{d(K/L)}{dt}, \qquad (16.3.38)$$

and

$$f(q_1^{**}) = q_1^{**}-\gamma, \quad \frac{\alpha_1^{**}}{\alpha_2^{**}} = -f'(q_1^{**}). \qquad (16.3.39)$$

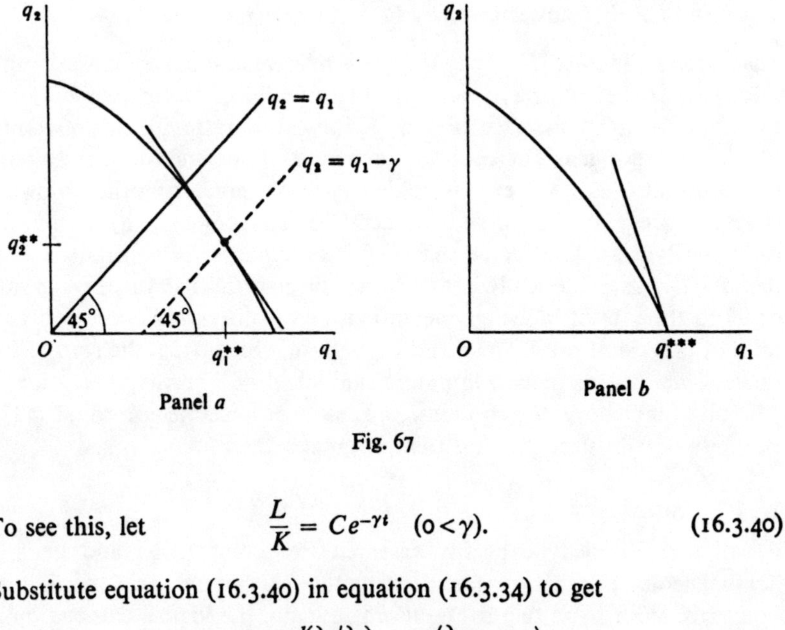

Panel a Panel b

Fig. 67

To see this, let

$$\frac{L}{K} = Ce^{-\gamma t} \quad (0<\gamma). \qquad (16.3.40)$$

Substitute equation (16.3.40) in equation (16.3.34) to get

$$\frac{1}{(\lambda_2/\lambda_1)}\frac{d(\lambda_2/\lambda_1)}{dt} = G\left(\frac{\lambda_2}{\lambda_1}Ce^{-\gamma t}\right). \qquad (16.3.41)$$

As a possible solution, try

$$\frac{\lambda_2}{\lambda_1} = Ye^{-\gamma t}. \qquad (16.3.42)$$

Taking the time derivatives, one obtains

$$\frac{\dot{Y}}{Y} = \frac{\dot{\lambda}_2}{\lambda_2}-\frac{\dot{\lambda}_1}{\lambda_1}+\gamma = G[CY]+\gamma. \qquad (16.3.43)$$

359

Equation (16.3.43) has a steady-state solution $Y = Y^{**}$ at the point where the proportionate rate of relative factor augmentation equals the rate of decrease in the labor–capital ratio. Thus setting $\dot{Y}/Y = 0$, one obtains

$$G[CY^{**}] = -\gamma. \qquad (16.3.44)$$

Equation (16.3.44) may have one or more real roots, just as equation (16.3.36), if the elasticity of substitution is sufficiently bounded away from unity. Further, if the elasticity of substitution is less than unity, there will be one or more equilibria that are stable. Samuelson also proved an extension of this result.[1] If labor grows at a constant exponential rate and if the saving ratio is a constant, the steady-state equilibrium will be characterized by Harrod-neutral technological progress (if the elasticity of substitution is less than unity). This equilibrium is illustrated by panel *b*, figure 67.

The results of this subsection may be summarized as

Samuelson's Theorem III: if capital grows relative to labor in natural units, there may exist equilibria in which the bias of induced factor augmentation exactly offsets the increase in the capital–labor ratio in natural units. Further, if labor grows at a constant exponential rate and the savings ratio is a constant, there will exist a golden-age state possessing the following characteristics: (i) Harrod-neutral technological progress, (ii) asymptotically constant relative factor shares, (iii) asymptotically constant rate of interest, (iv) asymptotically constant rate of growth of the real wage rate equal to the rate of labor augmentation, and (v) asymptotically constant rates of growth of capital and output, both of which equal the sum of the rates of labor-force growth in natural units and of labor augmentation.

In all of the above, the equilibria are stable or unstable according as the elasticity of substitution is less than or greater than unity.

16.3.7 Summary

Recall that Kennedy explicitly assumed free competition and linearly homogeneous production functions, although he did not specify the functions. With these two assumptions in hand, the logical companion is the assumption of competitive imputations. The three together imply the neoclassical theory of distribution. That is to say, within the model under consideration, the actual distribution of income is governed by marginal productivity theory. What Samuelson has shown is that given these assumptions, the Kennedy model with an explicit production function sometimes gives neoclassical results, sometimes not. When it does, it is a theory of distribution; but it is not a truly 'alternative theory' because

[1] Samuelson [1966*a*, pp. 447–8].

there are marginal productivity conditions embedded in it. Of course, within this model, when the Kennedy distribution differs from that of neoclassical theory, the 'induced innovations theory' is no theory at all.

In the paragraph above, I have stressed *within this model* because the model is Samuelson's, not Kennedy's. Indeed, Kennedy charged that in Samuelson's variant, 'the production function has swallowed up the innovation possibility frontier',[1] which is the opposite of Kennedy's intentions. To repeat the theme: without the introduction of an explicit production function, Kennedy's theory is a genuinely alternative theory of distribution; with an explicit production function, it is not.

16.4 Generalization of Samuelson's model

In the spirit of the Preface, let us agree to be neoclassical. That is, let us use a production function as well as the innovation-possibility frontier in discussing the theories of induced innovation and distribution. The analysis in this section is limited to the most interesting case, that in which there is a golden-age growth equilibrium characterized by Harrod-neutral, but Hicks-biased, technological progress.[2]

As in chapter 11, assume that there exists a production function

$$Y = F(K, L, t) \tag{16.4.1}$$

possessing all the usual neoclassical properties. Define the Hicks-rate (R) and Hicks-bias (B) of technological progress as

$$R = \frac{F_t}{F} = \frac{KF_{Kt}+LF_{Lt}}{F}, \tag{16.4.2}$$

$$B = \frac{F_{Kt}}{F_K} - \frac{F_{Lt}}{F_L}. \tag{16.4.3}$$

From equation (16.4.3), technological progress in the Hicks sense is capital using, neutral, or labor using according as $B \gtreqless 0$. Further, as shown in chapter 11, technological progress is Harrod-neutral if, and only if,

$$\left(1 - \frac{1}{\sigma}\right) R + sB = 0. \tag{16.4.4}$$

For technological progress to be progress, R must be positive. For stability of the growth model, σ must be less than unity. Thus Harrod-neutrality requires

$$B = \frac{F_{Kt}}{F_K} - \frac{F_{Lt}}{F_L} > 0, \tag{16.4.5}$$

i.e. there must be Hicks-capital-using or labor-saving technological progress.

---

[1] Kennedy [1966].
[2] The characteristics of the growth path as such are not discussed. For this, see Uzawa [1961a], Diamond [1965], and Ferguson [1968c].

Two more relations are needed before we turn to the model of induced innovation. First, from equation (16.4.2) it immediately follows that

$$R = (1-s)\frac{F_{Kt}}{F_K} + s\frac{F_{Lt}}{F_L},\qquad (16.4.6)$$

where s and $(1-s)$ are the relative shares of labor and capital respectively. Next, Harrod-neutrality requires a constant capital–output ratio at a constant rate of interest. By competitive imputations, the rate of interest (r) is

$$r = F_K.\qquad (16.4.7)$$

Hence

$$\frac{\dot{r}}{r} = \frac{F_{Kt}}{F_K} - \frac{s}{\sigma}\frac{\dot{k}}{k}.\qquad (16.4.8)$$

Similarly, the output–capital ratio (x) is

$$x = \frac{Y}{K} = \frac{F(K, L, t)}{K}.\qquad (16.4.9)$$

Thus its rate of growth is

$$\frac{\dot{x}}{x} = R - s\frac{\dot{k}}{k}.\qquad (16.4.10)$$

Setting equations (16.4.8) and (16.4.10) equal to zero and eliminating k/k, one obtains another expression for the condition for Harrod-neutrality:

$$\sigma\frac{F_{Kt}}{F_K} = R.\qquad (16.4.11)$$

Denote the output–labor ratio by y. From equation (16.4.1),

$$\frac{\dot{Y}}{Y} = (1-s)\frac{\dot{K}}{K} + s\frac{\dot{L}}{L} + \frac{F_t}{F}.\qquad (16.4.12)$$

Hence it follows that

$$R = (1-s)\frac{\dot{x}}{x} + s\frac{\dot{y}}{y}.\qquad (16.4.13)$$

Now, $\dot{x}/x$ and $\dot{y}/y$ show the reductions in capital and labor per unit of output respectively. Hence Kennedy's problem may be formulated as

$$\max R = (1-s)\frac{\dot{x}}{x} + s\frac{\dot{y}}{y} \quad \text{subject to} \quad \frac{\dot{y}}{y} = f\left(\frac{\dot{x}}{x}\right),\qquad (16.4.14)$$

where $f(\cdot)$ posseses, by assumption, the properties of Kennedy's innovation-possibility frontier. The constrained maximization yields Kennedy's results:

$$\frac{1-s}{s} = -f'\left(\frac{\dot{x}}{x}\right) = -f'(0),\qquad (16.4.15)$$

where $f' < 0$ and $f'' < 0$.

The model in expressions (16.4.14) and (16.4.15) is precisely the same as Samuelson's model with Harrod-neutral technological progress. But now

362

from equations (16.4.6) and (16.4.13), we may make an interesting substitution and reformulation of the model:

$$\max R = (1-s)\frac{F_{Kt}}{F_K} + s\frac{F_{Lt}}{F_L} \quad \text{subject to} \quad \frac{F_{Lt}}{F_L} = g\left(\frac{F_{Kt}}{F_K}\right), \qquad (16.4.16)$$

where $g' < 0$, $g'' < 0$. Naturally,

$$\frac{F_{Kt}}{F_K} \neq \frac{\dot{x}}{x} \quad \text{and} \quad \frac{F_{Lt}}{F_L} \neq \frac{\dot{y}}{y}.$$

However, equations (16.4.6) and (16.4.13) are equally valid representations of R, and hence expressions (16.4.14) and (16.4.16) are equally valid representations of Kennedy's problem. The only difference is that the innovation-possibility frontier in expression (16.4.16) is directly related to the production function and to Hicks' concept of biased technological progress.

The constrained maximization yields the familiar results:

$$\frac{1-s}{s} = g'\left(\frac{F_{Kt}}{F_K}\right). \qquad (16.4.17)$$

The ratio of relative shares so determined may be compared with the actual ratio dictated by marginal productivity·theory. The transition from equation (16.4.2), which is a definition, to equation (16.4.6), which is no longer a definition, is based upon the results of neoclassical distribution theory. Hence we may solve equation (16.4.6) for the marginal-productivity determined ratio of relative shares:

$$\frac{1-s}{s} = \left(\frac{R}{s} - \frac{F_{Lt}}{F_L}\right) \div \frac{F_{Kt}}{F_K}. \qquad (16.4.18)$$

If the Kennedy distribution is to be consistent with the marginal productivity distribution, the ratios of relative shares in equations (16.4.17) and (16.4.18) must be the same. Substituting $g(F_{Kt}/F_K)$ for F_{Lt}/F_L in equation (16.4.18) and equating the two expressions, one obtains

$$g'\left(\frac{F_{Kt}}{F_K}\right) - \frac{1}{F_{Kt}/F_K}g\left(\frac{F_{Kt}}{F_K}\right) = \frac{\sigma}{s}. \qquad (16.4.19)$$

Equation (16.4.19) is a first-order differential equation whose quadrature would, in principle,[1] determine the innovation-possibility frontier that makes the Kennedy distribution consistent with the marginal productivity distribution.

Equation (16.4.19) emphasizes two aspects of Kennedy's theory when a production function is added to the model. First, the Kennedy theory, if consistent with neoclassical theory, is clearly dependent upon marginal

---

[1] In the integration, σ/s cannot be treated as a constant. Hence equation (16.4.19) has no *general* solution (i.e. a solution independent of the specification of $s = s(F_{Kt}/F_K)$).

productivity theory. Hence it does not provide an alternative theory of distribution. Second, as a minor point, equation (16.4.19) shows that the transformation function must involve labor's relative share, as Samuelson suggested.[1] In addition, the neoclassical elasticity of substitution must enter the transformation function.

16.5 Conclusion

Neoclassical theory turns upon production functions; and it has been shown that when a model contains a production function, neoclassical results are obtained. That is just to say, so long as production functions are explicitly used in models of economic behavior, there are no 'alternative' theories. The models are essentially neoclassical and so are the results.

The import of chapters 15 and 16 has been to show that Kaldor's theory of distribution is unsatisfactory in a one-sector model and invalid in a two-sector model, that Mrs Robinson's implied theory of distribution becomes a neoclassical theory if competitive imputation is assumed, and that Kennedy's theory is not a genuine alternative if an explicit production function is introduced. This seems to suggest that the new-old neoclassical tale is worth the telling.

[1] Samuelson [1965]. After Kennedy raised an objection [1966], Samuelson left the point as a matter of doubt [1966a].

REFERENCES

ABRAMOVITZ, MOSES [1962] 'Economic growth in the United States', *American Economic Review*, LII, pp. 762–82.

AHMAD, S. [1966] 'On the theory of induced invention,' *Econ. J.* LXXVI, pp. 344–57.

ALCHIAN, A. A. [1963] 'Reliability of progress curves in airframe production', *Econometrica*, XXXI, pp. 679–93.

ALLEN, R. G. D. [1938] *Mathematical analysis for economists* (London: Macmillan and Co., Ltd).

AMANO, AKIHIRO [1964] 'Biased technical progress and a neoclassical theory of economic growth,' *Quarterly Journal of Economics*, LXXVIII, pp. 129–38.

ARROW, KENNETH J. [1962] 'The economic implications of learning by doing,' *Review of Economic Studies*, XXIX, pp. 155–73.

ARROW, KENNETH J., HOLLIS B. CHENERY, BAGICHA MINHAS AND ROBERT M. SOLOW [1961] 'Capital–labor substitution and economic efficiency', *Review of Economics and Statistics*, XLIII, pp. 225–50.

ASHER, H. [1956] *Cost–quantity relationships in the airframe industry*, R-291 (Santa Monica: The Rand Corporation).

ASIMAKOPULOS, A. [1963] 'The definition of neutral inventions', *Econ. J.* LXXIII, pp. 675–80.

ASIMAKOPULOS, A. AND J. C. WELDON [1963] 'The classification of technical progress in models of economic growth', *Economica*, New Series, XXX, pp. 372–86.

ATSUMI, HIROSHI [1960] 'Mr Kaldor's theory of income distribution', *Review of Economic Studies*, XXVII, pp. 109–18.

BAILEY, MARTIN J. [1954] 'Price and output determination by a firm selling related products', *American Economic Review*, XLIV, pp. 82–93.

BARDHAM, PRANAB [1965] 'On factor-biased technical progress and international trade', *Journal of Political Economy*, LXXIII, pp. 396–8.

BAUER, P. T. [1941] 'A note on monopoly', *Economica*, New Series, VIII, pp. 194–202.

BEAR, D. V. T. [1965] 'Inferior-Inputs and the theory of the firm', *Journal of Political Economy*, LXXIII, pp. 287–9.

BERGLAS, EYTAN [1965] 'Investment and technological change', *Journal of Political Economy*, LXXIII, pp. 173–80.

BÖHM-BAWERK, EUGEN VON [1959] *Capital and interest*, vol. II, *Positive theory of capital*, trans. by George D. Hurcke (South Holland, Ill: Libertarian Press).

BOMBACH, G. [1959a] 'Preisstabilität, wirtschaftliches Wachstum und Einkommensverteilung', *Schweizerische Zeitschrift für Volkswirtschaft und Statistik*, XCV, pp. 1–20.

[1959b] 'Die verschiedenen Ansätze der Verteilungstheorie', *Schriften des Vereins für Socialpolitik*, Gesellschaft für Wirtschafts- und Sozialwissenschaften, Neue Folge, XVII, pp. 95–154.

365

REFERENCES

BORTS, BEORGE H. AND E. J. MISHAN [1962] 'Exploring the "uneconomic region" of the production function', *Review of Economic Studies*, XXIX, pp. 300–12.

BOULDING, KENNETH E. [1953] 'The fruits of progress and the dynamics of distribution, *American Economic Review*, Papers and Proceedings, XLIII, pp. 472–83.

BOWLEY, A. L. [1924] *The mathematical groundwork of economics* (Oxford: The Clarendon Press).

BRONFENBRENNER, MARTIN [1960] 'A note on relative shares and the elasticity of substitution', *Journal of Political Economy*, LXVIII, pp. 284–7.

BROWN, MURRAY [1966] *On the theory and measurement of technological change* (Cambridge University Press).
[1967] 'Substitution-composition effects, capital intensity uniqueness and growth', Discussion Paper Number 2, Economic Research Group, State University of New York at Buffalo.

BROWN, MURRAY AND JOHN S. DE CANI [1963a] 'Technological change and the distribution of income', *International Economic Review*, IV, pp. 289–309.
[1963b] 'A measure of technological employment', *Review of Economics and Statistics*, XLV, pp. 386–94.

BRUNO, MICHAEL, EDWIN BURMEISTER AND EYTAN SHESHINSKI [1966] 'Nature and implications of the reswitching of techniques', *Quarterly Journal of Economics*, LXXX, pp. 526–54.

CARLSON, SUNE [1939] *A study on the pure theory of production* (London: P. S. King and Co., Ltd).

CASSELS, J. M. [1936] 'On the law of variable proportions', in *Explorations in economics* (New York: McGraw-Hill Book Co.), pp. 223–36.

CHAMBERLIN, EDWARD H. [1936] 'Monopolistic competition and the productivity theory of distribution', in *Explorations in economics* (New York: McGraw-Hill Book Co.), pp. 237–49.

CHAMPERNOWNE, D. G. [1935] 'Elasticity of substitution: A mathematical note', *Econ. J.* XLV, pp. 246–58.
[1953] 'The production function and the theory of capital: A comment', *Review of Economic Studies*, XXI, pp. 118–30.

CHATTOPADHYAY, PARESH [1966] 'Diminishing returns and linear homogeneity: Further comment', *American Economic Review*, LVI, pp. 181–2.

CLARK, JOHN BATES [1888] 'Capital and its earnings', *A.E.A. Publications*, III, pp. 89–149.

CLARK, JOHN BATES [1965] *The distribution of wealth* (New York: Augustus M. Kelley).

CLEMENS, ELI W. [1951] 'Price discrimination and the multi-product firm', *Review of Economic Studies*, XIX, pp. 1–11.

CLEMHOUT, SIMONE [1964] 'The class of homothetic isoquant production functions', paper presented to the Econometric Society, Chicago.

COASE, R. H. [1946] 'Monopoly pricing with interrelated costs and demand', *Economica*, New Series, XIII, pp. 278–94.

COBB, C. W. AND PAUL H. DOUGLAS [1928] 'A theory of production', *American Economic Review*, Papers and Proceedings, XVIII, pp. 139–65.

CURTISS D. H. [1941] 'Maxima and minima of functions of several variables', *Mathematical Monographs*, I (Evanston and Chicago: Northwestern University Press), pp. 1–43.

REFERENCES

DAVID, P. A. AND TH. VAN DE KLUNDERT [1965] 'Biased efficiency growth and Capital–Labor substitution in the U.S., 1899–1960', *American Economic Review*, LV, pp. 357–94.

DAVIDSON, PAUL [1960] *Theories of aggregate income distribution* (New Brunswick: Rutgers University Press).

DENISON, E. F. [1962] *The sources of economic growth in the United States and the alternatives before us* (New York: Committee for Economic Development).

DEWEY, DONALD [1965] *Modern capital theory* (New York: Columbia University Press).

DHRYMES, PHOEBUS J. [1964] 'On the theory of the monopolistic multiproduct firm with uncertainty', *International Economic Review*, V, pp. 239–57.

DIAMOND, PETER A. [1965] 'Disembodied technical change in a two-sector model', *Review of Economic Studies*, XXXII, pp. 161–8.

DORFMAN, ROBERT [1951] *Application of linear programming to the theory of the firm* (Berkeley: University of California Press).

DORFMAN, ROBERT, PAUL A. SAMUELSON AND ROBERT M. SOLOW [1958] *Linear programming and economic analysis* (New York: John Wiley and Sons).

DOUGLAS, PAUL H. [1934] *The theory of wages* (New York: Macmillan and Co., Inc.).

DRANDAKIS, E. M. AND EDMUND S. PHELPS [1966] 'A model of induced invention, growth, and distribution', *Econ. J.* LXXVI, pp. 823–40.

EDWARDS, EDGAR O. [1950] 'The analysis of output under discrimination', *Econometrica*, XVIII, pp. 163–72.

EISNER, ROBERT [1964] 'Income distribution, investment and growth', *Indian Economic Journal*, XI, pp. 400–12.

FABRICANT, SOLOMON [1959] *Basic facts on productivity change*, National Bureau of Economic Research, Occasional Paper No. 63 (New York).

FEI, JOHN C. H. AND GUSTAV RANIS [1963] 'Innovation, capital accumulation and economic development', *American Economic Review*, LXXX, pp. 282–313.

[1965] 'Innovational intensity and factor bias in the theory of growth', *International Economic Review*, VI, pp. 182–98.

FELLNER, WILLIAM [1956] *Trends and cycles in economic activity* (New York: Henry Holt, Inc.).

[1961a] 'Two propositions in the theory of induced innovations', *Econ. J.* LXXI, pp. 305–8.

[1961b] 'Appraisal of the labour-saving and capital-saving character of innovations', in Lutz and Hague, eds. *The theory of capital* (London: Macmillan and Co., Ltd), pp. 58–72.

[1962] 'Does the market direct the relative factor-saving effects of technological progress?' in R. R. Nelson, ed. *The rate and direction of inventive activity: Economic and social factors* (Princeton: Princeton University Press), pp. 171–88.

[1966] 'Profit maximization, utility maximization, and the rate and direction of innovation', *American Economic Review*, Papers and Proceedings, LVI, pp. 24–32.

FERGUSON, C. E. [1962] 'Transformation curve in production theory: a pedagogical note', *S. Econ. J.*, XXIX, pp. 96–102.

367

[1963] 'Cross-section production functions and the elasticity of substitution in American manufacturing industry, 1947–1958', *Review of Economics and Statistics*, XLV, pp. 205–13.

[1964a] 'Theories of distribution and relative shares', *Jahrbücher für Nationalökonomie und Statistik*, CLXXVI, pp. 23–37.

[1964b] 'The elasticity of substitution and regional estimates of capital and capital ratios in American manufacturing industry, 1954–1958', in Greenhut and Whitman, eds., *Essays in southern economic development* (Chapel Hill: University of North Carolina Press), pp. 404–49.

[1965a] 'Time-series production functions and technological progress in American manufacturing industry', *Journal of Political Economy*, LXXIII, pp. 135–47.

[1965b] 'Substitution, technical progress, and returns to scale', *American Economic Review*, Papers and Proceedings, LV, pp. 296–305.

[1965c] 'Saving and the capital-output ratio in the neoclassical theory of growth', *Quarterly Review of Economics and Business*, V, pp. 53–63.

[1965d] 'The elasticity of substitution and the savings ratio in the neoclassical theory of growth', *Quarterly Journal of Economics*, LXXIX, pp. 465–71.

[1966a] *Microeconomic Theory* (Homewood: Richard D. Irwin, Inc.).

[1966b] 'Production, prices, and the theory of jointly-derived input demand functions', *Economica*, New Series, XXXIII, pp. 454–61.

[1967] 'The theory of input demand and the role of "Inferior Factors" in the theory of production', *Revue d'Economie Politique*, LXXVII, pp. 413–33.

[1968a] 'The simple analytics of neoclassical growth theory', *Quarterly Review of Economics and Business*, VIII, pp. 69–83.

[1968b] '"Inferior Factors" and the theories of production and input demand', *Economica*, New Series, XXXV, pp. 140–50.

[1968c] 'Neoclassical theory of technological progress and relative factor shares', *Sth. Econ. J.* XXXIV, pp. 490–504.

FERGUSON, C. E. AND RALPH W. PFOUTS [1962] 'Aggregate production functions and relative factor shares', *International Economic Review*, III, pp. 328–37.

FINDLAY, RONALD [1960] 'Economic growth and the distributive shares', *Review of Economic Studies*, XXVII, pp. 167–78.

[1963] 'The Robinsonian model of accumulation.' *Economica*, New Series, XXX, pp. 1–12.

FISHER, FRANKLIN [1965] 'Embodied technical change and the existence of an aggregative capital stock', *Review of Economic Studies*, XXXII, pp. 263–88.

FORTENAY, PATRICK B. DE [1964], 'Diminishing returns and linear homogeneity: A comment', *American Economic Review*, LIV, p. 750.

FRANKEL, MARVIN [1962] 'The production function: Allocation and growth', *American Economic Review*, LII, pp. 995–1022.

FRIEDMAN, MILTON [1936] 'Note on Dr Machlup's article', *Review of Economic Studies*, III, pp. 147–8.

FRISCH, RAGNAR [1931] 'Einige Punkte einer Preistheorie mit Boden und Arbeit als Produktionsfactoren', *Zeitschrift für Nationalökonomie*, III.

[1965] *Theory of production* (Dordrecht: D. Reidel Publishing Company).

GAITSKELL, H. T. N. [1936] 'Notes on the period of production, Part I', *Zeitschrift für Nationalökonomie*, VII, pp. 577–95.

REFERENCES

GAITSKELL, H. T. N. [1939] 'Notes on the period of production, Part II'. *Zeitschrift für Nationalökonomie*, IX, pp. 215–44.

GAREGNANI, P. [1966] 'Switching of techniques', *Quarterly Journal of Economics*, LXXX, pp. 555–67.

GEORGESCU-ROEGEN, NICHOLAS [1935] 'Fixed coefficients of production and the marginal productivity theory', *Review of Economic Studies*, III, pp. 40–9.

[1951] 'Some properties of a generalized Leontief model', in T. C. Koopmens, ed. *Activity analysis of production and allocation* (New York: John Wiley and Sons, Inc.), pp. 165–73.

[1955] 'Limitationality, limitativeness, and economic equilibrium', in H. A. Antosiewicz, ed. *Proceedings of the Second Symposium in Linear Programming* (Washington, D.C.: National Bureau of Standards), vol. I, pp. 295–330.

[1960] 'Economic theory and agrarian economics', *Oxford Economic Papers*, New Series, XII, pp. 1–40.

GERAKIS, ANDREAS S. [1962] 'A note on linear and homogeneous functions and marginal products', *Economica*, New Series, XXIX, pp. 282–3.

GORDON, R. A. [1948] 'Short period price determination in theory and practice', *American Economic Review*, XXXVIII, pp. 265–88.

GORMAN, W. M. [1965] 'Production functions in which the elasticities of substitution stand in fixed proportion to each other', *Review of Economic Studies*, XXXII, pp. 217–24.

GRUNFELD, YEHUDA AND ZVI GRILICHES [1960] 'Is aggregation necessarily bad?' *Review of Economics and Statistics*, XLII pp. 1–13.

HAHN, F. H. [1951] 'The share of wages in the national income', *Oxford Economic Papers*, New Series, III, pp. 147–57.

HALTER, A. N., H. O. CARTER AND J. G. HOCKING [1957] 'A note on the transcendental production function', *J. Fm Econ.* XXXIX, pp. 974–96.

HANCOCK, HARRIS [1917] *The theory of maxima and minima* (Boston: Ginn and Co.).

HARROD, R. F. [1956] *Towards a dynamic economics* (London: Macmillan and Co., Ltd).

HEADY, EARL O. AND JOHN L. DILLON [1961] *Agricultural production functions* (Ames: Iowa State University Press).

HICKS, JOHN R. [1932] *The theory of wages* (London: Macmillan and Co., Ltd; second edition, 1963).

[1933] 'Notes on the elasticity of substitution: A note on Mr Kahn's paper', *Review of Economic Studies*, I, pp. 78–80.

[1936] 'Distribution and economic progress: A revised version', *Review of Economic Studies*, IV, pp. 1–12.

[1939] *Value and capital* (Oxford: Clarendon Press; second edition, 1946).

[1965] *Capital and growth* (Oxford: Oxford University Press).

HIRSCH, WERNER Z. [1952] 'Manufacturing progress functions', *Review of Economics and Statistics*, XXXIV, pp. 143–55.

[1956] 'Firm progress ratios', *Econometrica*, XXIV, pp. 136–43.

HOTELLING, HAROLD [1935] 'Demand functions with limited budgets', *Econometrica*, III, pp. 66–78.

INTRILIGATOR, MICHAEL D. [1965] 'Embodied technical change and productivity in the United States, 1929–1958', *Review of Economics and Statistics*, XLVII, pp. 65–70.

REFERENCES

JOHANSEN, LEIF, [1959] 'Substitution *versus* fixed production coefficients in the theory of economic growth', *Econometrica*, XXVII, pp. 157–76.

JOHNSON, W. E. [1913] 'The pure theory of utility curves', *Econ. J.* XXIII, pp. 483–513.

JONES, RONALD W. [1965a] 'The structure of simple general equilibrium models', *Journal of Political Economy*, LXXIII, pp. 557–72.

[1965b] '"Neutral" technological change and the isoquant map,' *American Economic Review*, LV, pp. 848–55.

JORGENSON, DALE W. [1966] 'The embodiment hypothesis', *Journal of Political Economy*, LXXIV, pp. 1–17.

KAHN, R. F. [1933] 'Notes on the elasticity of substitution: The elasticity of substitution and the relative share of a factor', *Review of Economic Studies*, I, pp. 72–8.

[1935] 'The elasticity of substitution: Two applications of the concept', *Econ. J.* XLVI, pp. 242–5.

KALDOR, NICHOLAS [1937] 'Limitational factors and the elasticity of substitution', *Review of Economic Studies*, IV, pp. 162–5.

[1955] 'Alternative theories of distribution', *Review of Economic Studies*, XXIII, pp. 94–100.

[1957] 'A model of economic growth', *Econ. J.* LXVII, pp. 591–624.

[1959] 'Economic growth and the problem of inflation', *Economica*, New Series, XXVI; Part I, pp. 212–26; Part II, pp. 287–98.

[1960a] 'A rejoinder to Mr Atsumi and Professor Tobin', *Review of Economic Studies*, XXVII, pp. 121–3.

[1960b] 'A rejoinder to Mr Findlay', *Review of Economic Studies*, XXVII, pp. 179–81.

[1961] 'Capital accumulation and economic growth', in Lutz and Hague, eds *The theory of capital* (London: Macmillan and Co., Ltd), pp. 177–222.

[1962] 'Comment', *Review of Economic Studies*, XXIX, pp. 246–50.

KALDOR, NICHOLAS AND JAMES A. MIRRLEES [1962] 'A new model of economic growth', *Review of Economic Studies*, XXIX, pp. 174–92.

KALECKI, M. [1938] 'The determinants of the distribution of income', *Econometrica*, VI, pp. 97–112.

[1939] *Essays in the theory of economic fluctuations* (London: George Allen and Unwin, Ltd).

[1942] 'A theory of profits', *Econ. J.* LII, pp. 258–67.

[1943] *Studies in economic dynamics* (London: George Allen and Unwin, Ltd).

[1954] *Theory of economic dynamics* (London: George Allen and Unwin, Ltd).

KEMP, MURRAY C. [1963] 'An extension of the neo-Keynesian theory of distribution', *Econ. Rec.* XXXIX, pp. 465–8.

KENDRICK, JOHN W. AND RYUZO SATO [1963] 'Factory prices, productivity, and growth,' *American Economic Review*, LII, pp. 974–1003.

KENNEDY, CHARLES [1961] 'Technical progress and investment', *Econ. J.* LXXI, pp. 292–9.

[1962a] 'Harrod on "neutrality"', *Econ. J.* LXXII, pp. 249–50.

[1962b] 'The character of improvements and of technical progress', *Econ. J.* LXXII, pp. 899–911.

[1964] 'Induced bias in innovation and the theory of distribution', *Econ. J.* LXXIV, pp. 541–7.

REFERENCES

[1966] 'Samuelson on induced innovation', *Review of Economics and Statistics*, XLVIII, pp. 442–4.

KEYNES, J. M. [1930] *A treatise on money* (London: Macmillan and Co., Ltd).

[1936] *The general theory of employment, interest and money* (New York: Harcourt, Brace and Co.).

[1939] 'Relative movements of real wages and output', *Econ. J.* XLIX, pp. 34–49.

KNIGHT, FRANK H. [1933] *Risk, uncertainty and profit*, London School of Economics Reprints of Scarce Works, No. 16.

KRAVIS, IRVING B. [1959] 'Relative income shares in fact and theory', *American Economic Review*, XLIX, pp. 917–49.

KRELLE, W. [1957] 'Bestimmungsgrunde der Einkommensverteilung in der modernen Wirtschaft', *Schriften des Vereins für Socialpolitik*, Gesellschaft für Wirtschafts- und Sozialwissenschaften, XIII.

KUENNE, ROBERT E. [1963] *The theory of general economic equilibrium* (Princeton: Princeton University Press).

KUHN, HAROLD W. AND A. TUCKER [1951] 'Nonlinear Programming', in J. Neyman, ed. *Proceedings of the Second Berkeley Symposium on Mathematical Statistics and Probability* (Berkeley: University of California Press), pp. 481–92.

KURZ, MORDECHAI [1963] 'Substitution versus fixed production coefficients: A comment', *Econometrica*, XXXI, pp. 209–17.

LANCASTER, KELVIN [1960] 'Mrs Robinson's dynamics', *Economica*, New Series, XXVII, pp. 63–70.

LEIBENSTEIN, HARVEY [1966] 'Allocative efficiency *vs.* "X-efficiency"', *American Economic Review*, LVI, pp. 392–415.

LEONTIEF, W. W. [1947a] 'A note on the interrelation of subsets of independent variables of a continuous function with continuous first derivatives', *Bulletin of the American Mathematical Society*, LIII, pp. 343–50.

[1947b] 'Introduction to a theory of the internal structure of functional relationships', *Econometrica*, XV, pp. 361–73.

LERNER, A. P. [1933a] 'Notes on the elasticity of substitution: The diagrammatical representation', *Review of Economic Studies*, I, pp. 68–71.

[1933b] 'The concept of monopoly and the measurement of monopoly power', *Review of Economic Studies*, I, pp. 157–75.

[1934] 'Notes on the elasticity of substitution', *Review of Economic Studies*, I, pp. 147–8.

[1936] 'The question of symmetry', *Review of Economic Studies*, III, pp. 150–1.

LEVHARI, DAVID [1965] 'A nonsubstitution theorem and switching of techniques', *Quarterly Journal of Economics*, LXXIX, pp. 98–105.

[1966a] 'Further implications of learning by doing', *Review of Economic Studies*, XXXIII, pp. 31–8.

[1966b] 'Extensions of Arrow's "learning by doing"', *Review of Economic Studies*, XXXIII, pp. 117–31.

LEVHARI, DAVID AND PAUL A. SAMUELSON [1966] 'The reswitching theorem is false', *Quarterly Journal of Economics*, LXXX, pp. 518–19.

LIEBHAFSKY, H. H. [1963] *The nature of price theory* (Homewood: Dorsey Press).

[1964] 'Diminishing returns and linear homogeneity: Comment', *American Economic Review*, LIV, pp. 739–44.

REFERENCES

LUNDBERG, E. [1961] *Produktivitet och rantabilitet* (Stockholm: P. A. Norstedt and Soner).

MCARTHY, MICHAEL [1964] 'Technical progress: A theoretical and empirical analysis of its effects on aggregate output and its sources', unpublished Ph.D. thesis, Southern Methodist University Library.

[1965] 'Embodied and disembodied technical progress in the constant elasticity of substitution production function', *Review of Economics and Statistics*, XLVII, pp. 71–5.

[1966] 'Quantity augmenting technical progress and two-factor production functions', *Sth. Econ. J.* XXIII, pp. 71–80.

MCFADDEN, DANIEL [1963] 'Further results on CES production functions', *Review of Economic Studies*, XXX, pp. 73–83.

MACHLUP, FRITZ [1935] 'The commonsense of the elasticity of substitution', *Review of Economic Studies*, II, pp. 202–13.

[1936a] 'Reply', *Review of Economic Studies*, III, pp. 151–2.

[1936b] 'On the meaning of the marginal product', in *Explorations in Economics* (New York: McGraw-Hill Book Co.), pp. 250–63.

MANSFIELD, EDWIN [1961] 'Technical change and the rate of imitation', *Econometrica*, XXIX, pp. 741–66.

[1962] 'Entry, Gibrat's law, innovation, and the growth of firms', *American Economic Review*, LII, pp. 1023–51.

[1963a] 'The speed of response of firms to new techniques', *Quarterly Journal of Economics*, LXXVII, pp. 290–309.

[1963b] 'Intrafirm rates of diffusion of an innovation', *Review of Economics and Statistics*, XLV, pp. 348–59.

[1963c] 'Size of firm, market structure, and innovation', *Journal of Political Economy*, LXXI, pp. 556–76.

[1964] 'Industrial research and development expenditures: Determinants, prospects, and relation to size of firm and inventive output', *Journal of Political Economy*, LXXII, pp. 319–40.

[1965] 'Rates of return from industrial research and development', *American Economic Review*, Papers and Proceedings, LV, pp. 310–22.

MARSHALL, ALFRED [1920] *Principles of Economics* (New York: Macmillan and Co., eighth edition).

MATTHEWS, R. C. O. [1964] 'The new view of investment: Comment', *Quarterly Journal of Economics*, LXXVIII, pp. 164–72.

MAUER, WILLIAM A. AND THOMAS H. NAYLOR [1964] 'Monopolistic-Monopsonistic competition: The multi-product, multi-factor firm", *Sth. Econ. J.* XXXI, pp. 38–43.

MEADE, J. E. [1934a] 'The elasticity of substitution and the incidence of an imperial inhabited house duty', *Review of Economic Studies*, I, pp. 149–52.

[1934b] 'The elasticity of substitution and the elasticity of demand for one factor of production', *Review of Economic Studies*, I, pp. 152–3.

METZLER, LLOYD A. [1945] 'Stability of multiple markets: The Hicks conditions', *Econometrica*, XIII, pp. 277–92.

MITRA, ASHOK [1954] *The share of wages in national income* (The Hague: Central Planbureau).

MOESEKE, PAUL VAN [1965] 'Diminishing returns and linear homogeneity: comment', *American Economic Review*, LV, pp. 536–9.

MOORE, HENRY L. [1929] *Synthetic economics* (New York: Macmillan and Co.).

REFERENCES

MORISHIMA, MICHIO [1964]   *Equilibrium, stability, and growth* (Oxford: Clarendon Press).

[1966]   'Refutation of the nonswitching theorem', *Quarterly Journal of Economics*, LXXX, pp. 520–5.

MOSAK, J. L. [1938]   'Interrelations of production, price, and derived demand', *Journal of Political Economy*, XLVI, pp. 761–87.

MUKERJI, V. [1963]   'Generalized SMAC function with constant ratios of elasticities of substitution', *Review of Economic Studies*, XXX, pp. 233–6.

MUNDLAK, YAIR [1964]   'Transcendental multiproduct production functions', *International Economic Review*, V, pp. 273–84.

NAYLOR, THOMAS H. [1965]   'A Kuhn–Tucker model of the multi-product, multi-factor firm', *Sth. Econ. J.* XXXI, pp. 324–30.

NEWMAN, P. K. AND R. C. READ [1961]   'Production functions with restricted input shares', *International Economic Review*, II, pp. 127–33.

NUTTER, G. WARREN [1963]   'Diminishing returns and linear homogeneity', *American Economic Review*, LIII, pp. 1084–5.

[1964]   'Diminishing returns and linear homogeneity: Reply', *American Economic Review*, LIV, pp. 751–3.

[1965]   'Diminishing returns and linear homogeneity: Reply', *American Economic Review*, LV, p. 539.

PAROUSH, JACOB [1964]   'A note on the CES production function', *Econometrica*, XXXII, pp. 213–14.

PASINETTI, LUIGI L. [1962]   'Rate of profit and income distribution in relation to the rate of economic growth', *Review of Economic Studies*, XXIX, pp. 267–79.

[1966a]   'Changes in the rate of profit and switches of technique', *Quarterly Journal of Economics*, LXXX, pp. 503–17.

[1966b]   'New results in an old framework', *Review of Economic Studies*, XXXIII, pp. 303–6.

PFOUTS, RALPH W. [1961]   'The theory of cost and production in the multi-product firm', *Econometrica*, XXIX, pp. 650–8.

PHELPS, EDMUND S. [1962]   'The new view of investment: A neoclassical analysis', *Quarterly Journal of Economics*, LXXVI, pp. 548–67.

[1963]   'Substitution, fixed proportions, growth and distribution', *International Economic Review*, IV, pp. 265–88.

PHELPS, EDMUND AND CHARLOTTE [1966]   'Factor–Price–Frontier estimation of a vintage production model of the postwar United States nonfarm business sector', *Review of Economics and Statistics*, XLVIII, pp. 251–65.

PHELPS, EDMUND AND M. E. YAARI [1964]   'Reply', *Quarterly Journal of Economics*, LXXVIII, pp. 172–6.

PIGOU, A. C. [1932]   *The economics of welfare* (London: Macmillan and Co., Ltd, fourth edition).

(1934)   'The elasticity of substitution', *Econ. J.* XLIV, pp. 232–41.

PIRON, ROBERT [1966]   'Diminishing returns and linear homogeneity: Further comment', *American Economic Review*, LVI, pp. 183–6.

PREISER, ERICH [1953]   'Erkenntniswert und Grenzen der Grenzproduktivitätstheorie', *Schweizerische Zeitschrift für Volkswirtschaft und Statistik*, LXXXIX, pp. 25–45.

[1961]   *Wachstum und Einkommensverteilung* (Heidelberg: Carl Winter).

REFERENCES

PUU, T. [1966] 'Les Effets de Substitution et D'Expansion Dans la Théorie de la Production', *Revue D'Economie Politique*, LXXVI, pp. 57–91.

RAPPING, LEONARD [1965] 'Learning and World War II production functions', *Review of Economics and Statistics*, XLVII, pp. 81–6.

REDER, M. W. [1941] 'Intertemporal relations of demand and supply within the firm', *Canadian Journal of Economics and Political Science*, VII, pp. 25–38.

ROBINSON, JOAN [1933] *The economics of imperfect competition* (London: Macmillan and Co., Ltd).

[1934] 'Euler's theorem and the problem of distribution', *Econ. J.* XLIV, pp. 398–414.

[1936] 'Dr Machlup's commonsense of the elasticity of substitution', *Review of Economic Studies*, III, pp. 148–50.

[1938] 'The classification of inventions', *Review of Economic Studies*, V, pp. 139–42.

[1953] 'The production function and the theory of capital', *Review of Economic Studies*, XXI, pp. 81–106.

[1955] 'The production function', *Econ. J.* LXV, pp. 67–71.

[1956] *The accumulation of capital* (London: Macmillan and Co., Ltd).

[1962] 'Comment', *Review of Economic Studies*, XXIX, pp. 258–66.

[1963] 'Learning by doing: A further note', *Review of Economic Studies*, XXX, pp. 167–8.

ROTHSCHILD, K. W. [1961] 'Some recent contributions to a macro-economic theory of income distribution', *Scottish Journal of Political Economy*, VIII, pp. 173–99.

ROWE, JOHN W., JR. [1964] 'Diminishing returns and linear homogeneity: Comment', *American Economic Review*, LIV, pp. 745–6.

[1965] 'Diminishing returns and linear homogeneity: Comment', *American Economic Review*, LV, pp. 532–5.

SALTER, W. E. G. [1960] *Productivity and technical change* (Cambridge University Press).

SAMUELSON, PAUL A. [1947] *Foundations of economic analysis* (Cambridge: Harvard University Press).

[1962] 'Parable and realism in capital theory: The surrogate production function', *Review of Economic Studies*, XXIX, pp. 193–206.

[1965] 'A theory of induced innovations along Kennedy–Weizsäcker lines', *Review of Economics and Statistics*, XLVII, pp. 343–56.

[1966a] 'Rejoinder: Agreements, disagreements, doubts, and the case of induced Harrod-neutral technical change', *Review of Economics and Statistics*, XLVIII, pp. 444–8.

[1966b] 'A summing up', *Quarterly Journal of Economics*, LXXX, pp. 568–83.

SAMUELSON, PAUL A. AND ROBERT M. SOLOW [1956] 'A complete capital model involving heterogeneous capital goods', *Quarterly Journal of Economics*, LXX, pp. 537–62.

SATO, KAZUO [1965] 'Induced bias in technical progress and the stability of equilibrium growth', mimeograph manuscript dated March, 1965.

SATO, RYUZO [1964] 'Diminishing returns and linear homogeneity: Comment', *American Economic Review*, LIV, pp. 744–5.

SCHEPER, WILHELM [1965] 'Produktionsfunktionen mit konstanten Substitutions-elastizitäten', *Jahrbücher für Nationalökonomie und Statistik*, CLXXVII, pp. 1–21.

374

REFERENCES

SCHNEIDER, DIETER [1964] 'Diminishing returns and linear homogeneity: Comment', *American Economic Review*, LIV, pp. 747–9.

SCHNEIDER, E. [1934] *Theorie der Produktion* (Vienna).

[1957] 'Einkommen und Einkommensverteilung in der makroökonomischen Theorie', *L'Industria*, II, pp. 256–68, translated as 'Income and income distribution in macro-economic theory', *International Economic Papers*, VIII (London: Macmillan and Co., Ltd), pp. 111–21.

SCITOVSKY, TIBOR DE [1943] 'A note on profit maximization and its implications', *Review of Economic Studies*, XI–XII, pp. 57–60.

[1964] 'A survey of some theories of income distribution', *The behavior of income shares*, Studies in income and wealth, XXVII (Princeton: Princeton University Press), pp. 15–31.

SCOTT, ROBERT HANEY [1962] 'Inferior factors of production', *Quarterly Journal of Economics*, LXXVI, pp. 86–97.

SEEBER, NORTON C. [1962] 'On the classification of inventions', *Sth. Econ. J.* XXVIII, pp. 365–71.

SEN, A. K. [1963] 'Neo-classical and neo-Keynesian theories of distribution', *Econ. Rec.* XXXIX, pp. 53–64.

SHEPHARD, RONALD W. [1953] *Cost and production functions* (Princeton: Princeton University Press).

SIMKIN, C. G. F. [1947] 'Some aspects and generalizations of the theory of discrimination', *Review of Economic Studies*, XV, pp. 1–13.

SMITHIES, ARTHUR [1935] 'The Austrian theory of capital in relation to partial equilibrium theory', *Quarterly Journal of Economics*, L, pp. 117–50.

[1936] 'The boundaries of the production function and the utility function', in *Explorations in economics* (New York: McGraw-Hill Book Co.), pp. 326–35.

SOLOW, ROBERT M. [1955] 'The production function and the theory of capital', *Review of Economic Studies*, XXIII, pp. 101–8.

[1957] 'Technological change and the aggregate production function', *Review of Economics and Statistics*, XXXIX, pp. 312–20.

[1958] 'A skeptical note on the constancy of relative shares', *American Economic Review*, XLVIII, pp. 618–31.

[1959] 'Comment', *Review of Economics and Statistics*, XLI, pp. 282–5.

[1960] 'Investment and technical progress', in P. Suppes, ed. *Mathematical methods in the social sciences* (Stanford: Stanford University Press), pp. 89–104.

[1961] 'Notes toward a Wicksellian model of distributive shares', in Lutz and Hague, eds. *The theory of capital* (London: Macmillan and Co., Ltd, pp. 245–65.

[1962a] 'Technical progress, capital formation, and economic growth', *American Economic Review*, Papers and Proceedings, LII, pp. 76–86.

[1962b] 'Substitution and fixed proportions in the theory of capital', *Review of Economic Studies*, XXIX, pp. 207–18.

[1963a] *Capital theory and the rate of return* (Amsterdam: North-Holland Publishing Co.).

[1963b] 'Heterogeneous capital and smooth production functions: An experimental study', *Econometrica*, XXXI, pp. 623–45.

[1964] 'Capital, labor and income in manufacturing', in *The behavior of in-*

come shares, Studies in income and wealth, vol. XXVII (Princeton: Princeton University Press), pp. 101–28.

SOLOW R. M., J. TOBIN, C. C. VON WEIZSACKER AND M. YAARI [1966] 'Neo-classical growth with fixed proportions', *Review of Economic Studies*, XXXIII, pp. 79–116.

SOPER, C. S. [1964a] An extension of the neo-Keynesian theory of distribution: A comment', *Economic Record*, XL, pp. 124–6.

[1964b] 'Elasticity of substitution and factor shares: A diagrammatic illustration', *Econ. Rec.* XL, pp. 571–5.

[1965] 'The elasticity of substitution', *Econ. Rec.* XLI, pp. 539–48.

SOSIN, KIM [1967] 'Joan Robinson's theory of distribution', *Nebraska Journal of Economics and Business*, VI, pp. 30–45.

SPENGLER, J. J. [1954] 'Limitational factors in population theory: A note', *Kyklos*, VII, pp. 227–43.

SRAFFA, PIERO [1960] *Production of commodities by means of commodities* (Cambridge University Press).

STIGLER, GEORGE J. [1939] 'Production and distribution in the short run', *Journal of Political Economy*, XLVII, pp. 305–27.

[1946] *Production and distribution theories* (New York: Macmillan and Co.).

STOBBE, ALFRED [1960] 'Kurzfristige und Langfristige Bestimmungsgrunde der Einkommensverteilung', *Schweizerische Zeitschrift für Volkswirtschaft und Statistik*, XCVI, pp. 131–55.

STONIER A. AND D. HAGUE [1955] *A textbook of economic theory* (London: Longsman, Green and Co.).

STURMEY, S. G. [1964] 'Cost curves and pricing in aircraft production', *Econ. J.* LXXIV, pp. 954–82.

SWEEZY, P. M. [1933] 'Notes on the elasticity of substitution: A note on relative shares', *Review of Economic Studies*, I, pp. 67–8.

TANGRI, OM P. [1966] 'Omissions in the treatment of the law of variable proportions', *American Economic Review*, LVI, pp. 484–93.

TARSHIS, LORIE [1934] 'Notes on the elasticity of substitution', *Review of Economic Studies*, I, pp. 144–7.

THANH, PHAM CHI [1966] 'Production processes with heterogeneous capital', *Economic Record*, XLII, pp. 430–46.

THEIL, H. [1954] *Linear aggregation of economic relations* (Amsterdam: North-Holland Publishing Co.).

TINTNER, GERHARD [1941] 'The pure theory of production under technological risk and uncertainty', *Econometrica*, IX, pp. 305–12.

[1942a] 'The theory of production under nonstatic conditions', *Journal of Political Economy*, L, pp. 645–67.

[1942b] 'A contribution to the non-static theory of production', in Lange, McIntyre, and Yntema, eds. *Studies in mathematical economics and econometrics* (Chicago: University of Chicago Press), pp. 92–109.

TOBIN, JAMES [1960] 'Towards a *general* Kaldorian theory of distribution', *Review of Economic Studies*, XXVII, pp. 119–20.

UZAWA, HIROFUMI [1961a] 'Neutral inventions and the stability of growth equilibrium', *Review of Economic Studies*, XXVIII, pp. 117–24.

[1961b] 'On a two-sector model of economic growth', *Review of Economic Studies*, XXIX, pp. 40–7.

REFERENCES

[1962] 'Production functions with constant elasticities of substitution', *Review of Economic Studies*, XXIX, pp. 291–9.

[1963] 'On a two-sector model of economic growth, II', *Review of Economic Studies*, XXX, pp. 105–18.

VINER, JACOB [1931] 'Cost curves and supply curves', *Zeitschrift für Nationalökonomie*, III, pp. 23–46; reprinted in A. E. A. *Readings in price theory* (Homewood: Richard D. Irwin, Inc., 1952), pp. 198–238.

WALTERS, A. A. [1963] 'Production and cost functions: an econometric survey', *Econometrica*, XXXI, pp. 1–66.

WELDON, J. C. [1948] 'The multi-product firm', *Canadian Journal of Economics and Political Science*, XIV, pp. 176–90.

WESTFIELD, FRED M. [1966] 'Technical progress and returns to scale', *Review of Economics and Statistics*, XLVIII, pp. 432–41.

WHITAKER, J. K. [1964] 'A note on the CES production function', *Review of Economic Studies*, XXXI, pp. 166–7.

[1966] 'Vintage capital models and econometric production functions', *Review of Economic Studies*, XXXIII, pp. 1–18.

WICKSELL, KNUT [1893] *Value, capital, and rent*, translated by S. H. Frowein from *Über Wert, Kapital und Rente* (London: George Allen and Unwin, Ltd. 1954).

[1901] *Lectures on political economy*, vol. I, translated by E. Claussen from *Vorlesungen über Nationalökonomie* (London: Routledge and Kegan Paul, 1934).

WITTE, JAMES M., JR., [1958] 'Productivity, relative prices, and income distribution', *Sth. Econ. J.* XXV, pp. 144–51.

WORSWICK, G. D. N. [1959] 'Mrs Robinson on simple accumulation: A comment with algebra', *Oxford Economic Papers*, New Series, XI, pp. 125–41.

WRIGHT, T. P. [1936] 'Factors affecting the cost of airplanes', *J. Aeronaut. Sci.* III, pp. 122–8.

YASUI, T. [1965] 'The CES production function: A note', *Econometrica*, XXXIII, pp. 646–8.

ZASSENHAUS, HERBERT, [1935] 'Dr Schneider and the theory of production', *Review of Economic Studies*, III, pp. 35–9.

ZOTOFF, A. W. [1923] 'Notes on the mathematical theory of production', *Econ. J.* XXXIII, pp. 115–21.

AUTHOR INDEX

Abramovitz, Moses, 278
Ahmad, S., 341, 342, 349, 350
Alchian, A. A., 293 n.
Allen, R. G. D., 79 n., 90 n., 94, 107, 144,
    152 n., 159 n., 187 n., 193 n., 194 n.,
    198, 199 n., 201, 235 n.
Amano, Akihiro, 224 n., 231 n., 249 n.
Arrow, Kenneth J., 293, 294 n., 303, 305,
    306, 307
Arrow, Kenneth J., Hollis Chenery,
    Bagicha Minhas and Robert M. Solow,
    62 n. 98, n., 101. 106 n,
Asher, H., 293 n.
Asimakopulos, A., 216 n.
Atsumi, Hiroshi, 314 n.

Bailey, Martin J., 201
Bardhan, Pranab, 224 n.
Bauer, P. T., 311 n.
Bear, D. V. T., 189 n., 192 n.
Berglas, Eytan, 272 n.
Blackburn, John O., 197 n.
Böhm-Bawerk, Eugen von, 251, 260
Bombach, G., 309 n., 314
Borts, George H., 120, 125 n., 126
Boulding, Kenneth, 309, 314
Bowley, A. L., 159 n.
Bronfenbrenner, Martin, 239, 243 n., 308
Brown, Murray, 98 n., 100 n., 101 n.,
    103 n., 105, 255, 264, 265 n., 268 n., 269,
    272 n., 275 n., 278 n., 279
Bruno, M., 251 n., 255, 258
Burmeister, Edwin, 251 n., 255, 258

Cani, John S. de, 98 n., 101 n.
Carlson, Sune, 1, 60 n., 79 n., 130 n.
Carter, H. O., 124 n.
Cassell, Gustav, 336
Cassels, J. M., 66 n., 77
Chamberlin, Edward H., 1
Champernowne, D. G., 90 n., 250 n.,
    271
Chattopadhyay, Paresh, 94 n.
Clark, J. B., 12, 250, 252, 253, 267, 269
Clemens, Eli W., 201
Clemhout, Simone, 124
Coase, Ronald, 201
Cobb, C. W. and Paul Douglas, 62 n.

Cournot, A. A , 312
Curtiss, D. H., 131 n.

Davidson, Paul, 2, 309 n.
David, Paul, 243 n., 244 n.
Denison, E. F., 278
Dewey, Donald, 5
Dhrymes, Phoebus, 201 n., 202 n.
Diamond, Peter, 224 n., 361 n.
Dillon, John L., 101 n.
Dorfman, Robert, 201
Drandakis, Emanuel, 224 n., 351 n.

Edwards, Edgar O., 201
Eisner, Robert, 314

Fabricant, Solomon, 321
Fei, John C. H., 224 n.
Fellner, William, 338, 340 n., 342
Ferguson, C. E., 2 n., 3 n., 90 n., 98 n.,
    101 n., 103 n., 124 n., 144 n., 154 n.,
    187 n., 223 n., 224 n., 240 n., 245 n.,
    277 n., 302 n., 314 n., 358 n., 361 n.
Findlay, Ronald, 314, 323 n.
Fortenay, Patrick B. de, 94 n.
Frankel, Marvin, 305, 307
Friedman, Milton, 90 n.
Frisch, Ragnar, 8, 17 n., 29, 47 n., 68 n.,
    69 n., 71 n., 79 n., 81 n., 171 n.

Gaitskell, H., 252 n.
Garegnani, P., 251 n., 252 n., 255, 258
Georgescu-Roegen, Nicholas, 8
Gerakis, Andreas S., 112 n.
Gordon, R. A., 201
Gorman, W. M., 101 n., 110 n.
Griliches, Zvi, 4 n.
Grunfeld, Y., 4 n.

Hague, D. C., 93
Hahn, Frank, 314
Halter, A. N., 124 n.
Hancock, Harris, 131 n.
Harrod, Roy F., 216 n., 219–24, 316,
    331 n., 348
Heady, Earl O., 101 n.
Hicks, John R., 1, 12, 90, 110 n., 189 n.,
    198, 216, 217–19, 225, 235 n., 237 n.,

Hicks (*cont.*)
238, 255, 258, 259 n., 261, 263, 264, 265, 267, 286 n., 328 n., 336, 337, 338, 340 n., 341, 343, 348
Hirsch, Werner, 293
Hocking, J. G., 124 n.
Hotelling, Harold, 131 n.

Intriligator, Michael, 272 n.

Johansen, Leif, 294
Johnson, W. E., 79 n., 159 n.
Jones, Ronald W., 231 n., 243 n., 249 n., 266 n.
Jorgenson, Dale, 272 n., 278, 279

Kahn, R. F., 90 n.
Kaldor, Nicholas, 1, 2, 90 n., 239 n., 254 n., 294 n., 295 n., 308 n., 309, 310 n., 311 n., 314, 316, 317, 322, 323, 343, 364
Kalecki, M., 309, 310, 312
Kemp, Murray, 314
Kendrick, John, 62 n., 101 n.
Kennedy, Charles, 216 n., 233, 341 n., 343 n., 344 n, 345, 346, 347 n., 349, 350, 351, 353 n., 356, 361, 363, 364
Keynes, J. M., 239, 309, 317
Klundert, Th. van de, 243 n., 244 n.
Knight, Frank H., 101 n., 125, 126
Kravis, Irvin, 239 n
Krelle, Wilhelm, 309 n., 314
Kuenne, Robert, 3 n., 261
Kuhn, Harold, 201, 202
Kurz, Mordechai, 272 n.

Lancaster, Kelvin, 232
Leibenstein, Harvey, 186
Leontief, W. W., 271, 280
Lerner, A. P., 90 n., 91 n., 311 n., 312 n.
Levhari, David, 258, 293 n., 300 n.
Liebhafsky, H. H., 93, 94 n.
Lundberg, E., 293

McCarthy, Michael, 243 n., 272 n., 275 n.
McFadden, Daniel, 101 n., 110 n.
Machlup, Fritz, 68 n., 90 n., 91 n.
Mansfield, Edwin F., 216
Marchal, Jean, 309 n.
Marshall, Alfred, 238 n.
Matthews, R. C. O., 272 n.
Mauer, William, 201 n.
Meade, J. E., 90 n.
Metzler, Lloyd A., 192 n.
Mirrlees, James, 1 n., 239 n., 310 n., 314 n.
Mitra, Ashok, 309, 310, 311, 312, 313
Mishan, E. J., 120, 215 n., 126

Moeseke, Paul von, 94 n.
Moore, Henry, L., 159 n.
Morishima, M., 251 n., 255, 258
Moroney, John, 168 n.
Mosak, Jacob L., 144, 187 n.
Mukerji, V., 101 n., 110 n.
Mundlak, Yair, 124 n.

Naylor, Thomas H., 201 n., 202 n.
Newman, P. C., 101 n., 124 n.
Nutter, Warren, 93, 94

Paroush, Jacob, 101 n.
Pasinetti, Luigi L., 2 n., 251 n., 255, 258, 309, 314
Pfouts, R. W., 101 n., 124 n., 201, 202, 209 n.
Phelps, Edmund S., 224 n., 272 n., 351 n.
Phelps-Brown, E. H., 309 n.
Pigou, A. C., 90 n., 201 n., 336, 337
Piron, Robert, 94 n.
Preiser, Erich, 314
Puu, T., 144 n., 187 n.

Ranis, Gustav, 224 n.
Rapping, Leonard, 293
Read, R. C., 101 n., 124 n.
Reder, Melvin W., 201
Robinson, Joan, 1 n., 90, 201, 216 n., 221, 231 n., 250, 255 n., 258, 271, 293 n., 309, 310, 314, 323, 324, 325, 326, 327, 328, 330, 331, 332, 333, 335, 364
Rothschild, K. W., 308, 309
Rowe, John W., 94 n.

Satler, W. E. G., 337, 344 n.
Samuelson, Paul A., 1, 7 n., 12 n., 55 n., 56, 58 n., 59 n., 130 n., 131 n., 138 n., 144, 163 n., 201, 250, 251 n., 252 n., 253, 255, 256, 257, 259, 260, 261, 264, 267, 269, 270, 271 n., 328 n., 341 n., 351, 353 n., 354, 356, 358, 360, 361, 364 n.
Sasser, Earl, 62 n.
Sato, Kazuo, 351 n.
Sato, Ryuzo, 62 n., 94 n., 101 n.
Scheper, Wilhelm, 101 n., 110 n.
Schneider, Dieter, 94 n.
Schneider, Erich, 8 n., 79 n., 130 n., 309, 314
Scitovsky, Tibor de, 186, 309 n.
Scott, Robert Haney, 189 n.
Seeber, Norton C., 216 n.
Sen, A. K., 314
Sheppard, Ronald W., 1, 124 n., 130 n.
Sheshinski, Eytan, 251 n., 255, 258

Simkin, C. G. F., 201
Smithies, Arthur, 7 n., 9 n., 60 n.
Solow, Robert M., 3 n., 124 n., 201 n., 239 n., 252 n., 257, 271, 272 n., 274, 275, 278, 280, 283 n., 287, 289, 290, 282, 294, 295 n., 304, 305
Soper, C. S., 314
Sosin, Kim, 325 n.
Spengler, J. J., 2 n.
Sraffa, Piero, 250 n., 258
Stigler, George J., 1, 71 n.
Stobbe, Alfred, 314
Stonier, A., 94
Sturmey, S. G., 293
Sweezy, Paul, 90 n.

Tangri, Om, 71 n.,
Tarshis, Lorie, 90 n., 91 n.
Thanh, Pham Chi, 287 n.
Theil, Henri, 4 n.
Tintner, Gerhard, 216 n.
Tobin, James, 272 n., 287 n., 314 n., 317 n.

Tucker, A. W., 201, 202

Uzawa, Hirofumi, 101 n., 110, 111, 216 n., 223, 231 n., 245, 249 n., 361 n.

Viner, Jacob, 155

Walters, A. A., 168 n.
Weldon, J. C., 201, 216 n.
Weizsächer, C. C. von, 272 n., 287 n.
Westfield, Fred, 272 n.
Whitaker, J. K., 101 n., 272 n.
Wicksell, Knut, 12, 251, 252 n., 258, 326, 334 n.
Witte, James M., 314 n.
Worswick, G. D. N., 323 n.
Wright, T. P., 293

Yaari, M., 272 n., 287 n.
Yasui, T., 101 n.

Zassenhaus, Herbert, 8 n.

SUBJECT INDEX

aggregate demand, factor shares and, 314–35
  Kaldor's model, 314–22
  Robinson's model, 323–35
average cost, 162–3
  and homogeneous functions, 163, 164–6
  elasticity of, 160
average product
  definition, 71
  elasticity of, 76–7
  fixed proportions production function, 19–24, 26–9
  homogeneous production function, 112–13, 116–20
  inhomogeneous production function, 71–2
  relation to marginal product, 116–20
  relation to total product, 116–20

biased technological progress, *see* Technological progress

Cambridge Criticism, 251, 254–5, 257–9, 265–9
capital theory
  and neoclassical theory, 253–4
  Cambridge Criticism of, 254–5
  heterogeneous capital models, Neoclassical views, 251–2
  real capital models, 252–4
CES production function, 62, 101–3, 215
  and cost functions, 163–6
  characteristics of, 103–7
Cobb–Douglas production function, 62, 76, 98–9, 215
  and vintage models, 272–5
  characteristics of, 99–101
complex inputs, theory of production with, 29–42
constant output demand curves, 138–41
  cross-elasticity of, 140
cost, theory of, 154–68, 176–9
  and function coefficient, 158–63, 178–9
  and marginal expense of input, 170–1
  cost functions, 157
  elasticities of cost, 158–63, 177–8
  expansion path and, 154–5
  variable input price, 169–86

cross-acceleration coefficient, 69
  and classification of input relations, 71

direct acceleration coefficient, 69
duality theorem, 133

economic ray, *see* Pareto ray
economic region of production
  complex inputs, 39–41
  homogeneous production function, 114–16
  inhomogeneous production function, 77–9
elasticity of substitution, 90–2
  complex inputs, 41–3
  definition, 91
  homogeneous functions, 95–7
  inhomogeneous functions, 90–2
  multiple production processes, 45–6
  partial, 107–11
  variable, 111
expansion path
  and variable input prices, 174
  definition, 142
  characteristics of, 142–3
  fixed proportions, 47–50
  homogeneous production function, 142–3
  inhomogeneous production function, 142–3
  isoclines, 142
  relation to function coefficient, 157–8
  relation to long-run cost, 154–8
extensive margin, 78

fabrication coefficient, 71
factor of production
  fixed, 7
  general, 60–1
  ingredient, 6
  specific, 60–1
  variable, 7
factor price frontier, 253–4, 256–7, 261–2, 285–7
  elasticity of, 266–9
fixed coefficients, 19–24
  derivation, 97–8
fixed proportions, 25–9

382

Frankel's variant, 305–7
function coefficient
  and elasticities of cost functions, 158–63
  definition, 79
  derivation, 81–3
  relation to output elasticity, 83

heterogeneous capital goods, 11–12
Hicks case, 259–61
homothetic production function, 124
Horndal effect, 293

induced bias of technological progress
  Ahmad on, 341–3, 349–50
  Fellner on, 338–40
  Hicks on, 337
  Kennedy on, 343
  Samuelson on, 351–61
inferior factors, 187–200
  and commodity price, 191–2
  and cross-elasticity of input demand,
    192–3
  and output effect, 193–9
  definition of, 189–91
input
  complex, 17–18, 29–31
  continuity factor, 68
  elementary, 15–17
  general, 60–1
  ingredient, 6
  limitational, 8–11
  limitative, 8–11
  redundant, 23–4
  specific, 60–1
  supply, elasticity of, 170–2
inputs, classification of relations, 71
input demand functions, 144–53, 179–85
  elasticity of, 235–9
  multi-factor model, 149–57, 179–85
  two-factor model, 145–9
intensive margin, 77
isocline
  definition, 86
  homogeneous production function, 113–
    14
isocost curves, 127–8
  shifting, 129–30
  with variable input prices, 171, 174–7
isoquants
  and comparative statics, 136
  definition, 63–4
  homogeneous production function,
    120
  inhomogeneous production function,
    63–7

Kennedy's theorem, 233
Kuhn–Tucker theorems, 202–4, 205–6,
  210–11

Law of variable proportions, 69
learning by doing, 293–307
  Arrow's model, 293–300
  Frankel's variant, 305–7
  growth path, 300–2
  neoclassical properties of, 302–4
  relative shares, 298–300
  social and private returns, 296–7
linear homogeneity
  and economic region of production,
    114–16
  and elasticity of substitution, 95–7
  classes of linearly homogeneous pro-
    duction function, 97–111
  cross-section production curves, 116–20
  definition, 94
  isoquant map, 120–2
  mathematical properties, 94–5

macroeconomic theory, 3–5, 215–16
marginal cost, 157–8, 162–3
  and homogeneous functions, 163,
    164–6
  definition, 157
  elasticity of, 161
marginal product
  definition, 67
  fixed proportions production function,
    19–24, 26–9, 31–4, 44–5
  homogeneous production function,
    112–13, 116–20
  inhomogeneous production function,
    67–71
  relation to average product, 75–6,
    116–20
  relation to total product, 73–5, 116–20
marginal rate of technical substitution
  definition, 84
  diminishing, 88–9
monopoly and relative factor shares,
  308–14
  Kalecki's theory, 310–11
  Mitra's theory, 311–14
minimum subset, definition, 19
multi-product firm, 201–11
multiple production processes, 43–6

neoclassical theory, 2–3, 251–4
neutral technological progress and relative
  factor shares, 240–1
'new view' of investment, 272, 278–80

optimal input combinations
    cost-minimization approach, 130–3, 172–3, 204–9
    output-maximization approach, 133–8, 173–4
output elasticity
    definition, 76
    elasticity of average product, 76–7
    function coefficient, 79–83
Pareto ray, 24, 26–8
    as an expansion path, 52–3
    as an isocline, 50–1
Pareto region, 34–9
production function
    definition, 7
    economic theory of, 127–53
    fixed proportions, 7–8, 25–9
    homogeneous, 93–126
    inhomogeneous, 60–92
    variable proportions, 7–8, 61–3

real-capital ratio, 325
relative factor shares
    aggregate demand as determinant of, see aggregate demand
    induced bias and theory of, see induced bias
    and biased technological progress, 241–54, 345
    and neutral technological progress, 240
    monopoly as a determinant of, see monopoly and relative factor shares

in factor-augmenting model, 243–5
in multi-sector model, 245–6
in two-sector model, 246–50
degree of mechanization and, 330
technological progress and, 330–2
reswitching of techniques, 262–5, 330, 334
returns to scale, and function coefficient, 80
ridge line, 88
Ruth Cohen Curiosum, 250, 251, 255, 258, 262, 330, 334

Samuelson's parable, 255–7
short run, 6–7
stages of production, 77–9
substitution region, 86–8
    definition, 87

technological progress, 216–34
    and relative factor shares, 239–51
    Harrod classification, 219–22, 232
    induced bias and, 336–61
    Hicks classification, 217–19, 231–2
    neoclassical theory of, 224–34
    relation between Hicks and Harrod classifications, 222, 228–9, 232–4

valuation of capital, 325–6, 333–5
vintage models, 271–92
    Cobb–Douglas model, 272–5
    factor-augmenting model, 275–80
    'new view' of investment, 272, 278–80
    with fixed proportions, 280–92